Government and economies in the postwar world

The chance to begin anew seldom occurs. Yet the nearly complete break-down of the world economy between 1939 and 1945, together with the dominant position of the United States at the end of the war, provided just this opportunity. A new international economic order was built on the ruins of the old. How this happened – and the role of government in economic performance – is the subject of this important and timely book.

Written by political scientists, contemporary historians and economists, it includes ten country studies covering all the major industrialized nations in the East and the West: the USA, USSR, Japan, West Germany, United Kingdom, France, Italy, Spain, Eastern Europe, and Scandinavia. In each chapter readers will find information on the main objectives and instruments of economic policy, the institutional framework, where the country started from at the end of the war, and a summary of what happened thereafter both in terms of policies and outcomes. Each chapter also contains data on the country's economic performance, a list of selected dates of important events, and a guide to further reading.

The book begins with an overview of the system of international trade and payments since the war, and ends with five commentaries drawing attention to contrasts and similarities between the nations. The commentaries feature David Henderson, Head of the Economic Division of the OECD, on the overall economic performance, Charles Feinstein on the influence of different starting points, David Marquand on the effect of different political and institutional structures, and Sidney Pollard on economic policies and traditions.

Learning from other countries' experience as well as understanding how they see their own problems is increasingly important with 1992, 'glasnost', and the problem of international policy coordination between the USA, Japan, and West Germany so high on the agenda. No other book provides such a wide-ranging account of how the industrialized world came to be where it is today. It is essential reading for policy makers, business people and all students of current affairs, economics and postwar history.

The New Routledge Library Of Economics

The New Routledge Library of Economics is designed to make books which have made an innovative contribution to their field available in paperback. The books are characterized by their original and exciting scholarship and research and will appeal to those with interests across the range of economics.

Other titles in the series:

Historians, Economists and Economic History
Alon Kadish

The Methodology of Economic Model Building: Methodology after Samuelson
Lawrence A. Boland

Government and economies in the postwar world

Economic policies and comparative performance, 1945–85

Edited by

Andrew Graham with Anthony Seldon

Routledge

London and New York

First published 1990
by Routledge
11 New Fetter Lane, London EC4P 4EE

New in paperback 1991

Simultaneously published in the USA and Canada
by Routledge
a division of Routledge, Chapman and Hall, Inc.
29 West 35th Street, New York, NY 10001

338.9009
G721

British Library Cataloguing in Publication Data
Government and economies in the postwar world:
  1. Economic development, history
  I. Graham, Andrew II. Seldon, Anthony
  330.9

  ISBN 0–415–07288–3

Library of Congress Cataloging in Publication Data
Government and economies in the postwar world: economic policies and
  comparative performance, 1945–85/edited by Andrew Graham with
  Anthony Seldon.
    p.   cm.
  Bibliography: p.
  Includes index.
  ISBN 0–415–07288–3
    1. Europe—Economic conditions—1945– 2. Europe—Economic policy.
  3. Japan—Economic conditions—1945– 4. Japan—Economic
  policy—1945– 5. United States—Economic conditions—1945– 6. United
  States—Economic policy. 7. International economic relations. I. Graham,
  Andrew, 1942– . II. Seldon, Anthony.
  HC240.G568   1989   88–10046
  338.9′009′045—dc20

Contents

v

Contents

Introduction; Objectives; Growth and fluctuations; Aspects
of equality; *Income differentials*; *Regional differentials*;
Towns and villages: agricultural and industrial workers;
Inflation
Part two: The case of Czechoslovakia
Policy before the establishment of exclusive communist
power; Tensions in the centrally planned economy;
Assessment of results; Efficiency – the problem of the day;
Conclusion

Contents

Part II

Acknowledgements

We would like to thank the Warden and Fellows of Nuffield College for hosting the conference in November 1987 at which many of the chapters in this book were initially discussed. We also acknowledge thanks to the OECD for statistics and other data; to the British Academy for support in meeting expenses connected with secretarial and technical assistance on the Eastern European chapter; Lord Bullock (an ICBH patron) for suggesting the idea; David Butler for chairing the conference; David Henderson for advice and encouragement and Stephanie Maggin of the ICBH for coordinating the conference and book.

A.G.
A.S.

Figures

Tables

Contributors

Dr Kathleen Burk, Lecturer in History and Politics, Imperial College, London

Sir Alec Cairncross has been both an economic adviser to Government and Master of St Peter's College, Oxford 1969–78

Professor Charles Feinstein, Reader in Recent Social and Economic History, University of Oxford, and Professorial Fellow of Nuffield College

Dr Graham Hallett, Research Associate in the School of European Studies, University of Wales College of Cardiff

Professor Philip Hanson, Professor of Soviet Economics, Centre for Russian and East European Studies, University of Birmingham

Professor David Henderson, Head of Economics and Statistics Branch, OECD

Professor Joseph Hogan, Head of Department of Government and Economics, Birmingham Polytechnic

Jaroslav Krejčí, Professor Emeritus, University of Lancaster

Dr Frances Lynch, Lecturer in Economic History, Department of European Studies, UMIST

Professor David Marquand, Professor of Contemporary History and Politics, University of Salford

Professor Ian Nish, Professor of International History, London School of Economics

Professor Sidney Pollard, Professor of Economic History, University of Bielefeld

Professor Paul Preston, Dean of Faculty of Arts, Queen Mary and Westfield College, London

Dr Michael Rose, Reader in Economic Life, University of Bath

Dr Patrick Salmon, Lecturer in History, Department of History, University of Newcastle upon Tyne

Dr Donald Sassoon, Reader in History, Queen Mary and Westfield College, London

Chapter one

Introduction

Andrew Graham

There are literally hundreds of books on the principles of economics, rather fewer on particular economies and very few on comparative economic performance. There is one good reason and one bad reason for this relative paucity of comparative material.

The good reason is that it is difficult to establish firm results. This is partly because there are no agreed criteria by which performance should be judged and partly because there is no way of establishing the counterfactual – what would have happened otherwise. Is the performance of Eastern Europe, for example, to be compared with what its performance might have been under capitalism (whatever precisely that may mean) or under 'economic reforms', or under more decentralized planning? The mere posing of these questions illustrates that the particular counterfactual chosen is at one and the same time both important and highly arbitrary. Also, even when chosen, it is incredibly difficult to describe – we simply do not have this degree of knowledge of the social world. Economists have models and carry out simulations, but, at best, these are no more than crutches to our thoughts; and, at worst, such simulations contain so many unrealistic assumptions that they hide more than they reveal. An alternative to the counterfactual is to make a comparison either with early periods of history or with other countries for the same period. This approach, which is used extensively in this book, has the advantage of being more straightforward – we know what we are doing – but, inevitably, many factors change at once and, for all its apparent simplicity, this method is ultimately just as arbitrary.

The bad reason for the lack of comparative work is the fallacious argument that because little can be established nothing can be learned. On the contrary, looking at different countries and at similar, if not identical, policies in different contexts can be a stimulus to our imaginations. It would be stupid to suppose that one country can transplant institutions from another – the circumstances are always subtly different – but looking at one country from the perspective of another may suggest possibilities that would not otherwise have been considered.

It is in this spirit that this book has been written. The method chosen was to invite 'country experts' to write about particular countries covering the period since the end of the Second World War and to see what differences and similarities emerged. These country chapters (chapters 3 to 12) form the core of the book and first drafts of these were presented at a conference at Nuffield College, Oxford in November 1987 and then revised in the light of the discussion. Contributors were left free to choose which factors to emphasize – there was no attempt to develop a 'line' – but they were asked to follow a broadly similar format so that for each country the reader will find information on the main objectives and instruments of economic policy, the institutional framework, where the country started from in 1945, and a summary of what happened both in terms of policies and outcomes thereafter.

These country chapters are complemented by two other contributions. First, to set the scene, chapter 2 describes the changing system of international trade and payments during the postwar period. Second, there are a series of commentaries (chapters 13 to 17) which look across the group as a whole. This allows features that would not be obvious at the level of a single country to emerge. For example, David Henderson (chapter 13) draws attention to the very general pattern of growth which has affected all of the countries discussed here. Similarly Charles Feinstein (chapter 14), by looking at the level and change in productivity of individual countries relative to the others, develops a thesis about the extent to which a country's ability to grow is influenced by the scope that exists for it to catch up with others.

Another feature of economic performance, which was emphasized at the conference at Nuffield, is the extent to which people attribute characteristics to particular countries and use these to explain behaviour. For example, it was alleged that the East Germans work much harder than employees in other countries and that this accounts for much of their economic success. Such arguments are sometimes unsatisfactorily stated since it is easy to confuse levels and rates of change – hard work may produce a lot of output, but it is less obvious that it produces high growth. Nevertheless it is not too difficult to think of links between cultural and institutional factors on the one hand and a willingness to invest and to innovate on the other which could produce higher growth. Moreover, while these factors are extraordinarily difficult to track down (and still more difficult to quantify), there is currently a somewhat greater willingness amongst social scientists to take them seriously. The final three commentaries therefore look at the influence of tradition (Sidney Pollard, 15), at what we know (and don't know) about the effects of hard work (Michael Rose, 16) and, still more difficult to pin down, at the influence of institutions in terms of the whole way that societies organize themselves (David Marquand, 17).

At one point in the planning of this book the intention was to finish with a chapter of 'Conclusions', but conclusions in a book of this kind are not really appropriate. The point of this book is not to find 'the truth', but to learn about countries with which one is unfamiliar and, perhaps as a result, to reconsider views about economic policy and performance in those countries which are well known already. This is a task for each reader rather than for the editor. Nevertheless, in the course of producing this book certain points inevitably made an impact.

One general observation is the difference in the perspectives that emerge in the commentaries and in the country chapters. The former seem more concerned with grander themes and larger trends; the latter more with the minutiae of policy. This contrast is to some extent both inevitable and intentional, but it raises the question, touched on especially by Alec Cairncross, in chapter 3 on the UK, of whether much of economic policy is not merely shuffling the chairs – all show and no substance.

One possible implication of this line of thought is that short-run macro-economic demand management policies do nothing and that policy should concentrate instead on long-term supply management through institutional change. (Admittedly one might go further and conclude that supply-side policies would have no effect either – everything is just in the grip of inexorable laws – but none of the contributors really suggest this.) The former position, namely that supply-side management is what matters, has certainly been highly influential in the 1980s, especially in the US and the UK, but we should be cautious about accepting it uncritically.

One reason for expressing some scepticism is that a further point to emerge from the country chapters is the extent to which economic policy appears to be influenced by the mood of the time. For example, the UK's interest in planning in the 1960s was a conscious aping of the planning in France a few years earlier and similar moves were occurring at the same time in Italy and even, on some readings, in West Germany. Similarly, in the late 1960s and early 1970s many countries experimented with prices and incomes policies of one sort or another and then in the 1980s we observe de-regulation and a renewed emphasis on markets (at least in domestic markets; as chapter 2 shows, at the international level the 1980s is notable for the renewed use of protectionist policies). This last swing in policy occurs on both sides of the Atlantic, both sides of the English Channel, and even both sides of the Iron Curtain. Of course, it is just possible that all of these changes were entirely the result of carefully considered reactions to common circumstances, but, without denying any role for events and rational calculations, the alternative interpretation is that there is an element of fashion to economic policy.

To be more blunt, in correcting for one error (excessive belief in the power of demand management in the 1950s and the 1960s) we must avoid falling into another (that demand is wholly irrelevant). Many years ago

Marshall compared demand and supply to a pair of scissors and commented 'When one blade is held still, and the cutting is affected by moving the other, we may say with careless brevity that the cutting is done by the second; but the statement is not one to be made formally, and defended deliberately' (Marshall 1890: 820). The same message almost certainly applies to policy: demand-side policies need (and help) supply-side policies and vice versa.

There are two further reasons for being sceptical of the view that supply is all that matters. First, it is difficult to read the country chapters without receiving the impression, that, at least in the eyes of many of the contributors to this book, demand management policies did in fact slow down or speed up particular economies quite substantially on a number of occasions. Second, David Henderson's comment shows very clearly that, leaving inflation aside, the economic performance of the whole OECD block was substantially better during the years 1950 to 1973 than during any earlier period of history or subsequently. Why this happened is still a matter of considerable contention, but in a recent careful study, covering seventeen OECD countries, Boltho concludes that

> via both automatic stabilizers and the confidence-enhancing role of the new demand management commitment to avoid cycles and unemployment, private sector behaviour was changed in a way that itself contributed to greater stability. Announced policy changes, far from being impotent, were actually more powerful than had they not been anticipated. (Boltho 1988: 21)

This is *not* to argue that demand management policies were always well chosen, still less to maintain that all countries could or should be attempting to fine-tune their economies at present. The changes in financial markets have substantially reduced the scope for this and, in some countries (especially the US) the institutional structure makes sensible short-run adjustment a near impossibility; there is, however, much to be said for a medium-term adjustment by the US, especially if co-ordinated with Germany and Japan. It is also important to stress that much of the Boltho argument operates through expectations and not primarily through the mechanistic plugging in of a certain quantity of expenditure. (The Keynesian models of the 1950s and 1960s with neatly calculable multipliers were as naive about human behaviour as was the stable velocity assumption of the monetarists who followed.)

A closely related point, and one which suggests much caution about being wildly enthusiastic about any particular policy prescription as some form of panacea in general, is the extent to which the context matters – both the other policies occurring at the time and the general climate of expectations in the particular country. It also matters whether policy is applied at the right moment and with intelligence. For example, the French devaluations of 1957 and 1958 seem especially well chosen and effectively carried out whereas the 'same' policy in the UK in 1967 looks noticeably less successful.

Another illustration of the importance of context is the case of Japan. The causes of Japanese growth are much disputed and undoubtedly several were at work at the same time. Nevertheless it is easy to see that if you have an efficient bureaucracy, an energetic private sector with technical skills, and a long way to catch up, then protecting domestic industry and importing foreign technology makes a lot of sense. Moreover it makes even more sense if external protection is combined with internal competition (as Japan, unlike Spain, seems to have achieved). But such an argument in no way proves the general superiority of protection over free trade (anymore than the benefits of free trade to the UK in the earlier part of the nineteenth century prove the converse).

Having so far emphasized the traditional macro-policies (primarily as a counterweight to contemporary concerns with supply) it remains to make two brief points about supply itself. First, many of the items that one would expect to be important on the supply-side – training, new technology, research and development – are precisely those areas in which traditional economic theory would predict market failure. Second, it seems to be a feature of those countries which have handled supply relatively well (Germany and Japan come to mind) that they have tackled these market failures by various forms of institutional coordination – or, as economists would say, they have internalized the externalities. In other words we should not think of policy as consisting just of markets on the one hand and state control on the other, but instead be using our imaginations to devise and create institutions that might solve, or ease, some of the problems of the market.

There is one other undercurrent on markets – an idea that surfaces every so often throughout the book, but most obviously in chapter 2 on the international environment. It is clear that during the last forty years countries have become more closely integrated with one another, at first through the expansion of trade and later through the growth of financial markets. It is also clear that, at least during the last decade, there has, on the whole, been more de-regulation of domestic markets and between countries within already existing customs unions. However, occurring alongside this there has been, first, a greater degree of trade protectionism and, second, the renewal of intervention in foreign exchange markets (and stock markets). One way of thinking about this series of interventions is to regard it as a measure of the extent to which someone somewhere is taking the strain in ways which they find unacceptable. In other words we are not in equilibrium. This is hardly surprising. But the point is that, if, in general, the whole world economy cannot achieve this state then we should not be surprised to find the market being supplanted. The question is not whether it will happen, but where. Equally, one of the roles for policy should be to decide who takes the strain – and there may be an important role here for fiscal policy and monetary policy acting as the shock absorbers.

Finally, to return to the problem of evaluating performance, it is worth emphasizing that, while most of the discussion of this book is in terms of the conventional economic outcomes (especially growth, unemployment, and inflation) none of us are unaware of the importance of other factors, even where these are less quantifiable. Jaroslav Krejčí's chapter on Eastern Europe, for example, refers to the 'de-levelling' of political rights that occurred alongside the levelling of incomes. Similarly, the chapters on France and Italy and, still more so, that on Spain show how their moves towards more rapid growth and industrialization were aided by the extent to which real wages were held down. But how is one to assess the costs and benefits of such policies? Even rejecting the Marxist thesis that all the benefits accrue to the capitalists (which is obviously not true is these countries), it is clear that, in the short-run, the shift in the distribution of income towards profits does temporarily help one group in society more than another, and, even in the long-run, the workers who eventually receive the benefits will almost certainly be different from those who made the initial sacrifice.

At this point it is time for the editorial introduction to cease (before it becomes too long). The chapters should now be left to speak for themselves and the reader left to draw his or her own connections and contrasts from the stories that the countries tell.

References

Boltho, A. (1988) 'Did Policy Activism Work?', *Applied Economics Discussion Paper* No. 60, University of Oxford.

Marshall, A. (1890) *Principles of Economics*, (ninth (Variorum) edn 1961), Macmillan & Co. Ltd, for the Royal Economic Society.

Part I

Chapter two

The international environment

Kathleen Burk

Introduction

The chance to begin anew seldom occurs. Yet the nearly complete breakdown of the world economy between 1939 and 1945, together with the extraordinarily dominant position of the United States at the end of the war, provided just this opportunity. Policy-makers in the US were determined to convince – and, if necessary, to compel – other nations to join them in building a new economic order on the ruins of the old.

The aim of the US (and to a lesser extent of Britain and Canada) was to establish a new scheme for international payments, which would have as its primary objective the avoidance of the competitive exchange rate depreciations of the 1930s, and, accompanying this, a new set of rules for international trade which would be designed to promote non-discrimination and the free exchange of goods and services. The first part of this twin approach was the Bretton Woods agreement (named after the place where the US plan was finally ratified by the United Nations), which set up the International Monetary Fund (IMF), and the International Bank for Reconstruction and Development (the World Bank). The second part, on which the US had less of its own way, became the General Agreement on Tariffs and Trade (GATT). This joint system, for good or ill and despite periods of non-operation, determined how most of the countries discussed in this book interacted with one another for much of the postwar period. This chapter therefore describes the initial establishment of the system, its evolution since 1945, and the main strains to which it has been subjected.

There are four main themes. First of all, from the late 1940s until the early 1970s, a system of fixed but adjustable exchange rates was in operation. However, as initially designed at Bretton Woods, this was supposed to be accompanied by freedom of capital movements – currencies were to be freely convertible – but this did not occur, even for the majority of the main currencies, until the late 1950s. In short, the Bretton Woods system was not fully operational until long after 1945. In addition, both before and after it was in full operation, it was subject to a series of crises, which were only resolved by a variety of *ad hoc* arrangements by the IMF and temporary agreements between Central Banks.

Second, despite these problems with international payments, the development of international trade was abnormally successful. The period began in a protectionist mode left over from the 1930s and reinforced by the postwar poverty in Europe, but this gave way under the general aegis of the GATT to a much more liberal regime – a move which almost certainly contributed to the spectacular increase in both output and foreign trade from the early 1950s to the mid-1970s. As Table 2.1 shows, not only did the output of the main industrial countries grow more rapidly than in any previous period of history, but the growth of trade was above that of output for most of the period. Moreover, while both slowed down after 1973, trade continued to grow more rapidly than output (at least up to 1979). But, accompanying the slowdown in output and the higher levels of unemployment that emerged, there was renewed recourse to protectionism, particularly in the form of non-tariff barriers and the greater emphasis on (the already existing) regional customs unions.

Third, when capital movements were liberalized (in a series of moves from the late 1950s onwards), there was an enormous expansion and integration of financial markets. The Eurodollar market, which hardly existed in 1960, grew to hundreds of billions of dollars by the 1980s; the turnover of foreign exchange exploded – it is estimated to have reached $150 billion per day by 1985 (Strange 1986: 11); and the growth of share dealing made the international financial 'global market-place' a reality by the end of the period.

Fourth, in the mid-1970s these capital flows, especially in combination with divergences in inflation rates from one country to another and with external shocks from oil price rises, made it impossible to sustain the original system of fixed exchange rates, and there was a widespread adoption of floating rates. However, at the very end of the period, the experience with floating rates (especially the large speculative capital flows and the associated swings in exchange rates) led to a renewal of co-ordinated intervention by central banks. This was not a return to the fixed

Table 2.1 Growth of world GDP and trade[a] 1870–1985 (average annual % changes)

	1870–1913	*1913–50*	*1953–63*	*1963–73*	*1973–9*	*1979–85*
World trade[b]	3.3	1.1	6.5	8.9	4.7	2.1
World GDP			3.7	5.2	3.1	2.1

a Market economies
b Average of exports and imports after 1953; exports before 1953

Sources: Maddison 1982 and Boltho and Allsop 1987.

rates of Bretton Woods, but took the form of attempts to hold some of the major exchange rates within broad 'zones' for periods at a time.

In other words, since 1945, not only has the international trade and payments environment changed almost beyond recognition, but even the initial design was never fully in place – or at least never worked as intended.

The establishment of the new system: Bretton Woods and GATT

Bretton Woods

On 27 December 1945, at a signing ceremony in Washington, DC, attended by thirty countries, the twin children of Bretton Woods came into existence. One was the World Bank, whose main duty was to supply development project loans. The other was the IMF, whose remit was the maintenance of exchange stability and, when balance of payments problems made this impossible, to facilitate any necessary adjustment. They were conceived as pillars of a new planned economic world in which governments would have considerable freedom to determine and carry out economic objectives, but in which they would be prevented from indulging in competitive depreciations and protectionism. To impose discipline, there would be fixed exchange rates and currency convertibility, based on a gold exchange standard in which the dollar would maintain its link with gold at $35 an ounce. The IMF would supervise the operation of the system and provide medium-term lending to those countries in temporary balance of payments difficulties; in the event of a 'fundamental disequilibrium' – the definition of which caused no little disagreement – the IMF would supervise the adjustment mechanism which permitted a country, with international agreement, to change its exchange rate.

The IMF found its medium-term lending function constrained almost before it had begun, largely because the US forbade those receiving Marshall Aid during the period from 1948 to 1952 from borrowing from the IMF. At the same time, the lack of convertibility until January 1959 of most of the major currencies meant that the IMF's role in this sphere was scarcely tested. It can therefore be argued that while legally the Bretton Woods system began with the outbreak of peace, only from 1 January 1959 was it able to carry out its prescribed duties.

Nevertheless, the arrangements planned for the international monetary system were at least in place in 1945; the same could not be said for the organization which the US wished to oversee the actual trading of goods, the International Trade Organization (ITO). In September 1945 a set of Proposals for the Expansion of World Trade and Commerce were hammered out between Britain and the US and then published in December 1945: each country was to pursue its own full employment policies so long as they did not harm the trade of the other countries; bilateral bargaining accompanied by the application of the most-favoured-nation approach was to lead to tariff reductions; and the United Kingdom's tariff system of imperial preference would 'eventually' be wound down. But the agreement fell a victim to increasing Anglo-American acrimony.

In 1947 in Geneva two types of discussion occurred alongside one another. Work continued on the ITO. At the same time, a range of countries began to negotiate bilateral tariff reductions. Eventually 123 sets of negotiations amongst 23 countries were embodied in a single General Agreement on Tariffs and Trade (GATT), signed in October 1947. At this stage GATT was meant to be an interim arrangement pending the setting-up of the ITO, and a conference met in Havana between November 1947 and March 1948 to discuss the charter for the ITO. However, profound discord was the theme. There were many sources of conflict, but basically, the then-called 'underdeveloped countries' argued for controls on international investment, trade preferences in their favour, and the right to impose quantitative trade restrictions. In short, they wanted the right to ignore multilateralism in the interests of their own economies. The US and the UK drew together and on 23 March 1948 refused to sign the Havana Charter. In the end only one country ratified the Charter, and it and the ITO were abandoned. This left only the GATT as a mechanism for tariff reductions.

Certain principles informed the GATT. First, there was to be non-discrimination: any privilege granted to one country had to be granted equally and immediately to all the other signatories of GATT (this is the most-favoured nation clause enshrined in Article 1). Second, if domestic industries must be protected, reliance should be placed upon tariffs, rather than upon more hidden, non-tariff, barriers. Third, trade disputes should be settled through a continuing process of consultation and conciliation.

By 1948, then, the most important structures for the co-operative, international management of the economy were in place. The Bretton Woods system dealt with payments and the GATT, despite being watered down from the US intentions, provided the framework within which most trade negotiations occurred. In practice GATT has proved considerably more resilient than the Bretton Woods arrangements, but then, it was much less ambitious.

The operation of Bretton Woods in practice

The period since 1945 has seen the decline of the pound sterling as a reserve currency, the rise and relative decline in the use of the dollar, and, latterly, the seemingly inexorable rise both in value and in use of the yen. During most of the period the Deutschmark has had the strength to become a reserve currency, but the Federal Republic has been reluctant to have the mark assume the role. The behaviours of these four currencies were the main determinants of when the procedures agreed at Bretton Woods were put into operation, and when they had to be terminated.

In 1945 there were two currencies of overwhelming importance, the pound and the dollar, the former of which was in great supply, while the latter was in great demand. At the same time it was the products which the dollar area had in great supply which were in great demand, and Europe's needs combined with Europe's lack of dollars produced the situation termed the dollar famine. Because Europe was exporting comparatively little to the dollar area, the US in particular ran a massive balance of payments surplus.

While lacking dollars, many individuals, companies, and governments possessed pounds, some held in other countries. In total some £3.5 billion (1945 figure) were banked in London, the so-called 'sterling balances' (Ellis-Rees 1962: 12). The pound had historically been central to the international monetary system, in demand particularly for international transactions, but during the war a regime of strict exchange controls had been put in place. If sterling could again be made fully convertible, this would facilitate a return to free trade (and non-discrimination against the dollar and American exports). The Americans therefore required full convertibility by the UK as a condition for a loan (the Loan Agreement of December 1945). On 15 July 1947 the pound became fully convertible. The result, hardly surprisingly, was that millions of pounds were sold to acquire dollars, and the ensuing crisis ensured that convertibility lasted only until 20 August, when the window was slammed shut: it was not to be re-opened until 1 January 1959.

An alternative method of dealing with the dollar famine was for the Americans to provide a supply. Over the period 1948–51, the Americans granted to the sixteen participating countries roughly $13 billion under the Marshall Aid programme (superseded in 1951 by the Korean War related Mutual Security Agency programmes). Whether or not this aid 'caused' European recovery is debatable: Milward, for example, has argued that European recovery was already in train, and, indeed, that the 1947 crisis was caused by the success of this recovery as expressed in a marked increase in capital goods imports from the US (Milward 1984: 465). Marshall aid, however, at least facilitated the continuance of this recovery. It also helped reduce political and social pressures by enabling capital investments to be made without further cuts in consumption.

Economic growth in the 1950s was accompanied by the strengthening of the European currencies, and this allowed steps to be taken towards convertibility. Intra-European payments were facilitated by the European Payments Union (EPU), which had been set up as part of the Marshall Aid programme. Indeed, the link between the EPU and the sterling area provided convertibility between western European currencies, sterling, overseas sterling-area countries, and others linked through an 'administrative control' by the Bank of England (Scammell 1983: 114–15), although not between this group and the dollar. Nevertheless, such full convertibility was the goal of the Bretton Woods agreement.

The UK authorities moved slowly in this direction by allowing the limited growth of free markets for sterling. In December 1951, British banks were allowed to hold balances of currencies and deal in foreign exchange on a very limited basis, and by 1954, 'transferable sterling' (i.e., sterling held in a particular set of countries, earned in current transactions, and used for settlement with one another) could be changed into dollars in centres such as New York and Zurich, with a discount of only 1 per cent. In February 1954 the Bank of England began to intervene in the free markets to support the free rate, and sterling was thus *de facto* convertible (Tew 1985: 36–7). But in 1955 balance of payments problems returned, followed in 1956 by the Suez adventure, when the pound came under strong attack (and the US refused to defend it), and by a further sterling crisis in 1957. Only in December 1958 was it deemed safe to agree to *de jure* convertibility for sterling for non-residents.

The pace, however, had been set by Germany and France. A substantial improvement in Europe's balance of payments had led to an increase in the gold and foreign exchange reserves in 1958, and indeed, those of western Europe and Japan had virtually doubled between 1952 and 1959 when they reached more than $22 billion (of a world total of $57 billion) (Solomon 1977: 26). In 1957, Germany allowed capital exports by German residents without restrictions, and in 1959 convertibility on capital as well as current account was allowed. But it was France rather than Germany which precipitated convertibility by making the franc freely convertible into dollars. This ended the European Payments Union, which had facilitated inter-European payments, and the others were forced to follow.

On 1 January 1959, therefore, the much-postponed Bretton Woods system was fully activated. It was to have a short, unhappy life, although when it ended is problematical. Was it in 1971, with the de-linking of the dollar from gold? Was it in 1973, with the abandonment of fixed exchange rates? Or was it in 1976, when the IMF Interim Committee recommended that *de facto* recognition of conditions as they had obtained since 1971 be made *de jure*? Regardless of when body as well as brain death was acknowledged, the system led an eventful life.

The Bretton Woods system faced three main problems. The first was that the fixed exchange rate system seemed to be designed for a world where countries were in equilibrium with one another. Of course, where there was 'fundamental disequilibrium', the system allowed for the exchange rate to be moved (the 'adjustable peg'), but this was where the second problem arose: in practice, countries were reluctant to change their exchange rates. Moreover, the resistance to exchange rate changes proved to be asymmetrical – the pressure on countries in balance of payments deficit to devalue was stronger than that of the converse situation. The result was that, on balance, more countries devalued against gold, and thus against the dollar, than revalued; and this was one of the factors that weakened the position of the US balance of payments and so contributed to the eventual crisis of the dollar.

While the first two problems primarily concerned the ability of the system to adjust, the third problem, that of liquidity, arose from the need – which any system has – for funds during the process of adjustment. In the case of Bretton Woods this liquidity issue took two forms, one concerning the IMF, the other the role of the dollar.

The problem for the IMF was that it had insufficient funds of its own to lend to countries whose currencies were under threat. During the 1960s this was addressed, first, by the General Arrangement to Borrow (GAB) in 1961, second, by further increases in IMF quotas in February 1966 and, third, by the creation of a new form of liquidity in 1967, the Special Drawing Rights. The GAB was set up in response to fears of a run on the dollar (although its initial use proved to be in defence of the pound); ten countries, seven European, the US, Canada, and Japan, stood ready to lend a total of $6 billion to the IMF, to be drawn upon by members. The GAB was notable for another reason, in that it officially recognized that while all members of the IMF were equal, some were more equal than others; these ten richest countries evolved in due course into the Group of Ten. The Special Drawing Rights (SDRs) were created, after prolonged controversy, by the IMF, as a reserve asset alongside the dollar; however, SDRs suffered because of political conflict amongst their creators and because they were created by fiat (Solomon: chapter 8).

In the short term, the first two of these new arrangements, as well as currency swaps organized by the Bank for International Standards (BIS), and the Gold Pool established by eight central banks in November 1961 to stabilize the price of gold, proved capable of handling the imbalances in the system in the early 1960s which manifested themselves almost immediately after convertibility was announced. At this stage the main concerns were the continuing weakness of sterling on the one hand (1960 saw a current account deficit of £258 million compared with a surplus the previous year of £149 million), and, on the other, the growing strength of the Deutschmark, with massive, export-led surpluses on the current account (surpluses which persisted in spite of a small revaluation in 1961).

In the medium term, exchange rates had to be moved. The most obvious of these was the devaluation of sterling in 1967 (see p. 17). However, neither *ad hoc* injections of liquidity nor exchange rate changes dealt with the more fundamental problem of the dollar. What happened in the late 1950s and early 1960s was that the dollar famine became a dollar glut. The result was a tension between two opposing features. On the one hand, the supply of dollars provided the liquidity that the system needed. Looked at from this point of view, everyone was using dollars for international transactions and thus everyone was content to hold more of them. On the other hand, the supply of dollars relative to gold, when placed in the context of a weakening US balance of payments position (the weakening of which was itself causing the supply), created doubts about the dollar's value: perhaps it was risky to hold.

During the 1960s this tension proved manageable. At this stage the US was still in surplus on the balance of exports and imports; the reason for the dollar glut was primarily a deficit on capital account as US corporations invested abroad, and the 'weakening' was caused largely by foreign aid and military expenditure (especially in Vietnam), rather than by any obvious loss of competitiveness. The response of the US government was to try to reduce private capital outflows. For example, the Interest Equalization Tax of 1964 taxed the purchase by Americans of foreign securities from foreigners, while in January 1968, under the Foreign Direct Investment Program, net transfers of capital by US investors for direct investment in advanced European countries and South Africa were subject to a moratorium.

These measures by the US had less effect on their balance of payments than had been hoped, but they had another result of considerable importance: they greatly stimulated the growth of the Euro-dollar market and uncontrolled short-term capital flows in general. The markets in foreign exchange had, of course, already been boosted by the resumption of convertibility in 1959. But Eurodollars, i.e. dollar deposits held in Europe rather than in the US, grew particularly because the US Federal Reserve stipulated, via 'Regulation Q' (dating from the 1930s), that interest paid by US banks on time-deposits was fixed, whereas dollar deposits in foreign banks were not subject to a ceiling. As a result, London banks bid for dollar deposits which they then lent back to the US. In addition, for geopolitical reasons, countries such as the USSR preferred to hold their dollar deposits outside the US. The upshot was that there grew up in London groups of both lenders and borrowers of dollars, both of whom could deal with much more flexibility about rates and conditions than they could in New York. The growth of the market was particularly stimulated by the activities of the British merchant and overseas banks, whose foreign exchange departments arranged many of the deals.

The presence of these large, and highly mobile, funds was really seen for the first time in a series of runs on sterling from 1964 to 1967. In most cases the movement of short-term capital was not the underlying cause; rather, they simply amplified movements in the current account. But the combination of 'hot' money with the one-way option provided by the adjustable peg system presented new problems to the Bretton Woods system.

During each of these crises of 1964 to 1967 the Bank of England and the British government utilized the support structures which had been established for this purpose, although not necessarily for this currency, with the crisis in October–November 1964 seeing the first use of the GAB which had been set up to support the dollar. By November 1967 the British government (although not the Bank of England) decided it was time to throw in the towel: economic recovery was a long-term problem, while aid to support the pound had come as short-term borrowings. The cost of trying to maintain the parity was underlined when on 17 November, the day devaluation was announced, Britain lost $1 billion from her reserves (Solomon 1977: 342–3; Burk *et al.* 1988: 44–5).

Many economists believe that the UK should have devalued earlier; but her attempt to maintain the rate of the pound had been strongly supported by the Americans, who believed that the pound formed the outer defence of the dollar, and that, if the pound went, speculators would then turn their attention to the other reserve currency. This, indeed, was just what happened, as the combination of American foreign and domestic policies deepened foreigners' distrust of the dollar.

The problems of the dollar came to a head in the early 1970s, but this crisis was part of a longer-term development in which power within the international monetary system shifted away from governments (especially the US) and international organizations and towards private traders. Private banks had played a large role as financial intermediaries earlier in the century, but the war and the plethora of exchange controls which accompanied it had cut them off, with the result that official capital flows dominated international payments in the 1940s and 1950s. As these controls were released, influence swung back in the 1960s (and much more so in the 1970s and 1980s) to private transactions. This development was not, by any means, the only cause of the turmoil of the 1970s and 1980s, but it undoubtedly contributed to it – and it was on the dollar that this new influence was seen most obviously.

The turmoil of the 1970s and 1980s

The dollar was not just another currency: the other IMF member-nation currencies were linked to it, and through the dollar's convertibility into gold at a fixed rate, it related all to gold. Thus the others could change their parities against the dollar, but that of the dollar could not be changed. All that the US could do, if other countries would not revalue their currencies, was to support the exchange rate of the dollar by selling gold. Gold consequently flowed out of the US, and by early 1971 the US gold reserve, which had totalled $17.8 billion in 1960, stood at only $11 billion, estimated as a five-year supply (Scammell 1983: 181). The state of the reserves, combined with a sharply deteriorating balance of payments, convinced the US authorities that they had to act.

Their actions fell in two stages, the so-called Nixon Measures of 15

August and the Smithsonian Agreement of 18 December 1971. By the Nixon Measures, the convertibility of the dollar into gold was suspended and a 10 per cent import surcharge was imposed, the latter to force Japan and Europe to revalue their currencies against the dollar. The results of the negotiations were embodied in the Smithsonian Agreement: there was a general revaluation of currencies relative to the dollar (West Germany by 13.6 per cent, Japan by 16.9 per cent, France and the UK by 8.6 per cent), and in exchange the US lifted the 10 per cent import surcharge, while devaluing the dollar 8 per cent by raising the price of gold from $35 to $38 per ounce (Scammell 1983: 182–3).

But the new dollar standard lasted only nineteen months. First of all, the parities established in December 1971 had been less market-based than bargain-based. When the chairman of the Federal Reserve System, Arthur Burns, called in May 1972 for monetary reforms which would include the ability to make more prompt changes in parities, other countries could be forgiven for showing reluctance to hold dollars (Solomon 1977: 219). Nevertheless, both Germany and Japan found themselves accumulating dollars at such a rate that they feared imported inflation. At the bottom of it all was the continuing large American balance of payments deficit (taking the current and capital accounts together).

What shocked the Europeans as much as anything was the priority given to domestic policy (the Americans charged the Germans and Japanese with the same heinous crime) and a seeming indifference to the international importance of the dollar. This *sauve qui peut* approach certainly encouraged the six members of the European Economic Community (EEC) to draw together in something approaching monetary union, and on 11 March 1972 they announced their intention to maintain their exchange rates within 2.25 per cent of each other (the snake in the tunnel). On 1 May the UK decided to join, but was shortly driven out again: sterling came under heavy pressure in June, and on 23 June 1972 the government announced that the pound would float. The other snake currencies shifted upwards in relation to the dollar, money flowed out of dollars into other currencies and foreign exchange markets were closed for two days.

This was symptomatic of the continuing pressure on the international monetary system for the subsequent eight months. There was a series of attempts to maintain fixed rates, but all of them were ultimately unsuccessful. The causes of this breakdown in the fixed rate system came primarily from four sources. First of all, there was confusion about what ought to happen to the dollar. Until 1972 the US had actually been in surplus on current account, so it was not clear that the problem was one of competitiveness. The real problems were the continuous long-term capital outflows and a loss of gold reserves. These, together with the large build up of short-term dollar holdings, produced a crisis of confidence pushing the dollar downwards; but even if a lower dollar would solve this liquidity problem, there was no obvious way of calculating how much lower it should be. Second, some other countries did seem to be in fundamental disequilibrium on current account. Germany, for example, appeared to have a persistent surplus. These countries therefore required a change in their *real* exchange rate – that is, a change that was not immediately wiped out by offsetting movements in money wages. Third, inflation was accelerating, and inflation rates were beginning to show greater divergence from one country to another. For this reason, changes in nominal exchange rates were required simply to keep real rates unchanged.

For all these reasons, the central banks were unclear as to what the new 'equilibrium rates' should be and, being unclear, were unable to agree on co-ordinated intervention. As a result, they lacked conviction and the markets knew this. Moreover, this confusion amongst the central banks occurred alongside the fourth factor, which was the enormous growth in the scale of actual and potential capital flows. Thus the market view of where rates should be grew in importance just when the other influence on rates – intervention – was declining. At the same time the scale of the market flows weakened still further the self-confidence of the central banks, and each factor fed on the other.

The final crisis came in February/March 1973. Between 1 and 9 February the German Bundesbank bought $5 billion to hold the Deutschmark down (and the dollar up), but on 10 February the Japanese ceased their support for the dollar and closed the foreign exchange market. On 12 February the US devalued the dollar a further 10 per cent, while the yen and the lira began to float (the Canadian dollar was already doing so). Despite this further devaluation, only just over a fortnight later (on 1 March) the European central banks found themselves spending a further $3.6 billion supporting the dollar, and were finally forced to close all their foreign exchange markets.

Thus on 9 March 1973 the finance ministers of fourteen countries signed the Paris Agreement which, *de facto*, ended the Bretton Woods system. Under this agreement, the EEC ministers announced a joint float of six countries with Britain, Italy, and Ireland floating independently; at the same time Germany revalued by 3 per cent. On 16 March they met again, and Sweden and Norway associated their currencies with the snake. Thus the dollar standard was ended and the dollar itself was left free to float. There was a mixed response from the other IMF countries: some pegged themselves to the dollar, a few to sterling, and some to a basket of currencies. In short, it was now a world of flexible exchange rates. But the *de facto* system could only be made *de jure* by the IMF, and a meeting of the Interim Committee at Jamaica in January 1976 proposed the legalization of existing realities. The two pillars of Bretton Woods had been gold as the monetary standard and fixed exchange rates with an adjustable peg. With regard to gold, its official price was abolished and its reserve role reduced; with regard to rates, their flexibility was legalized. In short, the determination of the par value of a currency was to be the responsibility of each country, rather than subject to international agreement.

It was just as well that the working arrangements had been changed in March 1973, because the old procedures would certainly not have held after the Israeli victory in their war with the Arab states in October 1973 and the consequent quadrupling of the oil prices. By early 1974 the price of crude oil was already US$10 a barrel, compared with US$3 a barrel the year before. The widespread use of oil was common to all of the industrialized countries, and the near-quadrupling of its price within three months gave a sharp stimulus to global inflation. But the price rise also acted as a deflationary regressive tax. This threw most countries into recession, giving rise to the newly coined term 'stagflation'. At the same time the oil price rise had pushed many countries, especially developing countries, into balance of payments deficit, so they had a financing requirement. Recession meant that the European and American commercial banks, the repository of much of the OPEC's unspent funds, had to find something to do with the money other than to invest it in the industrialized countries. The banks' common solution to the problem gave rise to one of the gravest international financial and political problems of the 1980s: the debt crisis.

Until the mid-1970s, the major sources of investment funds for developing countries were three: multinational aid from such as the World Bank, unilateral foreign aid, or investment by private corporations (usually multinationals). All three were unsatisfactory for various reasons: the World Bank imposed conditions on borrowers, aid from other countries carried with it expectations of influence and convergence of policies, while countries feared undue influence or dominance over their political and economic systems by foreign multinational corporations. In these circumstances, commercial bank loans came as a very welcome alternative. For the banks, oil-producing countries in particular were expected in the long term to be a good source of profits.

They were also deemed to be credit-worthy borrowers, partly because some of them had oil and partly because of an idea which grabbed the imagination of bankers. This was the belief that countries could not go bankrupt – there was, they thought, no 'country risk' – and therefore it was safe to lend to even the less credit-worthy of them. This was not a well-supported idea. History is full of cases where sovereign countries, whether represented by individuals or governments, have frequently defaulted – and default is the crucial aspect, not putative bankruptcy. In the sixteenth century the Fuggers (a famous German banking family) were virtually destroyed by repeated Spanish defaults; in the early 1880s, more than half of the loans to foreign governments listed in London were in default (Chapman 1984: 82); and in the twentieth century, all of the European countries except for Finland, and even including the UK, defaulted on their war debts to the US. It was therefore rather likely that the situation would end in tears.

The position was made more difficult because the less-developed countries borrowed in foreign currencies and at variable interest rates. This meant that they had no control over the interest rate, which was set by foreign central banks (especially the US Federal Reserve Banks), nor over the real value of their debts, which altered with movements in exchange rates. Moreover, the banks demanded payment in hard currencies, which many of these countries did not have. By the mid-1980s the total burden of world debt had grown from about $100 billion in the early 1970s to approximately $900 billion. Amongst the heaviest debtors were Argentina ($48 billion), Mexico ($97 billion) and Brazil ($99 billion) (Gilpin 1987: 316–17). But, by this time, the debtors were finding it increasingly difficult to service their debts. Much of the difficulty can be ascribed to the second oil price rise in 1979. This gave greatly increased encouragement to energy-conservation policies, and so, when oil demand began falling, even the oil producers were hit. But much more important, it was one of the major factors causing the world economy to go into a second major recession. As Table 2.1 shows, world GDP, which had slowed down after 1973, slowed down again after 1979 (and output actually fell from 1981 to 1982). As a result the debtor countries found it more and more difficult to export in order to finance their debts. Finally, during this period, debtor countries found themselves facing much higher interest rates when the US tightened monetary policy in 1979 and then again in 1980/1 (see chapter 11).

It was oil-producing Mexico which brought the crisis to a head, when in August 1982 it declared a moratorium on its interest payments. In order to protect the American (and international) banking system, the US Treasury and the Federal Reserve stepped in as lenders of last resort, easing monetary policy very noticeably in the second half of 1982 (Mullineux 1987: 69). If debtors to American banks default on interest payments, that renders the loans non-performing and thus substantially lowers their asset value; the amount of such debt held by major American banks was so great that in many cases they would have been deemed bankrupt had those loans been designated non-performing. Apart from the easing of monetary policy in 1982, the US government considered this to be a private sector matter. However, in a further switch of policy in 1985, the administration accepted that it was a problem requiring some contribution from the government. James Baker, the US Secretary of the Treasury, unveiled the Baker Plan in October 1985 at the IMF/World Bank meeting in Seoul, the main features of which were the recovery of the debtor economies through economic growth rather than through austerity, with privatization and the opening of the debtor economies to trade and foreign direct investment; all of this was to be lubricated by renewed lending by the commercial banks. The IMF was to have a supervisory role.

Occurring alongside this, and not unrelated, was a major reconsideration by the US of exchange rate policy. Higher interest rates had meant a much stronger dollar (measured against the OECD countries it had appreciated by more than a half from 1980 to 1985), and American exporters were finding it harder to retain markets for their goods. As a result, at a meeting of the central bank governors of the Group of Five countries (US, Japan, West Germany, France, and the UK) held at the Plaza Hotel, New York in September 1985, the US gained the agreement of the other countries that their authorities would intervene in foreign exchange markets and stimulate their own economies. This, together with the prospect of a cut in the US budget deficit, a lower price for oil, and the change in market sentiment that the co-ordinated intervention brought about, caused approximately a 33 per cent devaluation of the dollar by March 1986 (Gilpin 1987: 155–7).

The importance of this devaluation was that it was a policy change which the US would have found difficult if not impossible to effect on its own. This dependency was politically difficult to accept, in particular since the US government found that it could no longer act with quite the same indifference towards the outside world as had been the case for most of the period since 1945. This was underlined by the sudden realization by both policy-makers and the American public that the US was no longer top nation – at least financially – but had been replaced by Japan.

The new-found anxiety about the dollar, combined with the success of the co-ordinated action to devalue it, also stimulated the American administration to look anew at the possibilities of international financial co-operation as compared with national financial autonomy. In his State of the Union message to Congress in February 1986, Reagan proposed what he called 'policy co-ordination', the stated purpose of which would be to eliminate currency fluctuations and agree upon target zones for the major currencies (closely managed floats, which might be interpreted as virtually a return to fixed rates). At the Tokyo Summit of western leaders in May 1986, the US tried to convince the others that automatic rules should replace market-determined exchange rates; the idea was to lower the rate of the dollar further and thereby improve the US' huge trade deficit. But other countries did not agree with the view of the US, which was that their economies should be stimulated in order to close the gap in the rates of growth of the American and, e.g., the German economy. Rather, they, and Germany and Japan in particular, believed that the root problem was American financial indiscipline as exemplified by the budget deficit.

With their interpretations of the problem so at variance with that of the US, other countries did not want to put their economies at risk again from American indifference to the interests of its partners. The most they would agree to in May 1986 was 'enhanced surveillance' over rates and economic policies. This was to be carried out by a new international body, the Group of Seven (made up of finance ministers and central bankers of the Group of Five plus Canada and Italy), who would engage in 'close and continuous' co-ordination of the economic policies of the western powers; if and when there was a 'significant deviation', and the policy of one nation caused problems for others, the Group were to try and 'reach an understanding' on corrective action (Gilpin 1987: 159).

If it was not Bretton Woods II, it was the closest the US, with its new-found discovery of the benefits of rules, was likely to attain for some time. The international financial system had come full circle, with the US again attempting, primarily for its own but also for others' benefit, to establish international structures to allow the free play of private enterprise within agreed rules. But, this time, history got in the way: there was no longer a clean slate, and the US was no longer dominant. Other countries had suffered too much in the interim to put their own economies at risk from a self-absorbed US which might again turn rogue.

The development of trade

Coincidentally or not, postwar trade expansion was greatest during the period of Bretton Woods. Nevertheless, in spite of the fact that the events of 1973 marked a sharp decline in world economic growth, trade continued to grow faster than output (at least up to 1979, see Table 2.1). Considering the postwar period as a whole, certain themes stand out: the postwar recovery and the establishment of the EEC, the moves to liberalize trade, the growth in trade from the late 1950s to 1973, the impact of multinationals, and, in the 1970s and 1980s, the slowing of the growth of trade and the revival of protectionism.

The foundation of the postwar expansion was the recovery of the domestic economies of the industrial powers, with a steady increase in per capita incomes. The original impetus came from government spending and public and private investment, and it was later significantly fuelled by consumer demand. Marshall Aid facilitated this recovery; the US also helped by not plunging into postwar recession, as had been feared, but instead providing funds for private investment in Europe as well as a market for European exports. Expansion was encouraged, too, by trade liberaliza-tion, facilitated by the European Payments Union and then consolidated and expanded in 1957 with the establishment of the EEC, which provided for the progressive removal of tariffs within the Six. The setting-up of the European Free Trade Association (EFTA) in 1959 accounted for most of the remaining western European countries, and EFTA provided for comparable internal tariff reductions. At the same time, it is worth noting that the EEC also represented a more interventionist and discriminatory system. The Common Agricultural Policy is a good example of the former, while preferential trade relations with former Belgian and French colonies, linked as Associated States of the EEC by the Yaoundé Conventions of 1963 and 1969, are an example of the latter.

The US strongly backed these moves for regional customs unions. As noted above, it had attempted to establish multilateral free trade in the immediate postwar period, but, when this proved impossible, the US sanctioned trading blocks (e.g. the Sterling Area), even though these practised discrimination against dollar-area products. Elements in the US government expected that in due course these blocks would widen and link up, and thus it welcomed the EEC as providing an example of a large, internally free market. In retrospect it is amazing how little discussion there was amongst American policy-makers as to whether such a customs union might prove to be wholly to the benefit of the US.

The Americans also welcomed the EEC on political grounds, as providing a barrier to the expansion of communism in Europe, but their fears about the economic effects on the US rapidly grew. The renewal of the Reciprocal Trade Agreements Act in 1958 empowered the president to reduce American tariffs by 20 per cent, the object being to negotiate with the new EEC before it established itself as a discriminatory trade area (Scammell 1983: 169–70). Douglas Dillon, the American Under-Secretary of State, called in 1958 for a new round of tariff negotiations, utilizing the GATT, and in November 1958 ministers accepted the proposal. Negotiations began on 1 September 1960.

This fifth, so-called Dillon, round of negotiations lasted until 1962, but its achievements were relatively small, compared to the amount of effort expended: 44,400 tariff concessions were agreed, product by product. But because trade liberalization had gone some way by 1962, there was less scope for item reductions, particularly since the remaining core, by definition more important to the individual countries, tended to be supported by politically powerful groups. The answer was multilateral, across-the-board cuts, and this was the approach taken during the Kennedy Round (1963–7). The results were tariff cuts averaging 35 per cent on some 60,000 internationally traded products, but the outcome, at least for the US, was less satisfactory in the agricultural sector, with the failure to gain access to the EEC for its farm products (Scammell 1983: 172).

What also became clear during the Kennedy Round was the increasing importance of non-tariff barriers, and indeed, an Anti-Dumping code was concluded. But the decisive shift in emphasis to a preoccupation with non-tariff issues came with the Tokyo Round (1973–9). In addition to some tariff cuts, this round produced a series of supplementary agreements (known as 'codes') on a wide variety of subjects such as import licensing procedures, dumping, subsidies, and technical standards. However, subscribing to them was optional, and while widely acceded to by the industrialized countries, this was less the case for the developing countries.

The outcome, in short, was modest, and non-tariff issues were taken up again in the Uruguay Round, which began in September 1986.

The nature of the problem of trade liberalization, then, has changed over the postwar period, and the problems dominating the agenda after 1967 (and in particular after 1971) have lacked the transparency of tariffs; they are frequently buried deep in a country's economic system or even culture (the Japanese distribution system comes to mind here). But this should not obscure the important role played by liberalization in the spectacular increase in international trade. Between 1948 and 1970 trade in manufactures consistently grew more rapidly than world manufacturing output, with the former growing at 9 per cent a year. Trade expanded most rapidly between industrialized countries, and this provision of markets encouraged industrial investment and expansion.

One aspect of this was a great increase in foreign direct investment, notably by American multinational companies (although to some extent by the French and British), and the increase in the numbers and size of multinational corporations has changed the nature of international trade: within the general flows of exports and imports, a substantial proportion is now intra-firm trading. Indeed, one estimate made in 1977 suggested that 50 per cent of world trade should be regarded as taking place on an intra-firm basis (Scammell 1983: 160). This has probably increased as Japanese overseas investment has followed in the path of that of Britain, France, Germany, and the US. In response particularly to pressures in the 1980s, whereby both the EEC and the US sought to raise the barriers against Japanese export expansion, Japanese companies have progressively turned themselves into multinationals by establishing manufacturing plants in other industrialized countries (they had already done so in a number of Asian countries). Particularly since 1979, British companies too have resumed expansion abroad, with the US a prime target. In short, by the mid-1980s, large companies were more likely to be multinational than not, and an integrated global economy – serviced by a globally organized financial services industry – was no longer a pipe dream.

The growth in numbers and sizes of multinationals has been partly a reaction to the slowdown in the growth of international trade since 1973, as companies fought to maintain market share and/or profits and sought ways to get around increasing trade restrictions. Various fundamental developments in the 1970s, some of which have already been mentioned, contributed to this slowdown and to the revival of economic protectionism. By far the most important factor was the fall in output growth. Other developments included the shift to floating rates in 1973 and the consequent erratic behaviour of rates of exchange; the massive increases in the price of energy after OPEC I and II; the intensification of Japanese competition after 1971, and of the so-called newly industrialized countries, such as Taiwan and South Korea, whose technological attainments, when combined with low wage rates, made then highly competitive with the advanced industrial countries; the relative decline of the American economy, which has given rise to growing protectionist sentiment; the increasingly high barriers put up by the EEC against outsiders; and, providing the general context, global price inflation combined with recession (Gilpin 1987: 193). By the mid-1980s, however, inflation had been brought under control in most of the industrialized countries while economic growth had resumed. Nevertheless, restrictive habits had taken hold, and the goal of multilateral free trade seemed, even for the Americans, a dream for the past.

Conclusion

Looking at the broad sweep of developments, the overall picture is one of a system which, despite all of its trials and its non-operation, allowed countries to interact surprisingly successfully until the mid-1970s and which, even since then, has not fallen apart (as many predicted it would) under the twin strains of the oil shocks and Third World debt. It has evolved and changed, but it has not (yet) collapsed.

The changes are, however, changes of substance. In 1945 the US bestrode the world as hegemon, a junior partner or two at its side, but with other countries very much the underdogs. It used its power to set up, more or less in agreement with the other victors, organizations, designed to produce a world linked through an international monetary system and by ties of free trade. In practice the world economy has evolved in a very different manner. The system of fixed exchange rates with a gold–dollar standard at the centre has given way to a floating rate system; notwithstanding considerable liberalization of trade in the 1950s and 1960s, the ideal of multilateral free trade has not been achieved. Rather, it has been overcome by a world of organized trading blocs (the European Community, the Latin American Free Trade Area, the Central American Common Market, and the COMECON); and there is no longer a hegemon, but several powers of comparable economic strength.

What effects this system, and the major changes to which it has been subject, had upon the economic performance of countries is impossible to tell with any certainty. Nevertheless, the history of the postwar period suggests two broad observations about the interaction between countries.

First, there is a sense in which economic behaviour can be more (or less) than the sum of its parts. When the world economy is expanding, each country can do better than each separately expects, and expansion is thereby driven on by the favourable expectations that this engenders. Another possibility is that policies between countries can interact in cumulatively helpful ways: full employment, for example, is not only easier to sustain when other countries are growing, but also the presence of full employment makes trade liberalization more acceptable; this, in its turn, can further promote economic growth and employment. This optimistic view would be one way of characterizing the long boom from the end of the Second World War to the mid-1970s. Conversely, when one part of the framework gives way, holding the rest in place is that much more difficult – and again, this might characterize the problems besetting the world economy after 1973.

Second, the fundamental problem of the appropriate balance between intervention and markets remains on the agenda. During the postwar years, there has never successfully been freedom in all markets at once. Under Bretton Woods, exchange rates were fixed and trade and capital movements were gradually liberalized – but the fixed rates did not survive the full freeing of capital movements. Post Bretton Woods, exchange rates have been allowed to float, but protectionism has begun to creep back in, and the fluctuations in exchange rates have proved sufficiently large and disturbing to bring central bankers back into the game.

Therefore, while it may not be possible to pin down exactly how economic performance has been affected, there seems little doubt that the international environment of trade and payments has been an important influence on the economic policies of the different countries – and its effects appear and reappear constantly throughout this book.

Selected dates

December 1945	International Monetary Fund and the International Bank for Reconstruction and Development came into existence.
October 1947	Conclusion of the General Agreement on Tariffs and Trade.
November 1947– March 1948	Havana Conference to discuss a Charter for the abortive International Trade Organization.
1948–51	Roughly $13 billion in Marshall Aid granted to sixteen countries.
March 1957	Signing of the Treaty of Rome establishing the European Economic Community.
January 1959	Convertibility of the main European currencies: Bretton Woods system fully activated.
January 1960	Stockholm Convention signed establishing the European Free Trade Area.
September– December 1961	Setting-up of the General Arrangements to Borrow: set up by ten countries to lend $6 billion to the IMF, to be drawn upon by members to support their exchange rates.
1967	Negotiations leading to establishment of new form of liquidity, the IMF's Special Drawing Rights.

August 1971	Nixon Measures: suspended convertibility of dollars into gold.
March 1972	EEC countries announce they will maintain their exchange rates within 2.25 per cent of each other.
March 1973	Paris Agreement: floating exchange rates and *de facto* end of Bretton Woods system.
October–December 1973	Arab–Israeli War and consequent near-quadrupling of oil prices (OPEC I).
Spring 1979	Fall of the Shah and oil price hike of 40 per cent (OPEC II).
August 1982	Mexico ordered a moratorium on international debt interest payments and brought the international debt crisis to a head.
September 1985	US got agreement of Japan, Germany, the UK, and France that their governments would intervene in foreign exchange markets and stimulate their economies, to help devalue the dollar.
October 1985	Baker Plan unveiled in Seoul: recovery of debtor economies through growth rather than austerity, to be lubricated through renewed commercial bank lending.
February 1986	President Reagan called for 'policy co-ordination' to help eliminate currency fluctuations and agree upon target zones for the major currencies.
May 1986	Tokyo Summit agreed on 'enhanced surveillance', to be carried out by the Group of Seven.

References

Boltho, A. and Allsopp, C. (1987) 'Trade and trade policy', *Oxford Review of Economic Policy*, 3, 1.

Burk, Kathleen *et al.* (1988) 'The 1967 devaluation', *Contemporary Record*, 1, 4.

Chapman, Stanley (1984) *The Rise of Merchant Banking*, London: George Allen & Unwin.

Ellis-Rees, Sir Hugh (1962) 'The convertibility crisis of 1947', Treasury Historical Memorandum No. 4, T.267/3, London: Public Record Office.

Gilpin, R. (1987) *The Political Economy of International Relations*, Princeton, NJ: Princeton University Press.

Maddison, A. (1982) *The Phases of Capitalist Development*, Oxford: Oxford University Press.

Milward, A.S. (1984) *The Recovery of Western Europe 1945–51*, London: Methuen.

Mullineux, A.W. (1987) *International Money and Banking: The Creation of a New Order*, Brighton: Wheatsheaf Books.

Scammell, W.M. (1983) *The International Economy Since 1945*, 2nd edn, London: Macmillan.

Solomon, Robert (1977) *The International Monetary System 1945–1976: An*

Insider's View, New York: Harper & Row.

Strange, Susan (1986) *Casino Capitalism*, Oxford: Blackwell.

Tew, B. (1985) *The Evolution of the International Monetary System 1945-85*, 3rd edn, London: Hutchinson.

Guide to further reading

Brendan Brown, *The Flight of International Capital: A Contemporary History*, London, 1981.

Robert O. Keohane, *After Hegemony: Cooperation and Discord in the World Political Economy*, Princeton NJ, 1984.

Armand van Dormael, *Bretton Woods: Birth of a Monetary System*, London, 1978.

Chapter three

The United Kingdom

Alec Cairncross

Introduction

The United Kingdom emerged from the Second World War in what seemed, in comparison with most of her continental neighbours, to be a relatively favourable position. In 1946 industrial production was as high as at any time before the war and rising quite fast. By the end of the year exports had regained their pre-war level. There was little unemployment and retail prices were relatively stable. All this contrasted strongly with the situation in France, Germany, and Italy.

Yet appearances were deceptive. The British economy was overloaded from the start and faced with acute balance of payments difficulties. From being an investor in foreign securities on an unprecedented scale, with nearly one-third of her wealth overseas, the United Kingdom had become the largest external debtor in history. The net change on capital account during the war had amounted to $20 billion and was equal to the amount that the USSR sought in reparations from Germany. It completely offset the net addition to domestic assets since 1914, leaving the country no richer than thirty years earlier.

Since most of the debts contracted in wartime were short term, they represented a continuing overhang of liquid liabilities with damaging consequences in postwar years in the form of an abundance of sterling not in firm hands and threatening a flight from the pound. This limited the freedom of action of the government and contributed to that jerkiness of postwar growth that came to be labelled 'stop-go'. The loss of income from foreign investments and shipping earnings, which had paid for 35 per cent of pre-war imports, also added to Britain's balance of payments difficulties, and these were intensified by a sharp rise in the cost of imports in relation to the prices obtained for exports and by a large continuing outflow on military account as the United Kingdom undertook world-wide defence responsibilities in highly unsettled conditions.

The weakness of the postwar balance of payments had three important consequences for policy-makers. It was difficult to reconcile with the effort to maintain sterling as the leading international currency in which more than half the world's trade was conducted; it made it necessary to limit imports and spread them more thinly over an expanding economy – it was 1955 before the pre-war volume was regained; and it threatened to jeopardize the government's commitment to maintain 'a high and stable level of employment'.

The direction and character of British trade raised a second set of problems. A high proportion of British trade – about three quarters – was with countries outside Europe. Much of it was with Asia and Africa, i.e., the poorer, less developed countries; and much of it was with Commonwealth countries under preferential arrangements of diminishing force. In comparison with their competitors in Europe British manufacturers supplied a wider scatter of markets, heavily weighted by those that were poor and slow-growing. Trade links of themselves made the United Kingdom something of a world power, with global responsibilities and a disposition to look to international rather than European institutions. What was thought of as 'the special relationship' with the United States, arising in part from the two world wars, tended in the same direction. At the same time, continental countries and, under the Marshall Plan, the United States too, looked to the United Kingdom to take a lead in Europe both in economic reconstruction and in some form of economic integration. The dichotomy between world-wide and purely European connections and interests dominated much of British policy in the postwar years.

Britain's postwar trade problems had a further important consequence. The need to limit imports and boost exports was one of the main reasons for continuing in peacetime to use many of the administrative controls introduced during the war. These controls, which did little to promote rapid economic growth, were only gradually discontinued: food rationing and building controls, for example, lingered until 1954; the rationing of domestic coal ceased only in 1958; and exchange control was not given up until 1979.

Extensive controls over economic behaviour muffled incentives which were given freer play in some other industrial countries. High taxation told in the same direction. The standard rate of income tax remained at 45 per cent or more up to 1955 and the top rate was in some years as high as 97 per cent. Indirect taxation was correspondingly high. While for many such taxes may have been little discouragement to effort there were bound to be others whose inclination was to slacken off. Rightly or wrongly, the theme of inadequate incentives for management and workers alike recurs in the literature of the postwar years; and the attitudes current at the start tended to be self-perpetuating. Yet if other countries were more powerfully motivated it was not because of fewer controls or lower taxes but far more from the need felt by the individual worker and the individual enterprise to survive and re-build a livelihood. The compulsions in countries that had been bombed, occupied, or fought over were of a different order from anything in Britain even if there had been extensive bomb damage there too.

This points to one more weakness in the postwar British economy: the relatively high level from which it started and the strong expectation of better things to come. Unlike pre-war days, there was no lack of jobs and the pay was higher than before the war even if it could not all be spent on the things most wanted. GDP had no great distance to go to reach the pre-war level while on the continent there was a great gap to be closed. Where there was such a gap, the curve of output could slope steeply upwards and the momentum of recovery might prolong the rise by creating an atmosphere and attitudes congenial to further growth. Countries that started off with a high rate of growth tended to maintain a relatively high rate. In the United Kingdom, on the other hand, there could be no steep slope except through higher productivity, when the level of activity was already so near the ceiling.

Efforts to raise productivity were made in the years immediately after the war but were soon discontinued. The emphasis of policy was more on issues of distribution than on wealth creation. This was evident in the taxation system, rationing arrangements, food subsidies, and welfare benefits. There was also a tendency to defend the status quo and resist change. The British worker, for example, entered the postwar period with wages (and still more, earnings) that had risen faster than prices chiefly because of food subsidies. His (and her) consumption had been cut in wartime, not by a reduction in wages, but quite deliberately by rationing. Now that the war was over, they expected to see rationing removed without any offsetting contraction in income. The cost of rations had been held steady by government subsidies and this state of affairs, too, workers expected to continue even if world food prices rose or if the size of the ration was increased until rationing could be abandoned. They expected improved wages to be maintained whatever their own contribution to output and whatever the burdens war had bequeathed. They also looked to the state to maintain full employment and provide welfare benefits in health, education, pensions, and so on. Such expectations were not altogether unreasonable. But they could easily develop into an attitude of looking to others to provide what one feels entitled to consume. Such an attitude does not make for unstinted effort and a readiness to give priority to the common interest.

There had been none of the upsets in the British economy and social system that had made continental countries accept change as necessary for their survival. On the contrary, the quiet life had more appeal than ever for managements after the strain of war, while workers felt entitled to resume restrictive practices. Faced with labour shortages and lacking the necessary staff for careful planning and supervision, British managements tended to rely on piece rates to provide their workers with the necessary incentives and to surrender to them the power to plan their work in detail. The enhanced

bargaining power of the workers then either blocked the process of innovation or exacted a price that slowed it down. Managements in turn shrank
from the conflicts that change and innovation required. In these circumstances what is remarkable is that productivity increased as much as it did
rather than that there was any shortfall in growth in comparison with other
countries.

Two other circumstances reinforced these tendencies. One was the
apprenticeship system and the relative backwardness of systematic labour
training. This does not mean that there was an absence of skill – in some
industries there was, if anything, too high a reliance on labour skills – but
only that too small a proportion of the working population could claim to
be skilled and that the skills that were learned were acquired in on-the-job
training with a minimum of theoretical background. A second factor was
low elasticity of labour supply. The labour force grew very slowly and the
industrial labour force was not enlarged, as on the continent, by a large
outflow from agriculture. Employment in agriculture was no more, in the
early postwar years, than 4 per cent of total employment and the proportion
fell only slowly partly because balance of payments difficulties made it seem
desirable, in a country drawing over half its food from abroad, to make a
modest import-saving investment in agricultural expansion.

Together with the various weaknesses in the British economy there were
also a number of exceptional advantages. The United Kingdom was able to
borrow heavily from the United States and Canada; it had preferential
access to Commonwealth markets (although this proved to be a rapidly
wasting asset); and could pay in sterling for supplies from countries within
the sterling area if (as was not always the case) imports from them were in
excess of exports to them. The last of these advantages, however, was a
doubtful one since sterling area countries drew capital freely from the
United Kingdom on a scale that the country could ill afford.

In devising policies to deal with the situation the United Kingdom had a
highly centralized political and administrative machine. Power was concentrated in the Cabinet. Within the Cabinet responsibility for most aspects of
economic policy, external and domestic, usually lay with the Chancellor of
the Exchequer who, provided he could carry the Prime Minister, was in a
strong position to secure agreement to his proposals. His department, the
Treasury, united functions more commonly divided between several
different departments, including control of public expenditure and an
oversight over monetary policy. In matters of finance the Bank of England,
as the market operator and the Chancellor's financial adviser, also had an
influential voice, particularly with Conservative Chancellors, and preserved
its independence of judgement.

The two-party system operated in such a way that whichever party was in
power could rarely be removed from office except at election. This made for
stable government so long as there was no change of government but for

sharp reversals of policy when there was one. Even without a change of government, there could also be sharp reversals in mid-term under the pressure of events or because experience of office made a government change its mind. At the official level, reliance on an established non-political civil service made for continuity of policy and for efficient implementation of it. Here, too, there was a high degree of centralization, with the Treasury in a more dominant position than in pre-war years. Governments spoke with one voice and civil servants were not supposed to speak in public at all. The main institutions with which the government dealt were much less highly centralized. Neither the FBI (later the CBI) nor the TUC had much influence, let alone control, over their members. As a result it was difficult to secure their firm backing for government policy and count on them to deliver against any undertakings they could be induced to make.

Objectives

The dominant economic objective of government policy for most of the period after 1945 was 'a high and stable level of employment' as stated in the 1944 White Paper on *Employment Policy*. This objective was subject to a number of qualifications such as the need for 'moderation in wage matters' and it was at first interpreted – by officials at least – as implying a level of unemployment of about 5 per cent or possibly more. Beveridge, however, in his *Full Employment in a Free Society* proposed 3 per cent as a target and in 1951, after some years' experience of unemployment rates of under 2 per cent, the Labour government adopted publicly a target of 3 per cent as an operating average. It was a rate hardly ever exceeded before 1975 and never again achieved thereafter.

The absence of severe unemployment focused attention on a second objective – economic growth. This resulted partly from experience of a steadily growing GDP (and the availability in postwar years of regular official estimates of GDP) and partly from the spectacle of more rapid growth in continental countries. Once it became clear that this was not a purely temporary phenomenon, associated with recovery from war, British governments were under pressure to achieve higher rates of growth and to adopt the policies (such as indicative planning) that were thought to have made possible such rates in other countries. Since, however, different continental countries pursued very different policies while all enjoyed fast rates of growth it was not at all clear which policies were to be recommended. It was also very rare, after the early 1950s, for any country to experience an acceleration of growth such as was sought by the United Kingdom. On the contrary, there was some falling-off from the higher rates experienced earlier. It was natural to doubt, therefore, whether government policy played a part of much importance in continental growth rates.

With these objectives went two others that at times took precedence over full employment and growth; external and internal stability, or, in other words, balance of payments equilibrium and the absence of inflation. These might seem to be secondary and instrumental but became dominant and independent objectives. In the early postwar years, for example, many of the controls over the economy were directed towards bringing the international accounts back into balance and, for a long period, towards limiting outgoings in gold and dollars. At the other end of the period, from 1979 or earlier, control of inflation became the principal aim of policy without much regard to repercussions on employment or growth.

Nevertheless, at all times external and internal stability were either direct objects of policy or background concerns. Admittedly, for short periods one or other could drop off the political agenda, most obviously the balance of payments in the early 1980s when it was benefiting from both North Sea oil and the recession that the counter-inflation policies involved, but this respite was temporary. In the longer term governments could not be indifferent to the risk that their policies might involve a higher balance of payments deficit than they could finance or that they might give rise to a large outflow of funds endangering the stability of the economy. Equally they could not be indifferent to a rise in prices that created inflationary expectations. When inflation was thought to be due to excess demand, budget surpluses were used. When it was thought to be due to too much money the government turned to monetary policy. When it was thought to reflect higher wages, associated with the greater scarcity and bargaining power of labour and unaccompanied by higher productivity, governments sought to moderate the scale of wage settlements by some form of incomes policy. When the usefulness of such measures came to be doubted, governments turned to more drastic alternatives, relying again primarily on monetary policy.

Another objective akin to these two was to prevent too great an imbalance between the different regions and sectors of the economy. This meant an effort to temper any sudden decline in activity concentrated in one area or industry and afford more time for adjustment. It also meant an effort to put new life into declining areas with high levels of unemployment. What began in the 1930s as policy towards 'the depressed areas' developed in the postwar years into regional policy.

Economic objectives were combined with social objectives. One of these was greater equality; and a variety of policies was influenced by this aim. On the one hand, progressive taxation laid heavier burdens on the rich. On the other hand were all the welfare benefits met from public funds: education, health, housing, and pensions. So far as the cost of these fell on the taxpayer there was a transfer to the beneficiary, taxpayers being on the average better off than those who benefited. Egalitarianism entered more directly in the form of subsidies and price control. For example, the food subsidies of the early postwar years met 20 per cent of the public's expenditure on food in 1947 and a far higher proportion of expenditure on items such as bread. The subsidies and the rationing that accompanied them were partly designed to ensure 'fair shares', partly to keep consumption within the limits of what could be procured and paid for and partly to help in keeping money wages steady. Rent control, dividend control, control over prices (particularly in the public sector) were other examples of policies adopted on social grounds without much regard to economic side-effects.

Such policies reflected wider objectives. When Labour was in power the government sought to plan and regulate the economy almost as an aim in itself. The programme of nationalization after the Second World War, although defended at times on economic grounds, was primarily an attempt to bring under state control what were regarded as key economic activities before the policies to be followed in the nationalized sector had been worked out. Similarly, Conservative governments were disposed to treat as an aim of policy setting free the economy from state control. This might take the form of abolishing building controls or privatizing industries in public ownership or allowing the pound to float. In each case there would be a presumption on one side in favour of state control or ownership in the common interest and on the other a presumption against it.

Instruments

Until 1979 the main instrument of policy in pursuit of government objectives was the budget. This was not what had been envisaged in wartime. The Treasury, for example, had strongly resisted the inclusion in the White Paper on *Employment Policy* (1944) of proposals to vary taxation or the budget surplus in order to influence the level of employment or reduce inflationary pressure. Many Treasury officials continued to regard the use of taxation for purposes other than the raising of revenue as intrinsically objectionable. They had less objection to budget surpluses but were strongly against incurring deficits deliberately.

At the end of the war the Labour government continued to rely on wartime instruments of control and only gradually moved over to the use of the budget, in Cripps's words, as 'the most powerful instrument for influencing economic policy which is available to the government'. This did not, however, imply exclusive reliance on the budget; and for many years it was taken for granted that financial instruments of control would have to be supplemented by various forms of direct control. These were used, for example, to hold down prices, to ration consumer goods, to allocate materials, to limit imports, and to control investment and employment. To some ministers this added up to economic planning, and in consequence they favoured the indefinite retention of some at least of the controls. When a bill for this purpose was under consideration in 1950 it would have given the government statutory powers under all of the six headings just listed except labour controls. But the bill was dropped and in the course of the 1950s all five types of control were discontinued. Exchange control, which had been put on the Statute Book in 1947, was almost the only administrative control to be retained.

The gradual disappearance of direct controls was counterbalanced to some extent by the adoption of an active monetary policy by the incoming Conservative government in 1951–2 and the first use of hire purchase restrictions. These were imposed for the first time in 1952 and kept being tightened or loosened, removed and reimposed all through the next two decades.

Until the middle seventies demand management was the undisputed approach to economic policy. This meant the ascendancy of fiscal policy, with the support from time to time of 'packages' of other measures such as higher interest rates, credit restriction (including hire purchase restrictions on consumer credit), a tightening of exchange control, and the announcement of a wage freeze, or some other form of incomes policy. The use of a floating exchange rate, which had been much debated in the early 1950s, partly as a means of achieving earlier convertibility, partly as a substitute for import controls, was not resorted to until 1972.

Fiscal policy under the Labour governments of 1945–51 had been directed mainly towards eliminating excess demand through a succession of budget surpluses. From 1951 to about 1975 it was used in combination with monetary policy in the management of demand so as to stabilize employment. During that period the Conservatives not only revived the use of monetary policy but in 1957 revived also the quantity theory of money which made monetary policy the key to the control of inflation. Two years earlier they had treated tighter money as a means to lower income tax. While not much came of these ideas at the time, they returned at the end of the 1970s when policy aims underwent a major change.

The change was the result of alarmingly high rates of inflation. The stabilization of prices rather than employment became the dominant aim of policy. Indeed, employment policy seemed at times to be upside down and the government almost disposed to welcome higher unemployment in the interests of labour discipline. From about 1976 monetary policy emerged as a powerful instrument in its own right while fiscal policy began to assume a subordinate role. Instead of monetary policy being brought in to support fiscal policy, the first steps were taken to use fiscal policy in support of monetary policy. From 1979 this became the overt and declared policy of the government. A Medium Term Financial Strategy was announced, the government set about reducing the Public Sector Borrowing Requirement (PSBR) to 1 per cent of GNP or less, and various monetary targets were adopted in successive years, nominally in line with the medium-term strategy but in practice departing increasingly from it.

In the years after 1979 policy was completely dominated by the struggle with inflation. Other policies – employment policy, growth policy, incomes policy, regional policy – fell by the wayside. Similarly, the instruments of policy tended to narrow down and to be viewed largely in terms of their impact on the money supply. By 1985, however, the government had fallen silent on its earlier (monetarist) ideas and was clearly attaching more importance to the stability of the exchange rate than to any meaningful targets for the money supply.

Performance

If when we turn to economic performance we find it matching governmental objectives, there is a natural tendency to assume a causal relationship between the two. As we shall see, however, the government's influence was far more limited than would appear.

Employment

This is particularly true of growth but it applies also to employment. Until 1967 unemployment hardly ever rose as high as 2 per cent and this was taken as a sign of the government's success in maintaining 'a high and stable level' of employment. Similarly the abandonment of that commitment from 1979 tends to be associated with the increase in unemployment to over 3 million by 1985. The fact that boom conditions prevailed more or less everywhere in the first thirty years after the war makes it difficult, however, to attribute full employment in Britain entirely to policy in the UK. In the same way the rise in unemployment – although not to the same extent as in the United Kingdom – has been the common experience of nearly all industrial countries and cannot therefore be entirely due to the policy (or lack of policy) of the United Kingdom. On the other hand, the clear commitment to full employment did contribute to greater stability both directly through demand management and perhaps also by generating optimistic expectations in the earlier period. Similarly the rejection of this commitment may have intensified the slump in the early 1980s.

Despite its successful outcome British employment policy in the 1950s and 1960s had its critics, some opposed to full employment as such, some grumbling because the pressure of demand was not held completely constant but allowed to oscillate between stop and go. Fluctuations in the United Kingdom, however, were not appreciably wider or more frequent than in other countries: the only difference was that a slowdown in Britain might mean zero growth for a year or so while other countries on a higher trend line continued to grow.

Fluctuations in employment were heavily concentrated on manufacturing. Employment in the rest of the economy (accounting in 1985 for three-quarters of total employment) was remarkably stable throughout, with a slight upward trend. Between 1950 and 1965, when total employment grew by $2\frac{1}{2}$ million to 25 million, 1 million of the increase was in manufacturing and $1\frac{1}{2}$ million in services and other sectors. From 1965 to 1985, when total employment fell by ¾ million, the fall in manufacturing was $3\frac{1}{2}$ million while the rest of the economy absorbed 2¾ million more workers. Thus the non-manufacturing part of the economy grew faster in a period of growing depression than in a period of continuous boom.

What started as a lower rate of unemployment than in almost any other country became in time a higher rate than almost anywhere else. From less than 2 per cent up to 1965 the rate oscillated between 2 per cent and 4 per cent in the next ten years, doubled between 1974 and 1979 and more than doubled again in the next six years.

Although ministers were prepared to vary taxation to regulate the pressure of demand, they at no time committed themselves to budget deficits as a remedy for economic depression and the success of demand management was thus dependent on the continuation of the boom. In 1954, for example, when an expansionary budget seemed appropriate, the Chancellor, Butler, was confronted with revenue forecasts (which proved to be mistaken) of a vanishing surplus and was torn between his desire to get taxes down and his qualms over the impropriety (as he saw it) of a possible budget deficit. Even Robert Hall, the economic adviser to the government, agreed that 'the psychological effect of moving to an above-the-line deficit this year would be very damaging'. Similarly, when Butler cut the standard rate of income tax by 2.5 per cent at the height of a boom in 1955 he saw nothing wrong in such a move because he was 'giving away' only half the prospective surplus 'above the line'. Two years later prime minister Macmillan wrote: 'I believe that the view that high taxation is anti-inflationary has been pretty well exploded.'

It was not until the 1970s that employment policy collided with the need to finance a budget deficit. As the deficit swelled to a prospective £12 billion or over 10 per cent of GNP the Labour government in 1976 felt obliged to surrender full employment to the demands of debt management. This was partly in order to win help from the IMF: but more fundamentally it was because of the difficulty of financing the deficit through a weak gilt-edged market and the fear of aggravating inflation if it became necessary to resort to monetization of the debt. From then on, monetary targets, and later, foreign exchange targets, took precedence over the budget judgement. The budget deficit was limited by what the gilt-edged market would absorb and the scope for additions to shorter term debt that were consistent with the monetary target.

Growth

British policy after the war was not at first explicitly directed towards faster growth. The government did, however, attach importance to raising productivity; it sent teams to America to investigate what might be done, set up working parties in the consumer goods industries, and appealed to workers to improve their performance. More important perhaps was the Labour government's effort to give priority to exports and investment by holding down consumption between 1946 and 1951. Even so, labour productivity in the years 1948–51, which provide a fair test, grew by only 2.8 per cent per annum: lower than in the 1960s and much below the level in most continental countries in the first two postwar decades.

In spite of Butler's prediction in 1953 of a doubling of the standard of living in the next twenty-five years, not much was done by the Conservative government in the 1950s to increase the rate of growth except the introduction of an investment allowance in 1954 aimed at encouraging industrial investment. Then in 1961 Selwyn Lloyd set up the National Economic Development Council ('Neddy') with faster economic growth as one of its main objectives; and in 1965 George Brown prepared a National Plan for growth at 4 per cent per annum which in the end came to nothing.

From the mid-1960s growth policy switched to more hopeful lines of advance: management education, labour training, restructuring of industry through the Industrial Reorganization Corporation (IRC). Little Neddies were set up under the NEDC, somewhat along the lines of Stafford Cripps's working parties. But the relations between industry and government remained uneasy, with neither full-blooded competition on the American model nor the close co-operation practised in France and Japan.

With the first oil shock, talk of economic growth began to die away and productivity growth dropped sharply all over the world. By the time the Conservatives returned to power in 1979 the professed role of government had shrunk to an attack on inflation and although government continued to be a major factor in many different industries in one way or another, within the private as well as the public sector, ministerial statements expressed confidence that markets would produce better results than any fresh intervention could secure. This did not, however, prevent ministers from taking credit, as if it were traceable to their policies, whenever the movement of labour productivity took a favourable turn.

The record of growth in the forty years between 1945 and 1985 is generally admitted to have been disappointing in comparison with that of Britain's continental neighbours. For most of the time the growth of GDP remained close to 3 per cent. Then from the peak in 1973 there was a marked drop to half that rate over the next six years, a disastrous dip to negative growth between 1979 and 1982 and a recovery to the previous 3 per cent rate of growth in the next three years.

There were, of course, fluctuations in activity in the United Kingdom which affected the growth of GDP and employment, and, still more, output per head. Any measure of performance is therefore much affected by the span of time to which it relates. The dates selected in Table 3.1, however, are not such as to give rise to serious distortions.

The first three periods, covering the years 1948 to 1973 – the 'Golden Age' – show a fairly steady rate of growth irrespective of the rate of change in employment. Since employment grew more slowly, productivity growth accelerated, rising from a little over 2 per cent per annum to a little over 3 per cent annum. This was not, however, a steady upward trend. Productivity was growing faster in the first few years after the war. The early 1950s represented the low point and the early 1970s the high point in productivity growth.

Between the 1950s and the 1960s there was some acceleration of growth in the United Kingdom for reasons that are not very obvious but are likely to be connected with a rising level of industrial investment. No comparable acceleration occurred in neighbouring countries such as France and Germany which had set a much faster pace from the start and were not subsequently faced with the question of how to raise it to the level attained elsewhere.

Table 3.2 compares British growth performance with that of the OECD countries as a group leaving aside the early postwar years when countries starting from a very low level were able to achieve abnormal rates of growth. A comparison for the periods 1956–73, 1973–9 and 1979–85 brings out major changes.

Over the whole of the period the growth of GDP was more than half as fast again in the OECD countries as in the United Kingdom. After 1973, when growth slowed down, the falling-off was less proportionately in

Table 3.1 Growth in UK GDP, employment, and prices, 1948–85 (average annual rates of change, %)

	GDP	Employment	Output per worker	Prices[a]
1948–51	3.6	0.8	2.8	4.8
1948–56	2.9	0.8	2.2	4.7
1956–65	3.1	0.6	2.5	3.0
1965–73	3.1	−0.1	3.2	6.2
1973–9	1.5	0.2	1.2	16.0
1979–82	−0.7	−2.0	1.3	12.8
1982–5	3.1	0.7	2.4	5.1
1948–85	2.5	0.2	2.2	7.0

a GDP deflator

Source: OECD.

Table 3.2 UK economic performance 1946–85

		GDP	Employment	Output per worker	Inflation[a]	Unemployment rate[b]
			Average annual changes, %			%
UK	1946–56	2.5			4.9	
UK	1956–73	3.1	0.3	2.8	4.5	1.9[c]
OECD	1956–73	4.5	1.0	3.5	4.0	3.2[c]
UK	1973–9	1.5	0.2	1.2	16.0	4.2[d]
OECD	1973–9	2.6	1.1	1.5	9.0	5.2[d]
UK	1979–85	1.2	−0.6	1.8	8.9	9.8[e]
OECD	1979–85	2.3	0.6	1.7	7.1	7.8[e]
UK	1956–85	2.3	0.1	2.3	7.7	4.2[f]
OECD	1956–85	3.7	0.9	2.7	5.7	4.7[f]

a The Consumer Price Index from 1946–9. The GDP deflator from 1950–85
b The average level in the period as % of the total labour force
c 1960–73
d 1974–9
e 1980–5
f 1960–85

Note: The OECD totals for GDP and inflation are based on the exchange rates of 1980

Sources: OECD Historical Statistics, 1960–85 and the OECD database.

OECD but greater in absolute terms so that the rates in the United Kingdom and in OECD came closer together. Employment was also increasing faster in OECD throughout and the check to employment growth after 1973 was rather more marked in the United Kingdom. Taking the changes in output and employment together, output per worker was growing about 25 per cent faster in OECD in the years of rapid growth up to 1973 but very little faster after 1973. Indeed for the years from 1979 to 1985 output per head was rising slightly faster in the United Kingdom than in OECD although at a lower rate (1.8 per cent per annum) than before 1973. Thus if output has grown faster in other OECD countries since 1979 it has not been because productivity has risen faster. Whether the UK would still show to the same advantage if the world economy began to take in slack and growth rates in GDP returned to earlier levels in all countries is, however, a moot point.

Much the same results can be obtained by using manufacturing output per worker as a measure of the growth in labour productivity. Between 1948 and 1965 manufacturing output grew at an annual rate of 3.7 per cent and employment in manufacturing at 1 per cent, both rather faster than for the economy as a whole. Thus the growth in labour productivity in manufacturing averaged about 2.7 per cent per annum, also slightly faster than in the economy as a whole. In the next twenty years the record was very different. Employment in manufacturing contracted by nearly 40 per cent at an average rate of 2.5 per cent per annum while output grew annually by only 0.6 per cent. Thus, even with an unprecedented shedding of labour, the growth in output per head was no more than 3.1 per cent per annum. In contrast to the figures for the economy as a whole this represented an acceleration from the earlier average rate of growth. But it remained well below the rates achieved in other industrial countries. Again, however, the comparison looks quite different if it is confined to the six years 1979–85. For those years output per man-hour in manufacturing increased a good deal faster in the United Kingdom (at about 4 per cent per annum) than in Germany and Japan (which recorded very low rates in relation to previous experience – under 3 per cent), faster than in France and Italy, and at much the same rate as in Canada and the United States.

The improved performance of British manufacturing obviously owes something to the contraction of this sector of the economy in relation to the rest – an experience, however, that other industrial countries have shared – and to the large-scale shedding of labour over a period of twenty years, and particularly heavy since 1979. Higher labour productivity is usually the means to a higher standard of living but this is not so when employment falls simultaneously.

One aspect of growth, and to some extent a cause of it, is investment. Compared with continental countries, fixed investment formed a low proportion of GDP in Britain for most of the period, starting at 10.5 per cent in 1948 and rising to 22.2 per cent in 1973. The surprising thing is not that investment was low but that the ratio more than doubled and then that it was well maintained both in the 1970s (it was still 20.9 per cent in 1979) and in the 1980s as well (19.9 per cent in 1985). The reason for surprise is that on the one hand the return on capital fell to a low level in the mid-1970s and that on the other, investment in British industry yielded a much lower increment in output than in other industrial countries. Whether one takes total fixed capital formation or excludes from it dwellings and other social investment the rate of increase from 1948 to 1956 was 5.8 per cent and in the next period to 1973 it was only a little lower if housing and social investment are omitted and 4.8 per cent if they are included. The capital stock was increasing a good deal faster than output. Yet the return on capital was well below the return in other industrial countries.

Another indicator of economic performance is provided by foreign trade. In the early postwar years Britain's share of world exports of manufactures rose to 25 per cent and at the end of 1950 British exports of manufactures exceeded the combined total in France, Germany, and Japan. From then on, the British share fell steadily to 14 per cent in 1965 and 9.5 per cent in 1973. Thereafter only a small fall took place and by 1979 Britain's share was temporarily back to 9.5 per cent. There was then a renewed fall in the ensuing years, bringing the proportion down to 8 per cent in 1985, equal to that of Italy. A more dramatic change since 1965 (but beginning earlier) has been on the side of imports of manufactures. These grew rapidly throughout the 1960s and 1970s and by 1985 exceeded the value of exports of manufactures by about £10 billion when in 1980 the two were roughly equal. In the six years 1973 to 1979 imports of manufactures grew by 55 per cent and in the six years 1979 to 1985 by 40 per cent. These rates of expansion, in a period when the growth in the national income was only 1⅓ per cent per annum, was anything but reassuring.

Inflation

The average rate of inflation over the whole period from 1948 to 1985 was 7 per cent and it was rare that it fell below 3 per cent for any length of time, 1956–65 being one such period. Up to 1973 there was no great difference between the rate of inflation in the United Kingdom and in OECD but thereafter the British rate shot ahead and from 1973 to 1985 it averaged 12.4 per cent compared with 8 per cent for the OECD group. Even for the years from 1979–85 the British rate exceeded the OECD average at 8.9 per cent per annum compared with 7.1 per cent. The most that can be said is that the British rate of inflation fell further and was for a time below the OECD average.

Attempts to control inflation usually took one of two forms: deflation or incomes policy. Under the first Labour government deflation (or 'disinflation') meant withdrawing purchasing power through the budget. When the Conservatives came to power in 1951 they made use also of higher interest rates to dampen the inflation brought on by rearmament. In 1955 they again turned to 'a flexible monetary policy' to check inflation only to find it largely ineffective except in producing marked disagreement between the Treasury and the Bank of England. Two years later Thorneycroft invoked the quantity theory of money but resigned along with two other ministers (Enoch Powell and Nigel Birch) in January 1958 when the cabinet refused to agree to cuts in government expenditure on the scale he proposed.

The first Labour governments showed particular distaste for raising interest rates, and preferred to rely on requests to the banks or to other financial agencies to limit their lending. In contrast the first Conservative governments turned to monetary policy as a means of keeping taxes down. They had the greatest difficulty in reducing government expenditure and since they were opposed, almost in principle, to budget deficits this drove them to a reliance on credit restriction including restrictions on consumer credit for hire purchase. With public investment approaching half total fixed investment and a growing acceptance that inflation had come to stay, the forces pushing up interest rates strengthened steadily. The Bank of England could not sell enough bonds and the consequent abundance of liquid assets made it impossible to compress the banks' liquidity. Hence the frequency of credit squeezes.

Up to the mid-1950s monetary policy was seen largely in domestic terms as a weapon against inflation. With the revival of the use of Bank Rate in 1951, however, international factors came to exercise an increasing influence. In the various packages of measures used in the repeated exchange crises of the 1950s and 1960s, a higher Bank Rate came to be regarded as a necessary ingredient. This use of higher short-term rates as a fortification of the balance of payments continued throughout the sixties until the devaluation in 1967. At that point the money supply re-emerged as a matter of concern under the influence of the IMF (although the indicator they preferred was Domestic Credit Creation). From 1967 onwards, monetarist ideas began to win ground not only in government but in the City as well.

The British government was never fully monetarist but in the late 1970s they did come to believe that control of the money supply was the key to the elimination of inflation and that monetary contraction would work relatively painlessly. This meant rejecting the earlier view of the Radcliffe Committee that 'monetary measures will help but that is all'; and that, if monetary policy was used by itself to halt inflation, it would mean raising interest rates to crisis level and precipitate depression. Instead they expected tight money to tame the unions and limit wage increases with only a small increase in unemployment when all the evidence suggested that wages were not very sensitive to changes in the pressure of demand except when the pressure became intense. Whatever may be true of wages, prices are undoubtedly very sensitive to import costs and hence to the rate of exchange. An anti-inflation policy may therefore have to choose between holding to a money supply target and keeping the exchange rate steady. When the choice had to be made in 1980 the government elected to let the exchange rate rise to a fantastic level with disastrous consequences for employment. Since then an unannounced exchange rate target appears to have risen in importance in relation to the announced monetary target. It cannot be said that the kind of monetary targets now in use are treated with any seriousness or indeed make any sense. So far as British policy has not become purely opportunistic, the rate of exchange has taken over from monetary targets as the prime indicator for monetary policy.

Incomes policy

The possibility of using some form of incomes policy to combat inflation goes back well before the end of the war. The problem was how to give effect to the idea without abandoning or suppressing collective bargaining.

As Russell Jones has shown, 'every type of wage policy from an inflation tax to a public sector wage freeze' was put forward under the postwar

Labour governments and 'The roots of most more recent ideas on the subject can be traced back to this period' (Jones 1987). The early 1950s offered the first, and one of the few postwar opportunities, of introducing incomes policy in relatively favourable circumstances with prices almost steady in 1953, wages rising at under 4 per cent, and an absence of strong inflationary pressure. The opportunity was not taken. By the time the government was prepared to act, to the extent at least of issuing a White Paper in 1956, boom conditions again prevailed. The Conservative government's subsequent efforts to secure union agreement to a wage policy were not very adroit and the unions were by this time in a less accommodating mood. Neither the experiment of a price plateau nor the appointment of a Council on Prices Productivity and Incomes had much success.

In the early 1960s the Conservative government made a more spirited effort to limit wage increases by putting its call for a pay pause in the context of efforts to achieve faster growth through the NEDC but was unsuccessful in carrying the unions with it. The attempt to introduce a 'guiding light' in wage settlements administered by a National Incomes Commission had a brief life. George Woodcock, the General Secretary of the TUC, saw no way in which wage settlements could be held down for more than six months or so while the demand for labour remained intense.

Later efforts to evolve a pay and prices policy were largely unsuccessful and probably accelerated wage increases instead of limiting them. In the mid-1960s, when Aubrey Jones and the Prices and Incomes Board encouraged productivity bargaining, it certainly had this effect; the Board seemed at times more intent on legitimizing wage increases than on reducing them. The rapid increase in wages in 1964–5 while George Brown pursued agreement with the TUC on his 'Declaration of Intent' went far to make devaluation in 1967 inevitable. There was also a danger that foreigners holding sterling would be more discouraged by the breakdown of incomes policy than by the actual rise in wages.

The one major success of incomes policy in later years was in the scaling down of wage increases after the alarming rise in wages after 1974. The circumstances then were far more propitious, first because the rise in international prices was visibly slackening thanks to world reactions and second because the unions were themselves alarmed by the course of events and more willing to abide by a general limitation.

With the arrival of a new Conservative government in 1979 the ideas of Thorneycroft in 1957 came back to life. Ministers were not prepared to 'validate' wage increases by an appropriate expansion in the money supply and no doubt hoped as they did in 1957 that even a modest increase in unemployment would keep any rise in wages within limits. In this, not surprisingly, they proved mistaken since the pressure of demand and the movement of wages show little correlation except in the course of cyclical fluctuations. There is now no policy instrument by which the government seeks to exercise control over money wages except through the creation of unemployment of unspecified dimensions or a little bit of luck in the movement of the terms of trade.

Other policy objectives

Among other policy objectives, the aim of achieving a more equal distribution of income at one time ranked high but with the swing to reliance on market forces after 1979 the trend since then has been rather towards greater *in*equality.

There is no doubt that the increase in taxation in the first half of this century, especially in two world wars, fell heavily on the rich and contributed to a more equal distribution of income. On the other hand, taxation would not appear to have done much since the war to promote a further redistribution of income between rich and poor. It is true that in the twenty-five years between 1949 and 1974 the share in total personal incomes before tax of the top 10 per cent of income earners fell from 32 to 25 per cent. But on an after tax basis the change in share was *less*, from 26 per cent to 22 per cent. The forces making for greater equality seem to have lain outside the tax system. Moreover, these forces, whatever they were, operated much less powerfully after the early 1950s and there is strong evidence of a change in the opposite direction in later years on a pre-tax or, still more, on a post-tax basis. So far as action by the state has made for greater equality in the postwar period it has been far more through the expansion in the welfare benefits referred to (see pp. 35–6), particularly direct benefits in cash.

Changes in the distribution of personal wealth have been much more substantial especially if contributory and state pension rights are included. There is no continuous series of estimates on a constant basis, but there would seem to have been a fall in the proportion of wealth held by the top 10 per cent from about 49 per cent in 1971 to 34 per cent in 1981. The fall in earlier years was rather more gradual, probably by about 6 percentage points in the 1950s and perhaps another 5 in the 1960s. Again it is not altogether clear how far the change is attributable to state action apart from the grant of non-contributory pension rights.

Another objective was to secure a more even balance between regions in the pressure of demand. Governments tried by a whole series of measures to expand employment in the more depressed areas: by building factories for rent; by controlling the erection of new industrial premises; by favourable depreciation allowances; and by subsidizing industrial employment in regions with high unemployment through a regional employment premium. Claims have been made that these policies were highly effective particularly in the immediate postwar period and in the 1970s. There is no doubt that new industry was attracted to the favoured regions. But the long-term results are more doubtful. The regional pattern of unemployment rates remained obstinately the same except that the exploitation of North Sea oil yielded a more perceptible improvement in Scotland than had any government measures. The main impact of these measures would appear to have been on out-migration rather than on unemployment; and although the contraction of industry in areas of high unemployment may have been checked, the check was a rather minor one over the twenty years after 1965 when industrial employment (on which the measures concentrated) was contracting by 40 per cent over the country as a whole and at a correspondingly faster rate in the regions from the Midlands northwards.

Conclusion

It would seem that the performance of the economy over the postwar period has changed less than the policies adopted to manage it. After the trauma of the two oil shocks and the 1979–82 recession many features of the economy reassumed a familiar shape. The growth in output and in labour productivity between 1982 and 1985 was at a rate not very different from that in 1956–73 and the same was true of inflation. The balance of payments problems so familiar in the 1950s and 1960s began to reappear once North Sea oil production had passed its peak and as the economy expanded again. The outstanding contrast was the obstinately high level of unemployment, particularly long-term unemployment, which in 1985 had risen above 3 million and was still increasing.

When one turns to policy, whether employment policy, growth policy, monetary policy, or incomes policy, the influence of government on the events of the forty years from 1945 to 1985 has been small in relation to the effort that went to policy-making. Policy is an effort to foresee and influence the course of events. But the aims of policy are themselves influenced by events and the efforts of governments to manage or control the domestic economy are often little more than a reaction to events.

In the British case it is striking to find how in a situation not unlike the 1930s the ideas in vogue in the 1980s are also not unlike those of the 1930s. The Keynesian ideas that took over in postwar years were devised for situations like those of the 1930s and 1980s, while the ideas that have displaced them might be thought more appropriate to the boom years when they were out of fashion. If similar situations produce similar policy responses, can these responses be wholly wrong? Perhaps the lesson is that under boom conditions variations in the budget surplus yielded by the boom are sufficient to keep the economy in reasonable balance whereas in a slump it is extremely difficult to increase demand by budgetary action. It is also particularly difficult for one country to do it on its own.

The contrast is greatest between the beginning and end of the period. The proclaimed aim of policy after 1945 was full employment but the real preoccupations were external balance or, later, the dollar problem and internal balance or inflation. The preoccupations have remained: the aim of full employment has vanished. The change in aim goes with a policy environment that of itself makes full employment a more ambitious aim while lack of ambition is in turn an important element in the environment of policy. What is even more striking is the remarkable change in policy instruments.

The most obvious change is in the virtual disappearance of so-called physical controls. These were originally devised for a variety of purposes: to bring about changes in the use of resources by short-circuiting market mechanisms; to limit the pressure on resources, in total and at key points, by more peremptory methods than reliance on higher taxation or forced saving; to safeguard common access to the essentials of life at modest cost. These controls which uniformly implied a distrust of market mechanisms gave the government great power but at the cost of freedom of choice for the individual producer and consumer.

A second major change is the prominence now assigned to monetary policy. This was hardly used at all in the early postwar years and traditionally had more to do with keeping the international accounts in balance than with the control of inflation. When used in the 1950s to counter inflation it was largely ineffective; and even in the 1970s and 1980s it has included a large element of make-believe. The government's powers to manipulate the money supply, except through insupportable gyrations in interest rates, are extremely limited; variations in the money supply unless accompanied by large swings in interest rates are of little effect except via the exchange rate; and the common impression that it was monetary policy that brought down the rate of inflation in Britain, except in so far as high interest rates and the unforeseen overvaluation of the pound in 1980–1 produced a major depression, has little substance.

A third change is the presumption of impotence in face of external pressures. In the postwar years balance of payments policy was real and active. Domestic and external economic policy were intimately linked through the use of controls to thin out the dollar component of domestic spending, pending devaluation to promote the necessary adjustments. In the 1980s external pressures tend to be treated as exogenous and beyond the reach of domestic policy.

Yet another change is the abandonment of incomes policy. The years after 1945 saw the first, and perhaps the most successful, effort to operate an incomes policy (although not yet christened with that name). Thanks to the agreement made in 1948 with the TUC the government was able to hold the increase in hourly wage rates to less than 3 per cent in the eighteen months before devaluation in spite of an acute labour shortage; and in the year following devaluation, after the agreement between Cripps and Bevin and the TUC, the increase was just over 1 per cent. With unemployment far below present levels the average annual increase in hourly wages in the first five years of peace was no more than 5.5 per cent – well below the rate of increase in the 1980s.

Finally, the role of fiscal policy has changed. For Cripps and his successors the budget was the great instrument of planning and the budget judgement the centrepiece of economic policy. In the 1980s the budget has taken second place to monetary policy and has been treated almost as a tributary to monetary policy. Instead of relating the prospective surplus or deficit to the current economic situation, the Chancellor took pride in holding out the prospect of a fixed target for the PSBR of 1 per cent of GNP or, subsequently, zero and so denying himself the possibility of a judgement. A nil PSBR, moreover, was a far stiffer target than the 'surplus above the line' on which Chancellors used to concentrate and implied far more confidence in the power of the private sector to absorb current savings. However, the budget accounts continue to be as economically meaningless as they always were, the latest complication being the power of the Chancellor to eliminate a deficit by selling off government assets.

In the past forty years the instruments of economic policy have contracted steadily while international influences on the economy have become more and more powerful. Governments have less room for manoeuvre than in the past partly because they have deliberately abandoned their powers and partly because of the closer integration of the international economy. The contraction in the agenda of national economic management has meant a surrender not to national but to international market forces. On the other hand, the instruments and agents of international government, to which so much thought was given before the war ended, have not developed and expanded to keep pace with the functions they need to assume. The question needs to be asked whether it has been progress to deny ourselves some of the instruments of national economic policy before creating more powerful instruments of international policy.

Selected dates

August 1945	Labour government takes office under C.R. Attlee.
July 1946	US Loan Agreement ratified by Congress.
February 1947	Fuel crisis begins.
June 1947	General Marshall's Harvard speech on European Recovery.
August 1947	Convertibility of sterling suspended.
September 1949	Devaluation of pound sterling to $2.80.
May 1950	Announcement of Schuman Plan for European Coal and Steel Community.
June 1950	Outbreak of war in Korea.
October 1951	Conservative government under Winston Churchill.

November 1951	Bank Rate raised to 2.5 per cent: 'new monetary policy'.
February 1952	Cabinet sets aside plan to let pound float and make it convertible.
July 1954	End of food rationing.
February 1955	Government decision to support rate for transferable sterling.
November 1956	Franco-British armed intervention in Egypt.
September 1957	Bank Rate raised to 7 per cent.
December 1958	*De jure* convertibility of sterling.
November 1959	European Free Trade Area agreed.
July 1961	'Pay pause'. First use of tax 'regulator'.
October 1964	Labour government under Harold Wilson.
November 1967	Devaluation of the pound to $2.40.
June 1970	Conservative government under Edward Heath.
December 1971	Smithsonian agreement on exchange rates.
June 1972	Pound allowed to float.
January 1973	United Kingdom joins European Economic Community.
October–December 1973	First oil shock.
December 1973	Prime Minister announces three-day week from 1 January 1974.
March 1974	Labour government under Harold Wilson.
October 1976	Pound falls to $1.57. Negotiations with IMF begin a week later.
March 1977	Cash limits to government expenditure introduced in budget.
May 1979	Conservative government under Margaret Thatcher
October 1979	Exchange control discontinued.
October 1979–February 1980	Second oil shock.
March 1980	Medium-term financial strategy announced in budget.
November 1980	Pound peaks against the dollar at $2.4540.
April 1982	Argentina invades Falkland Islands.
June 1983	Conservative government re-elected.

References and guide to further reading

On economic policy, the fullest studies of the British economy since the war are those issued by the National Institute of Economic and Social Research:

Dow, J.C.R. (1964) *The Management of the British Economy 1945-60*, Cambridge: Cambridge University Press for NIESR.

Blackaby, F.T. (ed.) (1978) *British Economic Policy 1960-74*, Cambridge: Cambridge University Press for NIESR.

For the first half of the period there are two very readable accounts, now somewhat dated, in:

Shonfield, Andrew (1958) *British Economic Policy since the War*, Harmondsworth: Penguin Books.

Brittan, Samuel (1971) *Steering the Economy: the Role of the Treasury*, Harmondsworth: Penguin Books.

Useful studies of the period up to 1960 (also rather dated) were undertaken by a group of Oxford economists in:

Worswick, G.D.N. and Ady, Peter (eds) (1952) *The British Economy 1945-50*, Oxford: Oxford University Press.

Worswick, G.D.N. and Ady, Peter (eds) (1962) *The British Economy in the 1950s*, Oxford: Oxford University Press

More recent experience is dealt with in:

Dornbusch, R. and Layard, R. (eds) (1987) *The Performance of the British Economy*, Oxford: Oxford University Press.

For a good short survey see:

Wright, J.F. (1979) *Britain in the Age of Economic Management*, Oxford: Oxford University Press.

For an account of economic policy in the immediate postwar period see:

Cairncross, A.K. (1985) *Years of Recovery*, London: Methuen.

Cairncross, A.K. and Watts, N.G.M. (1989) *The Economic Section 1939-61*, London: Routledge.

For an American view in 1968 see:

Caves, R.E. (ed.) (1968) *Britain's Economic Prospects*, London: Allen & Unwin.

Specific aspects of policy covered in:

1. *Growth*

Matthews, R.C.O., Feinstein, C.H. and Odling-Smee, J.C. (1982) *British Economic Growth 1856-1973*, Oxford: Oxford University Press.

Elbaum, B. and Lazonick, W. (eds) (1986) *The Decline of the British Economy*, Oxford: Oxford University Press.

Feinstein, C.H. (1972) *National Income, Expenditure and Output of the United Kingdom, 1855-1965*, Cambridge: Cambridge University Press.

Oxford Review of Economic Policy (1988) *Long-run Economic Performance in the United Kingdom*, Spring.

2. *Money and finance*

Report of the (Radcliffe) Committee on the *Working of the Monetary System* (1959) Cmnd 827, London: HMSO.

Report of the (Wilson) Committee on the *Functioning of Financial Institutions* (1980) Cmnd 7937, London: HMSO.

Dow, J.C.R. and Savage, I.D. (1988) *A Critique of Monetary Policy*, Oxford: Oxford University Press.

3. *Employment and wages*

Employment Policy (1944) Cmnd 6527, London: HMSO.

Jones, R.B. (1987) *Wages and Employment Policy 1936-85*, London: Allen & Unwin.

Tomlinson, J. (1987) *Employment Policy: the Crucial Years 1939-55*, Oxford: Oxford University Press.

4. *Industry*

There is no recent conspectus such as was attempted in:

Burn, D.L. (ed.) (1958) *The Structure of British Industry: a Symposium*, Cambridge: Cambridge University Press for NIESR.

For industrial decline see:
Elbaum, B. and Lazonick, W. (eds) (1986) *The Decline of the British Economy*, Oxford: Oxford University Press.
Blackaby, F. (ed.) (1979) *Deindustrialisation*, London: Heinemann for NIESR.

Chapter four

France

Frances Lynch

Introduction

In 1945 the French economy had to be reconstructed not only from the effects of war and occupation but also from a decade of depression. France had been the only industrial economy not to recover from the international depression of 1929. Industrial production in 1938 was only 75 per cent of its peak level of 1929. The percentage of the labour force employed in industry had fallen from 37 per cent in 1929 to 32 per cent in 1938 while the agricultural labour force, although declining, still amounted to nearly one-third of the total by 1938. With food prices falling in the international economy throughout the 1930s the French government was unable to prevent agricultural incomes in France from declining. But due to the relative inefficiency of much of French agriculture, food prices were still considerably higher in France than in the international economy. This served to push up the cost of living and depress domestic demand. As a result French producers cut back investment and production and redirected exports to the limited but protected markets of the French colonies. Most governments abdicated responsibility for this industrial decline in the 1930s. Their reaction to the devaluations of sterling and the dollar and the disintegration of the international economy into protectionist trading blocs was to increase the level of protection for French industry and agriculture, and to reduce public expenditure. The autonomy of the Bank of France and its decision to defend the value of the franc was not challenged until 1936 when the Popular Front government under Leon Blum was elected.

Blum's policies aimed at stimulating recovery in the short term by increasing domestic demand. The longer-term strategy relied on increasing state control over the economy. To this end a new Ministry of National Economy was set up and steps were taken to reduce the autonomy of the Bank of France. However the failure of the short-term policies put paid to the long-term strategy. Blum's initial refusal to devalue the franc or to impose exchange controls in the face of higher domestic costs led to a speculative outflow of funds and a forced devaluation of the franc. The resulting export boom was then curtailed by the development of a labour shortage in France. Within a year the experiment had been abandoned.

Moreover, rapid defeat in 1940 revealed the extent of French economic backwardness. The Third Republic, which in its last decade had sacrificed economic growth in the interests of preserving financial stability, was bankrupt. So too was the Vichy state. By 1945 industrial production had fallen to 49 per cent of its 1938 level and the French population was the oldest in the world with 10 per cent aged over sixty.

The objectives and instruments of policy after 1945

The end of the war gave the new French policy-makers a unique opportunity to reshape the goals and institutions of French society. The outcome of the war had been a victory for the French Resistance. Although divided on many issues, the Resistance was united in its determination to extend the power of a democratic state over the economy. With the right-wing forces in French society discredited, the economy prostrate, and a set of instruments of economic control inherited from Vichy, the new provisional government was in a position to extend the power of the state over the economy. The institutional reforms which were implemented in the first two postwar years were based largely on the demands of the French Resistance and were to remain in place throughout the entire postwar period. With a couple of exceptions, they were all in place even before the constitution of the Fourth Republic had been agreed. They were left in place under the constitution of the Fifth Republic.

The institutional reforms included the nationalization of the main sources of energy, transport, and credit in the economy and the creation of a system of social security. State control over the training of top civil servants was to be effected through the creation of a public training school, the Ecole Nationale d'Administration (ENA). To counter the traditional weakness of French trade unions democracy was to be extended into the workplace with the compulsory institution of factory councils in all firms employing more than a hundred workers (this was subsequently reduced to fifty). And finally, to ensure co-ordination among all the new state economic agents, a planning commission was set up in 1946.

Thus the Bank of France together with the four largest deposit banks and insurance companies were nationalized. Responsibility for co-ordinating credit policy was vested in a new body – the National Credit Council (CNC). This brought together the Governor of the Bank of France and the Minister of Finance and was to issue instructions to banks based on the priorities set out in the national plan. Economic imperatives were to override financial stability as the principles guiding government policy.

Energy policy was to be co-ordinated with the nationalization of the 1,490 companies involved in the production, transportation, and distribution of electricity, as well as the 251 companies involved in gas and all the coal mines. Similarly, co-ordination of transport was to be ensured with the extension of state control over most of rail, air, and sea transport (André and Delorme 1982). To cope with the anticipated shortage of labour a National Office for Immigration was set up.

These changes came about because the shock of defeat in the Second World War had demonstrated to the French more forcibly than any other factor the weakness of the French economy and the backwardness of French industry and agriculture. All the parties in the first postwar coalition government, from the Communists to the newly-formed Christian Democrats (MRP) were therefore united on the need to promote recovery through rapid industrialization. This was seen to satisfy several objectives. In an age of total warfare the French attachment to the virtues of a balanced economy was seen as obsolete. An enlarged industrial sector was necessary if the state was to fulfil its primary purpose, namely to guarantee national security. A second, related objective was the conviction that industrialization was the motor for economic growth. Economic growth would bring higher living standards and thereby secure support and legitimacy for the new state. But rapid industrialization necessitated a high level of investment which the government, with the exception of the Ministry of Agriculture, agreed should come initially from the agricultural sector.

In the conditions of postwar scarcity, these difficult choices which had to be made were given legitimacy by placing them within the context of an overall national plan. The priorities of the Monnet Plan were to concentrate investment in energy, transport, steel, cement, and agricultural machinery. Satisfying the chronic needs for housing, consumer goods, and a more radical plan for improving agricultural efficiency were postponed.

Initially, the planners relied on the state exercising a wide range of direct controls over credit as well as prices, wages, distribution, and trade. In conditions of excess demand these controls were seen as crucial if a high level of private savings and investment were to be guaranteed. Public expenditure was to be partly financed through borrowing on the assumption that, as production increased, so would tax revenues. Inflationary pressure was also to be reduced by running a trade deficit in the medium term which would be financed through borrowing. An expansion of production and exports would thus be necessary if these loans were to be repaid.

This policy was modified in the course of 1947 under both domestic and international pressure. The government's failure to control prices, wages, and distribution effectively, led to rapid inflation, a deteriorating standard of living, and increasing discontent among the electorate. Wheat-growers, opposed to a price policy which depressed wheat prices relative to those of meat, cut back production. Their action, coinciding with a harsh winter in 1946/7, produced a bread crisis which forced the government to reduce rations to wartime levels and below. In the ensuing wave of industrial unrest the Communist Party for the first time since the war gave its support to the anti-government strikes in April 1947. This was to result in the dismissal of the communist ministers from government. Inflation, combined with the need to increase imports of American wheat, aggravated the trade deficit and resulted in the French government's acceptance of Marshall Aid.

International events then forced the French to forge a new consensus which revolved around the Atlantic Alliance, the almost permanent exclusion of the Communist Party from ministerial responsibilities, and a speedy relaxation of economic controls including controls over trade. Furthermore, the acceptance of Marshall Aid served to increase the power of the French Ministry of Finance through the creation of a special treasury account – the Fonds de Modernisation et d'Equipement (FME) into which the counterpart funds of Marshall Aid, which financed a large proportion of the planned investment, were placed.

The opposition to Marshall Aid of the main trade union, the communist-dominated Confédération Générale du Travail (CGT), led to the formation of the Force Ouvrière (FO) at the end of 1947. This created another division in an historically weak trade union movement. Unions in France were traditionally organized along both political and confessional lines. The CGT was the largest union by far with over 5 million members in 1946. The other main union, the Confédération Française des Travailleurs Chrétiens (CFTC) which was aligned with the Catholic Church and the Christian Democrat party had less than 400,000 members in that year. With the onset of the Cold War and the retreat of the Communist Party into opposition, membership of the CGT declined from its postwar peak but the other unions failed to expand into the vacuum. By the 1970s the proportion of the workforce that was organized in France was the smallest of any industrialized country. It amounted to about 20 per cent compared with over 30 per cent in West Germany and 50 per cent in Britain (Hall 1984).

In 1950, when controls over wages were abolished (apart from the minimum wage, the SMIG, which was guaranteed by government) and free collective bargaining was instituted, employers were sufficiently strong to ignore the unions altogether. Similarly the factory councils found themselves dealing with issues of social rather than economic significance. This remained the case until the events of May 1968 which led to the legal recognition of unions at the workplace.

Despite the dismantling of controls over wages distribution, prices, and an increasing amount of trade in 1950, the state still retained these instruments of control to be used if necessary. And, in spite of professed ideological differences, all governments in the Fourth and Fifth Republics resorted to most of the available instruments of control at one time or another. After the Monnet Plan came to an end the government's long-term economic objectives continued to be expressed in the form of a national plan. And the objectives continued to stress economic growth stimulated by a high level of investment and demand. But as the economy became increasingly integrated into the international economy in the 1960s the growth of exports came to replace that of domestic demand as a priority. The plan became increasingly selective concentrating on the promotion of investment in the most advanced sectors which were seen to have a future in trade among the industrialized countries.

With its emphasis on medium-term objectives the plan has frequently been revised in the interests of short-term financial stability. The stabilization policies of 1948, 1952/3, 1958/9, 1963/4 put short-term objectives before longer-term ones, but, apart from 1953 when no plan was in existence, these stabilization measures tended to take the form of reductions in private demand through increases in taxation rather than reductions in public expenditure. The main instruments of government policy for influencing the economy in the short term have been controls over credit, prices, foreign exchange, and in the 1950s over trade. While the planners had no specific powers of their own, the plan tended to be implemented through the government's control over the credit system.

Credit policy

One of the main purposes of the National Credit Council, set up in 1945, was to direct credit in accordance with the priorities of the plan. The CNC was to give instructions to banks to impose qualitative restrictions on credit. Thus, credit was to be allocated for investment purposes rather than to finance stockbuilding, for example. But since this rather vague policy was deemed to be contributing to inflation it was soon replaced by the imposition of quantitative controls on credit (Andrieu 1984).

Deposit banks were obliged to hold a percentage of their deposits in the form of Treasury bonds, thereby enabling the CNC to alter the credits granted to the economy by varying this percentage. These quantitative controls were occasionally supplemented again by qualitative controls. In order to safeguard investment in the priority sectors chosen by the planners credit was channelled through the FME and lent at preferential interest rates. A number of other funds were set up subsequently, each for a specific purpose and in 1955 they were brought together in the Fonds de Développement Economique et Social (FDES).

With the adoption of the second plan in 1954 the government instituted a system of 'programme laws' which guaranteed the financing of certain investments by removing them from the annual budgetary review. But because these programme laws reduced the flexibility of fiscal policy they were abolished in 1959. Thereafter the state retained its power to direct investment by offering loans at subsidized rates of interest.

Altogether in the 1950s the Treasury and the non-bank financial institutions under its supervision allocated on average 80 per cent of total investment credit. In the 1960s the government transferred some of this investment to the banking system. By 1979 while the financial institutions provided 80 per cent of the borrowing of non-financial enterprises, banks accounted for 65 per cent of the total domestic lending outstanding (OECD 1986/7).

The government was thus able to influence the funding of the economy largely by means of quantitative credit controls. Bank credit restrictions were imposed on a number of occasions: in 1957, 1963–5, 1969–70, and enforced on a systematic basis from 1972 to 1986. This undermined the role of interest rates in demand management, and throughout the postwar period they remained extremely low.

Controls over prices and incomes

The onset of the Cold War and the retreat of the CGT from any sort of co-operation with government effectively ruled out the possibility of using incomes policy as an instrument of economic control. The government controlled the minimum wage, which after 1952 was index-linked, as well as public sector incomes. But in order to influence private sector wages the government resorted to price controls, or to the threatened use of price controls with varying degrees of stringency, throughout the postwar era. They were in use frequently in the 1950s. After a professed aversion to such an illiberal policy by policy-makers in the Fifth Republic, they were used again after 1964, and with particular stringency in 1974 and 1977. Abolished with a flourish by Barre in 1978 they reappeared in 1982 when the Mitterrand government imposed a price and wage freeze for six months. This was then replaced with a more differentiated system of price controls in 1983. The system was gradually relaxed in 1985 and removed, yet again, in 1986.

The uninstitutionalized and fairly anarchic pattern of wage determination led to periodic strikes. These tended to start in the public sector where wages frequently lagged behind those in the private sector. In 1954 Mendès-France tried to establish a system of periodic meetings with the trade unions designed to bring wage increases into line with productivity (Bonin 1987: 245). To ease the growing discontent among peasants, agricultural wages were indexed to industrial wages. But in 1958 one of the elements of the Rueff-Pinay reforms was the abolition of all indexing apart from that of the minimum wage.

The industrial unrest which this produced, largely in the public sector where wages declined dramatically relative to those in the private sector, culminated in an abortive attempt in 1963 to enter into an agreement on incomes policy with the unions (Flanagan *et al.* 1983: 599). This was followed by the reimposition of price controls with infringement carrying a prison sentence. The Grenelle agreements which brought the national strike of May 1968 to a conclusion revived wage indexation, but this time the minimum wage was to be linked with the growth of the economy.

Immigration policy/employment policy

Due to its demographic position the French foresaw a problem of a labour shortage in the postwar period. The Conseil du Plan envisaged the need to import between 1 and 1.5 million foreign workers between 1946 and 1951. A state recruiting agency, the Office National de l'Immigration, was set up to that effect but the results proved to be disappointing. Lack of housing, relatively low wages, and exchange restrictions which inhibited the flow of remittances, all kept the number of legal migrant workers to a very low level. It was only after 1955, after several years of investment in housing, that the numbers of foreign workers entering France shot up. In 1956 the number of immigrants tripled reaching a total of 71,000. From 1957 onwards the number of immigrants represented a substantial proportion of the increase in the population and even more in the workforce. The average annual number of immigrants in the 1960s was 164,000 (Tapinos 1975). The large numbers of immigrant workers together with an increase in the numbers reaching working age in the early 1960s brought the tight labour market conditions of the 1950s to an end.

While unemployment increased progressively from 1964 onwards it was not until the early 1970s that measures were taken directly to reduce it. These included a law requiring official authorization for redundancies, measures to encourage the repatriation of immigrants, and increased subsidies for uncompetitive firms. In the 1980s specific measures included a reduction in the working week, early retirement schemes, and youth training programmes.

Trade policy and exchange controls

As early as 1946, in signing the Blum-Byrnes agreement with the US government which secured a line of credit of $650 million for French reconstruction, the French government pledged itself to the abolition of quantitative restrictions on trade and to a reduction in tariffs. The first concrete steps taken in that direction were within the trade liberalization programme of the OEEC. By June 1951 the French government had removed 75 per cent of the quantitative restrictions on its 1948 levels of trade within the OEEC. However, when faced with a chronic balance of payments problem within the European Payments Union (EPU), the government reimposed quotas in February 1952. Subsequent governments proceeded to a very gradual liberalization of trade as domestic prices became stabilized and exports increased. By June 1956, 86 per cent of quotas had been removed and in March 1957 the socialist government of

Guy Mollet signed the Treaty of Rome. Ironically, three months later the government of Gaillard and Pflimlin, faced with a huge balance of payments deficit and dwindling reserves, devalued the franc by 20 per cent and reimposed quotas and import licences. But this marked the last attempt to use trade policy to solve balance of payments problems. After the next devaluation of 17 per cent in 1958 trade became increasingly liberalized both within the EEC and with the rest of the world. It was not until 1982/3 that protection was seriously considered again as a policy instrument by the Mitterrand government – only to be rejected.

In contrast, controls over external payments for non-trade purposes have been in use almost continuously. The only exceptions were 1967/8, 1971/3, and 1980/1, but on each occasion when exchange controls were relaxed the subsequent net outflow of capital caused the experiment in liberalization to be soon abandoned (OECD 1986/7).

Exchange rate policy

In ratifying the Bretton Woods agreement in 1945 the French government devalued the franc and agreed to the principle of fixed exchange rates. Yet between 1945 and 1971 when the Bretton Woods system began to fall apart the franc had been devalued a further five times. Furthermore, between 1948 and 1949 a multiple system of exchange rates, some fixed and some floating, had been in operation. The French also have a reputation for using the exchange rate 'offensively'. The instance which most justifies this view was in 1957/8 when, as part of the Rueff-Pinay reforms (see p. 67) devaluation was used, in conjunction with policies to hold down the growth of money wages, in an attempt to achieve a competitive advantage at the beginning of the Common Market. Less obviously, the devaluation of 1969, which certainly took the foreign exchange markets by surprise, could be seen as a way of accommodating, rather than suppressing, the consequences of the wage pressures of 1968. However, to conclude from this that the French government readily used exchange rate policy as an instrument of economic management, would be to mislead. There were numerous occasions throughout the 1950s, 1960s, and even 1970s when the franc was over-valued, and devaluation eschewed. In 1952 Pinay preferred a combination of price controls, a loan, and trade protection to devaluation. In 1963 Giscard d'Estaing preferred deflation to devaluation and in 1968 devaluation was postponed for nearly a year resulting in a massive reduction in French reserves before the franc was devalued.

Exchange rate stability continued to be an objective of policy in the 1970s and was pursued rather unsuccessfully before 1976 through a combination of short-term interest rate adjustments, direct intervention by the central bank on the exchange market, exchange controls, and foreign borrowing. In 1979 France joined the European Monetary System thereby surrendering national control over the exchange rate in the interests of promoting European co-operation and trade.

The change in the policy mix

Over the postwar period the French state has remained unswerving in its commitment to promote industrial growth in France. The instruments of economic control which were devised after the war to enable the state to fulfil this objective have undergone some modifications since then. The direct controls over wages and distribution were the first to be removed during the period 1947 to 1950. The removal of controls over trade followed after 1958. The state retained its control over prices and the distribution of credit and it was this feature which most distinguished the French state in the postwar period from its neighbours or indeed from the Third Republic. The Ministry of Finance was able to exercise its influence over the Bank of France through their joint participation in the National Credit Council. This relatively greater strength of the Ministry of Finance *vis-à-vis* the Central Bank, at least as compared to some other countries such as the UK or Germany, probably contributed to the somewhat greater willingness of the French to use devaluation when its failure to control incomes led to external disequilibrium. Price controls were not an effective substitute for an incomes policy in periods of rapid productivity increases. But an incomes policy was not possible given the organizational weakness of the unions and their political opposition to collective bargaining with conservative governments.

In 1982 the majority Socialist government instituted a system of collective bargaining which was to give the state greater control over incomes than at any time in the postwar period. But control over the economy was undermined by the commitment to continued membership of the European Community and of the European Monetary System. This ruled out the possibility of using either trade controls or 'offensive' devaluations to stimulate recovery in the more depressed conditions of the 1980s.

Economic performance

An overview of the period

The performance of the French economy from 1945 to 1975 – a period known as the 'thirty glorious years' – was remarkable (Fourastié 1979). Growth rates of GDP averaged 6.8 per cent over this period compared with 4.8 per cent in West Germany and 2.4 per cent in Great Britain. This growth was not only remarkable in comparison with that of France's main competitors but as Table 4.1 shows it far surpassed growth in other periods of measured French history. Between 1870 and 1913 the French economy

Table 4.1 French macroeconomic indicators, 1945–85

	1870–1913	1945–75	1946–51	1951–8	1958–68	1968–73	1973–81	1981–5
			Average annual changes, %					
GDP	1.6	6.8	8.7	4.2	5.3	5.9	2.6	1.6
Inflation[a]			28.2	5.8	4.1	6.4	10.8	8.6
Employment					0.2	1.0	0.2	−0.4

	1952–9	1960–7	1968–73	1974–9	1980–5
Investment ratio[b]	16.8	22.3	23.5	22.7	20.3
Unemployment rate[c]	2.0	1.8	2.6	4.5	8.3
Current balance[d]	0.4	0.6	−0.1	−0.6	−1.5

a The consumer price index 1946–9. The GDP deflator 1950–85
b Gross fixed investment in % of GDP
c In % of the labour force
d In % of GDP

Sources: OECD database, OECD *Historical Statistics, 1960–85*, OECD Economic Surveys, France, *OECD Economic Outlook*, July 1988, and A. Boltho (ed.), *The European Economy. Growth and Crisis*, Oxford, 1985.

Table 4.2 French economic performance, 1946–85

		GDP	Employment	Output per worker	Inflation[a]	Unemployment rate[b]
		Average annual changes, %				%
France	1946–56	6.4			15.8	
France	1956–73	5.4	0.5	4.8	5.3	(1.7)[c]
OECD	1956–73	4.5	1.0	3.5	4.0	3.2 [c]
France	1973–9	3.0	0.3	2.7	10.6	4.5 [d]
OECD	1973–9	2.6	1.1	1.5	9.0	5.2 [d]
France	1979–85	1.5	−0.3	1.9	9.5	8.3 [e]
OECD	1979–85	2.3	0.6	1.7	7.1	7.8 [e]
France	1956–85	4.1	0.3	3.8	7.3	(3.9)[f]
OECD	1956–85	3.7	0.9	2.7	5.7	4.7 [f]

a The consumer price index 1946–9. The GDP deflator 1950–85
b The average level in the period as % of the total labour force
c 1960–73
d 1974–9
e 1980–5
f 1960–85

Note: The OECD totals for GDP and inflation are based on the exchange rates of 1980

Sources: OECD Historical Statistics, 1960–85 and the OECD database.

had grown at an annual average of only 1.6 per cent (when the German economy had grown at 2.8 per cent).

Even if we discount the postwar years, which it could be argued were spent catching up with technological developments achieved in other countries during the 1930s and the war, the French growth performance is still impressive. Between 1956 and 1973 the French economy grew at an annual average rate of 5.4 per cent compared with an average rate for the OECD countries of 4.5 per cent (see Table 4.2). Moreover, as Table 4.2 also shows, this impressive growth performance was even more marked in terms of productivity. Output per head grew at 4.8 per cent compared to 3.5 per cent for the OECD area as a whole. As a result by 1970 France had the second highest standard of living among major European countries (Hall 1984).

Furthermore, having been shielded from the full force of international competition since the end of the nineteenth century, French industry was increasingly exposed to European competition after the Treaty of Rome was signed in 1957. Yet French growth rates were even higher in the 1960s than in the 1950s, and the current account was in surplus in every year but one between 1959 and 1968. However, in the late 1970s growth rates began to falter and in the 1980s France has been overtaken by many of its OECD partners.

Rapid economic growth took place against a background of rising prices with only a brief period of price stability between 1953 and 1956. Inflation rates were particularly high in the immediate postwar years when supply was deficient. Over the entire period 1956–85 the average rate of inflation was 7.3 per cent making French inflation rates higher than the OECD average. The main reasons for the post-reconstruction inflation were the additional pressure of demand generated by budget deficits plus the government's failure to control incomes. But rather than deflate the economy and reduce investment the government preferred the option of periodic devaluation of the currency. This enabled high levels of investment to be sustained throughout the whole postwar period. Investment was higher in the 1960s than in the 1950s but higher still between 1970 and 1973 at a time when investment elsewhere in the OECD was declining. For the rest of the 1970s the investment ratio was higher than in the 1960s but this reflected rising public investment and declining private investment. The investment ratio declined still further in the 1980s and although it was still considerably higher than in the 1950s, growth rates failed to recover.

Over the whole period much of the investment was either directly attributable to the state through its control over the nationalized sector and its low interest rate policy, or indirectly attributable to it through its power to offer loans at preferential interest rates to selected industries or sectors of the economy.

The decline in private investment in the 1970s caused unemployment to rise for the first time since the war to over 3 per cent of the labour force. Since 1974 it has risen steadily each year reaching over 10 per cent in 1985. Even at the height of the depression in the 1930s unemployment only reached 4.5 per cent of the labour force – although this figure disguised considerable underemployment in the agricultural sector (Carré et al. 1976: 57). This has presented French governments in the 1970s and the 1980s with an entirely new problem and one which has undermined the consensus supporting state intervention in the economy.

The nature of the growth process

Early explanations of France's postwar growth concentrated on the role of supply factors such as the contribution made by new technology or the gains from the transfer of labour from low productivity agriculture to higher productivity industry. The role of government policy was seen at best as permissive (Carré et al. 1976: 57), and at worst as positively harmful to economic growth (Baum 1958). More recent analyses accord considerably more importance to the role of the state. It is argued that after the war there was a consensus of opinion in favour of rapid economic growth. The main exponents of this growth ideology were recruited to the new planning commissariat and the new training school for top level civil servants – the Ecole Nationale d'Administration. Between 1945 and 1975 these two institutions were able to convert the Ministry of Finance, the Bank of France, and French business to the virtues of investment and rapid growth. Increasing production was to be more important than its distribution, since only in that way could social conflict be resolved (Sautter 1985; Hall 1986). But arguments based on the 'growth consensus' fail adequately to explain the dramatic events of May 1968 or the success of the government's response to them. They also fail to explain why growth accelerated in the 1960s and then why the formula no longer worked so effectively in the 1970s and the 1980s.

Origins of growth: the postwar consensus

As we have seen the consensus which was formed in 1947 had a different social base from that of 1945. By excluding the Communist Party and therefore most organized labour, the centre parties depended for their survival in government on the ability of the state to deliver higher living standards. The combination of public investment under the first two plans and considerable labour mobility led to increased productivity and economic growth. With no history of chronic unemployment to restrain it, labour moved in great numbers both within the manufacturing sector and from agriculture into industry and services. Between 1949 and 1956 the greatest movements of labour were out of mining, the textile industry, and agriculture and into construction, the petroleum, chemical, and mechanical and electrical industries. It has been estimated that the movement from lower productivity agriculture into higher productivity manufacturing only contributed 5 per cent out of a 52 per cent rise in productivity between 1949 and 1959 (United Nations 1964). The largest contribution came from a shift within the manufacturing sector itself. However the increase in productivity in the service sector and in tourism in particular was higher than in any industrialized country except Austria. This stemmed from the fact that the service sector had to compete for high-cost labour which could find alternative employment. As a result new labour-saving machinery was installed in restaurants, and hotels were used to capacity.

The government also encouraged investment indirectly by showing its determination to open up the French economy to external competition. It did so gradually hoping that firms would respond positively to the colder climate. The institution of the European Coal and Steel Community was the first example of this. Then in April 1954 the rate of liberalization (i.e. the amount of trade free from any form of quantitative restriction) with OEEC countries was raised from 17.9 per cent to 53 per cent, although at the same time a tax of between 10 per cent and 15 per cent was imposed on those imported manufactured goods which had been liberalized. The trade balance did not deteriorate in the face of this partial trade liberalization and in 1954 and 1955 it was in surplus.

Exports increased more rapidly than imports between 1951 and 1955 and covered 90 per cent of imports by 1955. Imports of food and raw materials declined while imports of equipment increased fairly continuously from 1951 to 1955 (Lévi 1956). New equipment helped to increase productivity which in turn enabled wages to be increased without loss of profits. The resulting pressure of demand was contained through the partial liberalization of foreign trade.

However, after 1955 the pressure on weak centre and centre-left governments proved more difficult and ultimately impossible to contain. The commitment to public investment meant that it could not be cut to accommodate an increase in military expenditure. The resulting inflationary pressure was then fuelled by a decision to extend compulsory paid holidays from twelve to eighteen weeks and to index agricultural wages to industrial wages in 1957. The government of Gaillard and Pflimlin subsequently tried to reduce domestic demand by devaluing the franc by 20 per cent in 1957. This corrected the trade deficit but since it coincided with an international recession, the growth in exports was insufficient to maintain the previous rates of growth of domestic production. As a result the Fourth Republic came to an end not only in the midst of the Algerian War but also with the economy moving into recession.

The Rueff-Pinay reforms

The Algerian crisis brought de Gaulle back into power with a mandate to reshape the political system along the lines which he had envisaged in 1945. The strength of the president and the executive under the constitution of the Fifth Republic, together with a Gaullist majority, enabled de Gaulle to ignore the centre-left parties in the National Assembly. This was made even easier by the refusal of the Communist Party to develop a serious alliance with the Socialist Party. As a result de Gaulle was given a free hand to impose his economic policies.

The essential purpose of the Rueff-Pinay reforms enacted at the end of 1958 was to restore the power of capital over labour. Thus the system of wage indexation was abolished apart from that of the minimum wage which remained linked to consumer prices, and farm rents to the price of wheat. Public sector wages were reduced, the franc was devalued a further 17.5 per cent and made convertible. This 'offensive devaluation' together with the liberalization of 90 per cent of trade with Europe led to a surge in exports (Sautter 1985). The increase was accompanied by a dramatic change in their direction. By 1961 West Germany had overtaken Algeria as the main market while exports to former French colonies fell by 50 per cent between 1952 and 1962 (Adams 1987).

But the reduction of wages and salaries in the public sector, which in 1960 were not even at their 1957 level, produced a wave of resentment and strikes between 1961 and 1963. As a result wages were increased and prices rose to compensate. This increased the demand for imports which rose by 21.3 per cent in 1963. Since exports only increased by 11.3 per cent the trade surplus which had been building up since 1960 was almost wiped out.

The government's first reaction to the industrial unrest was to try to negotiate an incomes policy with the unions. But since the CGT was determined not to bargain with a conservative government the government preferred to ignore the unions altogether and impose wages restraint. External balance was to be restored not through devaluation or temporary protection but through the deflation of domestic demand. This took the form of Giscard d'Estaing's 'stabilization plan' of 1963 which replaced the official fourth plan. Private sector wages were controlled indirectly through the revival of price controls in 1964 (Flanagan *et al.* 1983: 599).

Because of the greater openness of the French economy the concern of the government, as enshrined in the fifth plan, was to increase the competitiveness of French industry. Thus, although economic growth, stimulated by high levels of investment, continued to be the main objective of economic policy, this was to be based less on supplying domestic demand, stimulated by a large public sector, and more on supplying the export market. At the same time the government encouraged investment to be financed out of private profits. For the first time under the fifth plan, income flows in actual prices were written into the plan. Profits were scheduled to rise at a rate of 8.6 per cent per annum while wages per capita were to rise at an annual rate of 3.3 per cent. Agricultural incomes were to rise at 4.8 per cent per annum (Sheahan 1967: 115). The plan selected what it considered to be the most competitive industries in the French economy, and encouraged them to reorganize into larger units. In 1965 France had the highest rate of mergers in western Europe. In return for getting guarantees on exports, investments, and wages the government relaxed its price controls and allowed firms to build up their profit margins. The firms thus favoured were in the large petrochemical, electronic, aeronautical, pharmaceutical, and data processing industries. The contracts remained secret (Hall 1986). In spite of considerable state support for exports in the 1960s an INSEE study concluded that the economy was specializing in those sectors which were in relative decline in international trade such as agricultural products, raw materials, and semi-finished goods. Table 4.3 shows both the increase in importance of trade in the economy as a whole (the ratios of exports and imports rise in almost all sectors) and the emphasis on agriculture (this is the only sector where the import ratio falls).

Table 4.3 Ratio of imports and exports to domestic production, 1959–72 (%)

	1959		1972	
	Imports	Exports	Imports	Exports
Agriculture	10.6	3.9	8.2	13.9
Food	10.3	7.6	12.3	11.8
Solid fuel	42.0	3.4	49.9	7.3
Iron ore, steel	15.0	41.6	38.3	39.9
Minerals and non-ferrous metals	87.0	24.6	117.3	53.1
Engineering goods	14.4	15.4	24.0	24.3
Electrical goods	5.7	13.3	21.3	24.0
Cars	3.9	34.7	20.3	41.4
Chemicals	20.6	23.7	33.7	34.6
Textiles	23.6	37.4	37.4	40.0
Other industries	4.9	19.7	14.7	20.9

Source: INSEE, La Mutation industrielle de la France, Collections de l'INSEE, série e, no. 31–2, 1975, 1:57.

The export performance of the French economy as a whole in the 1960s was average in comparison with its main competitors in the EEC. But because imports were increasing faster than exports, by 1969 France had a trade deficit with all the industrialized countries, and in particular with the rest of the EEC, in manufactures and semi-manufactures. The most critical deficits were in chemical products, transport machinery, and the category of 'other manufactures'. In the most technologically advanced industries such as electrical and electronic equipment the ratio of imports to domestic production increased from 5.7 per cent in 1959 to 21.3 per cent in 1972. The corresponding figures for the engineering and chemical industries were 14 to 24 per cent and 21 to 34 per cent respectively. Even in the car industry the ratio increased from 4 to 20 per cent but at the same time French car exports continued to expand rapidly and by 1972 over 41 per cent of the French car production was exported. More worrying was the fact that by 1972 the competitive sectors of the French economy were the same as in 1959.

1968 and its aftermath

As we have seen, the strategy of promoting economic growth was successful in the 1960s, at least in its own terms. However, the reason it was unable to continue was that it contained longer term problems. In particular, the industrial rationalization and wage restraint which were essential to the policy led to an accumulation of grievances in the labour market. Although real wages had continued to rise in the 1960s, after 1964 they had failed to keep pace with increases in productivity, as Table 4.4 shows, and the gap between the minimum wage and the average wage had widened.

Table 4.4 Growth of wages and productivity, 1963–8 (%)

	1963	1964	1965	1966	1967	1968
Change in real wages	5.2	5.7	3.7	3.5	4.0	6.9
Change in labour productivity	4.8	5.2	4.0	4.6	4.1	8.0

Source: Flanagan, Soskice, and Ulman 1983; 578.

Economic growth had brought social upheaval without any perceptible improvement in working conditions and by the late 1960s unemployment was beginning to increase. Despite the loose labour market, discontent was sufficiently strong for about half the French labour force to join in a national strike in May 1968. Not only was the scale of the strike different from the previous major strike of 1963 but so too was the political context in which it took place. Although the Gaullists secured a majority in the elections of June 1968, changes were taking place on the left which posed more of a threat to the right wing than at any time since 1958. The Confédération Française Démocratique du Travail (CFDT), which had broken its links with the Catholic Church in 1964, was strengthened by its support for the strikes in 1968 and began to move left politically. At the same time the internal reorganization of the Socialist Party was giving the Communist Party cause for concern. The fact that the Communist Party had not benefited politically from the strikes also forced it to reconsider its policy of opposition and isolation. Instead of deflating the economy as in 1963 and ignoring the unions the government agreed on a number of measures to improve wages and working conditions while at the same time trying to institute negotiations with the unions. Average wages were increased by 14 per cent, the working week was reduced to bring France into line with other European countries, and trade unions were given legal recognition at the company level for the first time.

The main concern of the government after May was to reduce the pressure on French prices resulting from these higher costs. Since excess capacity existed in the economy, the government hoped to expand output and increase labour productivity. Then when the increase in demand began to have an adverse effect on the external balance the government devalued the franc in August 1969. This devaluation was similar in many respects to that of 1958 (Sautter 1985). It served to curb domestic demand but increased exporters' profits so that investment rose and the economy moved into the 1970s with a faster rate of growth than in the 1960s and declining unemployment.

The energy crisis and its aftermath

Although the French economy grew more rapidly in the period between the two 'oil shocks' than the OECD average (3.0 per cent against 2.6 per cent) growth was still well below its postwar rate. The recession of 1975 marked the end of 'thirty glorious years' as after that date both inflation and unemployment increased, and growth rates slackened. While the origins of this weaker performance are to be found in the international economy, changes in French domestic politics contributed.

The signature of the joint programme of government by the Communist and Socialist Parties in 1972 significantly reduced the government's room to manoeuvre. Both the National Assembly elections of 1973 and the presidential elections of 1974 had revealed the very narrow majority of the right wing parties. This effectively meant that any policy based on reducing inflation through imposed wage restraint in order to restore competitiveness and exports, was ruled out. Instead, the government allowed wages to rise and reduced unemployment by tightening the law governing large-scale redundancies. Since wages were unofficially linked to prices, the quadrupling of the price of oil did not result in a decline in domestic demand but rather in industrial profit margins.

The government's reaction to the crisis took the form of a deliberate industrial and energy policy which was designed to change the structure of the country's system of production. High priority was given to the production of capital goods and other high value-added products, to nuclear energy, and to exports. This investment in nuclear energy, telecommunications, and high-speed trains was largely financed by raising funds on the international market in order to reduce pressure on the national capital markets, for private investment (Story 1983). Initially the strategy seemed to work. The economy continued to grow at a moderate rate, except for the recession of 1975, but this was due to the increase in private consumption and investment by public enterprises, as Table 4.5 shows. Private investment, despite negative interest rates in real terms, failed to pick up.

Raymond Barre, who replaced Jacques Chirac as prime minister in summer 1976, was determined to reverse the decline in private investment by restoring both productivity and profitability. The growing rift between the two parties of the left gave him an opportunity to adopt a less conciliatory policy towards labour. His plan was to put pressure on both prices and wages by refusing to devalue the franc, by allowing unemployment to rise,

Table 4.5 Volume of investment, 1974–9 (1973 = 100)

	1974	1975	1976	1977	1978	1979
Whole economy	100.6	97.9	101.3	100.0	100.0	103.2
Large nationalized firms	105.0	128.7	132.6	147.3	165.4	180.3

Source: R. Boyer (1987), 'The current economic crisis', in G. Ross, S. Hoffmann, and S. Malzacher (eds), *The Mitterrand Experiment. Continuity and Change in Modern France*, Oxford, p. 48.

and by controlling prices. But, even though unemployment increased from 4.4 per cent in 1976 to 5.2 per cent in 1978, in the absence of private investment, productivity did not increase by as much as he had hoped, and therefore neither did profits (Spivey 1982). After the legislative elections of 1978 Barre changed course, trying this time to reduce inflation and increase profits by liberalizing prices. This had the effect of stimulating private investment briefly before the second oil shock in 1979 once again increased costs.

Overall though, as a result of the fairly steady growth achieved partly through the selective public investment strategy, the French increased their share of the manufacturing output of eleven OECD countries in the 1970s, with the greatest increases being in the high skill intensity sectors. The most spectacular increase was in aerospace where the French share jumped from 4.7 per cent in 1970 to 14.3 per cent in 1980. Less spectacular increases were in electronics and electrical machinery (OECD 1986). But although exports of high skill intensity products increased, they tended to be concentrated to a growing extent on Third World markets, reflecting the predominance of state to state trading. In trade with the advanced countries – where products related to public procurement were of much less importance – the relative skill intensity of French exports tended to decline (Ergas 1986). Because of the declining competitiveness of French exports after 1973 there was a change in their geographic structure. In 1972 the OECD accounted for 76.5 per cent of French exports, the EEC of six accounted for 49.9 per cent and Germany alone 21.3 per cent. After 1972 the importance of Germany and the OECD declined and trade with Africa increased. By 1984 the OECD only took 66 per cent of French exports and trade with Germany had declined by a third. Whereas in 1973 the share of African countries in French trade was about 6.5 per cent, by 1980 this had risen to over 13 per cent (Spivey 1982) indicating certain parallels with the pattern of trade in the 1930s. The inexorable rise in unemployment was also a reflection, and a worse one, of that depressed decade and led to a Socialist victory in the elections of 1981.

The crisis of 1981/2

Excluded from power throughout the Fifth Republic, the left-wing government, under Mitterrand, sought to reverse France's economic decline and lay the basis for a democratic Socialist regime. This was to be done through a combination of short-term and long-term measures. The short-term policies, which were based on a quite different set of objectives and economic instruments from those of the previous government, placed the reduction in unemployment as the main priority. Under the interim plan for 1982/3 the government set itself the target of creating between 400,000 and 500,000 jobs in two years. This was to be achieved through a programme of income redistribution in favour of the lowest paid and a reduction in the official working week to thirty-nine hours with no loss of income. The longer-term objectives were to complete the programme of nationalizations begun by Blum's Popular Front government in 1936 and extended by the postwar coalition government between 1945 and 1947. The new nationalizations included five major industrial firms along with thirty-six banks and two financial companies. At the same time the nature of the planning process was to be changed with a return to the 1950s system of 'plan contracts'. These were negotiated for between three and five years with firms in the steel, chemicals, motor vehicles, aerospace, and electronics sectors (OECD 1986/7). But the other crucial aspect of the 1950s system of state economic control, namely, control over foreign trade, was rejected. With over 50 per cent of French exports going to the European Community, reimposing foreign trade controls was not viable on economic let alone political grounds.

Instead, the government hoped to be able to control the level of demand and prices within the economy by instituting a system of collective bargaining. Since the CFDT favoured such a policy more than the CGT, the Auroux Laws of May 1982 were to serve a dual purpose. On the one hand, they were to meet the desire of the Socialist majority to strengthen the power of organized labour without increasing the control of the CGT and therefore of the Communist Party and on the other hand they were to give the state greater control over wages than it had had since 1947 (Eisenhammer 1985: 282).

Another major innovation of the Mitterrand government was the creation of regional plans. For the first time since the Second World War regional policy-makers were to set medium-term priorities in consultation with central government rather than have policies and priorities imposed on them (Mény 1985).

Within a year the Mitterrand experiment, like the Blum experiment, had failed, but mainly for reasons beyond the government's control. The transfer of income to the lowest paid resulted in a surge in demand for imported consumer goods. However, the expected upturn in the international economy in 1982 did not take place so French exports failed to rise to compensate for the increase in imports. In 1982 the current account deficit more than doubled. Rather than leave the European Monetary System the government agreed to a devaluation of the franc in October 1981 and again in June 1982 and March 1983.

After the second devaluation, government policy, under pressure from Germany, began to shift towards trying to control inflation rather than expand demand. The central features of the new policy were a restrictive monetary and fiscal policy and an active prices and incomes policy. In June 1982 prices were frozen and wage increase agreements suspended. With a marked deceleration of wage costs, profits began to improve, and inflation rates fell. With the expansion in international demand in 1984 French exports increased by 7.1 per cent in real terms. But since the French economy hardly participated in this recovery, domestic demand remained fairly depressed and imports only rose by 2.8 per cent in 1984. Unemployment increased sharply and if the current account position improved this was as much a reflection of depressed demand as of increased competitiveness. The chief factor in the improvement in export performance in 1984 was the growth in exports of defence and civil aviation equipment, especially the Airbus. Exports by other sectors, such as chemicals, metals, and automobiles, stimulated by the upturn in both the American and European markets, also expanded, although to a lesser extent.

The economic record of the Mitterrand government in the early 1980s was widely interpreted as evidence of the failure of state control over the economy. As a result the emphasis began to swing back to the use of market mechanisms, a movement further reinforced when Chirac became Prime Minister, when great faith was once again placed on the functioning of free markets. In this new climate the prospect of the large European market being freed in 1992 was seen as acting as a stimulus to investment and expansion. Meanwhile in preparation for 1992 the system of economic controls in France was to be dismantled. The recently enlarged public sector was to be pruned back leaving only those enterprises of a public service nature under state control. Controls over prices, foreign exchange, and the labour market, which had been removed and then reinstated at various times over the postwar period, were once again to be dismantled. But the real innovation in policy was to be the attempt to end state control over the financial system. It was the state's ability to extend credit to selected firms or sectors, at preferential interest rates, which had been at the crux of the whole postwar system of economic control and planning. But in the conditions of rising unemployment and inflation in the 1980s this system was seen to be contributing to public sector deficits and lowering the price of capital relative to labour. A unified system of interest rates responding to the market rather than the state would, it was hoped, lead to a more efficient use of capital. In any case the government's membership of the European Monetary System had reduced the scope for altering interest rates for domestic policy purposes.

Conclusion

In the fifty years from 1936 to 1986 opinion regarding the role of the state in the French economy has almost come full circle. The consensus which underpinned an increased role for the state in economic management was born out of the failure of the market in the 1930s and the defeat of France in the Second World War. Between 1947 and 1958 government policy was aimed at maintaining a high level of investment in the economy in order to promote economic growth and higher living standards. Only in that way could support for the weak centre parties of government be secured. Through a combination of selective controls over trade and investment the government was able to stimulate a high level of demand and growth in the economy. But because of its inability to control wages which tended to rise faster than productivity this imparted an inflationary bias to the system, leading to two large devaluations of the currency in 1957 and 1958.

After 1958 conservative governments of the Fifth Republic pursued the objective of promoting growth and investment. But with the increased openness of the economy after the formation of the European Economic Community external balance could no longer be partially regulated through trade controls. As a result the government tried to exert tighter control over domestic demand and economic planning came to be replaced by selective industrial policies aimed at promoting advanced export-orientated industries. Public expenditure declined as a proportion of gross domestic production and investment was to be financed increasingly out of retained profits. Pressure on wages was exercised through direct and indirect price controls. The achievements of this strategy were limited. Not only did it widen the gulf between the modern and the traditional sectors of the economy, but it failed to make any appreciable difference to the export performance of the French economy as a whole.

The international recession of the 1970s and the deteriorating terms of trade demonstrated the precariousness of the French current account balance. But the government pursued its strategy of promoting investment in selected sectors of the economy in the hope that increased exports would help to cover the larger import costs. Since private investment remained depressed, productivity and profit margins did not rise.

In 1981 the Socialist strategy for economic revival rested on stimulating demand in the consumer goods sector of the economy on the assumption that this would stimulate domestic production. But after years of declining investment in these sectors the demand was met from foreign suppliers. In the absence of extensive trade controls the state's ability to manage the economy was called into question. The only way to stimulate private investment was to increase profit margins, which in the absence of rapid increases in productivity, could only be done by depressing wages. But since this reduced domestic demand and increased unemployment, revival of the French economy had to be stimulated by international demand. This undermined the role of the state in domestic economic management.

Those who had explained the deterioration of the economy in the 1970s in terms of the 'demise of planning' (Green 1978: 60–76) and a return to economic liberalism had to look for other explanations for the even worse performance of the economy in the 1980s. For some the failure of the Mitterrand experiment emphasized the fact that France had become an 'intermediate economy in an interdependent world' (Cerny 1985). Both the liberals and the planners were to turn to Europe to find a solution to the problems of the French economy. But whether the European solution was to rest solely on the liberalization of the market by 1992 or on its accompaniment by a further transfer of economic controls from the nation state to the European level, remained unresolved.

Selected dates

August 1944	Liberation of Paris.
December 1944–June 1945	Nationalization of Renault, air transport, northern coalfields.
October 1945	Creation of social security system.
December 1945	Nationalization of Bank of France, four deposit banks, and institution of National Credit Council.
December 1945	Ratification of Bretton Woods agreement and devaluation of franc.
January 1946	Creation of Commissariat au Plan.
April 1946	Nationalization of gas, electricity, and large insurance companies.
May 1946	Blum–Byrnes agreement.
January 1947	Adoption of Monnet plan.
April 1947	Strikes at Renault.
May 1947	Dismissal of Communists from government.
July 1947	Acceptance of Marshall Aid.
January 1948	Devaluation of franc.
October 1948	Devaluation of franc.
September 1949	Devaluation of franc.
February 1952	Indexation of SMIG.
January 1954	Adoption of second plan.
February 1956	Institution of three weeks' paid holidays.
August 1957	Unofficial devaluation of franc by 20 per cent.
September 1958	Adoption of constitution of Fifth Republic.
December 1958	Devaluation of franc and adoption of Pinay-Rueff plan.
March–April 1963	Large miners' strike.
1963	Stabilization plan of Giscard d'Estaing.
May 1968	General strike and Grenelle agreement.
August 1969	Devaluation of franc.
1973	First oil shock.
September 1976	Barre plan.
1979	Second oil shock.
1981	Election of left-wing government under F. Mitterrand. Nationalization of five industrial

	groups, thirty-six banks, and two financial companies.
Autumn 1981	Devaluation of franc.
June 1982	Devaluation of franc. Prices and wages frozen.
March 1983	Devaluation of franc and adoption of austerity plan.
March 1986	Return of a right-wing government.
April 1986	Devaluation of franc.

References

Adams, W.J. (1987) 'The exposure of French business to foreign competition since World War II', University of Michigan, unpublished paper.

André, Ch. and Delorme, R. (1982) *L'état et l'économie*, Paris.

Andrieu, C. (1984) 'A la recherche de la politique du crédit, 1946–1973', *Revue Historique*, CCLXX 1/2.

Baum, W. (1958) *The French Economy and the State*, Princeton, NJ.

Bonin, H. (1987) *Histoire économique de la IVe République*, Paris.

Brémond, J. (1987) *Dictionnaire d'histoire économique de 1800 à nos jours*, Paris.

Carré, J.-J., Dubois, P., and Malinvaud, E. (1976) *French Economic Growth*, London.

Cerny, P. (1985) 'State capitalism in France and Britain and the international economic order', in Cerny, P. and Schain, M. (eds), *Socialism, the State and Public Policy in France*, London.

Eisenhammer, J. (1985) 'Comment', in Machin, H. and Wright, V. (eds), *Economic Policy and Policy-Making under the Mitterrand Presidency 1981–1984*, London: Frances Pinter. 'Competition since World War II', unpublished paper.

Ergas, H. (1986) 'Does technology policy matter?', unpublished paper, July.

Flanagan, R., Soskice, D., and Ulman, L. (1983) *Unionism, Economic Stabilization, and Incomes Policies*, Washington, DC.

Fourastié (1979) *Les Trente glorieuses ou la révolution invisible de 1946 à 1975*, Paris.

Green, D. (1978) 'The demise of French planning', *West European Politics*, 1: 1.

Hall, P. (1984) 'Patterns of economic policy: an organizational approach', in Bernstein, S., Held, D., and Krieger, J. (eds), *The State in Capitalist Europe*, London.

Hall, P. (1986) *Governing the Economy. The Politics of State Intervention in Britain and France*, Cambridge.

Lévi, M. (1956) 'L'évolution et la structure des échanges commerciaux de la France avec l'étranger de 1951 à 1955', *Politique Etrangère*, November.

Mény, Y. (1985) 'Local authorities and economic policy', in Machin, H. and Wright, V. (eds), *Economic Policy and Policy-Making under the Mitterrand Presidency 1981–1984*, London.

OECD (1986) *Science and Technology Indicators*, Paris.

OECD (1986/7) *Economic Survey: France*, Paris.

Sautter, C. (1985) 'France', in Boltho, A. (ed.), *The European Economy: Growth and Crisis*, Oxford.

Sheahan, J. (1967) *The Wage–Price Guideposts*, Washington, DC.

Spivey, W. Allen (1982) *Economic Policies in France 1976–1981*, Michigan.

Story, J. (1983) 'Capital in France: the changing pattern of patrimony', *West European Politics*, 6: 2.

Tapinos, G. (1975) *L'Immigration étrangère en France 1946-73*, Institut national d'études démographiques. Travaux et documents, Cahier no. 71, Paris.

United Nations Economic Commission for Europe (1964) *Some Factors in the Economic Growth in Europe during the 1950s.*

Guide to further reading

The most important and comprehensive analysis of French economic growth from the beginning of the century until 1970 is: Carré, Dubois, and Malinvaud. A very interesting study of the role of the state in the economy with useful statistical material is: André and Delorme.

French statistical studies and sources are to be found in various publications of Institut national de la statistique et des études economiques (INSEE) such as: INSEE (1981), *Le Mouvement economique en France 1949-1979*, Paris. INSEE, *Fresque historique du système productif*, Collections de l'INSEE, série e, 1974 and 1975. INSEE, *Rapport sur les comptes de la nation*, série c.

Historical studies of the reconstruction period based on archival material are: Bloch-Lainé, F. and Bouvier, J. (1986) *La France restaurée 1944-1954*, Paris, and Kuisel, R.F. (1981) *Capitalism and the State in Modern France*, Cambridge.

Recent and interesting works in English on the role of the state in the economy are: Hayward, J.E.S. (1986) *The State and the Market Economy. Industrial Patriotism and Economic Intervention in Britain and France*, Brighton.

The most recent book in English specifically on French planning is: Estrin, S. and Holmes, P. (1983) *French Planning in Theory and Practice*, London.

An informative book on the role of trade unions is: Flanagan, Soskice and Ulman.

Finally, a most useful analysis of the French economy between 1945 and 1980 is Sautter.

Chapter five

West Germany

Graham Hallett

Introduction

After the Second World War, Germany was in a state of devastation not
known in Europe since the Thirty Years War. Millions of people were on
the move; in most cities half the housing had been destroyed; the average
calorie intake was half the normally accepted minimum level. A German
exile returning from the USA in 1947, saw

> a nation irremediably maimed in its biological structure – with a long-
> term sharp decline in its population inevitable – morally ruined – without
> food or raw materials – a nation whose social fabric has been destroyed
> by mass flight, mass emigrations, – a country where, amid hunger and
> fear, hope has died. (Stolper 1947)

Although his prognosis proved incorrect, his description of *Jahr Null* (year
zero) was valid. But, within a few years, West Germany was to experience
the most rapid recovery in modern European history. Economic growth
(per capita) continued at a level above the OECD average until the 1980s. In
1985 it was at the top of the league of European economies – apart from the
Scandinavian countries and Switzerland (see Table 5.1). Moreover, even
though it was still some 25 per cent behind the US, it was clearly ahead of
the US in terms of 'public goods' (public transport, environmental quality,
crime rates etc.) and in the extent of poverty: the 'problem districts' of West
German cities do not begin to compare with those of US (or British) cities.

The 'economic miracle' of the early years was assisted by a change in the

Table 5.1 GDP per head, 1985, US$ at purchasing power parities

US	17,300	Japan	11,800
Switzerland	14,100	UK	10,900
Sweden	12,700	Italy	10,800
Germany	12,100	Ireland	6,800

Source: OECD.

policy of the occupying powers. The Morgenthau Plan for 'pastoralizing' Germany was replaced in 1947 by Marshall Aid. But although this was a life-saver between 1947 and 1951, it cannot explain subsequent economic growth. Britain received more than twice as much Marshall Aid as West Germany. It is also true that, in spite of the destruction, it proved physically possible to bring the railways, roads and factories back into operation fairly quickly. But the tasks of recovery were nevertheless daunting. Much of the credit for the recovery must go to the German people, whose industriousness was given full play by the politico-economic constitution of the new West German state, the Federal Republic, founded in 1949.

The philosophy and institutions of the West Germany economy

The philosophy which came to be generally accepted was *soziale Marktwirtschaft* or the 'socially responsible market economy' (Mueller-Armack 1965, 1976). This, it has sometimes been suggested, was a pretentious German term for a combination of policies familiar elsewhere, such as 'Butskellism' in Britain. When judged by aggregates such as 'the size of the public sector', Germany is certainly not very different from Britain or most other west European countries. Public expenditure as a percentage of GNP rose in Germany from 36.7 per cent in 1966 to 47.2 per cent in 1985 (for Britain, the figures were 35.3 per cent and 47.7 per cent).

There have, however, been considerable differences between the relatively stable German policies and the constantly changing British ones. West Germany has never adopted either 'socialist' policies of prohibitive tax rates or 'radical Conservative' tax and benefit policies. (The maximum income tax rate has always been around 50 per cent, and there has also been a moderate wealth tax.) It has made far more use of subsidized non-state institutions, in housing, health services, etc. (*Subsidaritaetsprinzip*). It has not nationalized, or denationalized, whole industries, but has maintained municipal or regional public ownership of gas, water, and electricity. It has had hardly any private schools, and a state school system of reasonably uniform efficiency.

The most distinctive features of the 'German model', however, comprise a set of institutional characteristics which were introduced in the early years, and have remained largely unaltered. The most important of these are:

(a) a decentralized political constitution, characterized by checks and balances;
(b) an independent central bank;
(c) a legally enforced system of industrial democracy and industrial training; and

(d) a bank-based system for financing firms and monitoring their performance.

Together with whatever is attributed to 'national character', these four factors, which have acquired a quasi-constitutional importance, must be given most of the praise, or blame, for West German economic performance.

The political constitution was based on a high degree of devolution to the 'states' (*Länder*) and communities, and a considerable degree of institutionalized 'consensus'. All the federal governments have been coalitions – a situation encouraged by the element of proportional representation in the 'split vote' system. The mere possession of a majority in the Bundestag is not considered a justification for pushing through controversial legislation, and a strong second chamber, appointed by the *Länder*, ensures a slow and thorough review of legislation. Most major acts since the early 1950s have been initiated under one government and yet passed under a government of a different political composition. Similarly, tax reforms are discussed at length by experts and politicians before being introduced; finance ministers do not draw rabbits out of a hat on budget day. Snags thus tend to be discovered before, rather than after, legislation has been passed. In these respects, it might be said that Germany is not so very different from most other western countries – but it is clearly very different from Britain's 'elective dictatorship'.

Institutions remain effective, however, only as long as they enjoy public support, and are buttressed by unwritten rules. Consensus, 'fairness' (the English word is used), and self-denial by political leaders were hardly outstanding German characteristics in the century before 1945; they emerged only after the greatest disaster in German history. And even if consensus has become a little frayed under the impact of time and recession, it has by no means broken down.

The Bundesbank

Among the specifically economic institutions of the new state, pride of place must go to the Bundesbank (Federal Bank). Its predecessor, the Bank of the German States, played a key role in the currency reform of 1948, and was made independent of the federal government by the Allies. This Allied decision was, however, confirmed by the 1957 Act setting up the Bundesbank. The Bank was specifically charged with safeguarding the value of the currency; its directorate was elected in a way which guaranteed independence; and it was obliged to 'consider', but not be bound by, advice from the federal government. No other central bank has such a remit, or such a proven ability to resist government pressure. This power is based not only on law but on popular support, based on the experience of hyper-inflation in 1921-3 and suppressed inflation in 1945-8. In a report to SPD leaders in 1974, Chancellor Schmidt argued that 'we cannot indulge in any public disagreement with the Bundesbank; public opinion would not be on our side'.

The Bundesbank, while consistently taking a hard line on inflation, and using money supply targets since 1974, has never accepted monetarism, i.e., the doctrine that inflation is directly related to a particular, targetable measure of the money supply. Dr Emminger, a long-time director of the Bank, stressed in his memoirs that it is necessary to take into account a variety of indicators of monetary conditions, since fluctuations in the velocity of circulation can temporarily offset changes in the money supply (Emminger 1987: 439). (This is similar to the Radcliffe Commission's view – subsequently rejected by Conservative governments of both a Keynesian and a monetarist persuasion – that the basis for monetary policy should be 'the state of liquidity of the whole economy'.) Dr Emminger also stressed that monetary targets are as important for the signals they give to economic decision-makers as for their direct effects. This ties up with German 'incomes policy'. There have never been statutory norms for wage or price rises. There has always, however, been a dialogue between unions, government, and employers.

The priority given by the Bundesbank to price stability has been regularly criticized both inside and outside the country. But it arguably saved Europe from a 'Latin American' inflation in the 1970s and, for most of the postwar period, it seemed to be justified in terms of employment and economic growth. Since 1982, however, Germany has had an unemployment rate which – although lower than the Brtish figure or the OECD average – is clearly too high. Whether it can be attributed to policies under the ocntrol of the Bundesbank is a more open question.

Industrial democracy

The third institutional peculiarity of the 'German model' is industrial democracy. In 1953, a system of works councils and employee representation on company boards was introduced, which is still unique. Works councils, elected by all employees, have considerable managerial powers, and provide a forum for the resolution of workplace problems. Employees also elect a proportion of the Supervisory Board (of non-executive directors) – originally one-third, but one-half since 1973. The trade unions were also reorganized during the period 1947-9 into a small number of industrial unions, operating under labour laws which make contracts legally binding. The combination of industrial democracy with strong, but 'responsible', industry-wide, trade unions has provided stability, and relative peace, in industrial relations ever since. Figures on strikes are not an adequate measure of harmony, but those in Table 5.2 are still illuminating.

Table 5.2 Days lost through strikes, 1950–85 (per 1,000 employees) (yearly average)

	1950–70	1970–80	1980–5
Germany	37	48	99
Italy	835	1,418	911
UK	153	552	543
US	559	315	177
Japan	233	116	16

Sources: OECD, ILO.

Germany has the lowest number of strikes per year in each of the first two periods and would have been in the same position in the years 1980–5 except for the metalworkers' strike in 1984 (the average for the other years is only three).

Alongside this new postwar industrial relations system goes an industrial training system which originated in the 1870s, but has been up-dated. Nearly everyone obtains a qualification – either a degree or an apprenticeship certificate. Apprenticeship, which covers shoe selling or hairdressing as well as engineering, is based on practical experience combined with one to two days of 'school' training. The system is organized by quasi-public Chambers of Industry and Commerce. The importance of this comprehensive training system on shopfloor competence – and hence economic performance – can hardly be exaggerated. The backbone of German industry (as was pointed out before 1914!) is not so much the manager as the *Meister* (master craftsman) (Lawrence 1980; chapter 7; *NIER* 1988: 34). A series of comparative studies has shown that German industrial productivity is some 40 per cent higher than in Britain, not because of better, or more, equipment, but because of greater competence among workers (*NIER* 1985: 48; 1987: 84).

The banks and industry

Finally, there is the close link between the banks and industry, which again dates from the 1870s. The banks helped to rebuild German industry after 1918, and again after 1948. Firms rely extensively on loan, as against equity, finance, and the banks exercise an important monitoring role through their representatives on the Supervisory Board. The system has its critics, and there has been a slight shift towards equity finance. Nevertheless, the role of the banks tends to counter 'short termism', and provides a mechanism for reorganizing management in good time, when a company starts running into trouble. The 'turning round' of VW in the 1970s and AEG in the 1980s was organized by alliances of banks and other shareholders. (The full co-operation of the workforce – via the Works Councils and Supervisory Board – was also essential.)

Although the 'big three' commercial banks (Deutsche, Dresdner, Commerz) are private, they are flanked by public or quasi-public financial institutions. On one side are the municipally-owned 'savings banks'; on the other, the Finance Institute for Reconstruction, which was set up to administer Marshall Aid, and has continued as a public 'merchant bank'. This blend of public and private institutions is characteristic of the Federal Republic.

The politico-economic constitution of the federal republic – which has had a profound influence on business management at all levels, and hence on economic performance – is a mixture of new and old. Consensus and decentralization mark a break with National Socialism and Prussian absolutism, and a return to older traditions: works councils were one of the demands of the Frankfurt Assembly of 1848. On the other hand, many of the administrative systems of the Empire/Weimar Republic have been retained and adapted to new conditions. Anyone who studies local government, the school system, industrial organization, or vocational training must be struck by the continuity (temporarily interrupted by National Socialism) over the past hundred years.

Policy objectives

In the 1950s, the federal governments tended not to commit themselves to economic objectives – apart from price stability. Ludwig Erhard, as economics minister, emphasized the need to establish a liberal economic order, which would then produce economic growth. There was no official commitment to full employment, although in fact the 1950s were outstandingly successful in increasing employment and reducing unemployment.

The Economic Stability and Growth Act of 1967 committed the government to the 'magic triangle' of full employment, price stability, and external balance, and provided an armoury for counter-cyclical policies. In 1977, a commission representing the 'social partners' (i.e., both sides of industry) advocated a more structural, long-term, policy for achieving full employment. In the event, the 1980s have seen higher unemployment and a growing view that governments cannot do much about it – at least directly.

The political and economic institutions of the Federal Republic have not been without challenges. They survived the youthful and Marxist challenge of 1968, although absorbing some of the protesters' more acceptable ideas – such as more concern for the quality of life. In the 1980s, they have faced less dramatic challenges from both the Greens and the New Right, with a somewhat similar outcome. This stability and continuity can, however, be viewed favourably or unfavourably; those who are impatient for radical change – in various directions – tend to describe it as 'immobilism'.

Economic performance

In assessing economic performance I shall concentrate on the 'magic quadrilateral' of economic growth, full employment, price stability, and equilibrium in the balance of payments, with some discussion of the distribution of income. (The quality of life ought also to be discussed, but space allows only the assertion that, in the 1980s, Germany had, with Scandinavia, the lowest hours of work and the highest environmental standards in the OECD.)

In terms of individual material well-being, the relevant measure of economic growth is the change in GDP (or GNP) per capita, rather than the more usual figure based on national GDP or GNP. When dealing with changes over years or decades, the national and per capita figures can diverge considerably in countries (like Germany since the mid-1970s) in which population is falling, and countries (like the US) in which it is rising. The term 'economic growth' will therefore be used only in the per capita sense. Similarly, the change in employment (as distinct from unemployment) is a valuable short-term indicator, but can be misleading when comparing changes over several years in countries with differing rates of population growth or decline. If one wishes to measure the productivity of labour, the relevant figure is GDP per employee.

An overview

Germany's economic performance in the four periods is summarized in Table 5.3, in comparison with the OECD average. After devastation from 1945 to 1948, the period 1949 to 1956 saw the first stage of the German 'economic miracle'; output and exports increased much faster than the most optimistic prognoses, and, on any reasonable definition, full employment was achieved. The ensuing period, 1956 to 1973, was similarly successful, allowing for the fact that the initial recovery is almost always faster than the longer-term growth rate. This 'golden age' saw rates of economic growth and productivity growth of around 4 per cent, well above the OECD average; virtually the same moderate inflation rate of around 4 per cent; and almost no unemployment. Indeed, the main criticism of this period is that employment was over-full, leading to the importation of 'guest workers' – and an intractable racial problem.

The period 1973 to 1979 was more troubled, with inflation at 4.8 per cent, unemployment at 3.5 per cent, and economic growth and productivity growth below 3 per cent. In all these respects, however, Germany did considerably better than the OECD average. In the period 1979 to 1985, Germany continued to avoid the strong inflationary upsurge experienced by most countries, and had by 1985 achieved virtual price stability; on the

Table 5.3 West German economic performance, 1949–85

		GDP per capita	Employment	Output per worker	Inflation[a]	Unemployment rate[b] %
	GDP					
			Average annual changes, %			
W. Germany 1949–56	9.8	7.9	2.6	7.4	3.5	3.9
W. Germany 1956–73	4.8	3.9	0.5	4.3	3.9	0.8[c]
OECD 1956–73	4.5	3.1	1.0	3.5	4.0	3.2[c]
W. Germany 1973–9	2.3	2.5	−0.5	2.9	4.8	3.5[d]
OECD 1973–9	2.6	1.9	1.1	1.5	9.0	5.2[d]
W. Germany 1979–85	1.3	1.4	−0.3	1.6	3.4	6.5[e]
OECD 1979–85	2.3	1.7	0.6	1.7	7.1	7.8[e]
W. Germany 1956–85	3.6	3.2	1.0	3.5	4.0	2.8[f]
OECD 1956–85	3.7	2.6	0.9	2.7	5.7	4.7[f]

a The consumer price index 1949–50. The GDP deflator 1950–85
b The average level in the period as % of the total labour force
c 1960–73
d 1974–9
e 1980–5
f 1960–85

Note: The OECD totals for GDP and inflation are based on the exchange rates of 1980

Sources: OECD *Historical Statistics, 1960–85* and the OECD database.

other hand, economic growth fell below average, and a serious unemployment problem developed (even though it remained below the OECD average). Over the period 1956 to 1985, as a whole, Germany had above-average performance in terms of economic growth, productivity, inflation, and unemployment, but its lead was steadily eroded.

Devastation and recovery: 1945–56

Between 1945 and 1948, the economic situation in the three western zones deteriorated. The Iron Curtain severed the main lines of communication and cut off the food-surplus areas of the east, while millions of refugees flooded into the western zones. There was, however, a more fundamental cause of increasing shortages. National Socialism had developed into a command economy with excessive cash balances 'sterilized' by rationing and controls, i.e., suppressed inflation. After 1945, the command economy began to lose control; the outcome was a growth of the black market and barter, and a tendency for production to be shifted from price-controlled essentials to less essential products whose prices were not controlled. As Figure. 5.1 shows, the devastation was such that GDP did not regain its 1945 level until 1949.

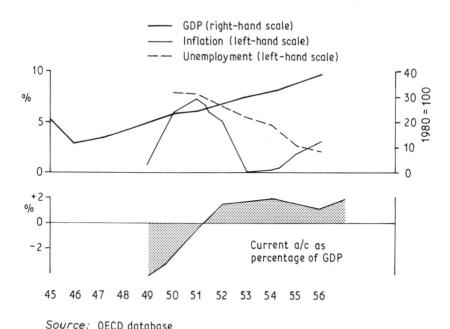

Source: OECD database

Figure 5.1 The level of real GDP, unemployment rate, inflation rate, and current account (as percentage of GNP), 1945–56

The currency reform of 1948 involved the withdrawal of existing currency and the substitution of a new currency – the Deutschmark. This draconian measure (combined with the end of rationing) removed the excess cash balances, and restored confidence in money. It eliminated the black market at a stroke, and brought goods back into the shops. The situation was nevertheless still bleak. In 1950, the German mark was the weakest European currency; there was a large current account deficit, and the chairman of an OEEC committee referred to a 'bankrupt Germany'. At the same time, unemployment was running at 8 per cent. Germany was then hit by the sharp rise in commodity prices which followed the outbreak of war in Korea – although the 'Korean boom' later assisted exports.

In the early months of 1951, Germany faced a severe balance of payments crisis. It was forced to seek a loan from the European Payments Union, which was granted only on condition that demand was curbed. Interest rates were raised – much to the displeasure of Chancellor Adenauer – and a quantitative restriction of credit was undertaken. Fiscal policy was tightened, and there were budget surpluses from 1951 to 1954.

The outcome was not the depression which some feared. On the contrary, unemployment continued to fall, and by 1956 virtually full employment had been reached. Exports increased so rapidly that, for 1951 as a whole, there was a slight current account surplus. From 1951 to 1956, there was near stability in prices and unit labour costs, although real wages rose by nearly half. The average annual increase in prices (using the GDP deflator) from 1949 to 1956 was 3.5 per cent – higher than in the US (2.4 per cent) but lower than in Britain (4.9 per cent. Exports rose from one-third of the British level in 1950 to near equality in 1956, and were higher by the end of the decade.

The remarkably rapid recovery – with only a slight, temporary, curtail-ment of the liberal policy instituted by Erhard – marked a turning point in the German and the west European economy. For Germany, it marked the changed from 'structural' deficit to surplus in the current account; for western Europe, it opened the way to relatively free trading arrangements and the establishing of the EEC. An economic breakdown in Germany, or the adoption of an autarkic policy, could have put western Europe on a different path.

Planning and non-planning

An eminent British economist wrote, in a 1951 report on Germany, 'It is surprising that there does not appear to be a really up-to-date German investment programme' – a criticism of non-planning echoed more strongly by some other commentators (Cairncross 1951: 30). It is true that there was no central plan for investment levels in all the major industries, backed up by raw material allocations, as practised in Britain from 1945 to 1952. Ludwig Erhard vehemently rejected this policy. But, as Wallich (1955) has shown, there was more planning than some observers realized – or than Erhard conceded.

In the first place, government expenditure was planned; which some might say is quite a large enough task for government. It included public investment (about a quarter of all investment at the time), subsidies, and tax expenditure or concessions. The peculiarities of the German system were twofold:

(a) some two-thirds of public investment (predominantly housing and public works) was delegated to the *Länder* and communities; and
(b) an important role was played by tax concessions and subsidies linked to private investment.

Most industrial investment was financed from retained profits, but this self-financing was encouraged by extremely generous provisions for depreciation. Loans made by individuals for investment could also be set against income tax, and there were tax incentives for exports. All these provisions (which were later withdrawn), were unselective, but some industrial investment of a targeted kind was undertaken by the Finance Institute for Reconstruction (Kredit Anstalt fuer Wiederaufbau).

The other main category of investment was housing, which was also financed by a combination of public and private money (Hallett 1977). There was a large programme of social housing, which differed from British council housing in that subsidies were made available to housing associations and even private individuals. Independently financed private building for rent was also encouraged by tax provisions. The outcome was an enormous volume of housebuilding of all types, which ended the acute housing shortage by the early 1960s. Thereafter, attention turned to the urban renewal, and Germany undertook what is – in relation to its population – probably the largest and most successful renewal programme in any OECD country (Hallett and Williams 1988). This programme has again been organized by the *Länder* and communities, and has involved a combination of public 'seed corn' and private investment.

By the end of the 1950s, the industrial and residential rebuilding of West Germany had been largely achieved. It is generally considered to have been a remarkable achievement, although some socialist academics are very critical (Kennedy 1984). The system under which rebuilding was undertaken may have been less 'socialist' than in some other European countries, but it was not *laissez-faire*. The federal government, the *Länder*, the communes spent large sums on infrastructure and services, and influenced the market through taxes and subsidies, although the actual construction was the responsibility of firms, co-operatives, and individuals.

Income distribution

It was a criticism of the Social Democrats at the time, and it has been a criticism of some economic historians since, that the gains of the 'economic miracle' were very unequally divided. The available figures suggest that there were divergent trends in the distribution of income and of capital. Many owners of bombed-out factories had, by the late 1950s, become owners of considerable capital, whereas most wage-earners still had little. The concentration of capital thus increased in the 1950s. The distribution of income was certainly not egalitarian, but it appears to have been more equal than under prewar National Socialism, and to have become slightly more equal after 1955. The figures in Table 5.4 suggest that the lowest 60 per cent of the population, in terms of earnings, gained at the expense of the top 20 per cent. These figures are pre-tax; post-tax figures would be more equally distributed. It seems reasonable to conclude that the 'economic miracle' was not (and probably could not have been) accompanied by an egalitarian distribution of income, but that it did not interrupt a secular trend towards a somewhat more equal distribution of income.

Table 5.4 Shares in national income, 1929–59 (by groups of earners) %

	1929	1936	1950	1955	1959
Top 5%	21	28	24	18	18
Top 20%	45	53	48	43	43
Bottom 60%	34	27	29	34	34

Source: Kuznets 1966: 208.

The long boom: 1956–73

The period 1956 to 1973 was one of a long boom, interrupted only by the brief recession of 1966/7. There was full (indeed over-full) employment, high economic growth, and generally low inflation. After 1969, however, inflation rose above the – for Germany – danger level of 5 per cent. Inflation was, to some extent, imported under the prevailing system of fixed exchange rates. When Germany inflation lagged behind the international level, there was a tendency for a balance of payments surplus to emerge. This caused an expansion of the money supply which, together with rising import prices, tended to boost inflation. German governments were slow to accept revaluation, but there were revaluations in 1961 and 1969.

The labour shortage of the time led to the importation of over 2 million 'guest workers' from southern Europe and Turkey, with no thought as to the long-term consequences. It was originally believed that, if the 'guests' were no longer needed, their residence permits would not be renewed, and they would be repatriated. After 1973, when the labour shortage ended, no new permits were issued, but most of the guests remained.

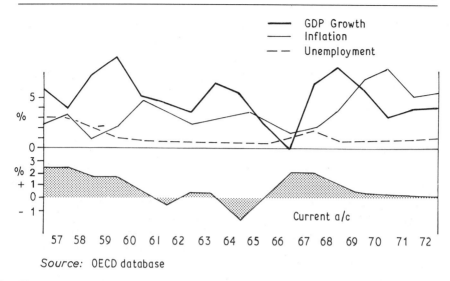

Source: OECD database

Figure 5.2 The real GDP change, unemployment rate, inflation rate, and current account (as percentage of GNP), 1957–72

At the beginning of the period, Germany had (with the benefit of hindsight) a fundamental disequilibrium in its balance of payments. As Figure 5.2 shows there was a persistent surplus of at least 1–2 per cent of GNP and a revaluation would have been appropriate. Such a move was, however, opposed by German industry (since it would curb exports), and by some members of the Bundesbank, who treated the exchange rate as sacrosanct (recalling the gold standard and the National Socialist economy, but overlooking the differences between those systems and 'Bretton Woods'). In 1961, however, the mark was revalued by 5 per cent, which contributed to a normalization of the balance of payments.

After a period of stability, there was a build-up of inflationary pressure in 1964/5, arising from both the cost and the demand side, which was not tackled by fiscal policy because of the slow-moving mechanism for changing tax rates. When the Bundesbank applied the monetary brakes, there was a short, sharp recession. Recovery from this recession was masterminded by Karl Schiller, the economics minister in the Grand Coalition, who was committed to a more active counter-cyclical policy.

The recovery of 1967–9 is generally considered to have been a successful example of fine-tuning, but it was accompanied by a large current account surplus and strong upward wage pressures. The Bundesbank favoured a revaluation, but some members of the government (notably Chancellor Kiesinger) were adamantly opposed to such a move, and it was delayed until October 1969, under the incoming SDP-led government led by Willy

Brandt. The – by German standards – inflationary mentality aroused at this time was reinforced in 1973 by the first oil shock, and the years 1969–74 saw price rises which reached 7 per cent per annum. In retrospect, Kiesinger was certainly wrong in delaying revaluation, although this issue pales into insignificance alongside his historic achievement in forming a coalition with the SDP, and thus paving the way for the SPD-led governments of 1969 to 1982.

Income distribution

During most of this period, the federal governments were CDU/Free Democrat coalitions, which were committed to a welfare state as well as a market economy. Their emphasis, however, was on alleviating poverty rather than on squeezing the rich. It appears that – whether as a result of the welfare system or full employment, or both – the poorest section of the population did in fact share in the prosperity of this period. The available figures on income distribution suggest that the top 20 per cent of earners were, after tax, relatively better off than their counterparts in (at that time) 'egalitarian' Britain, and nearly as well off as their counterparts in 'inegalitarian' France or Italy. On the other hand, the share of the bottom 10 per cent was relatively high, and rose steadily between 1950 and 1973. Similarly, a comparison of the proportion of the population in relative poverty in various countries in the early 1970s gave a figure of 3 per cent for Germany – lower than any other OECD country, even Sweden (see Table 5.5).

Germany's relatively good showing in the poverty stakes does not mean that there were no black spots. The occupationally based, contributory schemes for health and pensions – with a relatively low 'social help' safety net – cater well for normal households, but not so well for the rolling stones, the single-parent families, etc., and for a minority of pensioners: some widows have had extremely low pensions. Even greater problems have been faced by 'guest workers', especially Turks, many of whom were forced to accept low wages, dangerous working conditions and difficulties in housing and education.

Table 5.5 Poverty: international comparisons, 1950–1970s

	Share of post-tax income going to bottom 20%				% in 'relative poverty'
	1950	1960	1968	1970	early 1970s
Germany	5.4	6.0	6.2	6.5	3.0
UK		6.6	6.8	6.5	7.5
US					13.0

Source: George and Lawson 1980: 236–8.

The first oil shock: 1973–9

The period after 1973 was one of floating exchange rates. This enabled Germany to avoid imported inflation. The mark began a steady upward drift against a basket of other currencies (see Figure 5.3). The period was dominated by the first oil shock of 1973, which, in all OECD countries, caused an upsurge in inflation followed, in 1975, by a recession. Germany – which was now under a left-liberal government headed by Helmut Schmidt – survived these external shocks relatively well. Economic growth became negative in 1975, but then recovered sharply, giving an average of 2.5 per

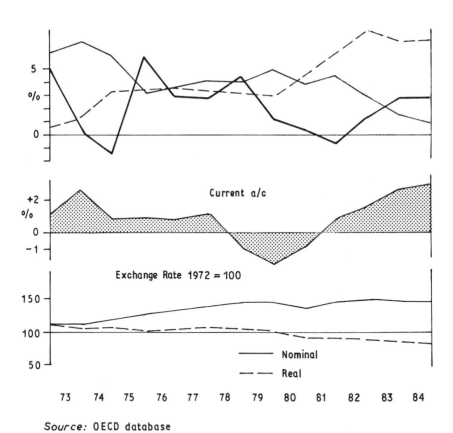

Source: OECD database

Figure 5.3 The real GDP change, umemployment rate, inflation rate, current account, (as percentage of GNP), and exchange rate, 1973–85

cent for the period. Inflation fell from a peak of 7.1 per cent in 1974 to 4.0 per cent in 1979. Indeed Germany was so successful in controlling inflation, relative to other countries, that while the nominal exchange rate rose, the real exchange rate fell slightly (see Figure 5.3). Unemployment peaked at 3.7 per cent in 1976, and then fell to 3.2 in 1979. This level of unemployment seemed very high after its virtual absence in the preceding twenty years, and in order to counter unemployment, the government pursued, after 1975, a policy which was called Keynesian but which was also close to what Milton Friedman once advocated – maintaining public expenditure at a constant level through booms and slumps, and allowing the fluctuations in tax receipts to act as automatic stabilizers. The public borrowing requirement (covering all tiers of government) rose from its previous level of well under 1 per cent to 5.7 per cent in 1975, before falling to 2.5 per cent in 1979. This was not an altogether unjustifiable level of borrowing. The Bundesbank estimated at this time that the normal borrowing requirement was 2 per cent – higher in bad times and lower in good. The borrowing was also matched by public investment, so that it went into tangible assets. (This had been a requirement of the original constitution, although it was relaxed in 1967.) The national debt as a percentage of GNP rose from 20 per cent in 1972 to 28.8 per cent in 1978. This was still well below the OECD average (40 per cent), but it began to arouse concern.

In 1978, the government increased public investment in response to pleas by other OECD governments that Germany should act as the 'locomotive' to pull the world out of depression. Unfortunately, this programme coincided with the second oil shock; thereafter, Germany was unwilling to act as a 'locomotive'.

Depression and 'recovery': 1979–85

This period began with the second oil shock. The effects of this can be seen in Figure 5.3 above. There was a plunge into a balance of payments deficit, from 1979 to 1981, a fall in the rate of economic growth, with a negative figure of 0.7 per cent in 1982, and a rise in inflation to 4.8 per cent in 1980. In all these respects, however, there was a rapid recovery. The current account was back in surplus by 1982, and rose to a near-record level (2.5 per cent of GNP) in 1985. Inflation fell to 1.6 per cent in 1985, and to zero in 1986. The recovery in economic growth was less spectacular, to 2.7 per cent and 2.6 per cent in 1984 and 1985. The one measurement which deteriorated and did not show any significant improvement was unemployment. After rising sharply from 3 per cent in 1980 to 8 per cent in 1983, it fell slightly, but levelled out at 7.1 and 7.2 per cent in 1984 to 1985.

In 1982, a coalition of Christian Democrats and Free Democrats came to power. The new Chancellor, Helmut Kohl, had talked of a *Wende* (U-turn) in policy; but in fact the changes were modest, apart from a greater emphasis on curbing borrowing and public expenditure. The public borrowing requirement fell from a peak of 3.7 per cent of GNP in 1981 to 1.1 per cent in 1985. (By 1985, the national debt had risen to 41 per cent of GNP, compared with an OECD average of 55 per cent.) Public expenditure as a percentage of GNP fell from 49.4 per cent in 1982 to 47.2 per cent in 1985. The expenditure cuts fell mainly on current expenditure; there was no drastic slashing of public investment.

During this period of depression and (partial) recovery, there was a marked shift from wages to profits. Real wages fell in 1982, 1983, and 1984, while profits, which had fallen in the 1970s, rose sharply after 1983, almost reaching the high levels of the 1960s. Industrial investment also recovered, although most of it took the form of 'capital deepening' to produce better products more cheaply, rather than 'capital widening; to produce more goods – with more employment.

Unemployment

The Kohl government repeatedly promised that the elimination of inflation and the supply-side improvements which it had allegedly encouraged would soon lead to a sharp fall in unemployment. This did not happen, and it became clear that the unemployment of the 1980s was more intractable than that of the early 1950s or 1966/7. In previous cycles, employment rose as output recovered: in 1982–5, it did not. Industrial output (1979=100) fell to 95 in 1982, before recovering to 103 in 1985. But this higher output was produced with a workforce which had fallen by 9.7 per cent; the fall was particularly severe in steel, shipbuilding and textiles. Although increased employment in other sectors partly offset the fall in manufacturing industry, total employment in 1985 was 0.5 million lower than in 1979. At the same time, the potential workforce was 0.9 million higher, because of a school-leaving 'bulge'. It was the rise in the potential workforce, combined with the fall in total employment, which caused unemployment to rise so sharply in 1981/2.

Although industrial production rose during this period by 3 per cent, the rise was substantially less than in the US (12 per cent) and Japan (28 per cent). Western Europe as a whole also had a 3 per cent growth of industrial production, and thus lost ground to the two other industrial superpowers.

Total employment bottomed out in 1984 and then rose, but the rise was matched by a rise in the potential workforce. The Federal Labour Office had warned in the late 1970s of this demographically determined development, and pointed out that economic growth rates of around 4 per cent would be needed for some years, if unemployment were not to rise (Hallett 1985).

The rise in unemployment was thus the result of demographic change, combined with a rise in industrial productivity and slow economic growth. It would be too facile to blame the rise in unemployment wholly on demographic change, since in the 1950s (when, however, there were short-ages of everything), a larger increase in the potential workforce was accom-modated. The fact that, after 1981, the rest of the economy did not take up the labour shed in manufacturing, and the school-leaving 'bulge', would seem to represent a failure of the economic system – but it was one common to most industrial countries at the time, and for which economists have no unanimous remedy. However, if demography aggravated the unemployment problem in 1979–85, it should (*ceteris paribus*!) alleviate it in the 1990s, when the potential labour force will fall sharply.

The debate on unemployment and growth

There are three (non-Marxist) schools of thought in the Federal Republic on the relatively low economic growth and high unemployment of the 1980s. They can be termed the supply side, or new classical; the demand side or Keynesian; and the 'hysteresis' school. The supply-side school – supported by some, although not all, industrialists and members of the Kohl govern-ment – argues that unemployment is the result of labour being too expensive. Excessively high wages ('political wages' to use a term from the 1920s) reduce the demand for labour; therefore union power and job security should be reduced, and the various employment taxes lowered. The demand-side school (for example, Davies 1987) argues, on the other hand, that the problem is a lack of demand. It blames the government for having cut the budget deficit too quickly, and supports a more expansive fiscal and monetary policy. The third, more eclectic, school (for example, Carlin and Jacob 1989) argues (by analogy with a phenomenon in physics called hysteresis) that unemployment feeds on itself so that what begins as a demand-side problem gradually becomes a supply-side problem. The argument is that the unemployed gradually enter a 'ghetto', and cease to compete in the labour market; they become increasingly demoralized, and their skills (if they have any) become obsolete. The recommendation is a Swedish-style employment policy; fiscal expansion should be targeted so as to benefit the unemployed, who should also receive intensive counselling and training (an 'active labour market policy').

It is, to some extent, possible to assess these three theories by reference to the facts. A sharp rise in real wages and a fall in profits, accompanied by a tendency towards rising inflation, would be evidence for the supply-side theory. This was the case – to a relatively mild degree – in the late 1970s. But the period 1983–5 saw falls in real wages, a sharp rise in the share of profits in national income, and the virtual elimination of inflation. These develop-ments (together with a savings ratio which has remained at around 12 per cent) tell against the supply-side, and in favour of the demand-side, theory. Against an unqualified demand-side explanation, however, must be set: (a) the large regional differences in unemployment; (b) the fact that the unskilled, or handicapped, are disproportionately represented among the unemployed; and (c) the rise in the number of long-term unemployed (in 1985 roughly 0.7 million people had been unemployed for over a year). These facts would tend to support the hysteresis theory.

There may, however, be something in all three theories. It is possible that wages are too uniform throughout the country, and should to a greater extend reflect the regional differences in employment which have emerged. And Germany's exceptionally heavy employers' taxes are probably an anachronism. As far as budgetary policy is concerned, it was (with the benefit of hindsight) almost certainly right for the Kohl government to reduce the budget deficit, if only for psychological reasons. But when (by 1984) the budget deficit had been substantially reduced, and the current account deficit eliminated, the government could have adopted a more relaxed stance, without running any inflation or balance of payments risks.

Income distribution

The data on income distribution for the periods 1973 to 1979 and 1979 to 1985 are sparse. There appear, however, to have been two divergent trends over the decade 1973–83 (Miegel 1983: 156ff). On the one hand, more people joined the middle income group, while the numbers of both rich and poor declined. On the other hand, the *gap* between rich and poor increased. In the 3–4 per cent of the population which can reasonably be classed as poor, living standards did not increase between 1973 and 1983 – as they had done before 1973. At the other end of the spectrum, the declining number of very rich became even richer.

It should finally be mentioned – since the discussion has been of economic performance – that there is no apparent correlation between economic performance and happiness. In a 1985 poll, carried out in twenty industrial countries, the happiest people, with 39 per cent saying that they were very happy, were the Irish, followed by the British; the least happy (10 per cent) were the Germans and the Italians (*The Economist* 1985: 23). Of course, such surveys should be treated with caution; market researchers know that people lie about facts, let alone states of consciousness – and the Germans tend to be unhappy unless they have something to worry about.

Retrospect and prospect

Many differing assessments have been made of the economic performance of the Federal Republic. In the early days, Dr (later Lord) Balogh denounced 'an iniquitous new economic and social system', which was producing far less than a centrally planned economy, fostering unemployment, and distorting production towards luxury goods (Balogh 1950: 72). Similar criticisms were made by German Social Democrats. But there were also criticisms from the right. The neo-liberal Freiburg School couched its prescriptions in very abstract terms but, fairly certainly, considered trade unions, industrial democracy, and social security to be incompatible with a free and successful economy (Eucken 1952).

Later assessments by British observers were equally varied. In the 1960s, Andrew Shonfield argued that Germany, handicapped by a decentralized structure 'wished on the Germans by their Allied conquerors', was 'not in the mainstream of modern capitalism' represented by France with its *planification* and Britain with its National Plan (Shonfield 1965: 273). In the first of a series of *Economist* supplements, by contrast, Norman Macrae pinpointed the labour relations and training systems, and the role of the banks, as mainsprings of Germany's impressive economic performance, but warned of the dangers for so export-dependent a country of a downturn in the world economy (*The Economist* 1966).

In the 1970s, many British commentators criticized Germany for being 'the only soldier in step' in its attitude to inflation, and in 1973 the British prime minister formally protested to the German chancellor that the Bundesbank's restrictive credit policy was contributing to the current sterling crisis (Emminger 1987: 274). German neo-liberal economists, on the other hand, maintained that the Schmidt governments were 'ruining the economy'.

The balance of payments deficits after 1979 were widely interpreted, in both Britain and Germany, as evidence of deep-seated economic failure. The subsequent swing into surplus produced some British articles with titles like 'An awesome mixture of old and new' (*Financial Times*, 18 December, 1984) and 'Away with Angst' (*The Economist* 1986) but *The Financial Times* (20 July 1987) was soon once again asserting that;

> Sluggish growth, high unemployment, high taxes, weak business investment, rigid markets and huge public subsidies; these are some of the characteristics of the West German economy in the late 1980s, and some of the reasons why the former miracle economy no longer deserves to be a model for the rest of Europe.

German neo-liberals have also criticized the Kohl governments for their failure to follow Britain's lead on 'union busting', deregulation, and privatization. Equally strong criticisms have, however, been made from a diametrically opposed standpoint (Leaman 1988).

Any country has the defects of its virtues. Nevertheless, some of these criticisms seem too strident. Let us examine four from the neo-liberal camp. One is of 'managerial rigidity'. In the 1970s, the difficulties of several large firms did seem to suggest that the Germans were good at the large-scale production of standardized items, but lacked the flexibility needed in an era of rapid change. German firms subsequently, however, showed considerable ability to adapt and to move to a higher level of technology – as evidenced by the balance of payments surplus (without the benefit of North Sea oil). In sophisticated industrial products, Germany had, in 1985, only one

Table 5.6 International patents registered, average 1983–5

	Total	Per million of population
Switzerland	1,873	288
Germany	12,552	206
Japan	12,923	107
UK	4,489	79
France	4,074	74
US	17,216	72

Source: Globus and OECD.

competitor, Japan, and its range of exports was even greater. Moreover, if innovative ability can be measured by the number of international patents, Germany scored extremely well. As Table 5.6 shows, in terms of patents per head of population, Germany was second only to Switzerland, and well ahead of the other industrial countries.

A second criticism is of over-regulation. Some standards may well be too perfectionistic but that is a question of degree, and of balancing different objectives. The radical neo-liberal *critique* of regulation is a different matter. It is longer on generalities than evidence; if examples are given, they are usually items such as shop closing hours or the high cost of the *Bundespost* telecommunication services. The shop hours (18.30 on weekdays and no Sunday opening) are certainly inconvenient for shoppers, and a slight relaxation has already been agreed, as has some liberalization of the *Bundespost* monopoly. But whether a 'free for all' in either field would increase economic growth or reduce unemployment is open to doubt; it would certainly run counter to German ideas of order. Moreover, the *Bundespost*, like the French PTT, is developing services for the mass of consumers (automatic metering of water and gas, electronic directories etc.), rather than concentrating on specialized business services, like the private British and US systems. Time will tell which is the better arrangement. The case for Thatcherism in health, safety, and environmental regulation, employee representation, town planning, etc., commands even less support: the free enterprise symbolized by *The Herald of Free Enterprise* is not favoured by many German managers.

A third criticism is of inflexible labour practices. This cannot refer to flexibility in the use of a firm's labour force, which is high. It means that managers are restricted in their ability to cut wages, and hire-and-fire in response to fluctuations in demand. Nevertheless, the general level of wages does respond to hard times; unit labour costs fell in 1967 and 1968, remained constant in 1976, and fell in 1983, 1984, and 1985. Moreover, there has been a trend towards a 'dual labour market', with a core of regular workers and a fringe of others who enjoy less security.

A fourth criticism is of the level of subsidies; of which agriculture, transport, and housing take the lion's share. Few economists would deny the need to reorientate agricultural support, but a more rational rural policy would not necessarily be cheaper. The subsidies for transport and housing contribute to a fine public transport system and a relatively small housing problem. These subsidies may need to be reviewed, but they are not necessarily uneconomic.

From locomotive to slowcoach?

There is room for argument on German policy of the 1970s and 1980s. The statistical record, however – in terms of the 'magic quadrilateral', and in comparison with other countries – suggests that Germany coped with the challenges of the time better than some criticisms of 'the German sickness' suggest. In the period 1973–9, Germany did considerably better than the OECD average on economic growth, inflation, and unemployment – an outstanding achievement in relative terms. In the period 1979–85, Germany acquired a serious unemployment problem. Nevertheless, the average unemployment rate (5.5 per cent) was below that for the OECD (9.7) and the US (6.3). Only Japan, Sweden, Finland, Norway, Switzerland, and Austria had lower rates. Germany was thus 'top of the second division' in the unemployment league. Moreover, there was a marked geographical division. South of the Main, there was something approaching full employment throughout the period. Economic growth in 1979–85 was slightly below the OECD average. Since, however, the German standard of living is so high, it can be perfectly rational for people, collectively or individually, to opt for modest economic growth, in favour of a better life – and there are signs that they are doing so.

It should also be pointed out that the usually quoted figures of national economic growth can be misleading. Miegel (1983:178) makes an illuminating comparison of the absolute increase in income per capita (in 1983 prices) in various periods. In the 1960s, the increase was DM 6,000. In the 1970s, it was DM 5,000 – lower, but equal to total per capita income in 1914. For the period 1983 to 2000 (when the population will fall by 2 million), an average national economic growth rate of only 1.5 per cent would still produce an increase of DM 8,000. Miegel argues that even such a low growth rate would be by no means a disaster. This is true – provided that unemployment can be reduced by other means. (The average national GNP growth from 1983 to 1988 was in fact 2.5 per cent per annum.)

In external trade, Germany was extraordinarily successful in recovering from the deficits of 1979–81; the term 'second economic miracle' is – in view of most economists' prognoses in 1980/1 – not unjustified. German industry was so good on the non-price side that a slight fall in the real exchange rate enabled it to achieve a large trade surplus, and become world's largest exporter, in four years. This 'success', however, has been criticized as a failure to achieve 'equilibrium in the external balance'. In fact, the issue is far from clear-cut. Equilibrium cannot mean that a country should have neither a surplus nor a deficit in the current account; there are times when it is justifiable to import capital, i.e., run a current account deficit, and times when it is justifiable to export capital. The German and Japanese surpluses of the early 1980s were the counterpart of the US current account deficit which, the Germans argue, resulted primarily from US economic policy – or lack of it.

The achievements of 1979–85 – notwithstanding the blemish of unemployment – were thus considerable. Inflation was eliminated, while retaining public services and a civilized framework for industrial relations. Industry became more competitive, without suffering the massive 'de-industrialization' of the UK. There was extensive training for stock, i.e., in anticipation of the expected labour shortage of the 1990s. The expansion of the apprenticeship scheme to cover virtually the whole of the school-leaving bulge was a most creditable achievement by German industry.

The Federal Republic has its period of rapid youthful growth behind it, but it has entered its middle-age without inflationary problems, balance of payments constraints, or skill shortages, and with a modern and well-maintained infrastructure. A balanced verdict on recent economic performance will perhaps be possible only in the 1990s; it is at least conceivable that British reports on the German economy could then be characterized more by envy than by *Schadenfreude*.

Selected dates

July 1945	Potsdam Agreement on the division of Germany into US, British, French, and Russian zones – while treating it as an economic unit – and the placing of 'former German territories' under Polish administration.
June 1946–May 1947	*Länder* governments elected.
June 1947	Marshall Plan announced.
April 1948	Bank of the German States set up.
June 1948	Currency reform announced.
May 1949	Constitution of the Federal Republic of Germany approved.
September 1949	Adenauer elected first Chancellor.
October 1949	Foundation of the German Trade Union Federation.
April 1951	Law on Co-determination in the Steel and Coal Industries.
October 1952	Law setting up Works Councils.
May 1955	West Germany becomes a sovereign state.

July 1957	Act creating the Bundesbank.
November 1959	Bad Godesberg declaration by Social Democrats, accepting a mixed economy.
March 1961	First revaluation of the Mark.
December 1966	Grand Coalition formed.
June 1967	Law on Economic Stability and Growth.
October 1969	Social Democrat/Free Democrat government formed.
March 1973	Floating of the Mark.
October 1982	CDU/Free Democrat government formed.

References

Balogh, T. (1950) *Germany, an Example of 'Planning' by the 'Free' Price Mechanism*, Oxford.

Cairncross, A.K. (1951) 'The economic recovery of West Germany', *Lloyds Bank Review*, October.

Carlin, W. and Jacob, R. 'Austerity policy in West Germany: origin and consequences', *Economie Appliquée* (forthcoming).

Davies, G. (1987) 'The German growth conundrum', *Goldman Sachs*, January.

Dresdner Bank, *Economic Quarterly*.

The Economist (1966) 'The German lesson', 15 October.

The Economist (1984) 'Down to earth', 4 February.

The Economist (1985) 21 December.

The Economist (1986) 'Away with angst', 6 December.

Emminger, O. (1987) *D-Mark, Dollar, Waehrungskrisen*, Stuttgart.

Eucken, W. (1952) *Grundsaetze der Wirtschaftspolitik*, Tuebingen.

Hallett, G. (1977) *Housing and Land Policies in West Germany and Britain*, London.

Hallett, G. (1985) 'Unemployment and labour market policies: some lessons from West Germany', *Social Policy and Administration*, 19:3 Autumn.

Hallett, G. and Williams, R.H. (1988) 'West Germany' in Hallett, G. (ed.), *Housing and Land Policies in Europe and the USA*, London.

Hardach, K. (1980) *The Political Economy of Germany in the Twentieth Century*, London.

Hellwig, M. and Neumann, M. (1987) 'The German recovery', *Economic Policy*, October.

Hennings, K.H. (1982) 'West Germany', in Boltho, A. (ed.), *The European Economy: Growth and Crisis*, Oxford.

Kennedy, D. (1984) 'West Germany', in Wynn, M. (ed.), *Housing in Europe*, London.

Kuznets, S. (1966) *Modern Economic Growth: Rate, Structure and Spread*, New Haven, Conn.

Lawrence, P. (1980) *Managers and Management in West Germany*, London.

Lawson, R. (1980) 'Poverty and equality in West Germany', in George, V. and Lawson, R., *Poverty and Equality in Common Market Countries*, London.

Leaman, J. (1988) *The Political Economy of West Germany 1945–85*, London.

Miegel, M. (1983) *Die Verkannte Revolution (1)*, Stuttgart.

Mueller-Armack, A. (1965) 'The principles of the social market economy', *The German Economic Review*, 3:2.

Mueller-Armack, A. (1976) *Wirtschaftsordnung und Wirtschaftspolitik*, Bern.

NIER (*National Institute Economic Review*) (1985) 'Productivity, machinery and skills in a sample of British and German manufacturing plants', February.

NIER (1987) 'A second look at productivity, machinery and skills in Britain and Germany' November.

NIER (1988) 'Productivity and management: the training of foremen in Britain and Germany', February.

Shonfield, A. (1965) *Modern Capitalism*, Oxford.

Stolper, G. (1947) *German Realities*, London.

Stolper, G., Hauser, K., and Borchhardt, K. (1967) *The German Economy: 1870 to the Present*, London.

Wallich, H.C. (1955) *Mainsprings of the German Revival*, New Haven, Conn.

Guide to further reading

The following publications can be recommended to non-specialists. For a historical background to the Federal Republic, Stolper (1947), Stolper *et al.* (ed.) (1967), or Hardach (1980). For a series of contemporary assessments of the economic situation, *The Economist* supplements. For studies of management and industrial relations, Lawrence (1980) and NIER (1985, 1987, and 1988).

Chapter six

Italy

Donald Sassoon

Introduction: the aftermath of the war

It is difficult to judge the extent to which Italy was ravaged economically by the war. Widely divergent and unreliable statistics make an accurate assessment virtually impossible (Daneo 1975: 5–6), but the view of most specialists at the time was that the industrial apparatus had not been unduly damaged.

From the point of view of economic reconstruction Italy was short of steel, required an appropriate supply of energy (the lack of natural resources was not new), and needed to reconstruct as soon as possible its internal transportation system which had unquestionably been seriously affected by the conflict.

There were, however, two fundamental questions of economic strategy which had to be resolved by Italy's first postwar governments (1945–7) which were broad national unity coalitions including the Christian Democratic Party (DC), the Communist Party (PCI), and the socialists (PSI) as well as smaller parties of the centre. These two fundamental questions were:

How should Italy's external economic relations be conducted? Should there be a continuation of fascist economic policy on the assumption that the country needed a strong dose of protectionism or should the economy be open to the international market? Should economic growth be based on a strong national market or should it be export-led?

What relation should there be between the state and the economy? Should Italy continue and perhaps develop the model of state interventionism which had been pioneered in the 1930s by maintaining the extensive network of state holdings built up by the fascist regime or should the country model itself according to the principles of economic liberalism?

Decisions such as these are, ultimately, determined by prevailing constraints. There were ideological preconceptions against autarchy because of its associations with fascism. There were economic constraints: Italy, having no oil, coal, or iron, was dependent on the outside world for most of the primary products needed for economic growth. There were political constraints given the obvious fact that, in a world about to be divided into spheres of influence, Italy was bound to be in a free trade area dominated by the USA. Having 'decided' to opt for international integration, Italy would have had to gear its economic development towards international trade. Prevented by politics from trading with the eastern bloc and by old (French and British) and new (American) empires from trading with what would eventually become known as the Third World, Italy had to produce goods which countries richer than herself would want, i.e., the countries of western Europe and North America. Thus by 1945–7 the overall co-ordinates of Italy's future growth were already established (Graziani 1971: 22–3).

Its internal economic relations were similarly constrained. State economic intervention was associated with fascism, planning with the USSR. The bulk of Italy's antifascist economists were committed liberals. The Liberal Party (PLI) itself, though small, had a key role in the coalition as the party representing the industrialists and because the Christian Democrats seemed to be content to let them have a disproportionate say in the running of the economy.

The PCI did not fight for a planned economy. Its leader, Palmiro Togliatti, was trying to elaborate a national road to socialism different from the Soviet model and – at a conference on economic questions specially convened in August 1945– had explicitly rejected central planning in favour of the principle of international economic integration (Togliatti 1984: 166). Moreover, neither the PCI nor the PSI were able to present a concrete alternative plan for the reconstruction of the Italian economy.

Internal and external liberalization could thus proceed without major impediments, all the more so as the left was expelled from the coalition government in 1947 and Italy was run from the centre from 1947 to 1962–3 when a new centre-left coalition which included the PSI (but not the PCI) came into existence.

It would be wrong, however, to imagine that Italian economic reconstruction was based on anything approaching *laissez-faire*. Italian economic decision-makers intervened to the extent of favouring economic growth based on low wages and sustained exports. Furthermore, the basic mechanisms of state intervention established by the fascist regime were not eliminated. The state holding company IRI was preserved. In steel the Sinigaglia Plan was carried out (partly with Marshall Aid funds) through an IRI subsidiary, Finsider. The plan (which was opposed by private steel interests) expanded production and lowered prices, thanks to the adoption of the integral cycle (i.e., beginning from raw materials and not from scrap metal). This facilitated industrial growth (Amoroso and Olsen 1978: 66). It also showed that what had been at issue between the right and the left in 1947 was not *laissez-faire* versus interventionism but the status of the public sector. With the defeat of the left it became clear that the role envisaged for the state sector was to be subordinated to the private sector. Nor did the establishment of ENI, the state oil company, modify this principle.

The role of the state would be to look after the provision of adequate infrastructures for economic growth. Otherwise economy policy was to be devoted to the implementation of orthodox finance and currency stability. In the short term, anti-inflationary policies prevailed (hence deflation, credit squeeze, etc.) at the expense of growth. The lira was allowed to be devalued from 100 lire in 1945 to 625 to the dollar in 1949 when the rate was fixed (and remained so until August 1971).

These policies helped the DC to obtain a massive electoral victory in 1948 (nearly 50 per cent of the votes) thus confirming the expulsion of the left from the government. The credit squeeze had already weakened the trade unions, paving the way for the anti-trade-unionism of the late 1940s and early 1950s. The consequent weakening of the labour movement prevented potential disputes and constrained wage bargaining with the net effect of keeping wages down. The low level of wages turned out to be the main pre-condition for the export-led growth which came to be known as the Italian 'economic miracle'.

The economic miracle

Trade union weakness was only one of the factors which ensured inexpensive labour. The low wage economy was a direct result of the existence of a cheap mass of labour in the Italian south. It was generally thought that this had a natural cause, namely, the age-old underdevelopment and backwardness of southern agriculture. This is a superficial view: some of the contributory factors were the often unintended results of government intervention. One of these was the agrarian reform of 1950 (caused by unrest in the south) which distributed 40,000 hectares of land in Calabria. A year later all land in latifundia areas was redistributed. The same agrarian reform law created the institution of the *Cassa per il mezzogiorno* (the Fund for the Redevelopment of the South). The *Cassa* did not so much promote development in the south as help to expand the market for northern industry by increasing incomes in the south through an extensive public works programme (establishing a clientele network for the DC-dominated coalition government). It also 'liberated' inefficient farmers from the land, providing the north with a reservoir of cheap labour. In this way the terrain was prepared for the 'free' economic growth of the second half of the fifties.

The state also facilitated growth by investing in agriculture, subsidizing private building development, and encouraging the growth of private transportation (and tourism) by an extensive public works programme in motorways.

Even in the early 1950s there was a recognition that some degree of public planning would be necessary. It was accepted by all except the most fanatical free marketeers that Italy's economic dualism between north and south could not be overcome without some measure of state intervention. In 1954 the DC-led coalition government prepared a document, the so-called Vanoni Plan, which established that the three main strategic objectives over the next ten years would be the creation of 4 million jobs in the non-agricultural sector, the elimination of the income gap between north and south and a balance of payments equilibrium (Castronovo 1975: 446). To achieve these objectives the economy would have to grow by at least 5 per cent a year.

As it turned out, the economy grew at a slightly higher rate than 5 per cent and the balance of payments reached equilibrium in 1958. The second target – job creation – was partly met: 2.4 million jobs (instead of 4 million) were created, whilst the north–south gap remained unchanged. The planners had little merit in this partial success. Of far greater importance were state intervention through the state holding network of IRI and ENI and Italian participation in the growth of international demand through the process of European economic integration. Sustained growth during the period 1950–8 led to an even higher rate in 1958–63 (see Table 6.1):

The integration of the Italian economy into the European one took some time. We can only begin to speak in terms of export-led growth after 1957, when foreign demand became important. Balance of payments surpluses up to then were due to tourism and to the export of labour with the consequent revenue accruing from remittances of Italians working abroad.

The actual rapid economic growth of the 1958–63 period depended not only on foreign demand (and hence on the end of protective tariffs in 1957) but also on the considerable growth of state fixed investment (public spending as such grew only in line with national income). In 1959 one-fifth of all investment came from the parastate sector. By 1964 it was one-third (Colajanni 1976: 17–18).

Government economic policy was thus crucial in promoting the kind of

Table 6.1 A comparison of economic growth, 1950–63

	1950–8	1958–63
	Average annual changes, %	
Japan	8.4	10.2
West Germany	7.9	5.6
Italy	5.6	6.5
France	4.4	5.5
US	3.0	4.0
UK	2.3	3.6

Source: OECD database.

economic growth which occurred in Italy. It follows that the lack of social infrastructure (housing, education, health, etc.) which characterized the country was also the result of a semi-deliberate policy of putting the state at the service of private enterprise.

Of all the many factors which would account for Italian economic performance in the late 1950s we should perhaps single out low wages: real wages were stagnant between 1950 and 1954 and between 1956 and 1961. In 1950 unemployment was 7.8 per cent, decreasing only slightly in the following ten years to 7.3 per cent, while average unemployment in the rest of Europe was only 1.9 per cent (and this in spite of the emigration of 1.7 million Italians) (Castronovo 1975: 461).

Low wages by themselves cannot explain the competitiveness of exports and hence Italian economic growth. Wages in underdeveloped countries were even lower yet there was no economic miracle there – at least not until much later. One of the advantages that Italy had over its potential cheap labour competitors was the fact that the general cultural level of the southern Italian peasant, however low it may appear to some, was already structured by the ethics and mentality of the technological world (De Cecco 1971: 982). It is this cultural aspect which allowed the rapid transformation of the southern peasant into a relatively high productivity assembly line proletarian in a short period of time; this cultural adaptability also meant that the line between the urban and the rural worlds was not broken as is generally the case in underdeveloped countries. In many of these the modern sector is like a cathedral in the desert, an island cut off from its rural shores. In the Italian case the revenues accruing to the former peasant, now a worker, would be sent to his village to form the basis of a market which would recycle these sums in the national economy. Thus the washing machine made by southern labour in the north could be bought by the relatives who had remained behind.

What was the role of monetary policy in economic growth? Very little. Monetary policy was in the hands of the Bank of Italy, the fiefdom of Italy's economic liberals. This was the only major economic institution which was never under the full control of the Christian Democratic Party. Its first governor, the respected Liberal Party economist, Luigi Einaudi, who then became the first elected president of the republic, ensured that it would remain in the hands of a largely meritocratic elite rather than become part and parcel of the clientele system of the DC thus sparing the Bank the fate which befell much of the rest of the public sector banking system. The ideology of the Bank remained staunchly anti-Keynesian. Its main achievement was the deflation of 1947 which blocked the postwar inflationary spiral and helped establish the regime of low wages. A restrictive policy was followed (unnecessarily) until 1955. Then a certain grudging *largesse* was adopted until 1963. Not that it made much difference: monetary policy can be effective only to the extent that interest rates are important for economic growth. This is the case only if growth is financed out of bank lending. But this was not the case until 1962. The level of profitability was sufficiently high to enable the private sector to finance itself from retained profits.

The economic miracle as such was concentrated in the years 1958 to 1963, though it should be said that from the early 1950s onwards Italy showed a steady advance. In the period 1954 to 1963 Italy was the third fastest growing economy in western Europe, after West Germany and Austria and well ahead of the average for the OECD countries. Even in the years from the end of the miracle (1963) to the oil crisis of the 1970s Italy performed fairly well and stayed marginally ahead of the average of the other European OECD countries. In fact throughout the period 1956–73 Italy outperformed (in growth terms) the OECD achieving an average of 5.4 per cent against an OECD average of 4.5 per cent (see Table 6.2 below). This is worth stating if for no other reason than that most of the Italian literature describes the 1963–73 decade as a period of economic crisis. One should note, however, that both inflation and unemployment were systematically higher in Italy than in the OECD as a whole throughout the 1946–85 period.

As always, Italian governments came and went throughout the 1950s, though it would be quite wrong to characterize the country as being the victim of chronic instability. This view can be held only if one adopts a

Table 6.2 Italian economic performance: 1946–85

		GDP	Employment	Output per worker	Inflation[a]	Unemployment rate[b]
		Average annual changes, %				%
Italy	1946–56	7.3			9.9	
Italy	1956–73	5.4	−0.3	5.7	4.5	5.2[c]
OECD	1956–73	4.5	1.0	3.5	4.0	3.2[c]
Italy	1973–9	2.6	0.8	1.7	17.1	6.6[d]
OECD	1973–9	2.6	1.1	1.5	9.0	5.2[d]
Italy	1979–85	2.0	0.4	1.6	14.9	8.8[c]
OECD	1979–85	2.3	0.6	1.7	7.1	7.8[c]
Italy	1956–85	4.1	0.1	4.0	9.1	6.4[f]
OECD	1956–85	3.7	0.9	2.7	5.7	4.7[f]

a The consumer price index from 1946–50. The GDP deflator from 1951–85
b The average level in the period as % of the total labour force
c 1960–73
d 1974–9
e 1980–5
f 1960–85

Note: The OECD totals for GDP and inflation are based on the exchange rates of 1980

Sources: OECD *Historical Statistics, 1960–85* and the OECD database.

purely formalistic approach to the question of government stability. In examining Italian governments, the key issue is the nature of the coalition, not the frequency of government change. All Italian coalitions from 1948 to 1962 were led by the Christian Democratic Party in alliance with smaller parties of the centre (the Liberals, the Republicans, and the Social Democrats). The opposition was divided between two parties (the PCI and the PSI) and had no hope at all of obtaining power. Thus, unlike France and Great Britain and like West Germany, the Italian executive was in the hands of the same group of people, who were in complete agreement as to the general framework within which the Italian economy should operate. As long as rapid growth was obtained there was little reason to alter the coalition, though there were always plenty of opportunities for intra-coalition discord. The fact that the coalition could not realistically be voted out of office meant that no penalties at all were attached to infighting.

However, it would be quite wrong to give unconditional praise to Italy's economic performance in the years 1954 to 1963. The country scored extremely well on one factor: growth. But economic performance cannot be assessed from one single criterion.

What the miracle did not do was to reduce the numerous structural distortions existing in the country: patterns of consumption, income differentials, productivity and, above all, the north–south divide. In addition inflation reappeared: 2.7 per cent in 1960, 2.8 per cent in 1961, 5.1 per cent in 1962, and 7.6 per cent in 1963.

The end of the economic miracle

The rapid growth and the consequent increase in employment revived trade union militancy which had hitherto been dormant (see Table 6.3). At the same time full employment had been reached in the north among the male workforce and in the advanced sector of the economy (i.e., in those areas which were directed towards export). The net effect was that the increase in money wages began to outstrip productivity significantly.

Up until this point Italy's handicaps (*vis-à-vis* her EEC partners and her other competitors) – constant emigration, scarcity of raw material, low productivity in agriculture, and poor technology – had been amply compensated for by exporting products of low technological content (e.g., household electrical goods) (Castronovo 1975: 417). However, from the early 1960s onwards, Italy was left increasingly exposed to competition from some Third World countries – whose labour was far cheaper than in Italy – and from advanced countries such as Japan and West Germany (whose exporting ability was based on their constant technological progress) (Onida 1977: 70).

The revival of working-class militancy in the early 1960s (which was the attempt, on the part of the northern proletariat, to share in the European-

Table 6.3 The effects of trade union militancy on wages, 1960–71

Year	Yearly % increase in		Millions of hours lost in strikes
	Real wages	Money wages	
1960	5.4	10.8	46.3
1961	5.9	11.1	79.1
1962	6.9	16.4	181.7
1963	11.1	21.6	91.2
1964	7.1	11.9	104.7
1965	4.1	5.5	55.9
1966	4.9	6.9	115.8
1967	5.1	10.6	68.5
1968	5.9	8.7	83.9
1969	5.4	10.1	302.6
1970	14.1	16.9	146.2
1971	9.1	15.1	103.6

Source: Sassoon 1986: 51 based on ISTAT data.

type high standard of living apparently enjoyed by the middle classes) coupled with full employment had precluded the possibility of expanding production through an expansion in employment. Expansion through an increase in productivity was difficult because this would need to be based on technological innovation.

Clearly Italy was entering a new phase. The political ruling classes of the time were deeply divided between a conservative tendency which was reluctant to innovate politically and was prepared to pay the price of economic stagnation, if necessary, and a 'progressive' tendency which was ready to adopt a policy of structural reform to reshape the Italian political and economic system. This division cut across the Italian governing coalition made up of Christian Democrats, Social Democrats, Republicans, and Liberals, as well as the industrial and financial establishment.

It became apparent to the 'progressive' Christian Democrats led by Aldo Moro and Amintore Fanfani that the existing coalition was no longer viable and that it was necessary to open up the political system to the Socialist Party which, since 1956, had demonstrated an increased desire to cut itself loose from its postwar ally, the Italian Communist Party. The involvement of the socialists in the governing coalition (and the consequent expulsion of the foremost conservative force, the Liberal Party) would have had three further positive effects (from the point of view of Christian Democracy). In the first place it would have the distinct advantage of splitting the opposition creating a semi-permanent cleavage between communists and socialists and confining the Communist Party in an oppositional ghetto. In the second place it would give radical credentials to a new coalition and provide a way for representing the working class inside the government. In the third place it would encourage the partial reunification of the Italian trade union movement. This had split along Cold War lines in the late 1940s resulting in three trade union federations: a Catholic trade union confederation (the CISL, the second largest) closely linked to the Christian Democratic Party; a 'third force' union (the UIL) whose leaders were close to the Republican and Social Democratic Parties; and the largest confederation, the CGIL, which had remained dominated by the Communist party even though it contained an influential socialist minority. It was hoped that the entry of the Socialist Party into the ruling coalition would lead to the break-up of the CGIL and the creation of a large non-communist trade union.

This general political plan was the most significant transformation of the Italian political system since 1948 and the equivalent of a change in government. The project of the new coalition was a modernization of the economy through systematic public intervention and planning. It was a shift to the left which paralleled that which occurred in Britain in 1964 with the advent of Wilson, and in West Germany in 1966 with the CDU–SPD coalition. By 1963 the whole of the Christian Democratic Party, with varying degrees of enthusiam, had accepted it, together with the Social Democratic Party and the Republican Party. The employers' association at first opposed it, but a significant and powerful group within it, led by FIAT and Pirelli, eventually won the day in the name of 'enlightened capitalism'. The Church had recently initiated its own *rinnovamento* and Pope John XXIII gave the new centre-left coalition his blessing (though many Italian bishops remained opposed to a coalition with a party – the Socialist Party – which was still formally Marxist). Finally the US administration, also in the hands of reformists (John Kennedy), gave the new Italian coalition the American approval which all Italian governments feel is essential.

Italian governments do not really control monetary policy. This remained the prerogative of the Bank of Italy, still a stronghold of the Liberal Party. It dealt with the end of the economic miracle in the only way it knew how: by continuing its traditional deflationary line. In September 1963, less than two months before the official entry of the Socialist Party into the governing coalition, the Bank of Italy imposed a harsh credit squeeze. With profits already much reduced the role of monetary policy was quite different from the 1950s and its effects were immediate. Investment decreased by 8.6 per cent in 1964 and by 7.5 per cent in 1965. Demand decreased and a depression ensued with consequent negative effects on employment which fell by 2.5 per cent by 1965 (by 4 per cent in the industrial sector alone (Castronovo 1975: 446).

Those who favoured the credit squeeze as a way of tackling inflation assumed that inflation was principally due to wage rises and, as the wage rise of 1962–3 seemed to have been a once and for all affair, they assumed that the inflationary spiral was a short-term phenomenon. Others, and these included all the supporters of the centre-left coalition government, believed that inflation and the balance of payments problems which followed were due to structural distortions in the economy and the lack of planning.

There is little doubt that the harsh credit squeeze had the desired effects: it dampened down inflation, improved the balance of payments and weakened the trade unions who renewed the labour contracts of 1966 with remarkable acquiescence.

The 'planners' could and did argue that this remedy treated only the symptoms and not the causes and they pursued their planning project with great vigour. Ugo La Malfa, leader of the small but influential Republican Party, was the main proponent of planning. In 1963 as budget minister he suggested the following framework as necessary in order to eliminate the gross distortions between agriculture and industry, between public and private consumption, and between the north and the south:

1. To concentrate public funding on projects which expand productive capacity.
2. To increase forced saving through taxation.
3. To plan the quantity and the direction of both private and public investment.
4. To obtain the co-operation of the trade union movement for a policy of wage restraint in exchange for an improvement in the social services.

This famous 'Additional Note' as it was known, achieved very little which was practical but it symbolized the end of the monopoly of neo-liberal economic thinking. What followed was a long saga of attempted planning (coinciding both in its chronology and in its failure with George Brown's National Plan in the UK) (Sassoon 1986: 52–3). No state institution emerged in control of planning. The apparently defeated neo-liberals maintained their strong position inside the Bank of Italy (Amato 1976:135). As they were able to resist becoming part of the Christian Democratic Party's clientele system they maintained intact their reputation for integrity and efficiency, a reputation which was, on the whole, well deserved.

Modernization did proceed but it was achieved through a spate of mergers and takeovers and an extension of public ownership rather than through planning. This process was initiated in 1962, even before the formal launching of the new coalition, when the electricity industry was nationalized. This also brought the telephone system under state ownership. The new state electricity company, ENEL, gave added impetus to the state holding system and this enabled the Christian Democratic Party to extend its political control further over the economic system, thus compensating for its shrinking bases in the rural sector, depleted by the growing rationalization of agriculture and internal migration.

All the efforts of the state, however, did little to protect the south. The recession of 1964–5 (caused by the credit squeeze of 1963) meant that there was little northern investment in the south despite low wages and weak unions. The crisis of profitability brought about by the end of the economic miracle was resolved not through capital investment but by the reorganization of the work process: more overtime and a speed-up of assembly lines (Salvati 1975).

Another important change brought about by state intervention in this period, the development of the tertiary sector, was determined by the expansion of the public sector. It was further fuelled by the considerable growth of the so-called *rentier* sector closely connected to real estate speculation. This development was in part due to the lack of a sustained public housing programme, as well as to the growth of highly paid sections of the professional classes, and of the higher echelons of the state bureaucracy, as well as the development of a strong managerial class. The high incomes achieved by these groups were invested largely in real estate.

Thus, the changes brought about by the end of the 'economic miracle' were considerable. It had a devastating effect on the vast array of small firms which had been the backbone of the 'miracle'. These now faced great difficulties which, however, would have been even worse if it were not for the fact that international demand was still strong in the mid-1960s and that the home market, thanks to the wage increases of 1962, was not as depressed as it would otherwise have been (Graziani 1971: 71–2).

By the end of the first phase of 'modernization' (1966–7) Italian industry had the structure of an iceberg: at the top there were three large public enterprises (ENI, IRI, and ENEL) and five or six private firms, including FIAT and Pirelli; at the bottom there were 72,000 small and medium-sized firms employing between 11 and 500 workers. (Castronovo 1975: 465).

Italy emerged from the recession of the mid-1960s with renewed gains in productivity achieved, as we have seen, through the speeding up of the work process, the reorganization of existing plants, and rationalization through mergers. After the wages shock of 1962, once again wage increases were matched by productivity increases. This temporary wage truce had the same function as an incomes policy. Instead of using direct means to control incomes, as the Labour government did in Britain in 1966, the Italian government, in spite of pressure from La Malfa's small Republican Party, preferred to use familiar indirect means – deflation and internal migration. But these techniques could no longer be as effective as they had been in the past. Internal migration was coming to a natural end and by 1969 deflation was politically difficult. The very high level of industrial conflict which occurred in the 'hot autumn' of 1969 meant that the labour movement had become too strong to be defeated by traditional methods.

The hot autumn of 1969 and its effects

This was the most serious social conflict since 1947. There were 302 million hours of strikes in 1969 and again 146 million in the following year (see Table 6.3). The main causes of the unrest were the following:

1. Intensification of the speed of assembly lines and a general worsening of working conditions.
2. A general dissatisfaction with the quality of life outside the factory, lack of public services, etc. This was due to the fact that rapid internal migration had not been supported by appropriate state spending on social infrastructure.
3. The inability of the state to resolve any of these problems in spite of the many promises of the centre-left government.
4. The lack of a clear economic decision-making system. There was considerable division within the government and within the economic elites. Furthermore, economic decision-making was parcelled out between four centres: Finance, Treasury, Budget, and the Bank of Italy.
5. There was a generalized dissatisfaction with the entrepreneurial classes who had been much admired during the years of the 'miracle'. Entrepreneurs were now busy exporting capital and trying not to pay taxes.

The economic and political importance of 1969 must not be underestimated. On the economic plane alone the effects on wages and prices were significant. Wage increases after 1969 were no longer matched by productivity gains. Hourly wage rates increased at a faster rate than the average for OECD countries (in the 1970s at double the rate). Between 1969 and 1970 alone, labour costs increased by 16 per cent. In manufacturing industry money wages rose by 9.1 per cent in 1969 and by 23.4 per cent in 1970. The share of the national income going to wage-earners went up from 56.7 to 59 per cent and in industry this share went up from 60.7 to 64.1 per cent. At the same time Italian inflation rates, which had been in line with the OECD throughout the 1960s, increased to twice the OECD average.

The 'hot autumn' was not only about wages. It occurred soon after the student unrest of 1968 (less intensive but more widespread and longer lasting than the French equivalent) and at a time when the whole of Italian society seemed to be in ferment. In qualitative terms the results of 1969 were the following:

1. Greater working-class control over the use of the labour force in factories. This meant that after 1969 employers could not easily reorganize the labour process to increase productivity.
2. Workers were able to acquire a greater degree of control inside the factories, thus becoming more independent of the official trade union confederations (these had found it difficult to control the movement). Workers, however, also obtained a uniformity of contracts and wage levels which had not existed previously.
3. The strength of the labour movement was such that the government had to pass a new law in 1970 known as the Workers' Charter (*Statuto*

lavoratori) which strengthened considerably the bargaining power of the workers and made illegal a number of anti-trade union practices. It became far more difficult to sack workers, the working week was shortened, and overtime was abolished in a number of large firms.

The centre-left government had collapsed and, until 1972, weak centrist coalitions governed the country. Their fragility was such that it was necessary to negotiate major pieces of legislation on the floor of the Chambers with the opposition. The resulting situation was highly paradoxical: during the so-called 'organic' period of the centre-left coalition (1963–8) not a single major reform was promulgated (in spite of all the rhetoric which had accompanied the birth of the coalition). During the following four years under the weak and unrepresentative centrist coalition major reforms received parliamentary approval: the most extensive widening of workers' power since the war (the Workers' Charter), the widest measure of devolution hitherto established (the legislation establishing the regions), and the 1970 divorce law which made divorce legal, are just some examples.

In the economic field the political situation prevented both a massive deflation and an incomes policy. What was introduced instead in the early 1970s was a semi-official policy of internal inflation coupled with devaluation. Domestic inflation was the inevitable result of full employment (though Italy never had as low a level of unemployment as the other European OECD countries), the constant increase in wages, and the prodigious growth of public spending. To maintain international competitiveness, devaluation ensured that external prices would not rise as much as internal ones.

The weakness of this strategy was that Italian imports became more and more expensive and this added to the inflationary spiral. Exporters granted wage demands readily in the expectation that the government would rescue them by devaluing the lira. The strategy was adopted in 1973 as Italian inflation rates reached a comparatively high level. This was also the year of the massive surge in oil prices. As Table 6.4 shows the devaluation of the lira proceeded constantly throughout this period against all other currencies:

Table 6.4 Lira exchange rate against selected currencies, 1973–85

Currency	1973	1977	1981	1985
US dollar	602	882	1,202	2,081
Swiss franc	191	368	658	749
Sterling	1,478	1,540	2,316	2,365
German mark	227	380	534	634
Yen	2.2	3.3	5.5	8.1

Sources: Bank of Italy, 1972–8 and *The Financial Times*.

Table 6.5 Measures of Italian outputs and inputs, 1959–74

Period	Average yearly rate of growth of national income	Average yearly rate of growth of industrial production	Ratio of investment to increase in income
1959–63	6.6	9.1	3.8
1964–70	6.0	6.2	3.5
1970–4	3.4	3.4	6.3

Source: Colajanni 1976: 8.

After 1973 the problem arose of covering the ever-growing deficit in the balance of payments. International loans, and in particular West German loans, were used frequently, but there was also another Bank of Italy credit squeeze which, as usual, hit the large firms much less than the others. This new credit squeeze stopped the recovery dead in its tracks and initiated the most serious economic crisis of the postwar period (Valli 1979: 135).

Looking back at the period 1959–1974 we see in Table 6.5 a constant drop in the rate of growth of the national income, of industrial production, and an increase in the ratio of investment to extra income (i.e., the amount necessary to invest in order to obtain an increase in income). In short, in this period the Italian economy was doing gradually less well both in terms of output and in the use of its inputs.

The government of national unity

At the local elections of 1975 the PCI scored a major success (32.1 per cent against 27.1 per cent in the 1972 general election). The DC was down to 35.8 per cent, the PSI gained two percentage points to 11.7 per cent. A year later the PCI further increased its share of the polls in the general elections to 34.4 per cent. The PSI, however, went down to 9.6 per cent whilst the DC regained much of the lost ground climbing back to 38.7 per cent. There were thus two victors: the DC and the PCI. On paper it would have been perfectly possible to reconstitute a centre-left government similar to the previous one, but the PSI attributed its poor results to its long-standing alliance with the DC and decided that it would no longer join in a coalition without the PCI. The PCI was willing to co-operate with the DC as part of its long-term 'historic compromise' strategy. All parties seemed to agree that the presence of communists in the government was not possible for 'international reasons' (i.e., the Americans would not like it). It was decided that the DC would form a government on its own and that the other parties (including the PCI) would abstain. A year later a programme was negotiated and the government could rely on the other parties' overt support in parliament. This government, inappropriately called the 'government of national solidarity', lasted until the PCI decided to withdraw at the end of 1978. By then the PSI was under the new leadership of Bettino Craxi and was more than ready to return to 'real' power.

The PCI's economic demands on the government were basically three. First, that there should be no attempt to modify the new agreement on the indexing of wages which had been reached the previous year (1975) between the employers' association and the trade unions (in fact between FIAT and the communist leader of the CGIL, Luciano Lama). The new agreement had introduced the principle of flat monetary increases for every percentage increase in inflation. The consequence of this was a tendency towards a narrowing of wage differentials. Second, that there should be no recourse to policies which would dampen down the economy, no massive deflation, no major increase in taxes, or severe cuts in public spending. Third, that there should be an interventionist industrial policy particularly directed towards the south and that this policy should be embodied in a major piece of legislation on 'industrial restructuring'.

The DC government largely upheld the first item of the package (an attempt to modify the indexation system in 1976 failed) which was given legal backing by parliamentary legislation. Employers constantly complained that the indexation was fuelling inflation and, later, the better skilled and white-collars workers complained of the narrowing of differentials.

The second point was more controversial also because the PCI demands were more vague. There was no out and out deflation but public services became more costly, various indirect taxes (on oil, tobacco, etc.) including VAT were increased. All in all between October 1976 and March 1977 these increases were worth 3.3 per cent of Gross Domestic Product (Chiaromonte 1986: 49).

Law No. 675 on industrial restructuring was approved in August 1977 in accordance with the joint programme agreed by the political parties. At first the PCI extolled the legislation but warned that it would be necessary to ensure that it be applied properly (Napolitano 1979: 228 and 296-7). Clearly this was not the case because, soon after the end of the period of 'national solidarity', PCI leaders, especially Napolitano and Chiaromonte, blamed the employers and the DC for emasculating the industrial policy (Napolitano 1979: 228; Chiaromonte 1986: 175) whilst admitting that the communists should have conducted a more decisive campaign throughout the country and tacitly implying that trade union support had not been as forthcoming as had been expected.

Law 675 was based on the assumption that the industrial policy depended virtually entirely on the central organs of the state (Vacca 1987: 112). The belief was that if one could control the largest firms one could shape the whole economy. Little account was taken of two other significant sectors:

the very large number of middle and small firms which dominate the Italian economy and the international economy.

Yet there was no question that Italy did need some major restructuring. One option would have been a restructuring around high technology. This would have required state intervention of a particular calibre: efficient and ruthless. But by the 1970s the state sector had become the political instrument of the Christian Democratic Party, its economic functions were totally subordinated to the requirements of ensuring the political survival of that party. In fact the path of 'high tech', though seriously considered in policies such as Law 675, was never really carried out. The avenue which was chosen (although the term 'chosen' implies some kind of conscious will: it was more a question of allowing events to happen) was the circumvention of the gains achieved by the working class in 1969–70 by reorganizing the system of production in such a way as to sustain the manufacture of traditional goods while resisting Third World competition. This was achieved through a decentralization of the productive system. Production was shifted from established firms (and often by these firms themselves) to an array of small firms and cottage industry. Employment in this sector assumed various forms: domestic labour, underemployment, juvenile and even child labour, casual and part-time labour (often performed by people who also had a 'regular' job in the open economy). The pressures towards the creation of a hidden or black economy were the desire to escape trade union constraints: payments in the 'hidden' sector did not have to correspond to wage rates offered in the open sector, health and safety regulations could be easily circumvented, and there were fewer or no strikes. Furthermore in the hidden sector it was possible for employers and employees alike to escape from the full burden of taxes and especially of the very high national insurance contributions (Sassoon 1986: 74–5). Tax evasion in 1984 was estimated to have been more than enough to wipe out the annual government deficit (*The Financial Times Survey, Italy*, 18 April 1988).

The 1980s

The effects of the decentralization of production towards the hidden sector permitted Italy to achieve a growth rate which, though not as high as that achieved in the golden years of the economic miracle was higher than that of most developed countries. OECD figures show that in 1980 GDP increased in Italy by 4 per cent against −0.2 per cent in the US, 1.4 per cent in France, −1.4 per cent in the UK, and 1.9 per cent in West Germany. Only Japan (4.2 per cent), Portugal (4.7 per cent), and Finland (4.2 per cent) did better. The successive five years included the period of greatest government stability in postwar Italian history – the administration of the socialist prime minister Bettino Craxi lasted from August 1983 to March 1987. This period

(1980–5), in spite of the claims made for it – including the overtaking of the UK by Italy in terms of per capita GDP – did not produce a specially pronounced growth. The 8.4 per cent achieved in terms of GDP volume was greater than West Germany, France, and Spain but lower than that of the US, Japan, the UK, Canada, Finland, Norway, and Denmark. One of Craxi's successors at the helm of the government (1987–8), the Christian Democratic leader Giovanni Goria, bitterly declared: 'The autostrade are overloaded and old, transport is inefficient, the postal system does not work, the telephones crackle, the bureaucracy is slow, costly and useless – this is not a modern country' (cited in the *Financial Times*, 18 April 1988).

One cannot attribute Italian growth in the 1980s entirely to the hidden economy though this may have been the only feature which was peculiar to Italy. The other conditions were paralleled in the rest of Europe: labour shake-outs, trade union weakness caused by unemployment (symbolized in the Italian case by a modification in the index-linked scale of wages upheld by a referendum), etc.

Nevertheless, much of the growth which was generated may have been achieved precisely because of the much criticized inefficiency and lack of authority of the Italian state. This allowed a *de facto* deregulation and a *de facto* tax reduction. Thatcher-type policies of public spending cuts could neither be advocated nor achieved in the political conditions within which the various Italian governments were operating. The repeated demands for modernization and efficiency which most Italian political parties, but especially the Socialist Party, would constantly advance, entailed an entirely different approach to economic reconstruction. As it turned out high growth was obtained precisely because nothing much was done about it. It is not surprising that the advocates of total deregulation have a secret admiration for the Italian model.

Sustained growth, particularly of this nature, of itself solves only one problem: that of low growth. Public spending continued to expand, the distortions in the labour market were further exacerbated, the activity rate remained exceptionally low, inflation in the period 1980–5 remained much higher than that of all other OECD competitors and unemployment in 1985 while lower than in Spain, the UK, the Netherlands, and Belgium, was higher than in all the other OECD countries. In 1987 unemployment was 12 per cent and highly concentrated in the south, among women, and the young. But the most serious problem remains that of the public sector debt which nearly equals GDP. All economists and all politicians agree that something should be done about it. One obvious solution is to cut public spending seriously, but 42 per cent of current spending (net of interest) is on health and old age pensions. No Italian government is likely to risk unparalleled unpopularity by significantly reducing social spending.

Of course, administrative efficiency, including the drastic decrease of tax evasion and the ability to deny clientele groups the public funds they ceaselessly demand may help. The problem is that the first would damage the hidden economy whilst the second would weaken the parties which form the present coalition. The only alternative coalition possible would have to include not only the Italian Communist Party (whose share of the vote has been declining since 1979) but also at least three of the five parties which are at present in power: the Socialists, the Republicans and the Social-Democrats. Such a heterogeneous coalition is unlikely to be any more stable than the present one; yet it remains the only possible way of breaking the mould of Italian politics.

Having said that, it remains unlikely that any new coalition government would be able to affect significantly Italy's economic performance in terms of growth rates. The national economy is so integrated with the international one that the level of interdependence is much too profound to allow national institutions and policies to have a radical effect. One can say this with a strong dose of certainty because there is very little evidence to suggest that national policies and institutions have had much effect on Italy's economic performance even when the degree of interdependence was lower.

The role of national politics has been that of facilitating a particular kind of economic development in the phase of sustained growth by removing constraints and helping to maintain a low wage economy. Subsequently, governments have tried to reduce social tensions, for example, by taking over loss-making firms thus maintaining employment or by acting as arbitrator in the general conflict between management and trade unions. Governments have had an impact in the *kind* of growth which has occurred and in the distribution of resources. The *rate* of growth, however, though it is frequently used by politicians as an index of government performance, has been determined only indirectly by political institutions.

In any case, it is evident that Italian governments have tended, on the whole, to worry far more about modifying the effects of growth on the national economy while at the same time allowing, within limits, the national economy to acquire a shape which would fit in with international requirements. In other words, the great successes of Italian governments (the economic growth rates of the late fifties and of the mid-eighties) have probably been due to an uncanny ability to bend with the prevailing winds rather than to a major insight into what are the conditions for economic growth.

Selected dates

April 1945	Liberation of Northern Italy. Coalition of National Unity.
June 1946	Referendum decides in favour of the republic. Election of Constituent Assembly.

May 1947	Communists (PCI) and Socialists (PSI) expelled from the government. Centrist coalition formed.
April 1948	Electoral victory of Christian Democrats (DC).
1949	Lira stabilized. Agrarian unrest.
1950	Agrarian reform. Constitution of *Cassa per il Mezzogiorno* (Fund for the South).
1953	Establishment of Ente Nazionale Idrocarburi (ENI)
March 1957	Rome Treaty (EEC) signed.
January 1960	*The Financial Times* (11 January) accords Italian lira the 'Oscar' for the most stable currency of 1959.
July 1960	General strike against the government.
November 1962	Electricity industry nationalized.
December 1963	Credit squeeze, PSI enters government.
1968	Widespread student unrest.
1969	Autumn: widespread strikes. Bomb in a Milan bank kills sixteen people: the start of ten years of terrorism.
1970	Parliament passes legislation legalizing divorce and establishing the regional system and the Workers' Charter.
1970–2	Last phase of centrist governments (DC plus the three small parties of the centre).
1974	Referendum upholds divorce legislation.
1975	Employers' and trade unions' accord on wage indexation.
1976	General elections: sizeable PCI gains. DC government supported by all parties (except far right).
March 1978	Aldo Moro, president of the DC and architect of the pact with the PCI is kidnapped and then killed by the Red Brigades.
1979	PCI withdraws from pact with the DC and loses votes at subsequent general election. Five-party coalition set up.
1983	At general election DC suffers major setback. PSI leader Bettino Craxi becomes prime minister.
1985	Government modifies wage indexation system. Decision confirmed by referendum in June.

References

Amato, G. (1976) *Economia, politica e istituzioni in Italia*, Bologna: Il Mulino.
Amoroso, B. and Olsen, O.J. (1978) *Lo Stato imprenditore*, Rome-Bari: Laterza.
Castronovo, V. (1975) *La Storia Economica. Storia d'Italia*, vol. IV, part I, Turin: Einaudi.

Chiaromonte, G. (1986) *Le scelte della solidarietà democratica, Cronache, ricordi e riflessioni sul triennio 1976-1979*, Rome: Editori Riuniti.

Colajanni, N. (1976) *Riconversione grande impresa partecipazioni statali*, Milan: Feltrinelli.

Daneo, C. (1975) *La politica economica della Ricostruzione 1945-1949*, Turin: Einaudi.

De Cecco, M. (1971) 'Lo sviluppo dell'economia italiana e la sua collocazione internazionale', *Rivista Internazionale di Scienze Economiche e Commerciali*, October.

Graziani, A. (ed.) (1971) *L'economia italiana: 1945-1970*, Bologna: Il Mulino.

Napolitano, G. (1979) *In mezzo al guado*, Rome: Editori Riuniti.

Onida, F. (1977) 'Il ruolo dell'Italia nella divisione internazionale del lavoro', in [various authors] *Lezioni di economia. Aspetti e problemi dello sviluppo economico italiano e dell'attuale crisi internazionale*, Milan: Feltrinelli.

Podbielski, G. (1974) *Italy. Development and Crisis in the Postwar Economy*, Oxford: Clarendon Press.

Salvati, M. (1975) *Il sistema economico italiano: analisi di una crisi*, Bologna: Il Mulino.

Sassoon, D. (1986) *Contemporary Italy. Politics, Economy and Society since 1945*, London and New York: Longman.

Togliatti, P. (1984) *Opere, Volume 5. 1944-1955*, Rome: Editori Riuniti.

Vacca, G. (1987) *Tra compromesso e solidarietà. La politica del Pci negli anni '70*, Rome: Editori Riuniti.

Valli, V. (1979) *L'economia e la politica economica italiana (1945-1979)*, Milan: Etas Libri.

Guide to further reading

On the political system in general see Joseph LaPalombara's debunking text *Democracy Italian Style* (New Haven, Conn.: Yale University Press, 1987). A good collection of articles is that of Peter Lange and Sidney Tarrow (eds), *Italy in Transition* (London: Frank Cass, 1980). See also *Italian Politics. A Review* vol. 1 edited by Robert Leonardi and Raffaella Nannetti (London: Frances Pinter, 1985). They were joined by Piergiorgio Corbetta for vol. 2, which contains interesting material on the economy (London: Frances Pinter, 1988), and for vol. 3 (London: Frances Pinter, 1989).

My *Contemporary Italy* (London: Longman, 1986) surveys the economic, social, and political development of Italy since 1945. On the immediate postwar period see S.J. Woolf (ed.), *The Rebirth of Italy, 1943-1950*, (London: Longman, 1972).

Interesting electoral studies in the broader sense can be found in the series edited by Howard Penniman: *Italy at the Polls, 1976* and *Italy at the Polls, 1979* (Washington DC: American Enterprise Institute, 1977 & 1981), and *Italy at the Polls, 1983* (Durham, NC: Duke University Press, 1987).

There is no major study on Christian Democracy in English but see Alan Zuckerman, *The Politics of Faction: Christian Democratic Rule in Italy* (New Haven, Conn.: Yale University Press, 1979). The southern patronage system of this party has been admirably examined in Percy Allum's *Politics and Society in Postwar Naples* (Cambridge: Cambridge University Press, 1973) and in Judith Chubb's *Patronage, Power and Poverty in Southern Italy* (Cambridge: Cambridge University Press, 1982).

I have dealt with the PCI in my *The Strategy of the Italian Communist Party* (London: Frances Pinter, 1981). The best book on the PCI's relation with the USSR is Joan Barth Urban's *Moscow and the Italian Communist Party* (Ithaca, NY: Cornell University Press, 1986).

On the trade unions those who can read Italian should try Alessandro Pizzorno, *I soggetti del pluralismo: classi, partiti, sindacati* (Bologna: Il Mulino, 1980). Note also Peter Lange, George Ross, and Maurizio Vannicelli, *Unions, Change and Crisis: French and Italian union strategy and Political Economy, 1945–1980*, (London: Allen & Unwin, 1982). For a fine reconstruction of the history of the labour movement since 1945 read Joanne Barkan's *Visions of Emancipation* (New York: Praeger, 1984).

On the economy one should turn to Guido M. Rey's contribution to Andrea Boltho (ed.), *The European Economy. Growth and Crisis* (Oxford: Oxford University Press, 1982). Less technical is D.C. Templeman, *The Italian Economy* (New York: 1981). For the 1950s and 1960s see also K.J. Allen and A. Stevenson, *An Introduction to the Italian Economy* (London: 1974) and Gisele Pobdielski, *Italy. Development and Crisis in the Postwar Economy* (Oxford: Clarendon Press: 1974). On the south see Augusto Graziani, 'The Mezzogiorno in the Italian Economy' in *Cambridge Journal of Economics* (Dec. 1978).

On Italy's stateholding system there is little new so the reader must turn to Stuart Holland (ed.), *The State as Entrepreneur: New Dimension for Public Enterprise, the IRI State Shareholding Formula* (London: Weidenfeld & Nicolson, 1972).

Chapter seven

Spain

Paul Preston

Introduction

The condition of the Spanish economy in 1945 is not readily comparable to that of most of the other countries examined in this book. Spain had not been directly involved in the Second World War. Nevertheless, as a consequence of the destruction of resources in its own civil war (1936–9), a repressive and autarkic economic policy, and the hostility of the western powers as a result of her clear association with the Axis, in 1945 Spain was one of the most economically backward and isolated countries in Europe.

In the early 1940s, the agricultural sector, which accounted for more than half of the active population, had seen its output reduced to pre-1914 levels as the effects of the civil war were exacerbated by severe and prolonged drought which devastated crops in many areas. The bulk of the agrarian population consisted of landless labourers dependent for their livelihood upon a small tightly knit elite of landowners whose privileged position had been reinforced by the agricultural policies of the first Francoist governments. This antiquated and inefficient structure was protected by an authoritarian and centralized state. The public enterprise sector was controlled by a single authority. Political parties and trades unions were illegal and strikes were banned. Labour and employers were regimented together in the official corporative syndicates.

The civil war had been fought and won to defend the interests of the agrarian oligarchy which had felt itself threatened by the mild land reforms of the Second Republic (1931–6) and by the growing militancy of anarcho-syndicalist and socialist trades unions. The Franco regime, which was created to defend the civil war victory of 1939 and thus to preserve the pre-1931 agrarian structures, was negotiated out of existence in the industrialized Spain of the 1970s. Between 1939 and 1975, Francoism reluctantly, some would say inadvertently, presided over the creation of a capitalist economy. In so doing, the dictatorship made itself a political anachronism (Clavera *et al.* 1973: I, 51–75).

The political economy of early Francoism: autarky 1945–51

Having annihilated the reformist challenge by military means, state activity in the economic sphere thereafter consisted of the suppression of left-wing political parties, the destruction of trades unions and the use of the Falangist Syndicates to control labour, particularly in the countryside (Amsden 1972: ch. 1; Aparicio 1982). The regime's repressive labour relations had the side-effect of creating conditions favourable for a capitalist take-off. Within the Francoist coalition, the agrarian elite was initially all-powerful, as befitted the preponderance of agriculture in the economy as a whole. Not surprisingly, rural values and support for agriculture were strong themes in early regime rhetoric (Estebán 1975: 85). Equally, the interests of industry, which had historically been subordinate to those of the agrarians, became a pressing concern of the state given the damage inflicted by the civil war and the need to reconstruct the economy. Moreover, the hegemonic crisis of the 1930s and its resolution brought a wider range of economic groups into the area of state concern and regulation. Thus, the Franco regime assumed a more active role than its predecessors, both to eliminate economic and social challenges and to maintain the cohesion of the competing social and political forces on which it relied for support (Snowden 1972: 293–5).

Until 1945, the regime's policy had aimed to preserve the 'balance' of agrarian, financial, and industrial interests that supported it, by piecemeal protectionist measures and rigid control of labour through the state-run syndicates. By cutting off Spain from world trade and economic relations, the regime made it clear that its priorities were the protection of its social base in a weakened agrarian economy and the use of dirigiste tools as a mechanism to create internal growth (Viñas *et al.* 1979: 252–3). Under autarkic conditions, an essentially fragile economic base could be maintained and hopefully nurtured, without exposing it to the vagaries of international markets or to the risks of liberal-democratic politics. Autarky was not, therefore, simply an 'aberration' or a failure of judgement, as the regime later attempted to portray it, nor an 'unfortunate' necessity in the face of international hostility. Rather it was an economic consequence of the Franco regime's social and political priorities (Viñas 1980: 63–5). Its immediate result was the removal of Spain from the evolution of the wider European economy as that responded to the effects of American Marshall Aid. Recovery was to be achieved in Spain without external aid or linkage to the world markets that the US tried to create. Autarky was essentially a system through which the dictatorship could suppress the dynamic effects of unbridled capitalism on an antiquated economic structure.

In the case of agriculture, the Franco regime was faced by the dilemma of having come to power to resist reform yet needing desperately to increase cultivation and production levels in order to feed a starving populace.

Accordingly, within the broad limits of the agricultural protectionism that lay at the heart of Francoist economic policy in the 1940s, some attempts at reform of the system took place. In consequence, a notable re-ruralization took place, reversing the trend to industrialization of the 1930s. Alongside calls to fight 'the battle for wheat' and to raise production, which led to the extension of areas of cultivation, the state aimed to create a numerous sector of smallholders through 'internal colonization' (Lieberman 1981: 73–4). By giving land to peasants, it was hoped to secure a solid block of pro-regime social support. However, to do this threatened to strike at the property rights of large landowners, as agrarian reform in the 1930s had tried to do, by reducing the size of large estates (the latifundias). By linking colonization with the irrigation programmes of the Instituto Nacional de Colonización in the late 1940s, newly reclaimed land could be passed to smallholders without undermining the latifundias which received the greater part of meaningful state support through the protectionism and pricing policy of the Servicio Nacional del Trigo (the National Wheat Board). However, the rate of reclamation was low and costs were high and passed on in their entirety to the new 'landowner' either through the purchase price or rental. Not surprisingly, the actual level of restructuring was low (Martínez Allier 1971: 20–2; Castillo 1979: 401–2). Real change within the countryside was minimal, but state intervention was still strongly felt in local society.

Its most obvious manifestation was the Syndicates' control over wages and the distribution of resources. Large reserves of surplus labour kept wages low anyway, but the local state machinery of appointed officials, the functionaries of the Falangist Movement and the Civil Guard made sure that any attempts at independent bargaining were suppressed. These bodies were also the channels through which food and raw materials passed as the regime extended rationing and regulated the granting of contracts and permits for all types of economic activity. Such tight control encouraged the emergence of a black market which was in effect promoted by local state functionaries. For consumers, a wide disparity existed between official food price levels and the reality imposed by local 'notables'. Large landowners, with their well established local bases and connections with the regime at a national level, were well placed to exploit the system. The Banco Urquijo concluded that the net effect of the efforts of landowners and state intervention was that considerable surpluses were accumulated by Spanish agriculture, although the bank was not able to ascertain how they were employed. As a regime of agrarian class domination, therefore, Francoism was highly successful in the late 1940s, in intensifying the extraction of a surplus from the land (Luis Leal *et al.* 1975: 29–37; Lieberman 1982: 77).

The transfer of capital from the land to other areas of the economy was inhibited, however, by the fragmented nature of state intervention. Without sources of outside support, industry was dependent on internally generated surplus for investment. The type of capital formation stimulated in Spain was not helpful to industry. In particular, the regime's concentration on the health of isolated sectors of the economy was little compensation for the lack of a national banking system. Private banks were heavily dependent on the state for support. (Lieberman 1982: 246; Walker 1948: 11–13). In the agrarian sector, this took the form of sponsorship of local savings banks (Cajas de Ahorro). The Cajas de Ahorro accumulated the savings which accrued to big landowners thanks to the control over wages decreed by the Ministry of Labour and imposed by the Falangist Syndicates, or Hermandades, as they were known in the countryside. The self-financing of agriculture was the aim but the consequence was often conspicuous consumption as well as long-term savings and short-term speculation. The conclusion of industrial banks such as the Banco Urquijo was that much potentially useful investment was 'lost', except where landowners decided to invest in national banks or in government-backed bonds issued through the Bank of Spain (Luis Leal *et al*. 1975: 37–69).

The trickle of finance produced a steady 1 per cent rate of growth in industry after 1945. Under the import substitution policy of the regime, the manufacture of light industrial goods requiring little heavy plant or technical expertise tended to dominate. The regime maintained direct control of contracts, raw material quotas, and production licences. Industrial production was inhibited by the combined effects of state regulations and agriculture's position as the virtual motor of the whole economic system. By the late 1940s, the regime's relationship with the economy encompassed a dramatic contradiction. It was politically committed to the survival of a structurally under-developed agrarian system which in turn was expected to provide potential investment for an advancing industrial base (Román 1971: 10). However, the primacy given to protecting the interests of landowners ensured that the role of the state at this point would be to suppress rising demands from industry.

Under autarky, the structure of imports and exports was regulated by bilateral trade agreements designed to ensure self-sufficiency in internal production (Viñas *et al* 1979: 571, Table). Energy and raw materials made up the greatest share of foreign trade, whilst price protection limited the possibilities for Spanish exports. An external stimulus to the economy through the import of capital equipment to re-equip industry, of machinery for agriculture, and of food was effectively denied by this policy. Strict control over quotas and import licences, often breached by corruption, had a number of consequences for the state's attempt to 'discipline' industrial production. Commercial autarky proved to be a double-edged sword. On the one hand, it protected the internal market, the operations of manufacturers, and especially the interests of agricultural producers. However, on the other hand, it also confined the possibilities for a dynamic expansion in production and the diversification of the industrial base to a domestic market dominated by agricultural scarcity. Whilst potential demand for goods and capital equipment was high, the actual means of encouraging that demand were limited. Given the delicate balance of benefits offered by the restriction of foreign trade, changes in autarky were hesitant.

Protection was a long cherished aim of Spanish industry. The price paid under the Franco regime was the strict controls of autarky. Under this cover, some rebuilding and modest growth had been possible, although this favoured already established industry. It also led to shortages of all kinds, uncertain supplies of raw materials and equipment, and bottlenecks in production. The attempt to substitute imports and to establish new industries in these conditions (particularly in the armaments field) led, in the late 1940s, to a changed role for Instituto Nacional de Industria (INI), created in 1939 as the channel for state aid to industrial reconstruction. This move to reduce imports took the form of attempts by the holding company to create new state industries in manufacturing areas such as steel and cars without regard to the opportunity costs involved or the ability of domestic buyers to pay for the product. (Lieberman 1982: 174; Clavera *et al.* 1973: I, 262–7). Equally, the state tried to encourage larger units of production through mergers and state direction of labour. Protection for Spain's backward industry helped tie business to the regime. However, efforts to rationalize and diversify a backward and ramshackle industrial base were bound to encounter major difficulties. The potential for 'change from within' was constrained by autarky. As a result, by 1948 industrial production had recovered to barely pre-civil war levels and a combination of inflation and stagnation was exposing the limits of autarky (González 1979: 39–45).

In fact, despite the import substitution policy of autarky, the economy continued to absorb much needed imports which diminished currency reserves and increased indebtedness. Multiple exchange rates and printing of money (through government loans) tightened the internal market and boosted inflation (on exchange rates see Lieberman 1982: 176–9; Viñas *et al.* 1979: 575–91). Businessmen and the state functionaries associated with them, in the Ministries of the Economy and Foreign Affairs, took advantage of the regime's diplomatic attempts at *rapprochement* with the western bloc to establish overseas commercial contacts. The process began with negotiations with American banks carried on 'privately', albeit with the support of the Ministry of Foreign Affairs. This culminated in the arrangements of loans, made with tacit US government approval, by the Chase Manhattan bank and to be followed by others from 1948 onwards (Viñas 1981: 43–63). A change in the regime's international position thus paralleled the turn whereby certain elements in the state apparatus and the economic elite began to seek commercial links outside the restrictions of autarky.

The beginnings of liberalization 1951–9

The regime's commitment to the modification of autarky had been signalled by the cabinet changes of 1951 and the promise of some 'liberalization' in state control of economic life. At the time, agricultural and industrial production had reached a ceiling which internal conditions and interrelationships would allow to develop no further. Further recovery required large expansion in imports of essential materials and equipment. The opening up of new opportunities through the tentative linkage of the economy to world trade and finance helped break the cycle of inefficiency and limitations which autarky had now reached, although it did not yet signal a fundamental regime decision about the economic future.

Although the 1951 programme showed an apparent acceptance of an internationalist free-market ideology for Spain, the real changes in the state's economic role were limited. The close connection that had developed between economic forces and the regime could not simply be abandoned or even drastically modified overnight. If anything, the changes that took place were more concerned with recognizing the importance of an industrial strategy for the state (Esteban 1975: 90). The first consequence of expanding the capacity to import and of relaxing direct controls over production was to stimulate industry. New supplies of capital equipment and raw materials allowed an expansion of industrial production above both the ability of industry to export and the internal demand for goods (Clinton Pelham 1951: *passim*). In effect, the 1950s saw the state simultaneously managing both dynamic changes and economic crisis, without freeing itself of the legacy of autarky.

A subtle redirection of autarky took place in the 1950s, bringing technical experts and notions of a 'growth' economy into the cabinet. The loosening of state economic controls, however, was not immediately evident. Considerable ambiguity existed as to the real orientation of policy. While the importance of industrial interests was now recognized, a rhetorical commitment to the ideology of agrarian society remained. The promotion of trade and the freeing of an internal market were not accompanied by any undertaking to modernize agriculture. However, pressure on the agricultural system could not entirely be ignored. Moreover, state penetration of rural society carried with it the spread of a more 'national' vision of markets. Although the regime remained tied to the socio-economic stability of the countryside, the 1950s saw a decisive undermining of this commitment.

Physically, the most dramatic manifestation of this was in migration from the countryside, from rural unemployment to developing urban industry whether in Madrid, the Basque country or elsewhere in Europe (Luis Leal *et al.* 1975: 200–4). In the period 1940–50, the rural population decreased by only 8–9,000, the following decade saw a loss of over

Table 7.1 Rural wages, prices, and implied rural real wages, 1935–72

	Rural wages	Prices	Rural real wages
1935	100	100	100
1940	154	189	81
1945	260	354	73
1950	424	698	61
1955	540	631	86
1960	1,125	916	123
1965	2,170	1,173	185
1970	3,787	1,289	294
1972	5,030	1,465	343

Source: Lieberman 1982: 77,80.

2000,000 (Bradshaw 1972: 74). Although the Syndicates tried to keep the labour force on the land, the decontrolling of many aspects of the economy that accompanied the 1951 changes rendered such efforts useless. A seepage of the pool of labour from the land began, pressures on agriculture increased as the urban demand for food grew, changes in diet reduced demand for wheat, and the end of controlled prices reduced profits as well. Most importantly, the key to traditional agriculture's successful operation, an abundant cheap labour supply, was also being eroded. As the rural population decreased, the relationship between labour costs and agricultural prices began to be inverted. As Table 7.1 indicates, rural real wages, which had fallen by about 40 per cent from 1935 to 1950, began to grow during the 1950s.

The impact of such developments was relatively slight in the fifties. Its longest-term significance lay in its effect on the agrarian social bloc which constituted the bedrock of the regime's political support. Rising production costs naturally hit the small producer with low economies of scale harder than the owners of the large estates or the agricultural exporters. Innovation was a difficult prospect in an already marginal existence. Consequently, while smallholders remained tied to 'traditional' patterns of production, the viability of their farms gradually declined under the pressure. Large landowners could resist such a process much better and were in a better position to innovate or to spread their capital holdings by turning towards business. The dictatorship continued to provide support for agriculture in the 1950s. National projects to promote irrigation and crop diversity, such as the Plan Badajoz, diverted state funds into the countryside. At the same time, the Servicio Nacional para la Concentración Parcelaria (SNCP), created in 1953, took over the role of the INC to encourage peasant settlement in the face of outside pressures which were exposing the shortcomings of agriculture (Sevilla Guzmán 1979: 184–92). Large landowners continued to gain disproportionately, and the illusion of a seamless web of agrarian social and economic cohesion was broken as state capitalism became more of a reality in Spain.

Parallel to this crisis, the secondary and tertiary sectors of the economy experienced the beginnings of a growth which the regime still sought to manage carefully (figures vary considerably, Lieberman [1982: 177] is more generous than Banco de España [1960]). Controls were not removed overnight. The essentials of autarky were retained but modified to free the potential for growth that had built up behind political barriers. The machinery of state intervention in industry was not abandoned. The effect on a weak industrial base could have been disastrous if overseas competition had been unfettered. Accordingly, the state encouraged only certain types of imports (Clavera *et al.* [1973: 37] shows that machinery imports grew rapidly). The shift was towards industrial and agricultural equipment, plus selected food products. Tariffs on manufactured goods remained in force in the hope that domestic industries would seize the opportunity provided by a captive market. Controls over raw materials imports, the labour force and wages also continued through the bureaucratic and Syndical apparatus. At the macro-economic level, the government aimed at balanced budgets, a programme of investment through INI and the encouragement of 'market levels' in pricing to eliminate the black market and bottlenecks. The regime was still concerned to maintain the balance of interests that autarky had protected, but internally and externally there was a shift towards allowing freer play of economic forces (Viñas *et al.* 1979: 830–49).

The immediate results of this opening were an increase in industrial output and a banking boom which began in the first half of the 1950s and accelerated noticeably in the second (González 1979: 125–7). Industrial growth was most marked in large concerns, particularly where INI provided state aid, such as steel or shipbuilding. However, the loosening of restrictions also saw the rise of small-scale enterprises producing for the domestic market. A monopolistic, state-aided sector, often linked to foreign capital, co-existed with a fragmented but widespread sector of small-scale production. However, this growth took place in a context of sluggish development of both the domestic market and the infrastructure. Consequently, tensions were not slow to emerge after the move from autarky and the subsequent industrial expansion. Crisis management of economic affairs became an urgent necessity for the dictatorship when overproduction coincided with a low capacity to export. Although imports stimulated production by releasing bottlenecks, domestic demand for goods was still low given the low purchasing power of consumers. Moreover, in world terms, Spanish goods were overpriced, which led to a balance of payments problem. Underconsumption brought a conflict between the regime's political and economic ambitions. The need to raise demand clashed with the wage restraint policy implemented by the Syndicates and the regime's specific aim of budgetary control.

The degree to which economic growth had become an acceptable goal, even if the reality of its costs had not, was revealed by the fact that, in 1954, the regime allowed wages to rise. In many ways, this also reflected the resurrection of the working class as a political force. The intrinsic structural problems and the contradictions between political Francoism and economic interests were to be starkly exposed in the mid-1950s by a political and social crisis which partial policy modifications could not resolve. After 1956, dynamic industrial elements linked up with state technocrats, particularly from the Catholic pressure group Opus Dei. They were backed by the important personal influence of Franco's *éminence grise*, his cabinet secretary, Luis Carrero Blanco. Impelled by rising middle-class aspirations, they pressed the regime for a wholehearted push on industrialization (Anderson 1970: 106, 111). Opposing such a path were those who favoured retrenchment and a return to the 'traditional' values of autarky, largely Falangists and agricultural interests threatened by change. As the spiral of overproduction, inflation, and dislocation deepened, so the regime became more distanced from its secure social foundation (Clavera *et al.* 1973: 30; González 1979: 49–57). This remained, however, an 'internal' crisis, with all the forces involved still tied to the future of Francoism.

A symptom of the crisis was the lack of co-ordination between different ministries, state bodies, and financial institutions. The Treasury distanced itself from the programme of de-regulation that heralded a structural crisis. Meanwhile, the Labour Ministry, dominated by the Falange's Syndical apparatus, pushed up wages. From the Ministry of Foreign Affairs, pressure was applied for the adoption of American models and the encouragement of foreign investment. Finally the banks, important sources of economic information and opinion, began to produce critical reports from their own experts echoing the arguments of the main Opus Dei technocrats, Laureano López Rodó and Alberto Ullastres. They warned that having ventured back into the world economy, the benefits accruing were now threatened by the likely total loss of foreign reserves. The consequences were conflict within the state's institutions, paralysis in the economy at large, and a clash between agricultural and industrial interests. Eventually, the structural and ideological shift that had taken place was confirmed by Franco's introduction of Opus Dei technocrats into the new cabinet of 1957 to pursue the industrial path that had opened up in the early fifties (Clavera *et al.* 1973: 163–4; Carr and Fusi 1979: 53; Gallo 1973: 248–9). Passivity was not an option in this period of transition away from the last vestiges of autarky, given that Francoism had always made a point of controlling economic affairs. To re-establish the regime's internal equilibrium and to undercut the opposition, the Oficina de Coordinación y Programación Económica (OCPE), was created. Closely linked to the very top of the policy-making apparatus, it was the forerunner of a series of planning and development bodies. Politically the aims were, as ever, to guarantee the stability and legitimacy of the dictatorship. Economically, the new men looked to full integration into the world economy and an industrial market-orientated pattern of development to underpin the regime (Clavera *et al.* 1973: 198–200; cf. Viñas *et al.* 1979: 50–65).

Stabilization and growth: 1959–73

Following the arrival of the new cabinet in 1957, there was a period of what has been called 'disorientation', during which public debt, inflation, and balance of payments problems continued (González 1979: 134–7). A twin process was pursued, of which the Stabilization Plan announced in 1959 was only a part. On the one hand, the regime fine-tuned the institutional arrangements that would allow growth to continue much as it had done since 1951. On the other, it massaged its political support at every level, to make acceptable the economic landscape that was developing. Economic change was now pursued as an explicit political aim. For critics of both left and extreme right, this seemed to be final confirmation that western capitalism had really triumphed in Spain, (Carr and Fusi 1979: 62–4; Tamames 1978: *passim*).

This 'liberalization' in the economic sphere proceeded, against internal opposition, on the basis of establishing closer links with major institutions of the western economy. Acceptance of Spain as a trading partner had to be extended beyond the bounds of the narrow American alliance if the benefits of a growing western economy were to be felt fully. To this end, the 1957 cabinet had already begun a series of discussions with the International Monetary Fund, World Bank, and OECD over the economic future and designed to pave the way for attracting foreign investment and imports on a sufficient scale to accelerate rates of growth (Viñas *et al.* 1979: 888–99). Membership of the IMF and World Bank permitted, from 1958, a process of consultations whereby the regime asked for 'advice' in the hope of discovering the terms on which international economic support could be secured. This was offered in a series of reports, the most important prepared by the International Bank of Reconstruction and Development (IBRD). It provided the 'objective' assessment of these expert agencies on the Spanish economy and was seen by the dictatorship's personnel as an expression of international capitalism's minimum requirements to make Spain an attractive prospect (Lieberman 1981: 216–21). The raising of confidence and the adoption of positive measures to satisfy such conditions were embodied in the Stabilization Plan of 1959 (Amado and Estapé 1986).

On the advice given, a number of adjustments were made to stabilize internal demand and inflation and, at the same time, to encourage foreign trade and investment. Externally the changes included the reduction of trade controls, and the establishment of the official exchange rate at 60 pesetas to the dollar, tantamount to a 42 per cent devaluation (Harrison

1985: 147). Priority was given to encouraging foreign investment by easing the controls both on repatriation of capital and returns and on maximum foreign participation in Spanish companies. Financial support for the Stabilization Plan was sought from a variety of interested international bodies which offered between $400 and $500 million in aid (Ruedo Ibérico 1966: I, 25; Harrison 1985: 148). Internally, the regime continued a policy, begun in 1957, of limiting public sector spending, of restricting credit facilities offered by banks, and of raising prices in public utilities. In addition, wage restraint was reintroduced and state support was restricted for agriculture as the main inflationary sector of the economy (Burgos López 1973: II, 955–6; Román 1971: 30).

The plan was a success in so far as it brought inflation down to 2 per cent and promoted an improvement in the balance of payments (Harrison 1985: 148). It also provoked a period of internal recession from which it was hoped that strong areas of economic activity would emerge renewed and the outworn 'traditional' past would go to the wall. Economic planners hoped thereby to leave Spain better adapted to function competitively in international markets. Imports fell in the wake of the devaluation of the peseta. Investment in industry declined as businessmen waited to see what the regime's change of policy really implied for them. A fall of 2.5 per cent in wages and a 10.7 per cent rise in unemployment in 1959 intensified the hostility between the Syndicates and the working class even further. The regime's repressive apparatus dealt brutally with the consequent industrial unrest. Production fell in every sector of industry, as wage and credit restraint bit into domestic demand. In 1960, unemployment rose a further 34.7 per cent on the previous year (Lieberman 1982: 206). To counter these negative consequences, agriculture was redeemed by a good harvest in 1959 and receipts from foreign tourism began, in 1960, the ascent which was shortly to make it one of the mainstays of the Spanish economy. The recession was relatively short-lived, however, thanks largely to the context of European growth in which it occurred. In 1961, an increase in industrial exports heralded the boom to follow (González 1979: 240–53). This trend also indicated that the balance of power within Spain's economy was swinging definitively towards industry and away from agriculture.

The key to industrial growth in the 1960s was a massive increase in productive investment after stabilization had been carried out. This reflected the effects of foreign investment, earnings from trade and services, and the direction of savings into industrial banks. From abroad, the US was the largest supplier of funds (40 per cent) followed by France and Britain. Much of this foreign investment capital went into the development of the infrastructure, especially construction, transport, and banking, or into new industries which experienced proportionally higher rates of growth, such as chemicals (Lieberman 1982: 230–1). Although the regime de-regulated overseas investment, except in the media and defence, after 1959 much of it seems to have been directed into areas that reflected demands in other economies, with a marked preference for chemicals, metals, real estate, pharmaceuticals, and food-processing. This left the rest of the industrial base to be expanded on the basis of internally generated investment from earnings. Levels of self-financing were low, even after businessmen began to borrow to invest after the recession of 1960–1. It was at this time that, with support from the regime, the five large banks gained control of the capitalization process. Consequently, a good deal of real control over development was forfeited by the regime. By this stage, agriculture was in no position to provide large-scale investment, although there is evidence that landowners were directing accumulated surpluses into the banking system (Luis Leal *et al*. 1975: 94–7). It was from tourism and receipts from workers overseas that the shortfall in investment was covered (Harrison 1985: 155). This wide variety of capital channelled into industrial production (the area to which both the stabilization measures and state action were directed) and into raising the capacity of the domestic market to absorb new goods and services, was the main growth agent in the process of development (Martínez Serrano *et al*. 1982). Much of this finance had been generated under autarky, particularly after 1951. The major change was that the regime now allowed its various sources to work together in an investment spiral that drove growth forward.

In opening up the economy to this type of investment-led growth, the regime in effect exchanged some of its direct powers over economic life for the political benefits that were expected from 'affluence'. The emergence of a new economic structure was naturally conditioned by that of the previous two decades. There was inevitable tension between the structural stability associated with autarky and the market 'values' now adopted by the regime. By comparison with the 1940s, industry and commerce were raised above agriculture (Sevilla Guzmán 1979: 181–4). Despite emphasis on industrialization, agriculture retained great importance within the overall economic system, but it had been marginalized in the process of rationalization. Thus, the OECD noted at the end of the stabilization period that agriculture employed some 45 per cent of the active population and accounted for more than half of the value of exports, yet it had not benefited from the policy of credit expansion (OECD Economic Survey 1961: section 18). Although investment was not forthcoming for agriculture, commercial values had an impact, thus exacerbating even further internal tensions. The OECD report for 1964 commented on Spain's need 'to apply the greatest possible effort to raise agricultural yields and reshape the pattern of production to fit the patterns of demand'.

State support for the agricultural system as a whole could not be as unconditional as it had been in the past. Nevertheless, the political support of this sector remained important to the regime. As industry grew, the processes of migration and demands on agriculture to feed the urban areas also intensified. State aid to palliate the effects of the falling supply of labour and the increased demand for food in the industrial centres were insufficient to prevent many small-scale landowners and tenants from having to leave the land in the 1960s to join the ranks of unskilled labour in the towns, or to emigrate abroad (Sevilla Guzmán 1979: 206-9). Large landowners, who had always received greater material benefits from the rigid structure and divisions of agriculture, were better able to adapt to meet more commercial conditions. The state embarked on a programme of concentration that abandoned smallholders to their fate (Sevilla Guzmán 1979: 209-19; Carr and Fusi 1979: 66-70). Demands for higher production could be met in· part by mechanization and by selectively increasing the size of cultivated areas. In effect, the number of tractors in use in Spain rose from 57,000 in 1960 to 260,000 in 1970. However, although some agricultural sectors adapted to the spiral of development and to international commercial conditions, others were simply left to wither away.

The regime encouraged urbanization and the formation of a cheap, unskilled workforce to underpin industrial growth. The drift of labour away from stagnating agriculture into industry created a new urban market for manufactured goods and imports. Equally, pressures on agriculture were lessened by imports of equipment and of food. Tractors and machinery, with which large landowners could replace scarce and expensive labour, boosted production. Shortfalls in meat and protein products were met by imports. In the 1960s, foodstuffs accounted for a steady 30 per cent of imports, which grew rapidly as Spanish industry remained unable to meet demand (Viñas *et al.* 1979: 299-306).

Once freed from the constraints of autarky, imports completed the cycle of growth. Technology transfers, raw materials, and above all cheap energy were vital to maintain the rise of productivity experienced after 1962. Export markets were opened up in EFTA and the US, helping to cover the balance of payments deficit that was the corollary of the new free market approach. At the same time, application was made to join the European Community which would bring distinct economic advantages for Spain in the early stages of industrialization, particularly in terms of agricultural exports. Rejection of the application was a long-term economic and political setback, but it was compensated by the so-called 'economic miracle' of sustained growth at unprecedented levels. For the period 1959-73, the annual rate of growth (admittedly from a low base) was 6.9 per cent; unemployment remained at below 3 per cent (see Table 7.2 p. 143) and industry definitively overtook agriculture as a percentage of GDP (García Delgado and Segura 1977: 76-88). The regime was committed to maintaining the cycle of growth. However, that cycle was itself altering the social make-up of Spain with obvious consequences in terms of the regime's basis of support.

One of the main aims of stabilization had been to raise economic confidence and to boost production; a successful policy thanks to the European boom and some breakdown of internal structural barriers to growth. However, although GDP rose rapidly from 1962, there was a low growth in living standards and low GDP/population ratio. This suggests that much of the early growth was dedicated to taking up slack demand suppressed under autarky. None the less, there were also longer term changes in the internal market taking place. While investment continued, it was dangerously dependent on keeping living standards low. This undermined the regime's determination to foster some degree of popular affluence.

Stabilization had no immediate effects on political life under the Franco regime. Nevertheless, the shift towards growth-oriented policies which had emerged from the dictatorship's internal crisis in the late 1950s inevitably re-shaped the state's role. The process of rationalization within the economy had presented the regime with difficult choices, most starkly in agriculture where it had undermined its own agrarian ideology and diminished the support of local elites. The institutional machinery of the state remained intact but a new rationale for its operation in an industrializing society had to be found. The regime's technocrats adopted the language of planning, mainly from French examples, to unite the internal forces of the dictatorship in a positive commitment to development. To this end, the OCPE announced the creation of the Comisaría del Plan de Desarrollo in 1962, with IBRD approval, as an institutional base from which the state could bargain with finance and business. In this sense, the regime simply changed the form of its economic intervention, going from a dirigiste approach to what was referred to as 'indicative planning'. Newspapers began to talk of a 'Gaullist' style whereby the regime based its appeal to society on the triumphalist rhetoric of material well-being rather than, as hitherto, on fidelity to the ideological tenets of the Falange (*The Economist* 30 March 1963).

This was the rhetoric of the first development plan produced for the period 1964–7. Growth was presented as a major justification for the regime's existence and private initiative was its core. Significantly, its publication in December 1963 coincided with the end of the first flush of economic growth. Its reanimation was a vital priority for the dictatorship. Far from loosening the relationship between the economy and the state, the clientelist nature of the regime's links with the dominant economic groups was reinforced. Important elements of continuity were thus retained and the divisions exacerbated between those inside the Francoist social coalition and those excluded. Internal conflicts which had appeared to endanger the overall health of the system were now mediated at the planning level and the economic interests of some groups, such as the peasantry, were ignored.

Despite the propaganda fanfares heralding the publication and operation of the development plan, co-ordination of state departments and budgeting was, in fact, minimal. This allowed flexible links to be established with lobbyists, but also constrained the amount of real direction that the regime could give to economic relationships (Gunther 1980: 92–105). The role of INI also changed; with control of its activities passing to the industry ministry in 1963. As before, INI was identified as an important instrument in the state's direction of economic development, now in the language of indicative planning, along the lines associated with Jean Monnet in France in the 1950s. INI was supposed to step in to fund ventures that private enterprise would not contemplate. Usually, however, its task tended to be the support of firms that were wilting under competition and in the financing of ventures in close co-operation with private capital (Schwartz and González 1981: ch. 5). For the purists of the OECD, however, state intervention was failing to come to grips with the economy at the macro-level at which state planning was supposedly aimed.

This criticism, often made in regard to agricultural productivity and the viability of new projects, failed to recognize the limits within which 'inter-vention' was operated. Strong elements of continuity in the regime's attitude to state activity still pertained. The level of state budgetary power was the lowest in western Europe giving little room for large-scale public sector spending (Martínez Serrano et al. 1982: 317–18; Gunther 1980: 46). Despite increases in wealth, taxation remained regressive, a reflection of the influence on public policy of business and large-scale agricultural interests. State activity therefore tended to follow formulas worked out by individual departments in concert with influential interests (Gunther 1980: 46–50, 73). The real significance of public policy tools as planning instruments was bound to be slight. In fact, control over monetary policy was the only one of any significance. An element of rationalization was necessary to maintain the momentum of development, particularly with regard to infra-structure. The degree to which the state could direct growth was thus highly constrained, despite its partnership position and its role as overseer of the economy. Therefore, planning had to pursue the job of rationalizing the contradictory aspirations of various groups and acting as a substitute for structural reforms.

One sign that the state was not simply directing operations from above came with the first real interruption to growth in 1964. This was the reappearance of inflation after the period of price stability enjoyed since the Stabilization Plan. The OECD saw this as a consequence of the fact that the more backward sections of the economy were slow to adapt themselves to the transformation accompanying rapid growth (OECD Economic Survey 1965: section 3). Inflation and the coexistence of developed and under-developed features, during what had become 'stop-go' growth, reflected rather fragmented state attention to financial stability and growing inequalities in every area of economic life. Special preference was given to firms and agricultural interests well connected with the regime. The tacit protection afforded to them encouraged the concentration of economic resources socially and geographically as a consequence of market growth.

Continued growth was intended eventually to overcome low living standards and remove barriers to 'affluence' at every level of society. However, inflationary tendencies in the mid-sixties militated against any redistribution of wealth by way of increasing wages. In order to stabilize prices in favour of producers, the regime devalued the currency in 1964, 1965, 1966, and 1967 which cut the real value of wages. High agricultural price levels and underproduction fuelled a spiral of inflation, the effects of which were borne by the working class (average rate for 1962–72 was 7.1 per cent). Although reliable statistics for real wage levels are not readily available, it appears that state policy reinforced an increase in wage differentials albeit against a background of continued growth. Intervention in the labour market through the Syndicates to keep labour costs down fostered growth. However, wage increases were soon to become a regular issue as the working class organized and responded to the expectations raised by the regime's propaganda. Control of labour was becoming increasingly difficult as the regime struggled with the effects of growing inequality and the need to provide material satisfaction, rendered all the more difficult by the inflation which accompanied growth.

Industrial production remained divided between small firms inadequately providing for the manufactured goods market and larger concerns, many of which had responded to export opportunities for cheap (in world terms) capital goods (Viñas et al. 1979: 326–33). Massive foreign capital and major state-linked enterprises both contributed to the general tendency towards monopoly. However, the majority of firms had a small workforce, were undercapitalized and technologically backward (Lieberman 1982: 305–8). Protection for some industries, such as steel and shipbuilding, also reinforced low levels of efficiency and the use of out-dated plant. As long as labour costs remained low and productive investment high, wide diversity in the size and scale of operation and efficiency of firms did not noticeably affect the general growth in industrial production. The state remained committed to growth as a focus for rallying business interests. However, its intervention was directed largely to big concerns well connected to world trade. Disparities between different sectors of industry began to be recognized in the second plan for social and economic development of 1968–70 which looked at the different requirements of light and heavy industry. While heavily subsidized export industries, such as transport, metals, and chemicals grew rapidly, manufacturing concerns producing mainly for the home market tended to lag behind (Wright 1977: 30–3). However, armed only with deflationary instruments, the state could foster production, but it could not guarantee the long-term viability or benefits of such production.

The social effects of industrial growth were areas of concern in the second and third plans. Mass migration from the countryside into the expanding urban centres, particularly in Madrid, the Basque country, and Catalonia, threatened to create two sets of problems. The first was to overstretch the capacity of the cities to absorb new people. Not surprisingly, the sixties saw a lot of excess labour soaked up into the housing construction industry. Generally, Spanish cities were blighted by poor apartment block developments, insanitary drainage, and bad services. The appalling living conditions of urban labour were a major factor contributing to the politicization that took place in the late 1960s (Sartorius 1975; Maravall 1978). The second problem was that the countryside was becoming depopulated and regional inequalities more pronounced in both absolute terms and as a proportion of GNP. The regime ignored the problem of urban squalor in favour of addressing localized problems, particularly in areas where its agrarian support had traditionally been strong.

Within the commitment to overall economic planning, regional inequality was singled out for special mention. However, this exposed the incompatibility between stimulating growth in general and piecemeal attempts to direct that growth into socially useful projects. 'Development Poles' of various types were adopted to favour regional investment and industrial development (Richardson 1974 gives an overview). In the third plan for 1970-4, more attention was paid to local initiatives. However, although some success was achieved in creating employment (Lieberman 1982: 262), really backward areas like Andalucia and Extremadura could not benefit from cosmetic measures which barely touched the agricultural system. In industrial poles, the transplanting of firms was noticeably less successful than home grown alternatives like the Mondragón co-operatives (Thomas 1980; González 1979: 337–42). These represented an attempt to stimulate new collective industry, self-financing and containing an element of educative/co-operative planning which experienced much more sustained and dynamic growth than other state directed projects.

Attention to such details was not possible in a centralized, nationally directed system of state-economy links which needed steady growth for its legitimacy and in which the political system was not responsive to new demands outside the carefully defined status quo. Francoism's political base within the financial and industrial elites, the urban middle-class professionals, and landowning class was losing its social cohesion. By the end of the 1960s, there was visible disjuncture between civil society and Francoist institutions (Maravall 1982: 4–19; *The Economist* 19 February 1972). This was apparent in the growth of clandestine labour organizations, middle-class discontent over rising prices, the desire of industrialists to join the EEC, and the beginnings of collective bargaining which by-passed the cumbersome mechanisms of the anachronistic official Syndicates (Preston 1976: 17–18). The nature of the dictatorship converted these essentially economic grievances into political challenges since they could not be satisfied without sweeping changes in the regime's structures. With the deceleration of economic growth which began around 1967 and was intensified by the world crisis of the early 1970s, both the limitations of Francoist authoritarianism and the consequent frustrations of the business class were exposed.

The use of police and even military force in response to strikes and the maintenance of rigidly ossified labour legislation were counter-productive. The situation called for flexibility and the co-operation of labour to achieve increased productivity and wage restraint in order to combat externally induced recession and a rising balance of payments deficit. Police brutality might have worked in the primitive rural economy of Spain in the 1940s but not in the sophisticated industrial economy of the 1970s. Repression no longer enjoyed the approval of most employers. Factory owners, construction magnates, shipbuilders, and financiers who had benefited from the 1960s development knew that strikes meant hours lost. Moreover, persistent industrial unrest deterred foreign investment. Its repression lessened the chances of Spain joining the EEC which was increasingly seen as a lifeline. Socially and economically, Spain was a very different country by the beginning of the 1970s from what it had been in 1939. The Franco regime's success in resisting political change had provided the stability which had helped promote that transformation. Paradoxically, the political rigidity which had served it so well in the 1940s and 1950s now diminished its ability to deal with the impending crisis of the 1970s.

The end of Francoism: 1973–7

The heavy dependence of the Spanish economy on foreign investment, revenues from tourism, and overseas trade made it especially vulnerable to fluctuations in the international situation. In addition, Spain was almost totally dependent on external sources for energy. In 1973, imported petroleum accounted for over 70 per cent of Spain's total energy needs (Barón 1982; Harrison 1985: 171–3; Martínez Serrano *et al.* 1982: 107–9). When OPEC raised the price, Spain was obviously obliged to take emergency action to cushion the blow. Yet, at first little happened. Because of long-standing good relations with the Arab world, Spain continued to receive ample supplies. Prices were not increased and no restrictions were placed on energy consumption. The reason for this economic irresponsibility was the political fear of the consequences of a drastic drop in living standards in a country in which the lack of liberty was justified by rises in material well-being. Moreover, the direction of the economy tended to take a back seat to political factional fighting in the years 1973–7.

This was the consequence of the uncertainty surrounding the future of the regime provoked by the assassination of Franco's right-hand man, Carrero Blanco, on 20 December 1973. With the demise of the octogenarian dictator inevitable, the descent into the bunker by some and the scramble for alliance with the moderate left by others took precedence over economic concerns, masking the seriousness of the situation and delaying its resolution (Fuentes Quintana, 1982; Pérez Díaz 1984). In the short term, the political crisis provoked by the assassination brought the regime's most conservative elements to the forefront. An inflexible team came to power as the international recession was leading to a dramatic reduction of foreign investment, and of Spanish exports, and a decline in industrial production. The 1973 trade deficit rose from $3,575 million to $7,069 million in 1974. The balance of payments on current account swung in the same twelve month period from a surplus of $557 million to a deficit of $3,245 million. By the end of 1975, the balance of payments deficit was $3,488 million (or 3 per cent of GDP) and continued to worsen until 1978 when a surplus of $1,633 million was registered (Harrison 1985: 174–5; Alcaide Inchausti 1984: 124–30). The increased cost of imported fuels raised production costs and in turn pushed up retail prices of manufactured goods. Consumer prices rose by 11.4 per cent in 1973 and at an average annual rate of 18.2 per cent, between 1973 and 1979 or twice the average of the OECD (see Table 7.2).

Table 7.2 Spanish economic performance, 1939–85

		GDP	Employment	Output per worker	Inflation[a]	Unemployment rate[b]
			Average annual % changes			%
Spain	1939–49	(3.3)			(12.0)	
Spain	1949–59	(5.4)			(5.7)	
Spain	1959–73	6.9	0.6	6.2	6.6	(2.5)[c]
OECD	1959–73	4.9	1.1	3.8	4.2	3.2 [c]
Spain	1973–9	2.5	−1.2	3.7	18.2	5.8 [d]
OECD	1973–9	2.6	1.1	1.5	9.0	5.2 [d]
Spain	1979–85	1.4	−1.6	3.1	11.8	17.4 [e]
OECD	1979–85	2.3	0.6	1.7	7.1	7.8 [e]
Spain	1959–85	4.6	−0.3	4.9	10.4	6.7 [f]
OECD	1959–85	3.8	0.9	2.8	6.0	4.7 [f]

a The cost of living index from 1939–49, the consumer price index from 1950–9, the GDP deflator from 1959–85.
b The average level in the period as % of the total labour force
c 1960–73
d 1974–9
e 1980–5
f 1960–5

Notes: (1) The data in brackets are significantly less reliable
(2) The OECD totals for GDP and inflation are based on the exchange rates of 1980

Sources: OECD Historical Statistics, 1960–85, the OECD database, Boltho 1982, and Cipolla 1976.

Unemployment also rose. This was as a result of decreased demand in the wake of the oil shock coming after the increased labour costs incurred by working-class militancy in the early 1970s and by a rise in employers' social security contributions. In addition, the European recession led to a shake-out of Spanish emigrant labourers who began to return home in large numbers. Between 1974 and 1977, the number of unemployed rose from 398,000 (2.9 per cent of the total labour force) to 832,000 (6.3 per cent) with pockets in the rural south and in the industrial belts around Madrid, Barcelona, and Bilbao where local rates far exceeded the national average (Banco de Bilbao 1982). Inflation and unemployment were to be the major problems concerning economic policy-makers in the course of the next decade.

Deprived of the safety net of world prosperity, the internal failings of the Spanish economy were starkly exposed. In spite of the pessimism of the OECD and indications that political uncertainty would deter foreign investment, the government of Carlos Arias Navarro which came into power in January 1974 failed to confront the country's economic problems. Moreover, after the death of Franco on 20 November 1975, and the eventual replacement of Arias in July 1976, the political situation continued to take priority over the economy. Arias's replacement, Adolfo Suárez, was totally absorbed in the complex task of overseeing a bloodless transition to democracy (Preston 1986: *passim*). The magnitude of the economic crisis precluded any attempt at solution which did not rest upon a consensus of employers, labour, and government. Until the structures of Francoism had been demolished, such collaboration, particularly from the labour movement which would bear the brunt of any austerity measures, was unthinkable. Moreover, hopes for economic recovery came to focus evermore on entry into the EEC and that too would require major political change as a prerequisite.

The economy in the transition to democracy: 1976–82

Aware that 'an economy in crisis constitutes a fundamental political problem' (Fuentes Quintana 1982: 16), the Suárez government set about the political reforms which were the essential prelude to adequate measures to resolve the economic crisis. The economic team believed that such measures would have to be gradual and reached by means of agreements between the social forces involved (Fuentes Quintana 1982: 18). Political parties and trade unions were legalized, the Francoist Syndicates dismantled, and democratic elections held in 1977. The stage was set for tackling the economic legacy of the Franco regime.

After his victory in the June 1977 elections, Suárez unveiled a two-pronged strategy for the economy. On the home front, the minister for the economy, Enrique Fuentes Quintana, presented a 'Programme for Rationalization and Economic Reform'. In the international arena, Spain applied in July 1977 for full membership of the EEC. The existing member nations of the EEC were already Spain's major trading partners. Full membership would provide even greater access to crucial markets. That was not only important in itself but it was seen as an incentive to extra-European investors looking for a base from which to springboard into Europe. Co-ordination with the Common Agricultural Policy was seen as a solution to rural underdevelopment (Preston and Smyth 1984: 66). In fact, EEC discussion documents make it clear that the optimum moment for Spain and the Community had probably passed by the end of the 1960s. With the Community equally affected by the oil shock, the ability of Europe to absorb Spanish exports, particularly of heavy industrial and agricultural products, was low. Nevertheless, the commitment of post-Franco governments to membership of the EEC never faltered.

Fuentes Quintana's 1977 rationalization programme was part of the preparatory groundwork essential for Spain to have a chance of being granted EEC membership. It contained a six-point proposal for the *saneamiento* (cleaning-up or rationalization) of an ailing economy: transfer of part of the investment and administrative burden from the state to the private sector; a progressive process of stabilization, reform, and reconversion in critical areas, particularly smoke-stack industries; gradual reduction of inflation through the control of labour costs; the encouragement of exports through exchange-rate and tariff controls; the modernization of existing economic institutions, especially the fiscal system and the adaptation of the productive infrastructure, with special emphasis on the energy, industrial, and agricultural sectors (Fuentes Quintana 1984: 19–23). This menu of objectives constituted the blueprint of Spanish economic policy throughout the presidency of Adolfo Suárez who resigned in early 1981. Indeed, its six principal goals remained the prime targets for later policy-makers after the Socialist Party came into power in October 1982.

The economy began to recover after 1976 thanks to increased foreign investment, a 20 per cent devaluation of the peseta in July 1977, increased revenues from income tax, and a rise in earnings from tourism. However, that growth was not sustained. Most crucially, the Suárez administration failed to come to grips both with unemployment, which rose from 6 per cent of the active population in 1977 to 15 per cent in 1981, and with inflation, which by 1981 was again running at 17 per cent. Furthermore, by the early 1980s, the balance of payments deficit had risen again to 2.5 per cent of GDP after having briefly registered a surplus in 1978 and 1979.

The Programme for Rationalization and Economic Reform reflected the Suárez government's belief that political solutions to Spain's economic problems were essential and inevitable but had to be gradual. The continuing problems of unemployment and inflation reinforced the belief that solutions involving austerity and wage control would only be feasible if they enjoyed the backing of a consensus of government, employers, trade unions, and opposition parties. This led to a series of negotiations between 8 and 13 October 1977 – the Moncloa Pacts. One feature of these accords was the imposition of a 20–2 per cent ceiling on wage increases at a time when inflation was running at 29 per cent together with the subsequent calculation of wage increases on the basis of the forecast inflation rate for any given year rather than of the rate actually registered in the previous year as had previously been the practice. In return for the unions' agreement, the government undertook to reduce inflation, to increase the state's contribution to the financing of social security, to reform the fiscal system, and to improve housing and the health service (Preston 1986: 136–8; Martínez Serrano *et al.* 1982: 247, 335).

Over the next three years, inflation dropped to 15 per cent, although remaining twice the OECD average. Monetarist policies led to a flood of bankruptcies and plant closures. The Moncloa Pacts were flawed from the very beginning by the refusal of the powerful employers' organization, the CEOE, to be bound by their terms, which were in any case obligatory for the public sector but only indicative for the private. Nevertheless, they marked a crucial watershed in the political economy of Spain. Hitherto, the parties of the left had been committed to making a clean break with Francoism. The signing of a pact between the socialist and communist parties on the one hand and a government containing many ex-servants of the Franco regime symbolized the continuity of economics between the dictatorship and the democratic regime. That in itself was a cause of chagrin on the left. Accordingly, when a brief period of growth petered out at the end of 1978 and a statutory incomes policy was announced for 1979, the unions felt as little inclined as the employers' organization to act in the conciliatory spirit of the Moncloa Pacts. On the one hand, wage increases were often conceded at levels above the 11–14 per cent band stipulated by the government and, on the other, there was an increase in strikes. In the three months prior to the general elections held in March 1979, 76 million man hours were lost through industrial action (Harrison 1985: 180).

Although Suárez's centre party, the UCD, won the elections, it had entered into a process of internal disintegration. That, together with the attrition of Basque terrorism and military conspiracy, sapped its energies. The government's inability to address the problems of the economy with anything like single-minded determination was compounded by the impact of the second oil shock. In response, the UCD announced a new Economic Programme followed, in the summer of 1979, by the National Energy Plan. Without the consensus of all the forces involved, however, such emergency measures were doomed to failure. The Economic Programme proposed a thoroughgoing liberalization prior to climbing aboard the EEC life-raft. In a context of national and international crisis, it was ill-timed and impracticable. The Energy Plan, which proposed to stimulate nuclear power, offended both the powerful traditional energy producing sector and the anti-nuclear trades unions. Moreover, UCD planners had underestimated the drop in export demand for Spanish goods and seriously overestimated the country's energy requirements (Harrison 1985: 180). Assistance came, however, from an unexpected quarter. In January 1980, the employers' organization, CEOE, and the socialist trades unions, UGT, signed the *Acuerdo Marco* (framework agreement) on collective bargaining of wage and work conditions. It reaffirmed the principle first elaborated in the Moncloa Pacts that wage rises would be based on expected rather than actual inflation. In effect, this enshrined the union's acceptance of the idea that part of any economic recovery would involve a sacrifice on the part of the workers.

The successor agreement to the *Acuerdo Marco*, the National Agreement on Employment, signed in 1981 by the government, the CEOE, and both the socialist and communist unions, went even further in confronting long-standing problems of inflation, inefficiency, and low productivity by fixing wage increases below inflation rates, making it easier for employers to dismiss workers or offer temporary employment and linking unemployment benefits to social security contributions paid. It was not, however, enough to resolve all of the problems of the Spanish economy. By 1982, inflation had been reduced slightly to 15.5 per cent but this was virtually the only positive trend. The rate of growth of GDP was stagnant at 1.7 per cent per annum over the period 1975–82. Unemployment had risen from 3.2 per cent of the active population in 1974 to 16.5 per cent in 1982. The balance of payments on current account was in deficit by more than 2 per cent of GDP and the public budget deficit was nearly 6 per cent of GDP. In a climate of growing public disenchantment, the UCD had completely lost its way. At the general elections of October 1982, the Socialist party achieved a landslide victory.

The Socialist Party in power: 1982–8

The new PSOE government inherited from the UCD more or less the same problems that Francoism had bequeathed to Suárez: inflation, external trade deficit, budgetary imbalance, decline of industrial production, and rising unemployment. This was the most politically sensitive issue and the PSOE programme had included a promise to create 800,000 new jobs. In the event, unemployment continued to climb, reaching a peak of 3 million (22 per cent of the active population) in December 1987. This was partly due to the continuing international recession. Even more, it was the consequence of the fact that in an era of dramatic technological development, Spain, with its characteristic use of a large, low-paid, unskilled, and semi-skilled workforce was ill-placed to compete. The policies pursued by the Socialists in order to remedy the defects of Spanish industry inevitably generated greater unemployment. The first Socialist Minister for Economic Affairs, Miguel Boyer, announced his economic programme in February 1983 as being the stabilization and restructuring of the economy as the prerequisite of its reactivation. The objectives were precisely those which the UCD had failed to meet because of its unwillingness to pay the political price of unpopularity. The PSOE, like the British Conservative Party, was able to enjoy the safety net of a large parliamentary majority and of a completely impotent opposition. Accordingly, it proceeded with dispatch and determination. Major efforts were made to stimulate private enterprise and to attract the support of the banking fraternity as well as of new sectors such as the electronics and communications industries, defence contractors, Spain's burgeoning media, and multinational interests.

Stabilization was seen as the keystone of a policy aimed at getting Spain into the EEC. Although political objections to Spanish entry had been wiped away, there remained major stumbling blocks in terms of Spain's ample agricultural output, especially in wine and olive oil, of her huge fishing fleet, of her over-capacity in steel and coal. Accession was not achieved until 1 January 1986 (for pre-entry negotiations, Preston and Smyth 1984: 66–80). The principal objectives were to reduce inflation, public sector deficits, and the balance of payments, to encourage foreign investment and to begin streamlining certain sectors in line with EEC policy. It was gambled that the negative consequences in terms of unemployment, increased taxation, and cuts in public services would be offset by rises in growth. Between 1983 and 1985, GDP grew at a rate of 2 per cent per annum, foreign investment revived, capital investment in machinery and equipment rose by 12 per cent. The external debt reached a peak of $31 billion in 1984 but was brought down to $28 in 1985. Inflation was brought down to 8.1 per cent by the end of 1985 and profits maintained an upward trend (OECD *Economic Survey* 1986: passim). The OECD predicted that 'prospects for self-sustained, though moderate, growth are probably better than at any time since the first oil shock' (OECD *Economic Survey* 1986: passim).

There were, however, clouds on the horizon. Unemployment at 22 per cent in 1985 was the highest of all the OECD countries. Labour shedding was especially dramatic in areas such as steel and shipbuilding. Accordingly, although average earnings rose by 9 per cent, the benefits were concentrated in the service sectors and in the growth areas of electronics and automobiles. Pockets of dire hardship were created in areas of declining heavy industry in the north. Discontent was met by government propaganda about the benefits of EEC membership, including a song entitled '¡Viva el IVA!' (Hooray for VAT!). The consequence of entry into the Community was a liberalization of conditions for exporting to and investing in Spain; the removal of protective mechanisms from Spanish industry and agriculture and the opportunity of receiving regional development funds.

Inflation was falling, there were better prospects for employment, revenue from tourism was reaching record levels, and international optimism about Spain was high. Entry into the EEC was perceived as a sufficient triumph to play a considerable role in helping the PSOE to win the October 1986 elections comfortably.

However, 1987 and 1988 saw an unexpected degree of industrial unrest with medical staff, teachers, bank employees, miners, and farmers especially militant. With a growth rate of 3.5 per cent in 1986 and an expected rate of 4 per cent in 1987, discontent was provoked by the government placing a 5 per cent ceiling on wage increases. Moreover, the unions were outraged that, while the government reduced social security contributions from employers to bring down labour costs, encourage job creation, and increase productivity, higher government revenues were not being channelled into infrastructural reform. If anything, government funds were financing, as well as a huge bill for unemployment benefits, an ever-increasing trade deficit with the EEC. Trade with the Community slid from a 200 billion peseta surplus in 1985 to a 500 billion deficit by the end of 1987 (International Country Risk Guide 1987: 40). A rift opened between the Socialist government and the socialist trade union, the UGT. Nevertheless, the commitment of the Socialist government to the economic programme initiated in 1983 has never wavered.

Conclusion

Since 1945, the Spanish economy has undergone a remarkable transformation. The goal of industrialization has been reached later than in other European countries but none the less Spain has passed from a predominantly rural to an industrial society. An economy until the 1970s based on the exploitation of a large, cheap, unskilled labour force now requires sophisticated technological, banking, and computing skills. An industry once ramshackle is now a serious competitor in the international marketplace. The bulk of this process has taken place since 1953. Before then, the Franco dictatorship was committed to policies of autarky. The consequent economic stagnation threatened the stability of the dictatorship. When Spain concluded the Pacts of Madrid with the US in 1953, she was not only concluding a military and diplomatic alliance but also expressing a commitment to the international capitalist order. This was also reflected in the work of the policy-makers who drafted the stabilization and development plans of the late 1950s and 1960s. Obedience to the recommendations of the IBRD or IMF, the aping of French planning models, were in stark contrast to the years of autarky and constituted an economic U-turn comparable to the political abandonment of fascism.

The development of the 1960s, however, took place almost in spite of the over-cautious intervention of Spanish planners. Development was above all the consequence of the combination of the domestic capital accumulation born of the repressive labour legislation of the 1940s, the receipts from emigrant workers and tourism, and foreign investment attracted by an anti-communist, anti-union regime. Ironically, having presided over, if not exactly masterminded, early growth and then seized upon growing material affluence as a source of political legitimation, the regime found itself rendered obsolete by the very pace of social and economic change. On the one hand, the industrial, banking, and business fraternities found themselves frustrated by paternalistic regulation of the labour market and by the political ostracism which kept Spain out of the EEC. On the other, a working class still deprived of political rights could no longer be bought off by constant increases in living standards after the first oil shock. A curious consensus between both was to lie at the heart of the transition to democracy. The first democratic governments under Suárez were hamstrung in reforming the economic legacy of Francoism, uneven development, and massive dependence on smoke-stack industries. Their initiatives were inhibited by grave political problems and an international crisis of enormous magnitude. The foundations were laid, however, for subsequent Socialist successes in the form of the beginnings made in the reduction of inflation. This was largely as a consequence of the considerable wage restraint accepted by the workforce which has also paid many of the hidden costs of Socialist economic achievements.

Selected dates

1945	End of Second World War: Spain excluded from postwar reconstruction projects and so reinforces its policy of economic autarky.
1947	Law of Succession: Franco declares Spain to be, in theory, a monarchy and thereby defuses international ostracism.
1948	A loan from the Chase Manhattan Bank is the first indication of a changing international attitude to Spain.
1953	Pact of Madrid: Spain receives economic, technological, and military aid from the US in return for airforce and navy bases.
1957	Appointment of new cabinet of Opus Dei technocrats committed to capitalist growth formalizes move away from Falangist autarky.
1958	Spain admitted to IMF, the World Bank and OECD.
1958	Law of Collective Bargaining initiates more flexible approach to labour relations.
1959	Stabilization Plan inaugurates a two-year period of

1962	planned devaluation, austerity, and recession as prelude to economic liberalization.
1962	Spain's first application for EEC membership.
1964	The First Plan for Economic and Social Development is introduced.
1966	The Organic Law of the State reasserts Franco's position as life-long ruler of Spain and attempts to institutionalize his regime.
1969	The Second Plan for Economic and Social Development is introduced.
1973	The first oil shock and the assassination of prime minister, Admiral Luis Carrero Blanco.
1975	Death of General Franco; restoration of monarchy under King Juan Carlos.
1976	Law of Political Reform opens the way for the legalization of political parties and trade unions.
1977	First Democratic elections since 1936, won by centre-right UCD.
1977	Moncloa Pact; beginnings of regular attempts to establish an annual prices and incomes policy.
1981	Attempted military coup revives popular support for democracy.
1982	Socialists win general elections and begin policy of thorough economic rationalization.
1986	Spain becomes a full member of the EEC.

References

Alcaide Inchausti, J. (1984) 'La distribución de la renta en España' in Linz, J.J. et al. *España: un presente para un futuro*, Madrid.
Amado, M. and Estapé, F. (1986) 'Realidad y propaganda de la planificación indicativa en España', in Fontana, Josep, *España bajo el franquismo*, Barcelona.
Amsden, J. (1972) *Collective Bargaining and Class Conflict in Spain*, London.
Anderson, C.W. (1970) *The Political Economy of Modern Spain*, Madison.
Aparicio, M.A. (1982) *El sindicalismo vertical y la formación del estado franquista*, Barcelona.
Banco de Bilbao (1982) *Informe económico*.
Banco de España (1960) *Informe Anual 1960*.
Barón, E. (1982) 'Ciclo económico y cambio político', unpublished manuscript.
Boltho, A. (ed.) (1982) *The European Economy: Growth and Crisis*, Oxford.
Bradshaw, R. (1972) 'Internal migration in Spain', *Iberian Studies*, Spring.
Burgos López, J.I. de (1973) 'El estado y el proceso económico', in Velarde Fuertes, Fraga Iribarne, M., and Campo, S. del (1973) *La España de los años 70*, vol. 2, Madrid.
Carr, R. and Fusi, J.P. (1979) *Spain: Dictatorship to Democracy*, London.
Castillo, J.J. (1979) *Propietarios muy pobres*, Madrid.
Cipolla, C.M. (ed.) (1976) *The Fontana Economic History of Europe*, 6 (2), London.

Paul Preston

Clavera, J. *et al.* (1973) *Capitalismo español: de la autarquía a la estabilización (1939-1959)*, 2 vols, Madrid.
Clinton Pelham, G. (1951) *Spain: Review of Commercial Conditions*, London.
The Economist (1963) 'Gaullism, Franco style', 30 March.
The Economist (1972) Report on Spain, 19 February.
Esteban, J. (1975) 'The economic policy of Francoism: an interpretation', in Preston, P. (ed.) (1975) *Spain in Crisis*, Hassocks.
Fuentes Quintana, E. (1982) 'Economía y política en la transición democrática española', unpublished manuscript.
García Delgado, J.L. and Segura, J. (1977) *Reformismo y crisis económica*, Madrid.
Gallo, M. (1973) *Spain under Franco*, London.
González, M.J. (1979) *La economía política del franquismo (1940-1970): dirigismo, mercado y planificación*, Madrid.
Gunther, Richard (1980) *Public Policy in a No Party State*, Berkeley, Calif.
Harrison, J. (1978) *An Economic History of Modern Spain*, Manchester.
Harrison, J. (1985) *The Spanish Economy in the Twentieth Century*, London.
Hooper, J. (1986) *The Spaniards: A Portrait of the New Spain*, London.
IBRD Report.
International Country Risk Guide (1987), London.
Luis Leal, J. *et al.* (1975) *La agricultura en el desarrollo capitalista española*, Barcelona.
Lieberman, S. (1982) *The Contemporary Spanish Economy: A Historical Perspective*, London.
Maravall, J. (1978) *Dictatorship and Political Dissent*, London.
Maravall, J. (1982) *The Transition to Democracy in Spain*, London.
Martínez Allier, J. (1971) *Labourers and Landowners in Southern Spain*, London.
Martínez Serrano, J.A. *et al.* (1982) *Economía española: 1960-1980*, Madrid.
OECD Economic Survey: Spain (1961, 1965, 1986).
Pérez Díaz, V. (1984) 'Políticas económicas y pautas sociales en la España de la transición', in Linz, J.J. *et al.*, *España: un presente para un futuro*, Madrid.
Preston, P. (1986) *The Triumph of Democracy in Spain*, London.
Preston, P. (ed.) (1976) *Spain in Crisis: Evolution and Decline of the Franco Regime*, Hassocks.
Preston, P. and Smyth, D. (1984) *Spain, the EEC and NATO*, London.
Richardson, H. (1974) *Regional Planning in Spain*, Farnborough.
Roman, M. (1971) *Los limites del desarrollo económico en España*, Madrid.
Ruedo Ibérico (1966) *Horizonte Español*, vol. 1, Paris.
Sartorius, N. (1975) *El resurgir del movimiento obrero*, Barcelona.
Schwartz, P. and González, M.J. (1981) *Una historia de INI*, Madrid.
Sevilla Guzmán, E. (1979) *La evolución del campesinado en España*, Barcelona.
Snowden, F. (1972) 'The social origins of agrarian fascism', *Archives Européenes de Sociologie*, xiii.
Tamames, Ramón (1978) *La oligarquía financiera en España*, Barcelona.
Thomas, H. and Logan, C. (1980) *Mondragón: An Economic Analysis*, London.
Viñas, A. (1980) 'Política exterior en el primer franquismo', *Revista de Estudios Internacionales*.
Viñas, A. (1981) *Los pactos secretos de Franco con Estados Unidos*, Barcelona.
Viñas, A. *et al.* (1979) *Política comercial exterior en España (1931-1975)*, 2 vols, Madrid.
Walker, J. (1948) *Spain: Review of Economic Conditions*, London.
Wright, A. (1977) *The Spanish Economy 1959-1976*, London.

Guide to further reading

In addition to the books listed below, and OECD reports, important annual reports and reviews are issued by several Spanish banks. Two of the best are the *Informe anual* of the Banco de España, which contains by far the most complete statistics and the Banco de Bilbao, *Informe anual*, which is more analytical. There is a useful synthesis of the latter in English translation.

Anderson, Charles W., 1970, *The Political Economy of Modern Spain*, Madison.

Carr, Raymond and Fusi, J.P., 1973, *Spain: Dictatorship to Democracy*, London.

Clavera, J. *et al.*, 1973, *Capitalismo español: de la autarquía a la estabilización (1939-1959)* 2 vols, Madrid.

González, Manuel Jesús, 1979, *La economía política del franquismo (1940-1970): Dirigismo, mercado y planificación*, Madrid.

Harrison, Joseph, 1978, *An Economic History of Modern Spain*, Manchester.

Harrison, Joseph, 1985, *The Spanish Economy in the Twentieth Century*, London.

Hooper, John, 1986, *The Spaniards: A Portrait of the New Spain*, London.

Lieberman, Sima, 1982, *The Contemporary Spanish Economy: A Historical Perspective*, London.

Maravall, José, 1982, *The Transition to Democracy in Spain*, London.

Martínez Allier, J., 1971, *Labourers and Landowners in Southern Spain*, London.

Preston, Paul (ed.), 1976, *Spain in Crisis: Evolution and Decline of the Franco Regime*, Hassocks.

Preston, Paul, 1986, *The Triumph of Democracy in Spain*, London.

Preston, Paul and Smyth, Denis, 1984, *Spain, the EEC and NATO*, London.

Viñas, Angel, *et al.*, 1979, *Política comercial exterior en España (1931-1975)* 2 vols, Madrid.

Wright, Alison, 1977, *The Spanish Economy 1959-1976*, London.

Chapter eight

Scandinavia

Patrick Salmon

Introduction

The four mainland Scandinavian countries – Denmark, Finland, Norway and Sweden – defy easy generalization despite their obvious similarities. Their differences, indeed, appear if anything to be becoming greater. According to one recent study, 'the notion of a common "Scandinavian model" seems futile', while *The Economist*, in a survey of 'The Nordic alternative' published in November 1987, confined its attention to Norway, Sweden, and Finland on the grounds that Iceland was 'too small to matter to anybody other than the Icelanders', whilst Denmark, the only Scandinavian member of the European Community, was coming increasingly under the influence of Brussels and Frankfurt (Mjøset 1987: 403; *The Economist* 1987a: 3). The very existence of such a survey, however, suggests that in the late 1980s the Scandinavian countries are being taken seriously in a way that they have not been, perhaps, since the early 1970s – though for rather different reasons. At that time foreigners chose to discern in Scandinavia (and in Sweden in particular) either the model post-industrial society or the Huxleyan nightmare of Roland Huntford's *The New Totalitarians* (Tomasson 1970; Huntford 1971). Now they are intrigued by the durability of the postwar Scandinavian achievement. It seems clear that the essence of that achievement – the creation of societies which are both rich and egalitarian, in which consensus is valued more highly than confrontation, and in which an extensive welfare state coexists with a competitive private sector – has survived the economic upheavals of the last decade and a half (*Scandinavian Studies* 1987).

This is an outcome which would have seemed improbable ten years ago. In the late 1970s the world looked on, not without a certain *schadenfreude*, as Scandinavian growth faltered and politics became more turbulent. Economic policies began to diverge sharply as Sweden and Norway tried to spend their way out of crisis – a strategy which worked in the short term for oil-rich Norway, but not for Sweden – while Finland and, to a lesser extent, Denmark, went in for policies more attuned to a harsher economic climate

(Andersen and Åkerholm 1982; DØR 1984; Mjøset 1987). But by the early 1980s Scandinavia was recovering its equilibrium as all four countries moved towards a more flexible approach to their problems. These problems have by no means been overcome: Denmark still faces recurrent balance of payments crises, while Norway has had to deal since 1985 with the consequences of falling oil prices. There remains, however, a large degree of consensus on the rules of the political game and the goals of government policy. The welfare state has not been dismantled in Scandinavia. Even though, therefore, the Scandinavian countries have differed in their responses to economic crisis, and though they may have become more like the rest of us, there is perhaps still something to be learned about the way they manage their affairs.

Variations in policy content and style are not, of course, of recent origin but reflect substantial differences among the four countries in terms of geographical location, resource endowment, and historical experience. Until the early 1970s Norway and Sweden enjoyed more stable growth than either Denmark or Finland not merely because their governments pursued more appropriate policies, but also because they possessed more diversified economies and produced goods for which there was a stable world demand, and because their political and social conditions created a framework conducive to rational decision-making. Denmark and Finland, by contrast, exported a narrower range of products for which prices and the rate of growth of demand were lower (Danish agricultural produce), or which experienced wide fluctuations in price (Finnish timber and paper products). They also had more fragmented political systems, and Finland in particular enjoyed much less social cohesion. In the 1970s, as we have seen, the conditions for success changed and the positions of the Scandinavian countries were partially reversed, with Finland in particular doing very well and Sweden very badly.

It is still possible, however, to make some initial generalizations about Scandinavian policy as a whole in the postwar period, and to identify certain shared perceptions and historical experiences. Two points in particular deserve special emphasis: first, the smallness and openness of the Scandinavian economies; and second, the existence of a political consensus whose centre of gravity has lain further to the left than in most other west European countries. Both of these considerations have led to policies designed to achieve stability rather than growth, and the distribution of wealth rather than its creation. The heavy dependence of the Scandinavian countries on exports, and their vulnerability to fluctuations in the world economy, place severe constraints on government policy. The attempt to pursue growth in isolation has rarely been made; and where it has, as in Norway in the late 1940s, it has been quickly abandoned. We would not, therefore, expect Scandinavian performance to deviate very much from the international norm, and in the main period of postwar growth, between 1950 and 1973, this was indeed the case.

Table 8.1 shows that over the whole period 1956–85 all four countries had growth rates of output and productivity close to the OECD average (though Finland enjoyed noticeably better than average productivity growth up to

Table 8.1 Scandinavian economic performance, 1946–85

		GDP	Employment	Output per worker	Inflation[a]	Unemployment rate[b]
			Average annual changes, %			%
Denmark	⎫	3.2			3.8	
Finland	⎬ 1946–56	5.5			11.8	
Norway	⎪	5.1			5.3	
Sweden	⎭	3.9			4.2	
Denmark	⎫	4.5	1.4	3.0	5.8	1.3[c]
Finland	⎬ 1956–73	4.9	0.4	4.5	6.3	2.1[c]
Norway	⎪	3.9	0.8	3.1	4.4	1.7[d]
Sweden	⎭	4.0	0.8	3.1	4.5	1.9[c]
OECD	1956–73	4.5	1.0	3.5	4.0	3.2[c]
Denmark	⎫	1.9	0.3	1.5	10.2	6.0[e]
Finland	⎬ 1973–9	2.3	0.7	1.6	12.6	4.4[e]
Norway	⎪	4.9	2.1	2.7	8.2	1.8[e]
Sweden	⎭	1.8	1.3	0.5	10.6	1.9[e]
OECD	1973–9	2.6	1.1	1.5	9.0	5.2[e]
Denmark	⎫	2.0	0.5	1.4	7.9	9.2[f]
Finland	⎬ 1979–85	3.4	1.3	2.1	8.7	5.2[f]
Norway	⎪	3.5	1.2	2.2	9.3	2.5[f]
Sweden	⎭	1.8	0.2	1.5	9.0	2.8[f]
OECD	1979–85	2.3	0.6	1.7	7.1	7.8[f]
Denmark	⎫	3.4	1.0	2.4	7.2	4.2[h]
Finland	⎬ 1956–85	4.0	0.6	3.4	8.1	3.3[h]
Norway	⎪	4.0	1.2	2.9	6.2	2.0[g]
Sweden	⎭	3.0	0.8	2.3	6.7	2.1[h]
OECD	1956–85	3.7	0.9	2.7	5.7	4.7[h]

a The consumer price index for 1946–9 (1946–50 for Sweden). The GDP deflator 1950–85
b The average level in the period as a % of the total labour force
c 1960–73
d 1964–73
e 1974–9
f 1980–5
g 1964–85
h 1960–85

Note: The OECD totals for GDP and inflation are based on the exchange rates of 1980

Sources: OECD *Historical Statistics, 1960–85* and the OECD database.

1973). Since 1973, of course, growth rates have fluctuated considerably; but until the early 1970s it was the consistency rather than the scale of Scandinavian growth rates which was most remarkable. It was here – in maximizing the advantages to be gained from foreign trade, and limiting the impact of externally induced fluctuations in the business cycle – that the main achievement of Scandinavian monetary and fiscal policies lay. Such policies have been designed to give as free a rein as possible to the business community: centralized planning and state ownership have played a smaller part in Scandinavia than in many other west European countries. At the same time, however, government reserves the right to take as much revenue as it needs to carry out its functions on behalf of the electorate. High levels of personal taxation and public spending, together with active labour market policies, reflect the priorities of electorates and powerful, well organized interest groups – above all the trade unions – which have kept socialist governments in power for very long periods: especially in Sweden and Norway.

The influence of the past

The roots of the postwar consensus lie deep in Scandinavian history and political culture: in the egalitarianism of societies which were until recently very poor and obliged to contend (as they still do) with harsh geographical and climatic conditions. But its immediate origins are comparatively recent (Elder *et al*. 1982). All four Scandinavian countries experienced class conflict and severe industrial unrest in the first three decades of the twentieth century, and in Finland these conflicts persisted into the postwar era. In each case conflict was resolved only when socialist parties achieved a secure hold on governmental power (Denmark 1929; Sweden 1932; Norway 1935; Finland 1966). The Scandinavian consensus is therefore, as Francis Castles (1978) has pointed out, a product of the political hegemony of the left. It represents an acquiescence in 'the social democratic image of society' on the part of all social groups – not merely the industrial working class – which is explained in part by the pragmatic character and successful record of Scandinavian socialism, but also by the historical 'weakness of the right' in Scandinavia. Castles explains this weakness by reference to two distinctive features of Scandinavian social and political development in the pre-industrial era: first, the existence of a strong and independent peasantry, less conservatively inclined than its counterparts elsewhere in Europe; and second, the corresponding absence of a powerful landowning aristocracy. The relative insignificance of the towns and of the urban middle class precluded the formation of united conservative parties, based on a merger of urban and rural interests or on a wide measure of working-class support (as in Great Britain); while the small farmers, represented by agrarian parties (renamed 'centre' parties in the postwar period) frequently formed political alliances with the socialists. A further point to note about the postwar consensus is its tendency to break down under stress. The outbreaks of industrial strife in Sweden in the late 1960s and the emergence of 'anti-system' parties in Denmark and Norway in the 1970s are obvious examples.

Consensus is not, however, merely an expression of political culture. It also represents a bargaining process between the leading interest groups – organized business and organized labour – with government as a more or less visible participant. The Scandinavian brand of corporatism is a product of the social and political changes associated with rapid industrialization in the late nineteenth and early twentieth centuries (Jörberg 1973; Turner and Nordquist 1982). Although parliamentary government came late to Scandinavia (Norway 1884; Denmark 1901; Sweden and Finland 1917), working-class political and trade union activity took on nationally based, centralized forms at an early stage. The creation of social democratic or labour parties in the 1870s and 1880s was followed at the turn of the century by the formation of central trade union organizations in Denmark, Sweden, and Norway (1907 in Finland, then still part of the Russian Empire) (Elvander 1974). This was followed in turn by the creation of employers' federations which, like their counterparts on the other side of industry, were far more disciplined and cohesive than the equivalent bodies in a country like Great Britain. In Denmark, then the most industrialized of the Scandinavian countries, agreement on the principle of collective bargaining between the two sides of industry was reached as early as 1899. But bitter disputes (notably the Swedish general strike of 1909) marked the industrial life of Sweden and Norway until the 1930s. Only the advent of socialist parties to power created a climate conducive to compromise. The 1935 Main Agreement between the Norwegian trade union organization *Landsorganisasjonen* (LO) and the employers', *Norsk Arbeidsgiverforeningen* (NAF), was followed in 1938 by the more famous Saltsjöbaden Agreement between their Swedish counterparts, *Landsorganisationen* (LO) and *Svenska Arbetsgivareföreningen* (SAF). In Finland a comparable arrangement was not reached until 1968 with the first Liinaama stabilization agreement; and the active participation of government ministers and senior civil servants, in contrast to the (ostensibly) non-interventionist stance of governments in Norway, and still more in Sweden, was a reflection of the relative weakness of the Finnish central organizations. In Denmark, despite the country's role as a pioneer of both voluntary and statutory constraints on industrial strife, their position is weaker still and the need for government intervention in industrial disputes, despite Denmark's *laissez-faire* ethos, has been correspondingly greater.

At the end of the Second World War there were considerable disparities in levels of development among the four Scandinavian countries, and these had been reinforced by differing wartime experiences (Jörberg and Krantz

1976). Sweden was by far the largest and most diversified of the Scandinavian economies: the only one of the four which could be described as fully industrialized. By the inter-war period Sweden already possessed a number of internationally competitive industries, notably in engineering and electronics; and many of the larger Swedish companies, like Electrolux, SKF, and ASEA, were multinationals. The Swedish economy had recovered rapidly from the depression in the 1930s, thanks to buoyant exports (especially of iron ore for German and British rearmament) and also (though this is still a matter for debate) to the social democratic government's experiments in counter-cyclical policy (Childs 1938; Lundberg 1957). In addition Sweden was the only Scandinavian country which managed to preserve its neutrality throughout the war: its economy therefore survived unscathed. Norwegian economic growth had been more uneven (Bergh *et al.* 1981; Hodne 1983). Industrial enclaves based on hydro-electric power had been established, notably in chemicals (Norsk Hydro) and in forestry products such as paper and pulp; and the Norwegian merchant fleet, among the largest and most modern in the world by the 1930s, was a major earner. But these had not been sufficient to counteract static or declining sectors of the economy like agriculture and fishing. The German war-time occupation had led to impoverishment and, in the far north, physical destruction; but there had been some German investment in the metallurgical industries and railway construction, and Norwegian shipping had made a large profit in Allied service (Milward 1972). Denmark, despite periods of industrialization at the turn of the century and again in the 1930s, remained heavily dependent on the agricultural sector for export earnings (Johansen 1987). She was dependent, too, upon a small number of very large foreign markets: Great Britain above all. Protectionism in Britain and Germany hindered Danish recovery in the 1930s, and dependence on the British market was to remain a source of instability in the postwar years. The Finnish economy was the least advanced of all (47 per cent of the population was still dependent on agriculture for its livelihood in 1950), and had suffered the most from war and its aftermath (Fredrickson 1960; Kindleberger 1987; Singleton 1987). The consequences of the two wars fought and lost against the Soviet Union between 1939 and 1944 included extensive territorial losses, a major refugee problem and a heavy reparations burden.

The objectives and instruments of policy

The making of economic policy in postwar Scandinavia has therefore proceeded from widely differing starting points which reflect significant differences in historical experience and levels of development. Variations in policy content and style emerge particularly clearly when we consider the fundamental question of the relationship between the state and the economy. Denmark, where governments have often been weak, has favoured a non-interventionist approach, but its governments have frequently been obliged to impose short-term crisis solutions owing to recurrent balance of payments crises, and in the absence of less drastic means of controlling the economy. As we have seen, the central trade union and employers' organizations are relatively weak, while the Danish central bank (still a privately owned institution) has found it difficult to control the expansion of lending by the commercial banks despite the new powers acquired by legislation in the 1960s. Sweden has made much of the autonomy of the wage-bargaining process between SAF, LO, and the white-collar unions in which, it is suggested, government intervention is unnecessary as well as undesirable. In practice, governments have always found means of making their wishes known to the two sides of industry in terms which ensure that they will at least be taken very seriously (Shonfield 1965); while the myth of non-intervention suffered severe damage when the government was obliged to bring the public service strike of 1971 to a forcible end.

In Norway and Finland the state has traditionally played a more direct role as a means of safeguarding newly won independence (dating from 1905 and 1917 respectively), making good war-time damage and (especially with the North Norway Plan of 1952) promoting regional development. The preservation of national energy resources from foreign control is a long-standing Norwegian preoccupation, stretching from the controversy over hydro-electric power in the early years of the century to the creation of Statoil in 1972, and beyond. The postwar labour government in Norway was also strongly committed, at least until the early 1950s, to socialist planning and state ownership. Through the nationalization of the Norwegian central bank in 1949, legislation to control the volume of lending by the commercial banks, and most of all through the establishment of state banks, governments have acquired a large degree of control over the supply of credit. The National Housing Bank of Norway (founded in 1946) has been responsible for half the total volume of lending since the war (Bergh *et al*. 1981). In postwar Finland only the state was capable of carrying through the enormous investment effort necessitated by war-time destruction and the peace terms imposed by the Soviet Union in 1944. The Finnish Central Bank has also exerted greater influence on economic policy than have its counterparts elsewhere in Scandinavia. It has been enabled to do so by the nature of the Finnish banking system, which is characterized by the indebtedness of the commercial banks to the Bank of Finland; by frequent changes of government; and by the Finnish tradition of having strong personalities as governor of the Bank. The relative ease with which such men can move between the political and financial worlds is well illustrated by the career of Mauno Koivisto, a former social democratic prime minister who dominated economic policy as governor of the Bank of Finland in the late 1970s, before going on to be elected president of the republic. Levels of state ownership remain higher in Finland and Norway than in the other Scandinavian countries, though still low by west European standards (Elvander 1981). In both countries, too, governments have frequently intervened in wage formation.

Differences between the Scandinavian countries are also revealed in their attitudes towards international economic co-operation and integration. Although they share a preoccupation with the preservation of national sovereignty, the four countries are pulled in different directions by differing political allegiances (Denmark and Norway to NATO; Sweden to neutrality; Finland to neutrality and a special relationship with the Soviet Union), and by the influence of domestic interest groups. Governments and the business community have generally been strongly committed to participation in international trade, but other members of society like Norwegian (but not Danish) farmers and fishermen, and economic isolationists at both ends of the political spectrum, have been much more sceptical and have occasionally been able to throw policy off course, as in the Norwegian EEC referendum of 1972. Whilst, therefore, the Scandinavian countries have participated actively in efforts, such as GATT or EFTA, aimed at reducing tariff barriers, as well as in the de-regulation of capital markets in the mid-1980s, serious difficulties have arisen in confronting organizations which imply economic or political integration even among themselves, let alone with non-Scandinavian countries (Miljan 1977). Finland, of course, has special problems arising from the need to take account of Soviet interests: Finnish membership of EFTA was accomplished only with the signature of a special FINEFTA agreement in 1961, and membership of the EEC is a political impossibility (although a free trade agreement with the EEC was signed in 1973) (Maude 1976). But the four countries failed to reach agreement either on a Nordic customs union in the late 1950s, or on the economic union, NORDEK, proposed by Denmark in 1968 (Haskel 1976; Wendt 1981). In each case negotiations were derailed by the rival attractions of broader European arrangements: EFTA and the EEC respectively. The question of EEC membership provoked the deepest divisions of all. Sweden showed considerable interest in membership in the 1960s – an interest still held strongly today by the business community – but eventually decided that it was incompatible with national sovereignty and neutrality (Waite 1974). In Norway and Denmark the issues were more complex (Allen 1979; Hodne 1983; Johansen 1987). Powerful economic interests and a traditionally close relationship with Great Britain led both countries to follow the British lead in applying for membership. In both countries, however, public opinion was sceptical; and whilst Denmark joined the EEC at the same time as Britain, in Norway an alliance of backwoods agrarian and radical left-wing sentiment led to rejection of membership by a narrow margin. The Scandinavian countries have therefore proved 'not only reluctant Europeans, but reluctant Nordics' (Miljan 1977: 284).

As we turn to examine the policies of individual countries, we should bear in mind the chronological distinction made earlier between the long period of stable growth up to the early 1970s and the period of instability thereafter. Each period, it was suggested, could be broadly associated with the policy approach of one or more countries. Norway set the tone for the first phase of postwar reconstruction as both Danish and Swedish social democrats sought (largely unsuccessfully) to emulate their Norwegian colleagues' commitment to the centrally directed economy (Lundberg 1957; Johansen 1987). From the mid-1950s onward it was the Swedes above all who seemed consistently more successful and more innovative than the rest in their pursuit of economic stability through active counter-cyclical policies. In the 1970s and early 1980s Norway enjoyed rapid growth in defiance of international trends, thanks to North Sea oil; but it was Denmark and, above all, Finland, which seemed to have adapted most successfully to a harsher economic climate.

Norway

The Norwegian postwar experiment had much in common with other western European efforts to avoid repeating the mistakes of the inter-war period, and to combine growth and social justice by means of social and economic planning (Milward 1984). Labour Party politicians and economists looked first and foremost to Britain as a model (Pharo 1984) but subjected the economy to controls over prices, consumption, and production which were 'more stringent than in other democratic countries' with the explicit aim of 'transforming society into a socialist order', as prime minister Gerhardsen put it (Hodne 1983: 143; Bourneuf 1958).

They also relied on 'national budgets' as instruments of economic forecasting, as well as on a large measure of direct investment. The liberalization of the international economy in the early 1950s, combined with business and, significantly, trade union opposition led to the dismantlement of much of the control machinery (although automobile rationing was not ended until 1960). But the government retained a large measure of control over the scale and direction of investment, thus contributing to one of the most distinctive features of Norwegian postwar development: a very high level of capital formation (see Table 8.2), much of it tied up either in large-scale industrial ventures like iron and steel or aluminium works, which yielded low returns; or in housing, much of it of very high quality, on which the return was naturally even lower. Norway was thus 'saddled with the highest capital coefficient among the OEEC countries' (Hodne 1983: 170). The reasons had to do, on the one hand, with the government's commitment to capital and energy-intensive industries which could utilize Norway's hydro-electric reserves, while at the same time contributing to the economic development of the more northerly regions (as well as, debatably, demon-

Table 8.2 Non-residential fixed investment, 1950–70 (as % of GNP at current prices) (average of ratios for years cited)

	1950–60	1960–70
Denmark	14.0	16.9
Finland	19.6	20.0
Norway[a]	23.7	23.8
Sweden	15.5	17.3
Western Europe (average)	15.4	18.1

a Includes some elements of repair and maintenance excluded by other countries

Source: Maddison 1976: 487.

strating the superiority of state over private enterprise); and on the other hand, with the social priority of improving living standards, in this case housing.

The relatively modest record of success enjoyed by state-owned industries did not, however, deter Norwegian governments from playing an active role in the exploitation of North Sea oil reserves in the 1970s (Noreng 1980; Alt 1987). Elsewhere in Scandinavia the extension of state ownership has generally been for pragmatic rather than ideological reasons. In Finland, where a modern industrial sector had to be established virtually overnight in order to meet Soviet reparations demands, an active state role was, as we have seen, unavoidable. Several state-owned concerns were set up in the immediate postwar period, and their number was augmented with the construction of enterprises such as steelworks in the 1960s and 1970s. Such enterprises appear to have a better management record than their counterparts in Norway or Sweden (Elvander 1981). The Swedish social democrats have been particularly cautious in their attitude towards nationalization since the vehement reaction to their radical twenty-seven point programme of 1944 on the part of the non-socialist parties. The establishment in 1969 of the state holding company AB Statsföretag to co-ordinate the management of existing state-owned firms was justified mainly on grounds of efficiency, while the main wave of postwar nationalization was initiated, as we shall see, by *non*-socialist governments after 1976 (Turner and Nordquist 1982).

Sweden

Conditions in Sweden after the war were exceptionally favourable for experimentation in counter-cyclical policy (Lundberg 1957, 1968; Lindbeck 1975). An unbroken period in office from 1932 onwards gave the social democratic government the confidence to learn from mistakes and avoid radical changes of course. The Swedish social democrats were open-minded and ready to accept the advice of economists who, in turn, were generally practical men with little liking for the ivory tower. The business community for its part was receptive to socialist experiments, not least because the socialists so clearly favoured an efficient business sector. The Swedish economy was, finally, small and easy to control (though, being small, it was also exposed to external pressures). Much could be achieved through informal contacts between a small number of people in key positions – in government, business, the labour movement and so on. Swedish policy was aimed not merely at straightening out fluctuations of the business cycle, but also at facilitating long-term growth and structural change in the economy. Two key principles were involved: first, control of the level and timing of aggregate investment; and second, manpower planning through control of the labour market. Both tasks (the second of which will be discussed below, p. 170) were entrusted to a characteristically Swedish corporatist institution, the Labour Market Board (AMS) which, by the late 1950s, had at its disposal a sophisticated array of instruments for influencing the level and timing of investment so that it could be increased during recessions and reduced during booms (Jones 1976). The most important of these were the incentives offered to both public authorities and private industry to time their investment decisions for the appropriate stage of the business cycle. Bodies in the public sector were encouraged to prepare a 'shelf' of investment projects which could be activated as soon as the AMS gave the word. Their incentive was simply the knowledge that if they did not have plans ready, other agencies would be allowed to fill the gap. Private firms were offered tax incentives. If they put part of their profits aside in special investment funds, the money was untaxed but could only be released for approved projects, at a time determined by the AMS. The sums accumulated in this way were very large indeed and could have a significant impact on investment levels. The 1,200 million kronor released for additional building in the winter of 1962–3 amounted to more than a quarter of all fixed investment in manufacturing and construction (Shonfield 1965). Business did not resent the intrusion, generally taking the view that, as a director of one large company put it, 'the tax advantages far outweighed any inconvenience' (Jones 1976: 24).

These methods appear to have worked well in the period 1955–63, but less well thereafter, mainly because the authorities found it easier to stimulate economic activity during recessions than to choke it off during booms (Lindbeck 1975). They may also have contributed to the growing uncompetitiveness of Swedish industry by favouring firms with high *past* profits rather than less well established but possibly more innovative ones. Above all, however, they encouraged complacency. In the 1970s 'the Swedish economy became the victim of its own success' (DØR 1984: 176). Traditional counter-cyclical remedies were applied in anticipation of an upswing that never came, while governments resorted increasingly to 'political interference in industrial decision-making' (Lundberg 1982: 218), most notably by means of subsidies to uncompetitive industries such as shipbuilding (Premfors 1984).

Post-1973

In *Sweden* the weakness in policy became particularly obvious after 1973. The greatest mistakes, ironically, were made by a succession of non-socialist coalition and minority governments between 1976 and 1982. Lacking the experience of their social democratic predecessors, sharing their commitment to full employment and welfare but not their readiness to tax, these governments presided over 'the most intense period of nationalization of private industry in Swedish history', as well as pushing industrial subsidies, budget deficits and foreign indebtedness to record levels (Premfors 1984: 266). Sweden's performance was among the weakest of all OECD countries in the late 1970s.

The position of *Norway* from the mid-1970s to the oil price fall of 1985 was entirely different from that of the other Scandinavian countries owing to the discovery and exploitation of North Sea oil (Noreng 1980; Alt 1987). In direct employment terms, the impact of oil was not very great, with fewer than 10,000 people directly engaged in oil production and drilling by 1985, and perhaps 64,000, or 3 per cent of the labour force, engaged in oil-related activities (OECD 1987b). But the overall impact has been enormous, with oil and gas accounting for 49 per cent of total Norwegian exports in 1985, against 9 per cent in 1975, and rising from 2 to 19 per cent of total government revenue over the same period. The government participated actively in oil exploitation through Statoil, which enjoyed a near monopoly position among Norwegian oil companies, and pursued a draconian taxation policy towards the multinationals. It also used oil to finance counter-cyclical policies similar to those of Sweden, with heavy subsidies to exposed industries such as shipping and shipbuilding. As oil prices rose, the government abandoned its initial caution, borrowing on the security of prospective oil revenues. As in Sweden, inflation and foreign indebtedness rose sharply and structural change in manufacturing industry was delayed. In the longer term 'domestic absorption of oil revenue was associated with cost and price pressures, causing severe loss of international competitiveness' (OECD 1987b: 7). The experience was similar to that of Great Britain, though the results were less severe: partly, it has been suggested, because the Norwegian krone was less exposed than the pound to speculative pressures (Alt 1987). Nevertheless, until 1985, Norway enjoyed years of stronger and more stable growth than did other European OECD countries, with very low unemployment and large balance of payments and budget surpluses.

Among the three non-oil economies, the performance of *Finland*, 'the Nordic "economic miracle" of the late 1970s' (Mjøset 1987: 443), was the most dramatic. Finnish policy since the war had been aimed at maximizing economic growth, with an emphasis on, for example, low interest rates as a means of encouraging investment. But strict budgeting, together with the price sensitivity of Finland's key export industries – timber, pulp, and paper – had made the Finnish economy vulnerable to cyclical fluctuations, leading to repeated balance of payments crises and a series of major devaluations (OECD 1986). The unusually deep recession of 1974–6 helped Finland to adjust earlier than most other countries to the first oil shock, but seems to have persuaded the Finnish authorities to adopt a new medium-term strategy aimed at stability rather than growth at any cost. Greater fiscal flexibility was reflected in highly selective taxation policies designed to increase investment and the competitiveness of specific industrial sectors, and in a rapid growth of cyclically adjusted spending. In one sense, therefore, Finland was belatedly turning to counter-cyclical policies reminiscent of those long practised by Sweden and Norway – a development paralleled by the growing stability of Finnish domestic politics. At the same time, however, 'the premises of the Finnish model involve a high level of conflict, high unemployment during the downturn, and a less developed welfare state than elsewhere in Scandinavia' (Mjøset 1987: 444). It should also be remembered that Finland gained considerably from the growth of her trade with the Soviet Union and other eastern bloc countries in the late 1970s.

Denmark, finally, represented a success story of a different kind in the early 1980s. Denmark's postwar transition from agriculture to manufacturing industry had been accomplished only with difficulty. As late as 1958 agriculture was still the dominant export sector, and it was for this reason that Danish performance in the 1950s was relatively poor, comparable only with that of Great Britain among west European countries (Johansen 1987). In the 1960s, however, the Danish economy grew very fast, with a proliferation of small, high-technology, and export-oriented industries. Growth was accompanied by a rapid expansion of both private and public spending: it was in this period that Denmark established a welfare state on the Norwegian and Swedish model. But the industrial sector, though healthy, was too small to support such a high level of spending. This is the fundamental structural weakness which still lies at the heart of Denmark's problems. It was exacerbated by the growing fragmentation of the Danish political system. The four parties which dominated the system up to 1973 bought electoral support, and achieved inter-party agreement when forming coalitions, by means of inflationary wage settlements and elaborate welfare provision. These were financed by a rapidly growing external deficit, and tax levels which rose from being among the lowest in Scandinavia to among the highest between 1968 and 1972 (Mjøset 1987). Political fragmentation was exacerbated in the early 1970s as voters abandoned traditional allegiances (notably to the social democrats) in favour of anti-system parties of both left and right, of which the most notorious was Mogens Glistrup's

Progress (anti-tax) Party. Following the 1973 general election the number of parties represented in the Danish parliament rose from five to ten. After years of hesitant 'stop-go' policies under a succession of weak Social Democratic-led goverments, and a deepening economic crisis in the early 1980s, a conservative-led coalition came to power in 1982 pledged to policies of unprecedented austerity. Accepting a much higher rate of unemployment (which had already reached 10 per cent by 1982) than had hitherto been acceptable in Scandinavia (apart from Finland), the Schlüter government squeezed wages and profits and attacked public spending. In the short term its success was spectacular. Budget and balance of payments deficits were cut, inflation fell, and investment rose. Danish growth rates were among the highest in Europe in 1984 and 1985.

Economic performance

Scandinavia's progress 'from subsistence to abundance' (Bergh *et al.* 1981: 1) over the past century has been an astonishing success story. Most of the progress has been made since the Second World War. By international standards, Scandinavian growth rates have not been exceptional; but, especially in Sweden and Norway, they have been remarkably stable over long periods and have been accompanied by lower levels of unemployment (see Table 8.1) and greater equality of distribution than in most other industrialized nations (Ringen 1987). Government policy clearly deserves much of the credit for these achievements. Against them must, however, be set more disturbing features. Scandinavia has been distinguished for much of the postwar period by inflation rates and levels of personal taxation and public consumption considerably higher than in other OECD European countries (see Tables 8.1, 8.3, and 8.4). Such disparities, maintained over long periods, have serious implications for Scandinavian competitiveness in foreign and domestic markets, as well as for profit margins and personal incentives. For these, too, government policy must take much

Table 8.3 The share of taxation[a] in output, 1955–79 (in % of GDP)

	1955–7	1962–4	1969–71	1977–9
Denmark	(25.1)	(28.4)	39.8	42.8
Finland[b]	(31.5)	(28.3)	32.3	37.0
Norway	(29.0)	(33.1)	40.2	46.6
Sweden	(26.6)	(32.7)	41.1	50.8
OECD Europe	(25.4)	(28.0)	31.5	36.9

a General government tax revenues
b Excluding contributions to some pension funds which in the other countries are considered part of taxation; in the late 1970s these would have boosted the output share by some 5 to 6 per cent of GDP

Source: Andersen and Åkerholm 1982: 613.

Table 8.4 The share of government consumption in output, 1960–85 (in % of GDP)

	1960–73	1974–9	1980–5
Denmark	17.9	24.2	26.9
Finland	14.0	17.5	19.2
Norway	15.9	19.6	19.0
Sweden	19.5	25.9	28.4
OECD Europe	14.8	17.4	18.8

Source: OECD 1987c.

of the responsibility; although inflation results also, as the well known 'Scandinavian model' of inflation suggests, from the impact of external price fluctuations on small open economies (Edgren *et al*. 1973; Aukrust 1977). The dilemmas of Scandinavian policy arise from the pursuit of ambitious social goals in such exposed conditions. Ironically, the stronger the national consensus and the more successful the government in its pursuit of non-economic objectives, the graver are the implications for enterprise, structural change, and growth. It is significant that Finland, the country where consensus is weakest, has, as we have seen, adapted more successfully than Norway and Sweden to the economic challenges of recent years.

In assessing Scandinavia's postwar performance we therefore have to bear in mind the relationships between, on the one hand, 'socialist planning' and 'market forces' and, on the other, 'internal decisions' and 'international factors' – to borrow the terms used by Hodne in his discussion of the Norwegian economy (Hodne 1983: 182–3). The international context, though in many ways the most important of all, has been discussed in Chapter 2. It is sufficient here to say that the Scandinavian countries participated fully in the unprecedented growth of the international economy after the Second World War, in which technological innovation and increased productivity; high levels of demand, savings, and investment; and the expansion of international trade, all played their part. We should be aware, however, of the magnitude of the structural transformation which all the Scandinavian economies have undergone. At the end of the war Scandinavian society was still largely rural. Even in Sweden, 20 per cent of the population was engaged in agriculture: by the early 1980s, the proportion had fallen to 6 per cent. All four countries have moved away from dependence on agriculture and the export of a narrow range of raw materials and semi-finished products, to become modern, urbanized societies with an increasingly diversified industrial base. The shift of the workforce from less productive sectors like agriculture and forestry into the manufacturing and service sectors (which was of course paralleled elsewhere in continental Europe) brought about a major increase in productivity and living standards but, as one Swedish banker reflected, it 'has been done once and for all. We cannot do it again. Many other industrial countries experienced such a change much earlier in their development' (Jan Wallander, in Nabseth and Wallander 1982: 76). The transformation remains incomplete: raw materials and food products still form a higher proportion of Scandinavian exports than they do in most other European OECD countries, exposing the Scandinavian countries to rapid price fluctuations – sometimes, but not always, to their advantage (Mjøset 1987: 422). And in exceptional cases, as in that of Norwegian oil, the trend towards diversification is reversible (Bergh *et al.* 1981: 14).

Nevertheless, what Hodne writes of Norway can be applied *mutatis mutandis* to all the Scandinavian countries: 'The motor of postwar growth was above all manufacturing, notably mechanical engineering and power-intensive industries' (Hodne 1983: 263). To understand Scandinavian growth we must therefore try to discover what has made Scandinavian industries so successful. The answer lies in two areas: first, management investment decisions; second, the nature of the workforce.

Although Scandinavian investment ratios have been high for most of the postwar period (the particular exception is Denmark after 1973, see Tables 8.2 and 8.5), success depends, as Jones (1976) has pointed out, on quality as well as quantity: on choosing the right concept at the right time. Swedish industry in particular has evolved sophisticated mechanisms for evaluating market potential, and has also been careful to assess the attitude of the work force towards technological innovation. It has been assisted by government not only through the investment funds discussed earlier, but also through special depreciation allowances to encourage modernization. Because so many of the major companies are multinationals, Swedish industry has also been able to spread its research and production costs to a greater extent than has been possible in the other Scandinavian countries. Opinions differ as to whether Swedish industries are sufficiently enterprising. Wallander, regarding Swedish corporations as 'highly imaginative and innovative' points to the creation of a Swedish car industry almost from nothing in response to war-time blockade, and to its subsequent capture of a world market in apparent defiance of commercial logic (Nabseth and Wallander 1982). Others, however, have noted the negative impact of taxation and profit-squeezing on investment levels, and have blamed the

Table 8.5 Gross fixed capital formation, 1950–85 (average annual changes, %)

	1950–60	1960–73	1973–9	1979–85
Denmark	5.3	6.4	−1.4	−0.7
Finland	7.6	5.5	−1.6	3.7
Norway	3.1	5.9	2.1	−1.2
Sweden	5.6	4.0	−0.6	1.6
OECD Europe	7.1	5.5	0.3	0.2

Sources: Andersen and Åkerholm 1982: 621; OECD 1987c.

bureaucratization of management and its close relationship with government for the absence of an 'enterprise culture' (Lindbeck 1975: *The Economist* 1987b: 75). Industry in the other Scandinavian countries has also come in for criticism. Research and development expenditure is low by international standards, and there is relatively little collaboration between the universities and industry (Hodne 1983). In Norway at least, tertiary education has tended to stress technological rather than commercial expertise: Hodne contrasts the commercial success of the Danish Bang and Olufsen company with that of the Norwegian Tandberg in the field of household electronic goods, despite the technical superiority of the latter's products (Hodne 1983). Yet a small selection of internationally known names – Elopak (Norway); Saab and Volvo (Sweden); Wärtsilä (Finland); Lego (Denmark) – suggests that there exists in all the Scandinavian countries a large measure of expertise in selling high quality engineering products on world markets.

The contribution of the labour force to Scandinavia's economic success can be judged first by its growth in absolute terms, and second by its qualitative improvement in terms of higher skills and attitudes towards change. In each of these areas government, management, and trade unions have been prepared to work together to match the labour supply to the demands of industry. The result, making due allowance for the aberrations of Swedish and Norwegian industrial policy in the 1970s, and for Danish and Finnish tolerance of rather higher unemployment levels, seems to confound the assumption that growth and full employment are mutually incompatible. Until the 1960s, the labour force grew only modestly in relation to the growth in total output. As we have seen, however, there was a marked shift in occupational structure, reflecting considerable geographical mobility within each country and also, to a lesser extent, between the Scandinavian countries (especially from Finland to Sweden). In Sweden in particular, mobility has been assisted by active labour market policies: help with the costs of relocation even extends to the purchase by the AMS of a worker's house or flat if he or she moves to a different part of the country. From the late 1960s the labour force grew much faster, partly for demographic reasons; mainly because of the growth of female employment; but again thanks also to government policy. Once again Sweden was the pioneer in expanding employment opportunities for disadvantaged members of society, notably the handicapped.

The qualitative improvement in the workforce has been due in part to the high level of capital investment noted earlier: new equipment both demands and teaches new skills. But it has also been based upon the traditionally high levels of education in Scandinavia, as well as upon retraining and the introduction of new working methods which have been promoted by government and unions as well as by management. There may well be an element of disguised unemployment in, for example, the large numbers of people engaged in training or retraining in Sweden; but, like every other aspect of labour market policy, they represent an active contribution to industrial restructuring. One function of such policies is to persuade the trade unions that rationalization need not mean unemployment.

There are other explanations, however, for the unions' generally positive attitude towards change. They enjoy a strong position in countries where union membership is high and still growing, and organized in a small number of industry-wide unions (the Swedish LO has only twenty-five members), but where, with the exception of Finland, strike activity has generally been low (see Table 8.6). In Norway and Sweden they have been in partnership with socialist governments for decades. They enjoy a close and usually amicable relationship with their opposite numbers on the management side. Above all, they have accepted the need for innovation in technology and working practices and – especially after the disastrous policy of subsidization in the 1970s – for the elimination of uneconomic industries: 'The Nordic unions, never Luddite, see no point in members producing goods that cannot be sold at a profit' (*The Economist* 1987a: 7). The unions extract, of course, a price for their acquiescence. They demand not merely higher living standards and improved working conditions for their members, but also a reduction in wage disparities. The resulting problem of 'wage drift' from the more productive to the less productive sectors of the economy has long been recognized as a major contributor to high inflation (Shonfield 1965). They also demand a voice in management decisions. 'Industrial democracy' in the shape of worker directors was pioneered in Norway and Sweden, as in West Germany, in the 1970s. In the

Table 8.6 Average number of working days lost through industrial disputes,[a] 1969–78

Country	Working days lost per 1,000 employees
Finland	1,143
Denmark[b]	575
Norway	79
Sweden[c]	42
W. Europe[d] (average)	627
Industrialized countries (average)[e]	749

a In the mining, manufacturing, construction, and transport industries
b Figures up to 1974 are only for manufacturing
c Figures to 1971 relate to all sectors of employment
d The four countries above plus Belgium, France, Germany, Ireland, Italy, Netherlands, Spain, and UK
e W. Europe plus Australia, Canada, Japan, New Zealand, and USA

Source: Elder et al. 1982: 162.

171

form, for example, of the wage-earners' funds envisaged in the Swedish Meidner Plan, democratization was highly controversial (Hodne 1983; Jones 1976; Childs 1980). But the presence of worker directors on the board has proved by no means disadvantageous to industry. Union leaders have a better understanding of difficult management decisions and are able to explain them to their members (*The Economist* 1987b).

Conclusion

Postwar Scandinavian policies have been viewed in a variety of lights: as highly successful examples of Keynesian economic management (Shonfield 1965); as object lessons in the dangers of too much interference in the free play of market forces (Hodne 1983); or as a sustained confidence trick practised upon the working classes by sophisticated capitalists and their social democratic collaborators (Hufford 1973; Christiansen 1984). None of these interpretations, needless to say, offers a sufficient explanation of the strengths and weaknesses of Scandinavian performance. It would be a mistake, however, to regard Scandinavian policy merely as an exercise in damage limitation – protecting the Scandinavian economies from economic forces over which they have little or no control. Scandinavian performance is always dependent on external conditions: this has been as true in recent years as it was during the main period of postwar growth up to the early 1970s. Fluctuations in the price of oil perhaps offer the clearest illustration. High oil prices benefited Norway until 1985 and contributed (through the bilateral relationship with the Soviet Union, Finland's chief oil supplier) to the rapid growth of Finnish-Soviet trade in the late 1970s, while falling oil prices boosted Swedish performance from 1986 onwards. From Scandinavia's position of dependence, with its attendant costs and benefits, there can be no escape.

But recent experience suggests that the Scandinavian countries also have considerable scope for influencing their own performance – at least in a negative sense. This is a matter of both official policy and public attitudes, and was most evident in the contradictory Scandinavian responses to the faltering of growth and the onset of 'stagflation' in the early 1970s. Policy reflected, on the one hand, overconfidence in the self-correcting mechanisms of the business cycle, and on the other, a resort to selective intervention on political grounds. Such 'fumbling', as Mjøset puts it, was especially evident, as we have seen, in Sweden and Denmark (Mjøset 1987: 419–20). Public attitudes towards the economy, the welfare state, and the environment were meanwhile undergoing a kind of crisis which manifested itself in a variety of ways. On the one hand, more was being demanded, in terms of better public services and higher living standards, than the economy was able to deliver. On the other hand, new demands were being articulated which wholly or partly rejected the tenets of welfare capitalism, and which ranged from the 'welfare backlash' (of which the right-wing Glistrup party was the most notorious example and the conflicts of Ingmar Bergman and Astrid Lindgren – both social democrats – with the Swedish tax authorities the most unfortunate) to a vocal espousal of environmental issues. Concern for the environment – in, for example, the controversies over nuclear power in Sweden, or the Alta River project in North Norway, or acid rain – is not, of course, unique to Scandinavia; but it is perhaps especially deeply felt among populations which are so sophisticated and yet so close to their rural roots.

By no means all of the problems that surfaced in the 1970s have been overcome. Many of the weaknesses of current Scandinavian policy to which the OECD, for example, frequently draws attention in its surveys – inflationary wage settlements; excessive public expenditure and so on – are directly attributable to the persistence of habits which became ingrained during the heyday of welfare capitalism. This may be true, too, of other, less familiar examples of Scandinavian improvidence such as the disincentives to saving which are built into the tax systems of Denmark and Norway (where interest expenditure enjoys unlimited tax deductibility) (OECD 1987b: 10; OECD 1988: 59; OECD 1987a: 47-8). Such problems are made all the more intractable by the continuing fragmentation of Scandinavian domestic politics: minority or near-minority government has become the rule, and there has been a proliferation of anti-system parties, populist and sometimes even racist in tone. The difficulties have been greatest in Norway, where the oil price fall hit an economy that was already overheated; and in Denmark, where repeated bouts of austerity have failed to cure an endemic balance of payments crisis. The inconclusive outcome of the 1987 general election, in which both the extreme left and the extreme right gained ground at the expense of the centre, is an expression of the political instability which has been intensified by the Schlüter government's failure, despite its brave start, to master the structural weaknesses of the Danish economy.

Yet the 1980s have also seen the economic revival of Sweden under a social democratic leadership which, if less charismatic since the death of Olof Palme, has not broken with the postwar consensus in its bid for growth. Most remarkably of all, perhaps, Finland has gone against recent Scandinavian trends to become more Keynesian in its economic policies and more consensual in its politics, while at the same time maintaining and deepening its special relationship with the Soviet Union. The election as president of the former social democratic leader, Mauno Koivisto, in 1981, and the coming to power of a conservative-led coalition in 1987 – both hitherto anathema in Soviet eyes – reflect the growing maturity of Finnish politics which has gone hand in hand with economic diversification.

We return finally, therefore, to the two general points made near the outset: international exposure and domestic consensus. For much of the postwar period a combination of good luck and good management enabled the Scandinavian countries to enjoy unprecedented economic growth and political stability. If the experience of the 1970s and 1980s has shown that 'economic growth, clearly, is not a gift, nor is it won once and for all' (Hodne 1983: 264), there remain considerable grounds for faith in the Scandinavian capacity to balance growth and welfare even under conditions of greater economic uncertainty.

Selected dates

1944	Armistice between Finland and Soviet Union. Twenty-seven point programme of Swedish social democrats.
1945	Liberation of Denmark and Norway. Norwegian Joint Programme on economic policy.
1946	First Norwegian National Budget.
1947	Finnish-Soviet Peace Treaty.
1948–53	Marshall Aid to Denmark, Norway and Sweden. Finnish-Soviet Treaty of Friendship, Cooperation and Mutual Assistance.
1949	Denmark and Norway sign North Atlantic Treaty. Norges Bank nationalized.
1950–3	Dismantlement of Norwegian pay and price controls.
1952	Formation of Nordic Council. North Norway Plan.
1954	Common Nordic labour market established.
1955	Finland joins UN and Nordic Council. Reform of Swedish investment funds system (introduced in 1938).
1959	Stockholm Convention: formation of EFTA.
1960	End of automobile rationing in Norway.
1961	Danish and Norwegian applications for EEC membership. FINEFTA agreement.
1963	'Totality Solution': government-imposed freeze of Danish economy.
1966	Establishment of broad left government in Finland. Public sector strike in Sweden.
1967	Second Danish and Norwegian EEC applications.
1968	NORDEK proposed by Denmark.
1968–9	'Liinamaa I and II' stabilization agreements in Finland.
1969	First major oil find in Norwegian Ekofisk field. Formation of AB Statsföretag in Sweden.
1970	NORDEK rejected by Finland at Nordic Council.

1971	First oil brought ashore in Norway. Public sector strike in Sweden.
1972	Referenda on EEC membership in Denmark and Norway: Danish acceptance; Norwegian rejection. Free trade agreement between Sweden and EEC. Formation of Statoil in Norway.
1973	Introduction of worker directors in Norway and Sweden. Free trade agreement between Norway and EEC. Finnish free trade agreement with EEC and agreement with Comecon. General election doubles number of parties represented in Danish parliament.
1976	Meidner Plan approved by Swedish LO Congress. 'Bergman affair'. Formation of liberal-conservative coalition in Sweden.
1977	Working Environment Acts passed in Norway and Sweden. Change of government economic policy in Finland.
1979–80	Campaign against Alta River hydro-electric project ends in defeat for Norwegian government.
1980	Referendum on nuclear power and major industrial conflict in Sweden.
1981	Mauno Koivisto elected President of Finland.
1982	Return of Swedish Social Democrats to office: 16 per cent devaluation of krona. Formation of conservative-led coalition in Denmark.
1986	Finland becomes full member of EFTA. Assassination of Olof Palme. 'Potato Diet': Danish austerity package.
1987	Formation of conservative-led coalition in Finland. Danish general election returns Schlüter government in weakened position.

References

Allen, H. (1979) *Norway and Europe in the 1970s*, Oslo: Universitetsforlaget.

Alt, J.E. (1987) 'Crude politics. Oil and the political economy of unemployment in Britain and Norway, 1970–85', *British Journal of Politics*, 17: 149–99.

Andersen, P.S., and Åkerholm, J. (1982) 'Scandinavia', in A. Boltho (ed.), *The European Economy: Growth and Crisis*, Oxford: Oxford University Press.

Aukrust, O. (1977) 'Inflation in the open economy: a Norwegian model', in L. Krause and W. Salant (eds), *Worldwide Inflation*, Washington, DC: The Brookings Institution.

Bergh, T., Hanisch, T.J., Lange, E., and Pharo, H. (1981) *Growth and Development: The Norwegian Experience 1830–1980*, Oslo: Norwegian Institute of International Affairs.

Bourneuf, A. (1958) *Norway: The Planned Revival*, Cambridge, Mass.: Harvard University Press.

Castles, F. (1978) *The Social Democratic Image of Society: A Study of the Achievements and Origins of Scandinavian Social Democracy in Comparative Perspective*, London: Routledge & Kegan Paul.

Childs, M.W. (1938) *Sweden: The Middle Way*, 2nd edn, New Haven, Conn.: Yale University Press.

Childs, M.W. (1980) *Sweden: The Middle Way on Trial*, New Haven, Conn. and London: Yale University Press.

Christiansen, N.F. (1984) 'Denmark: end of the idyll', *New Left Review*, 144: 5–32.

DØR, Copenhagen, ETLA, Helsinki, IFF, Copenhagen, IUI, Stockholm, and IØI, Bergen (1984) *Economic Growth in a Nordic Perspective*, Copenhagen: Det Økonomiske Råd, Sekretariatet.

The Economist (1987a) 'The Nordic alternative', special supplement, 21 November.

The Economist (1987b) 'Swedish multinationals: a hard act to follow', 1 August.

Edgren, G., Faxén, K.-O., and Odhner, C.-E. (1973) *Wage Formation and the Economy*, London: George Allen & Unwin.

Elder, N., Thomas, A.H., and Arter, D. (1982) *The Consensual Democracies? The Government and Politics of the Scandinavian States*, Oxford: Martin Robertson.

Elvander, N. (1974) 'The role of the state in the settlement of labour disputes in the Nordic countries: a comparative analysis', *European Journal of Political Research*, 2: 363–83.

Elvander, N. (1981) 'State intervention and economic freedom', in E. Allardt *et al.* (eds), *Nordic Democracy*, Copenhagen: Det Danske Selskab.

Fredrickson, J.W. (1960) 'The economic recovery of Finland since World War II', *Journal of Political Economy*, 68: 17–36.

Haskel, B.G. (1976) *The Scandinavian Option: Opportunities and Opportunity Costs in Postwar Scandinavian Foreign Policies*, Oslo: Universitetsforlaget.

Hodne, F. (1983) *The Norwegian Economy 1920–1980*, London: Croom Helm.

Hufford, L. (1973) *Sweden: The Myth of Socialism*, London: Fabian Society.

Huntford, R. (1971) *The New Totalitarians*, London: Allen Lane.

Johansen, H.C. (1987) *The Danish Economy in the Twentieth Century*, London: Croom Helm.

Jones, H.G. (1976) *Planning and Productivity in Sweden*, London: Croom Helm.

Jörberg, L. (1973) 'The nordic countries 1850–1914', in C.M. Cipolla (ed.), *Fontana Economic History of Europe*, 4 (2), London: Fontana.

Jörberg, L., and Krantz, O. (1976) 'Scandinavia 1914–1970', in C.M. Cipolla (ed.), *Fontana Economic History of Europe*, 6 (2), London: Fontana.

Kindleberger, C.P. (1987) 'Finnish war reparations', in C.P. Kindleberger, *Marshall Plan Days*, London: George Allen & Unwin.

Lindbeck, A. (1975) *Swedish Economic policy*, London: Macmillan.

Lundberg, E. (1957) *Business Cycles and Economic Policy*, London: George Allen & Unwin.

Lundberg, E. (1968) *Instability and Economic Growth*, New Haven, Conn.: Yale University Press.

Lundberg, E. (1982) 'Perspectives on the future of the Swedish economy – two extreme alternatives', in B. Rydén and V. Bergström (eds), *Sweden: Choices for Economic and Social Policy in the 1980s*, London: George Allen & Unwin.

Maddison, A. (1976) 'Economic Policy and performance in Europe 1913–1970', in C.M. Cipolla (ed.), *Fontana Economic History of Europe*, 5 (2), London: Fontana.

Maude, G. (1976) *The Finnish Dilemma: Neutrality in the Shadow of Power*, London: Oxford University Press.

Miljan, T. (1977) *The Reluctant Europeans: The Attitudes of the Nordic Countries towards European Integration*, London: C. Hurst.

Milward, A.S. (1972) *The Fascist Economy in Norway*, Oxford: Oxford University Press.

Milward, A.S. (1984) *The Recovery of Western Europe 1945–51*, London: Methuen.

Mjøset, L. (1987) 'Nordic economic policies in the 1970s and 1980s', *International Organisation*, 41: 403–56.

Nabseth, L., and Wallander, J. (1982) 'Can Sweden remain a leading industrial nation?', in B. Rydén and V. Bergström (eds), *Sweden: Choices for Economic and Social Policy in the 1980s*, London: Allen & Unwin.

Noreng, Ø. (1980) *The Oil Industry and Government Strategy in the North Sea*, London: Croom Helm.

OECD (1986) *Economic Survey of Finland*, Paris: OECD.

OECD (1987a) *Economic Survey of Denmark*, Paris: OECD.

OECD (1987b) *Economic Survey of Norway*, Paris: OECD.

OECD (1987c) *Historical Statistics 1960–1985*, Paris: OECD.

OECD (1988) *Economic Survey of Norway*, Paris: OECD.

Pharo, H. (1984) 'Domestic and international implications of Norwegian reconstruction', EUI Working Paper No. 81, Florence: European University Institute.

Premfors, R. (1984) 'Coping with budget deficits in Sweden', *Scandinavian Political Studies*, 7: 261–84.

Ringen, S. (1987) *The Possibility of Politics: A Study in the Political Economy of the Welfare State*, Oxford: Oxford University Press.

Scandinavian Studies (1987) special issue: 'Rethinking the welfare state', 59 (2).

Shonfield, A. (1965) *Modern Capitalism*, London: Oxford University Press.

Singleton, F. (1987) *The Economy of Finland in the Twentieth Century*, Bradford: University of Bradford.

Tomasson, R.F. (1970) *Sweden: Prototype of Modern Society*, New York: Random House.

Turner, B., and Nordquist, G. (1982) *The Other European Community: Integration and Co-operation in Nordic Europe*, London: Weidenfeld & Nicolson.

Waite, J. (1974) 'The Swedish paradox: EEC and neutrality', *Journal of Common Market Studies*, 12: 319–36.

Wendt, F. (1981) 'Nordic cooperation', in E. Allardt *et al.* (eds), *Nordic Democracy*, Copenhagen: Det Danske Selskab.

Guide to further reading

For Scandinavia as a whole the chapter by Jörberg and Krantz in the *Fontana Economic History of Europe* (1976) provides a useful introduction to twentieth-century economic development. More recent economic events, from the early 1970s onwards, are surveyed in two valuable short studies, by Andersen and Åkerholm (1982) and Mjøset (1987) and, with reference to the demands of social policy, in Eric S. Einhorn's contribution to the 1987 special issue of *Scandinavian Studies*, 'Rethinking the welfare state'. Coverage of the policies and performances of individual countries since the Second World War is very uneven. Sweden is served best, with authoritative studies by Lundberg (1957) and Lindbeck (1975). Hodne's volume on Norway in the Croom Helm series *Contemporary Economic History of Europe* (1983) is trenchant, informative, and opinionated. Johansen on Denmark in the same series (1987) is reliable but much less entertaining. On Finland the main work is Singleton (1987). Kindleberger (1987) has written interestingly on Finnish war reparations.

Among works dealing with more general aspects of Scandinavian politics and society, Turner and Nordquist (1982) offer a lively account of economic and political developments in each of the four countries since the turn of the century, with the emphasis on the postwar period. As the title of their book suggests, they also devote considerable attention to Scandinavian efforts at co-operation. The nature of Scandinavian consensus politics and decision-making is explored by Castles (1978), Elder, Thomas, and Arter (1982), and in an important new book, *Policy and Politics in Sweden: Principled Pragmatism*, by Hugh Heclo and Henrik Madsen (Philadelphia: Temple University Press, 1987).

Chapter nine

Eastern Europe

Jaroslav Krejčí

Part one: the group as a whole

Introduction

Similarities and differences between countries are largely a matter of perspective. What strikes most western lay observers is how different from the west are the forms of political and economic organization in eastern Europe, yet how similar they are as a group. They are all to a greater or lesser degree centrally planned. They all became communist dominated at, or soon after, the end of the Second World War. Except for Yugoslavia and Albania they are members of the same trading and military blocs, the Council for Mutual Economic Assistance (CMEA or COMECON), and the Warsaw Pact, which were set up in 1949 and 1955 respectively. CMEA was formed as a response to Marshall Aid, the offer of which initially included also the east European countries, but the USSR chose to establish its own organization instead. Many countries in this group are also still highly secretive with economic data and those which they produce often have to be treated with some scepticism.

In contrast, to those more familiar with eastern Europe, what stands out is the diversity within the group. The case of Yugoslavia is the most obvious. In the Second World War, Tito had led the largest resistance movement in Europe and its genuinely national roots, together with the absence of Soviet armies in the country at the time of liberation or after, were powerful factors contributing to Yugoslavia's ability to break away in 1948, and to pursue its own 'associational socialism' as compared to the 'state socialism' of the remainder. However, other countries too tried to achieve varying degrees of independence from the Soviet Union (East Germany in 1953, Hungary in 1956, and Czechoslovakia in 1968), but all these attempts were suppressed by the Soviet army. Only Poland's attempts at emancipation, in 1956 and then more seriously in the early 1980s, were allowed to be checked by internal forces.

There are also significant economic differences within the whole group.

Table 9.1 Approximate estimates of GDP per head in 1965 (US$)

East Germany	1,437
Czechoslovakia	1,427
Hungary	1,015
Poland	989
Bulgaria	877
Romania	697
Yugoslavia	692[a]
Western Europe (average)	1,532

a Indicators of total consumption, however, put Yugoslavia higher than Romania

Source: UNECE 1970: 150.

Czechoslovakia and the territory which became the German Democratic Republic (East Germany) had both been relatively industrialized before the war, whereas Bulgaria, Romania, and a greater part of Yugoslavia were primarily agricultural and relatively backward; even though much of East Germany's industrial equipment was moved to the USSR after the war (as part of reparations payments), it maintained its joint lead with Czechoslovakia. Bearing in mind the qualifications made above about the quality of official data, we may use for the sake of comparison a tentative estimate of the UN Economic Commission for Europe based on physical indicators expressed at average prices in US dollars. This estimate (Table 9.1) shows that, in 1965, in the middle of the period here reviewed, East Germany and Czechoslovakia had GDPs per capita almost comparable to the average of western Europe (western in the political sense, i.e., including Greece) and roughly twice that of Romania and Yugoslavia and still well above Bulgaria, with Hungary and Poland lying in the middle.

The extent of the socialized sector and of central planning is another factor which has varied both between one country and another and over time. Thus in Yugoslavia and in Poland most agriculture is in private ownership, and Yugoslavia operates with a managed market rather than a centrally planned economy. A further point of diversity is the extent of regional differences which in multiethnic countries such as Yugoslavia and to a lesser extent in Czechoslovakia have produced particular problems.

Finally, also, the degree of secrecy varies. At one extreme is Albania which provides no suitable data at all (and which is therefore omitted from the following discussion). East Germany, Bulgaria, and Romania were also always highly secretive and remain at this end of the spectrum. Poland, Czechoslovakia, and Hungary, on the other hand, achieved a degree of statistical *glasnost* from the mid-1960s onwards, publishing data which can be to a considerable extent recalculated in accordance with the system of standard national accounts (SNA) used in the west; and Yugoslavia has, at least since 1967, supplied figures directly in SNA form.

These variations in the quality of the data together with differences in geography, natural endowments, history, and habits necessarily limit the force of any generalizations that can be made about the group as a whole. The first part of this chapter is therefore an inevitably selective examination of the objectives and performance of this group of countries which only touches on the most salient features of their economic development. This is then supplemented in the second part by a somewhat more detailed examination of the particular case of Czechoslovakia: a country with a fairly developed economy (and thus comparable to the west), a reasonable amount of data and well known to the author from personal experience.

Objectives

The main aim of all these countries was the achievement of sustained economic growth that would be faster than under capitalist conditions. At the same time the new system was supposed to achieve greater efficiency and above all to abolish the classes and thus to achieve greater equality in three particular respects: between individual professions, between the more and less prosperous regions, and between town and country. The cherished idea was to make of a village a factory in which machinery would do all the hard work and collective farmers would have time to take part in the cultural life of the cities.

Consistent with the earlier example of the Soviet Union which provided the paradigm for central planning, growth was to be achieved by ambitious industrialization, especially in the producers' goods sector. A faster growth of production of the latter than of consumer goods has become an axiom.

Growth and fluctuations

How the various eastern European countries performed on these objectives cannot be answered until the data problems referred to above have been faced. Table 9.2 shows data drawn from the official publications of each of these countries and compares it with a measure of GNP based on physical outputs weighted by a factor cost estimate prepared by Alton (1987). The gap between the growth rates derived by these two methods can be interpreted as an approximate indication of the bias in the official statistics. It is smallest for Yugoslavia and highest for Romania, a finding that accords well with *prima facie* considerations about the relative secrecy of these countries.

Nevertheless, despite these data problems, Table 9.2 shows that, over the whole period, on both the official figures and Alton's estimates of GNP, Romania has the highest growth rate and Czechoslovakia and Hungary the lowest. It also seems reasonably clear that the east European countries slowed down in the late 1970s and yet again in the 1980s. For example, on

Table 9.2 A comparison of growth rates of output based on official indices of NMP and Alton's estimates of GNP,[a] 1950–85

		1950–5	1955–60	1960–5	1965–70	1970–5	1975–80	1980–5	1950–85	Ratios of growth of NMP: GNP 1950–85
Bulgaria	NMP	12.2	9.6	6.7	8.7	7.8	6.1	3.7	7.8	1.7
	GNP	6.2	7.2	6.5	5.0	4.7	1.0	0.8	4.5	
Czechoslovakia	NMP	8.2	6.9	2.0	6.9	5.7	3.7	1.8	5.0	1.6
	GNP	3.4	6.4	2.4	3.4	3.4	2.1	1.2	3.2	
East Germany	NMP	13.1	7.1	3.5	5.3	5.4	4.1	4.6	6.1	1.7
	GNP	6.3	5.1	2.9	3.2	3.4	2.3	1.7	3.6	
Hungary	NMP	5.7	6.0	4.1	6.8	6.2	2.8	1.3	4.7	1.5
	GNP	5.4	3.8	4.0	3.1	3.3	2.0	0.7	3.2	
Poland	NMP	8.6	6.6	6.1	6.0	9.8	1.2	-0.8	5.3	1.5
	GNP	4.6	4.7	4.4	4.0	6.5	0.7	0.6	3.6	
Romania	NMP	13.9	6.9	9.0	7.7	11.2	7.3	4.4	8.6	1.8
	GNP	7.3	4.4	5.4	4.9	6.7	3.9	1.9	4.9	
Yugoslavia	GMP[b]	5.1	7.9	6.8	5.8	5.8	5.6	0.7	5.4	1.1
	GNP	4.4	7.1	5.7	4.4	4.5	5.6	1.2	4.7	
Memorandum item: Total OECD GDP		4.8	3.3	5.3	4.6	3.0	3.3	2.5	3.8	

a Average compound annual changes, %
b Gross Material Product = NMP plus amortization

Sources: Statistical Yearbooks of the respective countries: T.P. Alton, *National Product of the Planned Economies of Eastern Europe*, New York, 1987, reprinted in M.C. Kaser and E.A. Radice (eds) *The Economic History of Eastern Europe 1919–1975*, vol. 4, Clarendon Press, Oxford, forthcoming; OECD database.

both measures they all decelerate after 1975 (except for Yugoslavia on Alton's figures) and they all decelerate further after 1980 (except for East Germany on the official figures). In addition, if we use the GNP figures, which are better for the purposes of this comparison, then we see that these countries straddle the growth rate of the OECD group: Romania (4.9), Yugoslavia (4.7), and Bulgaria (4.5) are slightly above; Poland (3.6) and East Germany (also 3.6) are very close, and Czechoslovakia and Hungary, each 3.2, are a little below.

It is also clear that individual countries have had considerable fluctuations and occasional setbacks throughout the thirty-five-year period. Table 9.3 shows a measure of this, giving maximum and minimum growth rates and the standard deviation of these rates. These are all based on the official series and so need to be interpreted with some caution. This is especially the case with the early 1950s, when these economies started from a very low postwar level, and when many economic activities formerly performed within households became industrialized and thus for the first time entered the statistical evidence. Some of the setbacks are due to the political upheavals such as that of 1956 in Hungary, or that of 1979–82 in Poland; some fluctuations are due to weather conditions (alternating good and bad harvests) in countries whose national product and foreign trade depend heavily on agriculture (actually all in this group with the exception of East Germany and Czechoslovakia); some, however, may also reflect

Table 9.3 Fluctuations in growth,[a] 1950–85

		1950–85			1960–85
	Average growth	Max	Min	Standard deviation	Standard deviation
Bulgaria	7.8	41 (1951)	−1 (1952)	7	2
Czechoslovakia	5.0	11 (1952)	−2 (1963)	3	3
GDR	6.1	25 (1951)	2 (1961)	4	1
Hungary	4.7	23 (1957)	−11 (1956)	6	3
Poland	5.3	11 (1954, 1957, 1972, 1973)	−12 (1981)	5	5
Romania	8.6	31 (1951)	−7 (1956)	6	3
Yugoslavia	5.4	21 (1957)	−14 (1952)	6	3

a The average growth rates are the annual average percentage change over the period. The maximum and minimum are the percentage changes in particular years with respective years shown in brackets

Source: Statistical Yearbooks of the respective countries.

inadequacies in the statistical service. This again is most likely with respect to the 1950s. Nevertheless, according to the official figures, all these countries, except Poland, show less fluctuation after the 1950s and the steadiest of all is East Germany. This is also the country which, again using official figures, has not slowed down in the 1980s. Poland's high rates of growth in the early 1970s were due to the foreign credit spree and over-investment which then cost the country so dearly.

Consistent with the picture of overall growth is the progress of industri-alization that occurred in all seven countries. Even the fairly developed countries such as East Germany (GDR) and Czechoslovakia (ČSSR) preferred to enlarge their secondary sector at the expense of a wide range of services. Only the government sector, both civil and military, experienced everywhere a considerable expansion. In the absence of a reliable assess-ment of value added, structural change can best be evaluated on the basis of labour force distribution (Table 9.4). Unfortunately the published data do not include the so-called unplanned sectors, such as the armed forces, the police and, except Yugoslavia, also the Communist Party. Thus the tertiary sector is incomplete.

With this qualification, during the thirty-five years the distribution of the labour force in the seven countries shows a moderate tendency towards con-vergence. In spite of a strong industrialization drive most countries under

Table 9.4 Structure of civil employment, 1956–81

		I	*II*	*III*
Bulgaria	1956	64	19	17
	1985	21	46	33
Czechoslovakia	1950	39	37	24
	1985	14	47	39
GDR	1952	23	45	32
	1985	11	48	41
Hungary	1950	50	24	26
	1985	22	39	39
Poland	1950	57	23	20
	1985	30	37	33
Romania	1950	74	15	11
	1985	29	44	27
Yugoslavia	1953	67	12	21
	1981	29	31	40

Note: Primary (I), secondary (II), and tertiary (III) sectors of economy as % of the civil labour force

Sources: Statistical Yearbooks of the respective countries.

study still employ 20 to 30 per cent of their labour force in agriculture. Even the GDR and ČSSR have a higher percentage in the primary sector (in 1985, 11 and 14 per cent respectively) than the comparable west European countries such as West Germany (FRG) and Austria (5 and 9 per cent). The latter, however, produce more per hectare than the GDR and ČSSR. (In the FRG and Austria the yields of cereals per hectare are 6 to 18 per cent higher). Also the development of the service sector is, with the exception of Yugoslavia, everywhere slower than in the west. Furthermore, the relative size of the secondary sector seems to have reached a ceiling in Czechoslovakia, the GDR and, unexpectedly, also in Hungary.

Aspects of equality

Income differentials

The goal of levelling which these countries have pursued has been most successful with respect to income differentials between blue and white-collar workers. This was partly due to the general tendency after the war when the more developed countries such as the GDR and Czechoslovakia had a relatively more abundant supply of white-collar workers than of other labour. Everywhere government policy favoured workers in heavy industries and, across the board, the technical against the administrative staff. The scarce statistical data show, especially in the earlier period, a more or less continuous decline of income differentials between manual and non-manual workers. Also, other differences between these two categories, such as in social insurance, in conditions of pay, and in the length of holiday were widely reduced or even abolished. All this however applies to the 'planned sector' only. As is well known, the armed forces, the police, and the party leadership enjoy special facilities not only in extra pay but also in the privileged access to the scarce and/or quality goods, to special health care, etc.

This significant exception in the levelling trend is further accentuated by the emergence of new, tangible differentials between the leaders and the rank and file. Many activities which earlier were either free or depended solely on one's financial means became subject to administrative rationing, and access to higher education, better jobs, foreign travel, and various scarce amenities became dependent on political screening. In the late eighties this trade-off between, on the one hand, material levelling and, on the other hand, de-levelling of personal rights and liberties is especially conspicuous in the more orthodox (conservative) state socialist countries such as Bulgaria, Czechoslovakia, and the GDR. Yugoslavia and recently also Hungary, however, moved in the opposite direction: some levelling of rights and liberties has been matched by some de-levelling of incomes, at least as far as the planned sectors are concerned. On the other hand, Romania's record has been disappointing on both counts. Her ambitious investment and economic mismanagement did not give her working people any bonus of industrialization and the situation there is still getting worse. Poland in the late seventies fell into a similar trap; but, in contrast to Romania, in Poland the de-levelling of rights and liberties did not reach such abysmal depths. In this respect the Poles have been for long better off than their state socialist neighbours.

Furthermore, in all countries discussed here there are many economic activities (legal and illegal) which are unaccounted for. The secondary or parallel economy provides a considerable corrective of income distribution through the official channels. It is however difficult to assess whether these unofficial incomes have a levelling or de-levelling effect on the population as a whole. In as far as they are earned by the poorly paid they tend to decrease income differentials. On the other hand, people with access to scarce commodities or providing special qualified services may increase already high personal incomes thus widening differentials. Unfortunately, even with respect to official incomes only, the trade-off mentioned earlier cannot easily be assessed.

Regional differentials

As far as the other types of levelling are concerned, achievements can best be assessed with respect to the regional differences.

Yugoslavia was the least successful, but also the country which had to work against the heaviest odds. None of the other countries has been confronted with such tremendous regional discrepancies in the level of both cultural and economic development. The fact that, in contrast to the USSR, Yugoslavia eventually turned the federal constitution from a fiction into reality (the most important step in this direction was the federalization of the Communist Party), as well as the policy of a managed market rather than a centrally planned economy, proved in several ways an impediment to a more vigorous policy of transfer of funds and equipment from the richer to the poorer areas and of labour in the opposite direction.

As is well known, the regional differences in Yugoslavia are amplified by ethnic and cultural variations of a complex nature implying different attitudes to family life, working habits, and entrepreneurial activity. Though the dominant language, Serbo-Croat, is spoken as a mother tongue by over 70 per cent of the population, the three historical cultures, Orthodox Christian, Roman Catholic, and Islamic, cut across the hard core of the main linguistic group. Outside the Serbo-Croat orbit, the thoroughly westernized Slovenia contrasts more sharply with the predominantly Muslim Kosovo; and, in spite of high investment into the socialized sector in Kosovo, the gap between the two continues to increase. This increase in inequality between the rich and poor regions is seen clearly in Table 9.5.

Table 9.5 Regional differences in Yugoslavia, 1955–85 (the whole of Yugoslavia = 100)

	Per capita GMP[a]		Unemployment		
	1955	1986	1965	1985	Level of development
Slovenia	175	203	45	17	Far advanced
Croatia	122	125	105	56	Average and above
Vojvodina	94	118	80	101	average
Serbia	91	100	105	104	
Bosnia	83	69	60	94	Below average
Montenegro	77	78	70	145	
Macedonia	68	66	215	155	
Kosovo	43	28	145	174	Far behind

a Gross material product (društveni proizvod) = net material product plus amortization

Source: Statistički Godišnjak Jugoslavije 1986: 417, 419; 1987: 415.

This shows per capita GMP and unemployment for each region relative to the national average in particular years. Thus, while in 1955 the per capita GMP was four times higher in Slovenia than in Kosovo, by 1986 it was more than seven times higher. (On the other hand, the annual rate of natural increase of population in Slovenia declined from 11 to 4 per 1,000, whereas in Kosovo it remained stable at over 25 per 1,000.) There was also a widening of the gap in unemployment. As the national average rose (from 2 per cent in 1965 to 6.9 per cent in 1985) virtually full employment was sustained in Slovenia (0.9 per cent in 1965 and 1.2 per cent in 1985), whereas in Kosovo the registered unemployment rose from 2.9 per cent to 12 per cent (all these figures ignore any change in disguised unemployment among the rural population).

Out of the state socialist countries only Czechoslovakia has had a regional problem underscored – like Yugoslavia – by ethnic differentiation between the Czechs and Slovaks. Yet, as can be seen from Table 9.6, here the levelling widely succeeded because the circumstances for such a policy were favourable. First, there were only two partners in the game, whilst in Yugoslavia there were eight. In Czechoslovakia the region which gave up resources, the Czech Lands, was stronger both in terms of population and in economic development, and the gap between the Czech Lands and Slovakia was on all counts closer than that between the most and the least developed parts of Yugoslavia.

Second, the Czech-Slovak economic levelling had a special political aspect. In the 1946 elections, Slovaks showed that they were much less inclined to embrace communism than the Czechs, and as the cause of this

Table 9.6 Regional differences in Czechoslovakia, 1948–83 (Slovakia in % of the level in the Czech Lands)

	1948	1968	1983
Industrialization[a]	54.5	82.0	91.4
Mechanization[b]	58.0	86.5	91.0
Per capita NMP	61.2	79.9	84.2
Gross money income of:			
workers' households	79.7[c]	83.1	88.3
co-operative farmers' households	61.9[d]	78.2	87.8

a Employment in the secondary sector in % of the civil labour force
b Productive assets per person employed in material branches of economy
c 1951
d 1953

Source: Calculated from the data in the *Yearbook of Historical Statistics ČSSR*, Prague – Bratislava, 1985.

was seen in a less numerous working class, the decision to industrialize Slovakia had to be carried through, not only in the Slovaks', but also in the Czech communists' interests. After communist rule in Czechoslovakia had become firmly established (1948), a transfer of funds for investment in Slovakia was in a way a compensation for the progressive curtailment of her autonomy achieved in 1945; the stages of curtailment being first in 1947, then in 1948, and finally by the constitution in 1960 which proclaimed Czechoslovakia a socialist republic.

The communists believed that once the socioeconomic differences between the Czechs and Slovaks were abolished, the occasional expressions of ethnic tension would disappear. This, however, was not the case. In 1968, as one of the measures of the general reform, the until-then highly centralized Czechoslovak Socialist Republic was transformed into a federation composed of the Czech Socialist and Slovak Socialist Republics. Significantly this constitutional change was the only part of the reform which survived the return to the status quo imposed on Czechoslovakia by the military might of the Soviet Union. The reason was again political. This time, unlike in 1946, the Slovaks happened to be more co-operative than the Czechs. Since then the levelling has continued but at a slower pace. It should also be noted, that after 1968 Slovakia could rely more on her own human resources which were not as much affected by the punitive measures against unreliable intelligentsia as in the Czech Lands.

In the other countries surveyed here, regional differences did not become political issues of primary importance. Consequently, their accounting was not given much attention. Macro-economic data referring to individual counties in Poland, Hungary, East Germany, etc. are virtually non-existent.

Towns and villages: agricultural and industrial workers

Unfortunately there is also not too much to be built on when we want to test the other socialist target, namely, the abolition of the cultural and economic gap between town and village. As has been said already, the idea was to make of a village a factory; with vast, balkless tracts of land, huge stalls, cowsheds, and pigsties, and above all, machinery which would do all the hard, monotonous work. Collectivization was supposed to be the shortest way to this end. Yet, as experience has shown, it was the general technological progress resulting in the transfer of the peasant population to other professions, mainly to industry in the towns, rather than a special policy that narrowed the economic gap between the urban and rural population – in short the same development as in the capitalist west but achieved at a much slower pace.

There was little difference whether the farms were collectivized or not. The gap between farmers' income and that of other working people narrowed as much in Czechoslovakia and in Hungary where almost all agriculture had been collectivized, as in Yugoslavia and Poland where most of it remained in, or returned to, private ownership.

From such data as exists we can see that in Poland there was a declining disparity between wages and salaries and farmers' incomes. In 1970 when 90 per cent of the workforce in agriculture were self-employed, their average income equalled 56 per cent of the average employees' income, whereas by 1985, when the private sector comprised 85 per cent of those working in agriculture, their average income had risen to 76 per cent of the wage and salary earners. A similar trend can be observed in Yugoslavia from the structure of the GNP at factor cost (SNA method). Per capita value added in agriculture as a proportion of value added in the economy as a whole rose from 37 per cent in 1971 to 46 per cent by 1981. There is, however, conclusive evidence that in the less developed regions of Yugoslavia the gap between the towns and countryside is much wider than in the advanced republics and regions.

In the case of Czechoslovakia the relevant information is provided in the accounts of the representative samples of various households and, ignoring the position of the state farms, these show that farmers' incomes caught up with those of workers. In 1953 the per capita money income in the households of the co-operative farmers was 67 per cent of the per capita income of the workers' households, whereas by 1968 it was up to 97 per cent. Taking into account income in kind, it may be inferred that the gap not only disappeared but that the co-operative farmers were on average better off than the workers. We have also to bear in mind that the number of those working in the co-operative farms declined considerably: from 14 per cent in 1961 to 9 per cent of the total labour force in 1970. Since then, the decline in numbers of the co-operative farmers has continued, but at a slower pace

(7 per cent in 1980), while their per capita money income has remained roughly level with that of the workers (in 1985 it was 97 per cent).

In Hungary also the living standard of co-operative farmers caught up with that of the blue-collar workers. The per capita expenditure of the co-operative farmers' households (which do not include income in kind) reached, in 1980, 94 per cent of the corresponding expenditures in workers' households. A juxtaposition of the structure of the labour force and the structure of gross money income of the working population, though not strictly comparable, points to a considerable narrowing of the gap between these two social groups between 1960 and 1985.

The contrast with the pre-war period is striking. Then, under Admiral Horthy, whose regime claimed to have its power base in the rural population, the economic interests of the peasantry were sacrificed to those of industry which continued to grow even during the world-wide recession of the 1930s. Under Kadar, whose regime was supposed to have its power base in the industrial workers, it was the diminishing number of farmers whose living standard achieved the greatest gains.

Although income equalization between farmers and workers was almost identical in Czechoslovakia and Hungary, the liberalization of marketing in the latter produced a greater increase in production at the same time. Between 1968 (the year of economic reforms in both countries) and 1983, gross production in agriculture, according to the official figures, increased in Hungary by over 50 per cent but in Czechoslovakia by less than 30 per cent.

Inflation

A particular programmatic requirement of economic policy in the state socialist countries has been stability of prices: if there was to be any price movement it should have been downwards not upwards. All the ambitious investment and expanding government consumption was to be financed from government revenues (a kind of forced savings) in which the differentiated turnover tax (discriminating against consumers) was to play the key role. The Treasury was supposed to operate with balanced budgets or, to be on the safe side, with surplus. To achieve these aims, the labour productivity had to grow faster than wages (under the circumstances of the aforementioned price policy real wages should not differ from nominal wages). As part of this policy the norms set for piece work should be raised periodically.

Reality, however, developed differently. Even those countries which withstood the lure of a revitalized market, like East Germany, Czechoslovakia, Bulgaria, and Romania, experienced various types and levels of inflationary pressure. To conceal the effect of inflation, carefully selected price indices were to be made available to the public. Yugoslavia is alone in not having attempted to disguise her grave inflationary problem. From 1955 to 1965 the Yugoslav retail price index increased by 100 per cent, from 1965 to 1975 by 300 per cent, and from 1975 to 1985 by over 1,500 per cent. Recently, Poland has become more open in revealing her pace of inflation. From 1975 to 1985 the official retail price index increased by 460 per cent (100 percentage points of this occurred in one year, 1982). The free market prices went up by a much higher percentage. Hungary admits for the same period a doubling of retail prices. Czechoslovak and Bulgarian official retail price indices show a 32 per cent increase between 1967 and 1985. However Bulgaria's 'bazaar' (i.e., free) market prices are reported to have increased in that period by more than 100 per cent. East Germany appears in this respect exemplary: from 1950 to 1960 her official retail price index went down from 190 to 100 points and from then until 1986 it remained remarkably stable. Occasionally published data on prices of intermediate goods, however, reveal that if this stability is true, it is achieved only at the cost of increasing price subsidies. Romania, for her part, prefers not to disclose price developments at all.

Part two: the case of Czechoslovakia

Policy before the establishment of exclusive communist power

The coalition government which ruled Czechoslovakia immediately after the Second World War took important measures which were to change the socio-economic structure of the country. In chronological order these were: first, all mines, enterprises of key industries, joint stock banks, private insurance companies, and other big firms (defined by the number of employees – between 150 and 500 according to industry) were nationalized (Law of 24 October 1945). This measure affected more than half the labour force in industry. Apart from this, there were large-scale confiscations of property of 'traitors' and 'collaborators' with the German occupation regime. In order to extend nationalization as far as possible, the communists tended to define 'collaboration' beyond the true meaning of this term.

Second, on 1 November 1945 a comprehensive monetary, price, and wage reform was inaugurated. Its aims were: (a) to check the inflationary pressure from the war-time accumulated savings; (b) to alleviate the burden of indebtedness; and (c) to remodel the price and wage structure. During the war both prices and wages were subject to government regulation (especially strict in the German occupied part of the state) and the machinery of regulation was taken over by the reconstituted Czechoslovak republic.

The main features of the monetary reform of 1945 were as follows. The holdings of the population were exchanged for cash only up to 500 korunas (10 US dollars at the official exchange rate introduced by the reform) per person and the rest had to be deposited in blocked accounts, to be released only for specific, mainly social, reasons. Deposit savings, life insurance, securities, and bonds were similarly frozen. Enterprises received exchange money for operational needs for one month. This meant that the amount of money in circulation was reduced from 120 billion to less than 20 billion korunas. On average the price and income level was about three times that at the beginning of 1939. However, rent and some services such as public transport were kept at the 'stop' level at the beginning of the war. (This upset the price–cost relationship in the construction of housing.) Wages and salaries were restructured; on the whole, in favour of low income recipients.

Taking the combined measures of this reform into consideration, they had the most penetrating income-levelling effects of the postwar period. At the beginning of 1946, real wages for men (blue-collar workers) were, on average, about 20 per cent higher, and those of women about 28 per cent higher, than in 1939; on the other hand, real salaries for men (white-collar workers) were lower by 30 per cent, women's real salaries by 14 per cent.

Third, during 1946 the process of socio-economic change was complicated by the expulsion of the German ethnic minority from Czechoslovakia (agreed at the Potsdam Conference of the US, UK and USSR). According to offical statistics, Germans who underwent the so-called organized transfer numbered 2.25 million. Outside of this scheme about 0.75 million left the country. Together it made up 20 per cent of the total population and 22 per cent of the labour force in industry. The loss of the labour force affected mainly the following industries: glass 45 per cent, textiles 40 per cent, stone and earthernware 38 per cent, paper 38 per cent, and mining 33 per cent. As a result of population transfer and other measures 23 per cent of the acreage in the whole state was confiscated and redistributed amongst the Czech and Slovak settlers. As both agricultural land and most of the industrial plant remained intact, and the effective demand was kept high by significant unfreezing of the blocked savings, the main problem was the scarcity of labour rather than unemployment.

Fourth, in 1946 Czechoslovakia worked out her first economic plan, scheduled for two years; 1947 and 1948. Though the two-year plan was of a merely rudimentary nature (it contained altogether 142 basic targets in physical units and overall indicators for economic growth) it nevertheless created the necessary apparatus which gradually became a powerful instrument of government economic policy.

Already during the first year of planning the question of the further orientation of the Czechoslovak economy emerged. As Czechoslovakia was still ruled by a coalition of political parties the issue was to be decided between them. Apart from the communists who came with an ambitious plan of economic restructuring, only social democrats put forward a detailed alternative for the first five-year plan. The main issues at stake were the extent of planning and the amount and structure of investment.

According to the social democrats, who wanted to give the market more leeway, the amount of gross capital formation should not exceed 25 per cent of GNP and, with respect to physical output, investment should not exceed productive capacity and energy supply. For the communists who preferred to restrict the market as far as possible, this was too timid. They planned a much faster rate of growth and their stress was on a rapid extension of the iron industry; in fact, more than three times as much as the social democratic proposal. According to the stratagem devised by Stalin all plans should always anticipate hidden reserves which should be 'mobilized' by increased efforts.

Tensions in the centrally planned economy

The orientation of further development, however, was not decided by negotiation. The communists outmanoeuvred their opponents, and, having their men in command of the armed forces, in February 1948 staged a successful *coup d'état* after which they took absolute power in the country. Their concept of economic development won the day. To satisfy the requirements of the USSR, they pushed the reconstruction of the Czechoslovak economy still further. Czechoslovakia was to provide the whole Soviet dominated bloc with steel and heavy machinery. The already very high targets for investment in heavy industry were further increased.

The first two years of the first five-year plan (1949–53) brought about drastic shifts not only in the economic but also in the social structure of the nation. The whole private sector except agriculture and apartment houses was socialized. The expropriation was partly based on law, partly on various kinds of punitive measures because of more or less fabricated offences. Consequently, there was a large, partly enforced transfer of labour force to the preferred branches of industry. The newly introduced turnover tax fell almost exclusively on consumer goods. The rationing of a wide range of consumer goods which was in 1947 near abolition had again to be extended. As almost all relevant economic data were kept secret the magnitude of the resulting disequilibrium could be only suspected.

By 1953 the inflationary pressure mounted so high that a drastic monetary reform had to be undertaken. Unlike the monetary reform of 1945, which had only blocked the pent-up demand and allowed for the freeing of limited amounts of assets when the social conditions of individual owners justified it, the monetary reform of 1953 combined the exchange of notes and coins with further redistribution and, above all, confiscation of wealth. It established a double, highly discriminatory rate of conversion: one for claims by 'society' (government, socialized enterprises, etc.) and the other for those by the population.

The basic conversion rate of 5 old korunas to 1 new koruna was introduced for all wage payments, pensions, and other social benefits, for all obligations towards government and socialist enterprises, and for cash balances up to 300 korunas in the new currency. For all other private cash balances and all other individual dealings with the government and socialized enterprises the conversion rate was fixed at 50:1, which meant a 90 per cent confiscation. The blocked deposits in pre-1945 currency were completely annihilated. Saving deposits in post-1945 currency were converted at the basic rate of 5:1 for deposits up to 5,000 korunas and above that level at a progressively depreciating rate. Rationing was abolished, and unified prices, somewhat higher than former rationed prices but lower than former free (legal market) prices, were deflated at the rate of 5:1. This raised the cost of living index for families buying only rationed goods by about 10 per cent. (Only lower wages and salaries and also wages of some categories of workers such as those in mines and heavy industry were increased by a few percentage points.) By this act of economic crafts-manship (it was the Soviet experts who masterminded this reform) all uncontrolled sources of income were abolished and the collectivization drive, which had already been started in the countryside, intensified.

Unfortunately, it is impossible to assess the impact of the above-mentioned confiscations on the different groups of population. However, judging from the reaction of the population in different parts of the country, we may reasonably infer that this reform hit not only the former capitalists but also the workers who, especially in the privileged branches of industry such as mining, metallurgy, and heavy engineering had accumu-lated large savings. The workers' demonstrations in several cities especially in Plzeň bear witness to this fact.

A particular aspect of the 1953 monetary reform was the 39 per cent revaluation of the koruna (official exchange rate) in terms of the US dollar. From then on, vital exports often had to be subsidized, even if exports were not, as a matter of principle, taxed by the turnover tax. On the other hand, the advantages of cheaper imports were to a considerable extent invalidated by several factors such as the dependence on low-grade iron ore from Soviet Russia, the embargo on some badly needed materials from the west and the inducement by the plan's indicators (gross output) to use raw material lavishly, which for industrial use had mostly to be imported.

After the socialization of private businesses, great and small, in 1949–51, and after the confiscation of most savings in 1953, came the farmers' turn. Whilst, in 1955, 56 per cent of cultivated land was still privately owned, by 1960 this share had dropped to a mere 9 per cent representing mainly holdings below 5 acres in infertile hill areas. At the same time the private owners of apartment houses had been ruined by the maintenance of rents at the 1939 level. Thus, as all potentially profitable means of production were socialized, Czechoslovakia could be proclaimed, in the new constitution promulgated in 1960, a socialist republic.

Meanwhile, however, the economists began to realize that the immense economic inputs were not generating corresponding outputs either in quantity or quality and that something had to be done. The first 'reform move' was directed towards reducing the number of indicators (about 15,000 quantitative measures were in use at that time) and decentralizing decision-making. In the bitter-sweet atmosphere which spread throughout the Czechoslovak power elite after the Twentieth Congress of the Soviet Communist Party (where Khrushchev disclosed and criticized Stalin's blunders) the reform ideas were incorporated into the resolution of the general Communist Party conference on 15 June 1956. Not much, however, happened in reality. The administrative machinery put into operation five to eight years earlier had become so strongly established and the people in top positions so well accommodated that they had no interest in a change.

Another attempt to shift decision-making from the top to lower organs and to rationalize the system of indicators, especially to lay much more stress on qualitative aspects of production, was undertaken two years later. Beginning in 1959, enterprises were allowed to accumulate funds from participation in increased profits and in depreciation allowances, and also some half-hearted steps were taken to give greater material incentives to employees for increased contribution to production. All of these modest reforms, however, served only to put additional strains on the already strained relationship between the monetary and real processes within the economy. Retained profits in enterprises bolstered the amount of investment, and continuous increases in wages stimulated effective consumer demand. This, in juxtaposition with the exhaustion of the labour reserve which occurred at about that time, led inevitably to new inflationary pressure, to a slowdown in investment and, eventually, to a reduction in production. In about three years the 'reform' had to be withdrawn. Only greater stress on agricultural production brought some good results. Higher purchase prices, higher investment, and a better supply of fertilizers bolstered both agricultural production and the living standard of co-operative farmers.

In 1962 however, the economic growth expressed in official indicators dropped to a mere 1.4 per cent, in 1963 turned to a 2.2 per cent decline, and in 1964 stagnated with a merely 0.6 per cent increase. This gave impetus to fresh thought and the authorities became more inclined to listen to the economists who were becoming increasingly aware of the insufficiency of the established methods of planning and management.

Already a resolution of the Twelfth Congress of the Czechoslovak Communist Party of December 1960 had postulated the following changes: (a) the gradual introduction of continuous planning (i.e., abolition of the uncertainty before the end of the planning period); (b) the reintroduction of balances with provision for reserves (i.e., abolition of the Stalinist system which set targets beyond the resources available); (c) the improvement of the system of indicators (especially abolition of the use of gross production for computation of productivity); and (d) the more effective use of material and semi-products. Stress was not on decentralization but on higher efficiency, without however the explicit statement of how this was to be achieved. This was in a way an advantage because it opened the door wider to specialist discussion from which eventually the need to revitalize the market emerged as the only practical way out.

The revitalization of the market, however, was *not* understood in the sense of a free market economy. The market ought not to become the decisive or regulating factor of economic growth, but rather a lubricant for its more efficient development. A socialist market economy had to be introduced stage by stage, using administrative methods for the transitional period. Of all good intentions however, only one – the re-structuring of prices with effect from 1 January 1967 – survived the subsequent scrapping of the reform.

This restructuring of prices resulted from the quest for 'a rational price formula'. Several alternatives were elaborated, taking into account various combinations of labour and capital cost. The result was a compromise between divergent interests. Although it did not abolish all political determination of prices (price subsidies provided at various levels of production were reduced by only about a half), it significantly reduced the gap between wholesale and retail prices, a gap which from the early 1950s had a strongly discriminatory effect against consumers. On the whole, retail prices remained almost unchanged (there was an increase of a mere 1 per cent) whereas wholesale prices were put up by almost 30 per cent.

The invasion of Soviet and other Warsaw Pact armies in August 1968 did not bring an instantaneous end to the new economic policy. The reformers' rule continued for more than a year until the pro-Soviet elements were restored to a full control. The Communist Party was purged of about a third of its membership; the traditional method of central planning and management became the substantial feature of 'normalization', the catch word for the return to the pre-reform practices in all walks of social life.

From 1970 until 1987 no attempt has been made to alter substantially the type and method of political and economic command. Economic policy has, however, had to cope with various challenges, partly external and partly internal. The most shattering external challenge came with the steep rise in oil prices in 1973 which strongly affected the structure of Czechoslovak foreign trade. Internally, the most worrying have been the accelerated decline of efficiency of fixed assets, the continuous wastage of raw materials, and the increasing damage to the natural environment.

Only in 1987, under the impact of developments in the USSR, did the Czechoslovak Communist Party feel compelled to embark on a new course of reform. Compared to 1968, however, the communist leadership has chosen to proceed cautiously. Up to the summer of 1988 they had produced two documents concerning the principles and execution of what was presented as a far-reaching reform to be implemented between 1988 and 1990. As the first practical measure to this end a new law regulating the position of the socialist enterprises was published. It remains to be seen whether and to what extent words will be followed by deeds and whether the rattling with the reform and democratization verbiage is, or is not, merely window dressing destined to appease big brother whose present reform-mindedness is considered a temporary phenomenon. The prospect that any loosening of economic grip might spill over to the political sphere is seen as a danger which has to be avoided even at a high economic cost.

Assessment of results

As was shown in Table 9.1, comparison of various indices of overall growth puts Czechoslovakia into the median position on the scale of discrepancies between official and private indices. Turning to the main item in the material product – industry (manufacturing, mining, and quarrying) – we find amazing discrepancies between various official indices themselves. As Table 9.7 shows, net industrial production from the 'national income produced' (or, net material product) series (line 3) is reported as having increased more than seven times from 1948 to 1985; the gross industrial production in the official social product series (i.e., net material product plus amortization, plus immediate consumption of raw material, semi-products, energy, etc.) (line 2) increased more than eight times, whereas the official index of industrial production under the heading 'industry' (line 1) increased more than thirteen times. In contrast, the private (Lazarcik/Alton's) index suggests that over the same period industrial production in Czechoslovakia increased less than five times.

Whatever virtues individual methods of calculation may have, it is clear that of all official indices that which is related to the NMP, that is line 3 in Table 9.7, is least affected by an upward bias. The official sources, however, especially when making international comparisons, tend to use the index with the highest figures (obviously the least realistic). As we have no other yardstick to assess the real growth in the Czechoslovak economy we must be satisfied with the assumption that between 1948 and 1985 the material product increased about five times and industrial production about six times.

Bearing these qualifications in mind we may ask how the growing product was used. The official figures, which refer only to material goods and services, indicate that between 1948 and 1985 output and investment grew more than private consumption (output by over 50 per cent more and gross investment by almost 75 per cent more).

More comprehensive figures can be obtained from the main shares of the GNP by final use calculated according to the SNA method (see Table 9.8). In order to show the impact of communist policies Table 9.8 also contains

Table 9.7 Czechoslovakia: various indices of industrial production, 1958–85 (1948 = 100)

	1958	1968	1978	1985
1 Official index of industrial production (Section 'Industry') of the Statistical Yearbooks	300	582	1,078	1,322
2 Gross industrial production in the official social product series at constant prices	239	433	735	836
3 Net industrial production in the official national income produced series at constant prices	220	370	640	735
4 Lazarcik/Alton *et al.*'s value added index	184	320	427	475

Sources: Lines 1, 2, 3: *Yearbook of Historical Statistics ČSSR*, 1985: 85, 89, 242; and *Statistical Yearbook ČSSR* 1986: 31, 129, 130; line 4, Lazarcik 1969, and Alton *et al.* 1984, 1987.

Table 9.8 Czechoslovakia: shares of GNP by final use, 1929–84 (% at current prices, SNA method)

	Managed market economy				Centrally planned economy			
	1929	1933	1937	1948	1959[c]	1968	1975	1984
Private consumption	67.7	75.7	67.9	65.1	50.4	52.0	47.8	47.8
Government consumption	11.0	12.6	16.1	17.0	20.0	18.7	20.5	23.5
Gross fixed investment	19.4	10.4	17.1	15.1	23.5	24.0	27.5	22.9
Foreign balance	0.3	−0.3	0.5	−1.3	1.1	0.5	−1.1	3.1
Increase in stock	1.6	1.6	−1.6	4.1	3.6	3.7	4.2	1.8
Losses	n.a.	n.a.	n.a.	n.a.	1.4	1.1	1.1	0.9
Extended private consumption[a]	71.1[b]	84.0	75.0	77.2	60.0	64.0	61.9	62.5

a Private consumption plus government expenditure on education, culture, health service, and social care plus investment in dwelling houses
b 1930
c Data adjusted to the wholesale/retail price ratio established from 1 January 1967 (see p. 196)

Sources: Krejčí 1968 (no. 6: 583; no. 11: 1049); Krejčí in Kaser and Radice, forthcoming (vol. 4) updated. For more detail, see also Krejčí 1982.

selected pre-war years covering the 1929–37 economic cycle. These, together with 1948, show how GNP was used under the conditions of a more or less managed market economy. The rest shows the respective proportions in the centrally planned economy.

All these data are at current (1988) prices which creates problems of comparability when prices are formed under different economic systems. Fortunately for our comparison the domestic market price relationship was only gravely distorted in the period between 1950 and 1966 and then again, but to a lesser degree, in the 1980s. The price reform with effect from 1 January 1967 achieved a substantial reduction of the gap between retail and wholesale prices, which had been created after 1948. Although this gap began to reappear in the late 1970s it only attained half its previous size.

Keeping the problems about prices in mind, Table 9.8 shows that the share of private consumption was sharply reduced under the centrally planned regime. In the pre-war economy it had fluctuated between two-thirds and three-quarters of GNP; in the postwar, planned economy it was cut to 50 per cent or less (it increased slightly in 1968, the peak year of the economic reform, but has slipped again since then). Government consumption, by contrast, has been increased. Part of this increase occurred pre-war with rearmament and at the time of the communist takeover it was high again (though the military requirements in 1948 were very modest in comparison with 1937). However, it has increased further since then and there has been a tendency to further growth in the 1980s.

The share of fixed investment which had proved to be extremely sensitive to the economic cycle of the 1930s kept well above the 20 per cent mark during the whole period of the centrally planned economy; the peak of almost 28 per cent was reached in 1975. An item of particular relevance for the state socialist economies is the investment in stocks. Judging from the repeated official criticism of the high level of stock increases, their magnitude in the structure of the GNP apparently reveals a failure in the efficiency of planning. Together with fixed investment which is not completed on schedule, the increases in stocks are officially considered as the main flaws on the output side of the economy. Reported losses are a special item separately disclosed in the Czechoslovak statistics (since 1948). They may be considered as a balancing item which reflects mainly the depreciation of stocks and production rejects.

Another factor to be borne in mind (both in western and state socialist countries) in comparing pre-war and postwar developments is that the part of government consumption which directly benefits the private consumer is higher since the Second World War than before. Taking into account all government expenditure (current and capital) on education, culture, health service, and social care, and also all public investment in dwelling houses, and adding these items to the private consumption, we arrive at 'Extended Private Consumption'. This is undoubtedly a fairer measure of the full share of consumers in the final use of the GNP. But, even with this adjustment, the share of the consumer in the years of the 'centrally planned economy' remains substantially below that of the 'managed market economy'.

As far as the foreign balance is concerned, little can be derived from the data throughout the period; with the exception of 1984 the fluctuations appear in comparable limits. However, after the communist takeover in 1948, there was, of course, a dramatic reorientation of foreign trade towards the USSR and other state socialist countries. Their combined share of Czechoslovak foreign trade increased from about 40 per cent in 1948 to 70 per cent in 1960, then it levelled out, but by the mid-1980s it had increased to almost 80 per cent.

There were also substantial changes in the terms of trade, especially at the beginning and towards the end of the period under study. In the first post-war years the terms of trade proved to be very favourable for Czecho-slovakia (UN Trade Statistics 1950, show the export/import unit value to be 20 per cent above the parity of 1937). But, during the 1950s this advantage was more than lost. A slight improvement in the 1960s has been followed since 1970 by a continuous deterioration which gathered momentum in the mid-1970s. As a result, by 1983 the export/import unit value was 27 per cent below the parity of 1970 (*Yearbook of Historical Statistics ČSSR* 1985: 322).

Efficiency – the problem of the day

The crucial issue for the further development of Czechoslovak (as of any other) economy is the efficiency of factors of production. The Czecho-slovak authorities became increasingly aware of this problem from the early 1960s and allowed more data to be published. As Table 9.9 shows there was a significant decline of efficiency of fixed assets after 1953 (the year of drastic monetary reform), a partial recovery in the late 1960s during the period of economic reform, and then a further decline from 1970 to the present. Czechoslovakia, however, continued to invest: from 1970 to 1985 the yearly increases of productive assets per person employed were even higher than in any previous period. In the case of labour productivity, after a remarkable recovery in the late 1960s this declined considerably, especially in the most recent five-year period (1980-5). With declining productivity of both labour and capital at the end of the period there is little doubt that the reformers' call for intensive growth based on increasing the productivity of all factors of production instead of extensive growth based on simple increases of the magnitude of inputs has not been heeded.

A further disadvantage of the emphasis on extensive growth has been the waste of material. The stress on the fulfilment of planned targets in physical units led to neglect of costs and this was one of the reasons why the

Table 9.9 Czechoslovakia: economic growth and efficiency (official data), 1949–85 (average growth rates per annum in % at constant prices or physical units)

	1 Net material product[a]	2 Employment in material production	3 Productive assets per person employed[b]	4 Productivity of labour[c]	5 Efficiency of assets[d]
1949–53	9.3	0.1	2.9	9.2	6.1
1954–5	6.8	2.1	2.2	4.7	3.1
1956–60	7.0	−0.1	4.6	1.5	−2.9
1966–70	6.9	1.2	3.0	5.6	2.5
1971–5	5.6	0.3	5.3	5.3	0.1
1976–80	3.7	0.4	5.5	3.3	−2.4
1981–5	1.8	0.4	4.9	1.3	−3.3

a National income produced
b Both indicators refer to material production only
c National income produced per person employed in material production
d National income produced per 1,000 korunas of productive assets in material production

Sources: Statistical Yearbooks ČSSR 1975: 23, 24; 1978: 129; 1982: 150; 1986: 131, 184. *Yearbook of Historical Statistics ČSSR* 1985: 146, 166.

reformers wanted to re-establish the profit motive. It is difficult, however, to find a suitable indicator for the extent of material wastage. The one used by the Czechoslovak economists and planners is a comparison of the rates of growth of national income produced (NMP) and of intermediate consumption. Intermediate consumption is the amount of inputs counted at the enterprise level (i.e., that part of gross production which does not constitute value added; which includes also the amortization of fixed assets and all semi-products – the last of these is particularly unreliable since it changes with the demarcation of enterprises). The indicator, labelled 'material claim on the production of national income', is defined as the volume of intermediate consumption per unit of national income produced. According to this indicator, between 1949 and 1965 wastage was on an ascending scale; the quinquennial averages increased from 0.6 to 3.1 per cent per annum. Since then the quinquennial averages have been close to zero, whilst the per annum values fluctuated within the range of plus or minus 1.7 per cent. However, repeated complaints in the press comparing the use of raw material for production of particular products in Czechoslovakia with other industrial countries show that the situation is still far from satisfactory.

Conclusion

On the strength of facts and figures discussed above it is clear that the Czechoslovak economy has shown both positive and negative features. On the one hand state socialist Czechoslovakia succeeded in attaining a more or less sustained economic growth, but this was not without fluctuations and at a decelerating pace. It also succeeded in achieving some more equality in socio-economic terms, such as between the blue and white-collar workers, between earnings in towns and villages and, last but not least, between the Czech and Slovak part of the state. There was also no question of unemployment: on the contrary, the ambitious investment targets required an extensive mobilization of labour reserves including, in the 1950s, a measure of forced labour.

On the other hand, however, quantitative growth was accompanied by decreasing efficiency and, what matters most for the bulk of the population, its main fruits were targeted towards capital formation and government consumption neither of which brought commensurate benefit to the consumer. Overmanning in administration and in the production of producers' goods as well as general wastage played a considerable role in the decline of efficiency. At the same time, the political leadership and the armed forces, including the police, were exempt from the drive towards more equality and the socio-economic levelling of the rank and file was offset by a substantial delevelling in the political sphere. Moreover, highly concentrated political power and the extension of its scope to all walks of life created a precarious state of civic inequality. Those who can, look for compensation in the 'second', alternative, economy which provides scope for a new type of socio-economic differentiation. Another, but narrower, escape route is that of the alternative culture which struggles for self-assertion at the border of legality.

In a word, this is the paradox of a system in which the requirements of the blueprint have clashed with the conditions of feasibility.

Selected dates: Czechoslovakia

April 1945	Coalition government declares the principles of economic policy.
April 1945	Slovakia's autonomy established.
October 1945	Big business nationalized by law.
November 1945	Beginning of the first monetary reform.
1946	German minority expelled; resettlement of the borderland.
October 1946	First Economic Plan (for two years) declared by law.
Spring 1947	Rationing reduced to minimum but soon extended again.
February 1948	Communist *coup d'état*; one party dictatorship established; Slovakia's autonomy limited.
April 1948	Further nationalization by law followed by expropriations outside law.
October 1948	First Five Year Plan declared by law.
January 1949	Czechoslovakia takes part in the constitution of the Council of Mutual Economic Assistance (CMEA).
June 1951	Decision to intensify collectivization of agriculture.
June 1953	Second monetary reform.
May 1955	Warsaw Pact concluded (Czechoslovakia founding member).
June 1956	First attempt at economic reform (resolution of the Communist Party conference).
July 1960	New Constitution: Czechoslovakia declared Socialist republic; Slovakia's autonomy virtually abolished.
December 1960	Second attempt at economic reform (12th Congress of the Communist Party).
May–June 1966	Third attempt at economic reform inaugurated (13th Congress of the Communist Party).
January 1967	Comprehensive price reform.
January 1968	Beginning of the reformers' rule.
August 1968	Soviet invasion; subsequent end of the reformers' rule.
January 1969	Czechoslovakia becomes federation of the Czech and Slovak socialist republics.

July 1987   Draft of a new law on the national enterprise (Fourth attempt at economic reform?).

References

Adam, J. (1979) *Wage Control and Inflation in the Soviet Bloc Countries*, London: Macmillan.

Alton, T.P., *et al. Economic Growth in Eastern Europe*, Research project on national income in East Central Europe, OP 80 (1984), OP 95 (1987), New York.

Brown, A., and Gray, J. (eds) (1979) *Political Culture and Political Change in Communist States*, 2nd edn, London: Macmillan.

German Institute for Economic Research (1979) *Handbook of the Economy of the German Democratic Republic*, London: Saxon House.

Graham, L.S., and Ciechocinska, M.K. (eds) (1987) *The Polish Dilemma, Views from Within*, Boulder, Col. and London: Westview Press.

Hare, P., Radice, H., and Swain, N. (eds) (1981) *Hungary, A Decade of Economic Reform*, London: Allen & Unwin.

Kaser, M.C., and Radice, E.A. (eds) (1986) *The Economic History of Eastern Europe 1919–1975*, Oxford: Clarendon Press, vols 2, 3; vol. 4 forthcoming.

Krejčí, J. (1968) 'Vývoj československého hospodářství v globální analýze', *Politická ekonomie*, 6.

Krejčí, J. (1968) 'Vývoj československého hospodářství v letech 1926–1937', *Politická ekonomie*, 11.

Krejčí, J. (1972) *Social Change and Stratification in Postwar Czechoslovakia*, London: Macmillan.

Krejčí, J. (1982) *National Income and Outlay in Czechoslovakia, Poland and Yugoslavia*, London: Macmillan.

Lazarcik, G. (1969) *Czechoslovak GNP 1937 and 1948–1965*, New York: Columbia University Press.

OECD *Economic Survey (1973–86) Yugoslavia*, Paris.

Sirc, L. (1979) *The Yugoslav Economy under Self-Management*, London: Macmillan.

UNECE (1970) *Economic Survey of Europe in 1969*, part 1, New York.

Statistical Yearbook ČSSR (1985, 1986), Prague.

Yearbook of Historical Statistics ČSSR (1985, 1986), Prague.

Chapter ten

The Soviet Union

Philip Hanson

Introduction

In a book on economic performance and policy in the developed world, chapters on the Soviet Union and eastern Europe might be said to deal with a world apart. This is most strikingly the case for the Soviet Union. Politically the USSR is a one-party state with (even now) an official doctrine, censorship, and a large internal security force. The economy is centrally administered, so that direct central control takes the place of market-forces-plus-central-intervention. (To call the Soviet economy centrally planned begs too many questions about the meaning of planning. To call it a command economy 'implies a more top-down, military style and more obedience than there has in fact been, at any rate since Stalin.)

If the record of Soviet economic performance and policy carries any lessons at all for western policy-makers, they can only be of a very general kind. The lesson that seems to emerge is this: for all their formal powers, Soviet policy-makers have often been unable to steer their country's economy in the direction they wanted. In arriving at that conclusion, this chapter pursues a course that is slightly different from that of most of the other chapters. This Introduction therefore covers three topics: the special political overtones of Soviet economic performance, the problem of Soviet statistics, and the traditional Soviet growth model and its recent decline.

The remainder of the chapter describes the objectives and instruments of Soviet policy (both are quite different from those of the west) and then reviews alternative analyses of the central policy problem now faced in the USSR: the long-term slowdown in growth. Finally there is a consideration of the major policy shifts since Stalin and of the connection of these with the economy's performance.

The politics of Soviet economic performance

The Soviet Communist Party long ago set the Soviet nation the task of 'catching up and overtaking' the economies of the west. This historic project is intended to show the superiority of Soviet socialism over capitalism, to increase Soviet international influence and to enable the USSR to maintain a strategic balance with the west – some would say, to achieve political domination over the west. In the 1961 Party Programme, adopted under Khrushchev, dates were put on this catching up and over-taking. By 1980 the USSR was to have overtaken American output levels and to be entering the blissful state of full communism. In fact the Soviet economy grew fast up to the 1960s but has since decelerated. From 1974, Soviet official statistics show Soviet output no longer catching up that of the US but stuck at about two-thirds of US final material output.

The new party programme gives no hostages to fortune in the form of deadlines. But Mr Gorbachev has said on several occasions that 'the future of socialism in the world' depends on the Soviet economy growing faster than it has recently been doing. In other words, the superpower status of the Soviet Union is in jeopardy. For that reason, improved performance is the central aim of current policies.

Measurement problems

With issues like these lurking in the background, it is harder to assess Soviet growth objectively than it is, say, to assess British growth in comparison with French, German, or American. None the less the task would be much easier than it is if Soviet economic data were acceptable for the purposes of international comparisons. They are not. First, there is the relatively minor issue of definitions: the Soviet definition of national income excludes most services and depreciation; the Soviet definitions of industrial and agri-cultural output are both gross or turnover series, combining the sales figures of all basic reporting units. This would be no great impediment to compari-sons if the official statistics were acceptable measures of what is, in principle, being measured. The most serious problems are to do with the reliability of the numbers themselves.

There are several defects in the Soviet statistics. All have been well discussed in the western specialist literature (Hardt and Treml 1972; Marer 1985; Pitzer 1982; Treml 1988). Briefly summarized, the main deficiencies are the following. Many of the Soviet statistics that are published are not clearly defined, or their derivation explained, in Soviet sources. For much of Soviet history there has been a tendency to tendentious presentation, such as the use of Laspeyres volume indices with valuation in the prices of a distant base-year. In addition, industrial output, investment, and capital-stock suffer especially from an under-accounting of inflation; in other words, there is hidden inflation within what purport to be constant-price or 'volume' series, and so real growth is overstated (Hanson 1984). Finally, there are gaps in what is published, which hamper both the re-calculation of

Soviet series and the analysis of the sources of Soviet growth: military production, money supply, and labour input data, especially.

There is also a profound problem of the meaning even of carefully recalculated Soviet growth rates. Actual Soviet prices are more heavily administered than prices in western countries. Shortages and surpluses of products are numerous and substantial. The relationship between total output of any nation, valued at its final prices, and economic welfare is imperfect under the best of circumstances; in Soviet conditions, where waste, shortages, and disequilibrium in general are pervasive, and prices are remote from equilibrium levels, it is tenuous in the extreme. The prevailing producer prices, moreover, do not lend themselves even to meaningful measures of productive capacity, since rates of return on capital differ very widely among different parts of the economy and rental payments for land are not systematically levied.

Western methodology for recalculating Soviet and East European national output is based on the 'adjusted factor cost' approach pioneered by Abram Bergson. It provides, in principle, a measure of productive potential rather than economic welfare. Even in this role, it has its limitations: reliance on a limited sample of output data by product, heroic assumptions in the calculation of appropriate rates of return for capital, and (in CIA estimates of Soviet GNP by end-use) an acceptance of Soviet 'constant-price' investment and capital-stock series that contain hidden inflation.

In the discussion that follows, a studious attempt will be made to treat the various assessments of Soviet growth impartially. But it is as well to be clear

Table 10.1 A comparison of Soviet and western measures of the growth rates of output and investment in the USSR, 1950–85 (average annual changes, %)

	Net material product (official series)	GNP (CIA estimate)	Investment (official)	Investment (CIA)
1950–5	11.4	5.5	12.3	12.4
1955–60	9.2	5.9	13.0	10.5
1960–5	6.5	5.0	5.4	7.6
1965–70	7.7	5.1	7.5	5.3
1970–5	5.7	3.0	6.9	5.4
1975–80	4.2	2.3	3.3	4.0
1980–5	3.5	1.9	3.5	3.5
Total change (1985 as a multiple of 1950)	10.2	4.1	12.0	10.4

Sources: Narodnoe khozyaistvo SSSR (various years), *Pravda*, 24 January 1988, and Bornstein and Fusfeld 1962:2.

from the outset that the estimates available are subject to margins of error considerably larger than is the case for developed western nations. An indication of the scale of this problem can be seen in Table 10.1 which compares the 'official' measures of the growth of output and investment with estimates prepared by the CIA. On the official series output grows tenfold between 1950 and 1985, whereas on the CIA estimate the growth is only fourfold. On the face of it, there is greater similarity in the measures of investment with both series showing a very high rate of growth, but this must be treated with considerable caution as the CIA figures for investment, unlike other elements in the CIA estimates, rely heavily on Soviet official data. (Further details of the official series, including an analysis by leadership periods is given in Tables 10.2 and 10.3.)

The traditional Soviet growth model and its decline

Despite the difficulties of measurement, on any assessment, the long-term growth rate of the Soviet economy has been high by international standards. At the start of the Soviet industrialization drive, in 1928, Soviet per capita GNP was about one-fifth that of the US (Eckstein 1962). In 1985, according to the CIA estimates of the geometric mean of 1970 ruble and 1976 dollar valuations, the ratio was between two-fifths and one half (CIA

Table 10.2 Soviet economic growth (official series), 1945–87 (average annual changes, %)

	1940–5	1945–50	1950–5	1955–60	1960–5	1965–70
NYP	−3.2	14.6	11.4	9.2	6.5	7.7
GIO	−1.7	13.6	10.4	8.6	8.6	8.5
GAO	−7.0	10.5	4.0	5.9	2.3	4.2
I	−1.4	16.1	12.3	13.0	5.4	7.5
Population			1.7	1.8	1.6	1.0

	1970–5	1975–80	1980–5	1986	1987
NYP	5.7	4.2	3.5	4.1	2.3
GIO	7.4	4.4	3.6	4.9	3.8
GAO	0.8	1.6	2.1	5.3	0.2
I	6.9	3.3	3.5	8.3	4.7
Population	0.9	0.9	0.9	1.0	1.0

Notes: NYP = national income (net material product) produced; in 1926/7 prices through 1950; in 1951 prices, 1951–5; in 1956 prices, 1956–8; in 1958 prices, 1959–65; in 1965 prices, 1966–80; then in 1982 prices
GIO = gross industrial output; in 1926/7 prices through 1950; in 1952 ex-works prices, 1951–5; in 1955 ex-works prices, 1956–67; in 1967 ex-works prices, 1967–80; then in 1982 ex-works prices
GAO = gross agricultural product; in 1926/7 prices through 1950; in 1951 prices in 1951–6; in 1956 and then 1958 prices, 1956–60; then in 1973 prices
I = gross investment; in 1969 estimate prices through 1964; in 1984 estimate prices thereafter

Sources: Narodnoe khozyaistvo SSSR (various years) and Pravda, 24 January 1988.

Table 10.3 Soviet growth (official series) by leadership periods, 1945–87 (average annual changes, %)

	Stalin 1945–53	Khrushchev 1953–64	Brezhnev 1964–82	Andropov–Chernenko– Gorbachev, 1982–7
NYP	13.2	8.7	5.6	3.4
GIO	13.5	9.3	6.4	4.2
GAO	7.0	5.0	2.3	2.2
I	13.9	10.3	5.8	4.7

Notes: see Table 10.2

Sources: *Narodnoe Khozyaistvo SSSR* (various years) and *Pravda*, 24 January 1988.

Table 10.4 Hypothetical projections of growth rates, and the date of 'catch-up' of USSR with US (beginning 1962)

US growth rates (% per annum)		2.5	3	4
USSR growth rates (% per annum)	6	1981	1985	1996
	7	1976	1978	1985
	8	1973	1975	1978

Source: Bornstein and Fusfeld 1962: 2.

1986). The historic aim of catching up has therefore been partly achieved: at least, over half a century, the Soviet lag behind the most powerful capitalist country has been reduced.

Indeed, until the early 1970s the USSR seemed to many western observers to be on course to complete the agenda of catching up and overtaking. In the first edition of their book of readings on the Soviet economy, in 1962, Morris Bornstein and Daniel Fusfeld illustrated the catching-up process with Table 10.4 of projected catch-up dates on the basis of what seemed at the time to be plausible extrapolations of the growth rates of real GNP in the two countries. (The dates are of the years in which total Soviet GNP would equal that of the US.)

Over a decade later, when Soviet growth had clearly slowed since the 1950s and 1960s, it was still reasonable for the authors of another American textbook to suggest that Soviet growth since the late 1920s was on average above that of any capitalist country, even Japan, from the beginning of its industrialization to the 1960s (Gregory and Stuart 1974).

All these authors were careful to point out that there was no guarantee that Soviet growth would remain as high in the future as it had been in the past. All pointed to the gross inefficiency of the Soviet economic system in resource allocation in a static sense. Most western specialists also stressed that the Soviet economy had grown fast by mobilizing resources at great speed – and at horrendous human costs – rather than by raising the productivity of resources used with any special rapidity. Moreover, there was a consensus among western specialists that the Soviet official claims about growth rates were exaggerated, even though the alternative recalculations offered were far from unanimous. It is now clear that many Soviet economists make the same judgement (Khanin 1981); Khanin and Selyunin 1987). Still, the general view was that the Soviet system did have advantages when it came to sheer growth – at any rate during the process of industrialization.

The chief advantages of the Soviet growth model were the following. First, the central policy-makers could and did impose a high rate of saving and investment. Today, gross fixed capital formation is estimated at about 23 per cent of Soviet GNP: not exceptional, but still above the share in the US (CIA 1986). Second, the heavy industry strategy entailed the concentration of investment in the producer-goods sector. This raised production capacity over time with particular rapidity, though with an infinitely delayable pay-off to consumption; in other words, there was a tendency to produce machines to produce machines to produce machines – the cultivation of what Peter Wiles called a 'solipsistic enclave'.

Third, the social and economic regime was one that facilitated the rapid mobilization of labour reserves – the initial late 1920s pool of unemployed people and the mainly female part of the working-age population which had not previously entered the labour force. By the same token, Soviet-style 'planning from supply' (that is, planning production to use up all available resources) guarantees the absorption of labour-force entrants into employment. (A high proportion of people past retirement age also work in the USSR.)

Finally, and this is a point that is not usually stressed in western accounts of the Soviet growth model, the emphasis on accumulation of capital has extended to human capital and to research and development (R and D) expenditure. Given its development level, the Soviet Union has spent heavily on technical and scientific education and on the employment of research scientists and engineers. The number of Soviet research scientists and engineers in recent years has been about 50 per cent higher than that in the US, though the Soviet population is less than 20 per cent larger (Hanson and Pavitt 1987). This heavy investment in R and D has been concentrated on the copying of western technology and on military programmes, but it has been at least a potential source of growth.

To a considerable extent, then, the rapid growth of Soviet output over some sixty years has been due to the rapid growth of inputs mobilized by the Soviet authorities. This style of growth is the product of a mixture of policy and system: the policy-makers have put growth first and have had to hand a social system that facilitates such mobilization. Moreover, traditional Soviet priorities among sectors, favouring industry and construction over agriculture and services, have led to a particularly rapid build-up of resources in sectors where the level and growth rate of labour productivity have been relatively high. The transfer of labour out of agriculture into industry, usual in all industrialization processes, went ahead particularly fast in the USSR, and the subsequent shift of resources into the service sector has been slow by international standards.

One result is that capital stock has grown much faster than man-hours, and continues to do so. Only Japan, amongst capitalist countries, has had a similarly rapid growth of the capital to labour ratio in the postwar period. Another result is that the industrial sector (whose weight in Soviet official measures of national income has been biased upwards by the distorted system of established 'market' prices) bulks exceptionally large in Soviet output, even when the latter is assessed at adjusted factor cost. These features of the Soviet pattern of growth can be seen in Tables 10.5 and 10.6.

Table 10.5 contains what might be called 'conventional' estimates of the growth rate of total factor productivity (TFP) in the Soviet economy: the growth of output not attributable to the growth of inputs of capital and labour. TFP I is an estimate in which the growth of capital and labour inputs combined is estimated with weights that would be typical for many western economies. TFP II uses weights approximating those used by the CIA, which are derived from CIA estimates of appropriate factor shares in Soviet GNP, and attach a much larger influence to capital. In both cases, productivity growth is depicted as low or negative, and deteriorating, throughout the period. This representation of the Soviet growth process reinforces the view that the Soviet growth model relies on extensive (resource-mobilizing) rather than intensive (productivity-enhancing) development.

The objectives and instruments of Soviet economic policy

Objectives

The Soviet economic agenda is set by the west. The main objective of Soviet economic policy since the war has been to maintain faster economic growth than the west in general and the US in particular. The political rationale for that objective has been the achievement and maintenance of the status of a military superpower and the demonstration that Soviet socialism was a superior economic system that would catch up and overtake the capitalist world in productivity and consumer prosperity.

One subsidiary objective that is not entirely reducible to a means to this end has been to copy, adopt, and diffuse western product and process technologies. Absorbing technology from industrially more advanced countries is a normal feature of the growth of late-developing economies. But for Soviet policy-makers, with their centrally administered system, it is a large part of the policy agenda. The Soviets have shown less readiness than the Chinese to develop alternative or 'appropriate' technologies, and less ability

Table 10.5 Soviet growth (CIA estimates), 1950–87 (average annual changes, %)

	1950–5	1955–60	1960–5	1965–70	1970–5
GNP	5.5	5.9	5.0	5.1	3.0
Ind. output	10.2	8.3	6.6	6.4	5.5
Ag. output	3.5	4.2	2.8	3.4	−2.3
Investment	12.4	10.5	7.6	5.3	5.4
Per capita cons.	3.1	3.8	2.7	5.3	2.8
Capital stock	7.9	9.2	9.7	7.4	8.0
Labour inputs	1.9	0.6	1.6	2.0	1.7
TFP I	2.1	3.2	1.4	1.7	−0.3
TFP II	0.9	1.4	−0.2	0.7	−1.5
Memorandum item:					
OECD GDP	4.8	3.3	5.3	4.6	3.0

	1975–80	1980–5	1986	1987
GNP	2.3	1.9	3.9	0.5
Ind. output	2.7	1.9	2.5	1.5
Ag. output	0.2	1.2	8.2	−3.1
Investment	4.0	3.5	6.0	4.7
Per capita cons.	1.9	0.7	−2.0	0.7
Capital stock	6.9	6.2	5.4	5.3
Labour inputs	1.2	0.7	0.4	0.4
TFP I	−0.3	−0.2	2.2	−1.1
TFP II	−1.5	−1.3	1.2	−2.1
Memorandum item:				
OECD GDP	3.3	2.5		

Notes: Output figures at 1970 rubel factor cost through 1965; at 1982 rubel factor cost thereafter. Investment at 1970 prices through 1965; at 1973 prices thereafter. Capital stock is gross; at 1955 prices through 1965; at 1973 prices thereafter. Both investment and capital stock growth are probably overstated. Consumption at 1970 factor cost through 1960; thereafter at 1982 established final prices. Labour inputs in man-hours as estimated by the Bureau of the Census of the US Commerce Department. TFP = total factor productivity, combining labour and capital only, with fixed weights
TFP I: capital weight = 0.25, labour weight = 0.75
TFP II: capital weight = 0.45, labour weight = 0.55

Sources: US Congress Joint Economic Committee, *USSR: Measures of Economic Growth and Development, 1950–80*, Washington, DC: US Government Printing Office, 1982, for output and investment through 1965 and consumption through 1960; Laurie Kurzweg, 'Trends in Soviet gross national product', US Congress Joint Economic Committee, *Gorbachev's Economic Plans*, Washington, DC: US Government Printing Office, 1987, 1: 126–66, for output after 1965, consumption after 1960, investment in 1986 and capital and labour series for 1966–86; *CIA Handbook of Economic Statistics 1986* for investment 1966–85; Padma Desai, *The Soviet Economy. Problems and Prospects*, Oxford: Blackwell, 1987: 146, for the capital stock and labour series for 1950–65; CIA/DIA, 'Gorbachev's economic program: problems emerge', report to the Subcommittee on National Security Economics of the US Congress Joint Economic Committee, 13 April 1988.

Table 10.6 Percentage shares of Soviet GNP by sectors of origin, 1950–85 (selected years) (western estimates in adjusted ruble factor cost)

	1950	1965	1985
Agriculture	30.6	22.9/30	19
Industry	20.4	30.5/28	34
Construction	4.3	7.1/7	8
Transport, communications, trade	9.5	15.5/13	17
Services	29.5	21.5/18	18
Other	5.9	2.4/3	2

Notes: The 1950 shares and the first of the two shares given for 1965 are in 1970 ruble factor cost. The second of the 1965 figures and the 1985 figures are in 1982 ruble factor cost

Sources: 1950 and the first set of figures for 1965: US Congress Joint Economic Committee, see Table 10.3. The second set of figures for 1965 and the 1985 shares: CIA, Handbook of Economic Statistics 1986: 67.

than the Japanese to move from copying through modification to indigenous innovation (Hanson and Pavitt 1987).

There are other elements in the Soviet agenda that are perhaps best seen as constraints rather than as additional objectives. There has been an implicit social contract with the population that certain traditional features of Soviet life would not be disturbed: full employment, a high degree of job security, low work effort, stable prices for 'necessities', and rather stable and narrow money-income differentials.

There has also been a requirement that social welfare provision and the ownership of productive assets should remain 'socialist'. So far as social welfare provision is concerned, the evidence is that this is a popular arrangement that could be seen as a part of the implicit social contract. So far as ownership is concerned, the evidence about popular appeal is unclear. The preservation of party rule, however, has almost certainly been seen as requiring it. The other important constraint has been the maintenance of a strong balance of payments in convertible currencies (low debt–service ratio and high reserves – though both are state secrets). That reflects an understandable caution about borrowing from and 'dependence' on the west.

The rigidity of these constraints should not be exaggerated. Consumer price stability applies to rented housing and public transport (at rates set before the Second World War) and to basic food items in state shops (at prices fixed in 1955 or 1962, depending on the product). Changes in product-mix and the over-pricing of new manufactured consumer goods have led to an officially unacknowledged upward movement in retail prices of about 2–3 per cent a year. Similarly, unemployment does not officially exist (and unemployment benefit does not exist at all), but there is a small margin of frictional unemployment at any given time. In any case, full employment and a regime of high job security have been a by-product of the shortage economy. Enterprises are rewarded for meeting output targets and not penalized for bidding for more resources than they need or for wasteful use of resources allocated to them. There is therefore a chronic excess demand for labour, along with all other inputs. So long as the micro-economic rules of the game remain the same, policy-makers do not have to worry about full employment as a macro-economic objective; it will be maintained anyway.

During the Brezhnev period (1964–82) the policy constraints and the policy objectives began to come into conflict. As was pointed out (p. 216), Soviet growth slowed to the point where the gap with the US was no longer narrowing. Slow growth emerged as the most fundamental policy problem, followed closely by a key structural problem: the near stagnation of per capita food production and worsening consumer shortages. The notion that these problems arise from the constraints listed above (or at least from some of them) has now been acknowledged by Mr Gorbachev and his allies. Current public discussion, encouraged by Gorbachev himself, calls into question four of the constraints: job security, narrow income differentials, fixed prices of necessities, and socialist ownership (at least the traditional identification of it with state ownership). Legislation is already beginning to show an intention to change some of these constraints: most notably a draft law on co-operatives, published in March 1988, that could drastically alter ownership arrangements in the Soviet system. This chapter deals only with policies and performance up to the late eighties, but there is no doubt that major changes are now under way.

Policy instruments

Soviet economic policy instruments are determined by the economic system. The import bill, for example, is controlled by direct administrative decisions ('cut imports by 10 per cent') and not by deflating domestic demand or manipulating the exchange rate. In general, macro-economic policy in the western sense of influencing aggregate demand does not exist. There have been inflationary pressures but their consequences are not of the kind encountered in market economies. Most prices are nominally controlled and politically sensitive prices are controlled very effectively. However, the stability of certain prices, despite rising production costs, has created a budgetary problem: a high and rising level of budget subsidies, not easily supported by budget revenues. That in turn seems to have been dealt with by an expansion of the money supply that has added to inflationary pressures (Pavlov 1988). But it is still possible for policy to be conducted through exclusively micro-economic measures. The existence of a budget deficit was admitted only in 1988, money supply data are not published, and the built-in systemic guarantee of full employment plus the insulation of domestic prices and output quantities from world-market influences make the penalties for ignoring aggregate demand tolerable. The idea that the money supply might be a proper object for major policy decisions is only just beginning to be aired.

The policy-makers have acted above all through resource-allocation decisions in physical or in fixed-price ruble-value terms. The scope of policy-making in these respects is far greater than in the west. The planners have to come up with annual and five-year targets for the output of a large number of products and product groups. Supporting those targets are detailed plans for the allocation of some 18,000 product groups between specific producers and users. (Changes in these arrangements were announced in 1988.) Correspondingly, the central policy-makers are responsible for deciding, not just influencing, the level and branch and regional allocation of investment and the volume and composition of imports and exports.

The innovation process, similarly, is not something to be merely indirectly influenced by science policy and industrial policy. Each five-year plan in recent times has contained 150 to 200 priority programmes for research, development, and innovation, with designated performers, targets, and resources. Lower-priority technology programmes are also incorporated in the plans, though at the level, broadly speaking, of branch plans.

These tools of economic policy are hard to distinguish from routine management procedures. (It is not at all fanciful to think of the Soviet economy as a single giant corporation, with the Politburo as the board of directors.) In any comparison with western policy-making, however, it seems reasonable to identify the following as the main instruments of Soviet economic policy: priority setting (between end-uses, between regions, between industries, between foreign and domestic sources of supply, and in investment allocation); price policy; and changes in economic institutions.

The last of these is central to Soviet policy but only intermittently important in the west. This is because the Soviet economic system has very little capacity for institutional change 'from below'. Almost all changes of any significance in institutions and standard operating procedures have to be decreed by the authorities. Small software firms, new types of markets, new financial instruments, and so on cannot simply evolve under the pressure of market influences. Officially, at least, they have traditionally had to be approved from above. Institutional change (not necessarily 'reform' in the usual sense of decentralization, but including reform) is perennially on the agenda of government. The party–state authorities are responsible for organizational structure as well as for performance.

For this reason organizational changes in the Soviet economy are apt, when they do come, to be rather clumsy. For example, from 1987 a number of production enterprises (about 100, by mid-1988) have been given the right to conclude foreign transactions for themselves instead of having to go through the traditional foreign trade organizations under the foreign trade ministry. Having been given these rights, the enterprises in question were *required* to set up their own foreign trade firms; when two enterprises wanted to set up a joint foreign trade firm – as was the case for the ZIL and Moskvich motor plants – they were not allowed to do so. In general the legislation and regulations covering economic management are based, not on the principle that whatever is not forbidden is allowed, but on the basis that only what is explicitly required, recommended, or permitted may be done.

Rapid growth and slowdown: the standard interpretation

In the CIA's annual *Handbook of Economic Statistics* a regular table shows the results of a simple growth accounting exercise that purports to measure changes over time in the productivity of labour, capital, and land combined in Soviet production. Such measures are apt to raise more questions than they answer. Nevertheless, this sort of measure – which might be called the standard version of events – will serve as a starting point for an assessment of the forces behind the Soviet growth slowdown.

According to this version of events, Soviet growth has been achieved by the rapid mobilization of labour and capital, and of the most readily available natural resources. The growth of productivity has been low or negative, reflecting a low rate of 'technical change' and/or mounting inefficiency both in the allocation of resources and in the use of resources.) This pattern of growth was compatible with a relatively fast increase of output so long as there were substantial additional resources available to be mobilized.

In the 1960s and 1970s, however, according to the standard account, such reserves dwindled. It became virtually impossible to raise the population's participation rate in the labour force any further, so labour-force growth came to depend very largely on the growth of the working-age population, and this growth was slowing. In addition, the most readily accessible reserves of fuel and minerals in the western parts of the USSR began to be depleted, and the exploitation of reserves east of the Urals entailed sharply increasing infrastructure investment and transport costs, and in some cases increasing extraction costs.

Other things equal, these influences might have been offset by faster growth of the capital stock. But investment growth and capital stock growth had been high for a long time. An acceleration of the growth of investment when other factors were dragging down output growth would have required an increase in the investment share of GNP, putting pressure on the growth of consumption and defence. In fact, the Soviet authorities chose in the mid-1970s to hold back the growth rate of investment (Table 10.1 above shows the slowdown on both the official and the CIA measures).

Another way of ending the slowdown would have been to achieve an acceleration of productivity growth. No doubt this was highly desirable but the system was not equipped to provide it. The conclusions of a series of case studies of Soviet technology levels have been widely cited to support this view. Across a wide range of technologies, Soviet production does not seem to have reduced significantly the technology lags behind the west that existed in the 1950s. So long as productivity growth is interpreted as a measure of technological change, or as strongly influenced by technological change, the conclusion seemed plausible: the Soviet system was bad at generating rapid technological change; therefore its productivity growth was slow; therefore, short of a major reform, Soviet growth could not be reinvigorated through faster technological change.

Some problems with the standard interpretation

This view of the Soviet slowdown has been summarized so baldly as to do less than justice to some of the more thoughtful expositions. Bergson's careful exercise in growth accounting, in which he tried to identify and measure 'technological progress proper' within the residual, is one such (Bergson, 1983). Nevertheless, there is much that is convincing in the standard account. Certainly Soviet growth has entailed rapid capital accumulation and rapid mobilization of labour supplies. Certainly those sources of growth have shrunk, and a more rapid growth of productivity would have offset the retarding effect of that shrinkage. Much of the analysis, indeed, has been implicitly accepted by Soviet policy-makers in their search for a change to so-called 'intensive' growth.

At the same time, there are problems with this account. The structure of the Soviet economy has been rapidly transformed since the 1920s, and this process continued for much of the postwar period (see Table 10.6). Certain highly aggregative approaches to separating different sources of Soviet growth have found total factor productivity growth to be slow. But it is hard to believe that this finding is really telling us that output growth due to the introduction and diffusion of technologies new to the USSR has been slow. If new technologies have not been introduced into Soviet production at a considerable rate, the words 'industrial development' must have lost all meaning. As for the slowdown in output growth, it is one thing to note that input growth has slowed, and quite another to show, as the conventional measures do, that productivity growth has also deteriorated. If measured productivity growth is a reflection chiefly of technological change, what has been happening that would have produced a rapid deceleration of technological change?

There is no firm answer to these questions, but some provisional answers can be put forward.

First, the simple measures of total factor productivity growth for the economy as a whole are heavily influenced by the changing composition of output. The modernization of the Soviet economy has entailed a rapid increase in the share of sectors and branches where the initial level and subsequent growth of output per unit of inputs has been relatively high. This is true within the industrial sector alone, and *a fortiori* in the economy as a whole. After a time, however, this process of structural change has slowed down, and as a result measured productivity growth could also be expected, other things being equal, to slow (Gomulka 1986).

Second, measures of the kind cited here are based on heroic assumptions about the aggregate production function: in particular, that it makes sense to analyse a whole economy as though there is such a thing as an aggregate production function and that a Cobb-Douglas function with fixed input weights derived from factor shares appropriate to a perfectly competitive economy are appropriate to the Soviet economy. For the Soviet industrial sector alone, and for sectors of industry. Padma Desai has shown that Cobb-Douglas production functions can be estimated, and give quite a good statistical fit. Her estimates, however, yield 'weights' (elasticities of output with respect to capital and labour inputs) that vary substantially from sector to sector and mostly bear little resemblance to factor-share weights (Desai 1987). It is true that Desai also endorses the view that total factor productivity growth has been low or negative in Soviet industry, and declining over time. However, that conclusion is vulnerable to the data problem that constitutes our third objection to the standard account.

The western estimates of Soviet output growth are generally preferable to the Soviet official figures. They may be slightly downwards biased because of their reliance on a fixed sample of products that understates (though it does not totally exclude) the impact of rapidly growing new products, but they are probably the best output measures available. The standard western estimates for recent years (those of the CIA), however, accept Soviet measures of investment and capital stock that contain hidden inflation. As the CIA assessments exclude such an upward bias on the output side, the Agency's measures of total factor productivity growth are almost certainly downwards biased, and probably increasingly so in recent years (Hanson 1984). In general, the weight attached to capital accumulation in most western accounts of the Soviet growth model and the slowdown, is probably exaggerated. The Soviet track record on productivity growth, at least in recent years, is probably better than it looks in these accounts – though not necessarily good by international standards.

The final observation to be made about the standard version of the Soviet growth slowdown is that technological change in the sense of the introduction and diffusion of new products and processes should not be identified with productivity growth, however the latter is measured. Technological change (with respect to processes but not products) may be a major source of measured productivity growth in most economies in the very long run. As Edward Denison's studies of western economies have shown, however, productivity growth can be decomposed into a number of elements, of which advances in knowledge are only one. Changes in the age and sex composition of the labour force, changes in resource allocation between branches, changes in educational level of the workforce, economies of scale, increases in crime rates, increases in expenditure on environmental protection, and so on can all have an influence. Major once-for-all errors in resource allocation and intangibles such as large changes in popular mood and morale could, by the same token, also have an influence. The 'stagnation' of the later Brezhnev period probably derives from a combination of factors of this kind.

Policy shifts and their effects

The first major shifts in Soviet economic policy came after the death of Stalin in 1953. They were initiated by a collective leadership in which Malenkov was the *primus inter pares*, and followed up by Khrushchev. They consisted of a shift in publicly stated priorities in favour of consumption as against investment and, associated with this, a shift of resource allocation in favour of agriculture. The more favourable treatment of agriculture took the form of raising state procurement prices paid to the farms, which had been held down to punitive levels under Stalin, reducing some of the administrative controls of the farms. The immediate effect of the price changes was to improve incentives and raise rural incomes. The end result is not easy to detect but Tables 10.3 and 10.5 indicate some narrowing of growth-rate differentials between agriculture and industry and Table 10.5 shows, between the first and second halves of the 1950s, an improvement in consumption growth alongside a slowdown in the growth of investment.

In the late 1950s Khrushchev's enhanced priority for agriculture took the particular form of the ploughing-up and cultivation of a huge additional land area – the Virgin Lands Scheme. That campaign raised agriculture's share in total investment, though it is possible that the policy-makers did not think of that share as a policy variable. At all events, Khrushchev presided over a long-term policy change that was adhered to, and even accentuated, under Brezhnev.

Other policy changes under Khrushchev included the following: a shift of resources out of military and into civilian end-uses in the form of large cuts in military personnel; the only postwar attempt to raise prices of necessities, in the form of increased state prices for meat and dairy products in 1962 (provoking at least one major riot, with considerable loss of life); the launching of a major programme of housing construction; an opening of trade relations with the western world (starting with imports of chemical plant as part of the 'chemicalization' drive launched in 1958); and a major institutional change: the switch from a branch to a regional structure of planning and management, which was made in 1957, somewhat modified in the early 1960s and then reversed in 1965 after Khrushchev's removal from office the previous year.

Khrushchev's policy changes were all a matter of changing priorities and changing the price structure, with the exception of the territorial reform of planning and management. This latter has generally been treated as a failure in subsequent Soviet writings.

For all the ridicule subsequently heaped on Khrushchev in the Soviet Union for so-called 'hare-brained schemes', two lasting achievements of economic policy can be put to his credit: an opening, albeit limited, of the Soviet economy to the outside world and an enhanced priority for household consumption and agriculture. If Stalin's priorities and his treatment of the farm sector had continued unchanged, the substantial growth of per capita consumption and of farm output between the early 1950s and the late 1970s would be barely conceivable.

In the Brezhnev era Soviet economic policy-makers came up against severe limits to policy. It should however be remembered that Brezhnev tended on the whole to maintain Khrushchevian priorities for consumption and for agriculture, and that much of the improvement on both those fronts occurred while he was in power. In the last few years, however, from 1978 to 1982, farm output stagnated, and the general slowdown of the economy left consumption levels growing at a rate estimated by the CIA at 1 per cent a year between 1975 and 1985.

Institutional reforms

The attempted institutional reform of 1965–7, the so-called 'Kosygin' reform, is generally considered to have failed to change economic behaviour. It was a somewhat limited, semi-market reform in intention, and was not accompanied either by more open discussion of economic problems or by any attention to the underlying system of property rights. In general, policy changes under Brezhnev after 1967 were overwhelmingly a matter of shifts in priority. Changes in price structure and substantial changes in institutions were avoided. State prices for 'necessities' were left unchanged, apparently for fear of discontent. As a result (given that production costs moved upwards, particularly in agriculture), shortages and the volume of subsidies tended to grow. There had been a general shift in 1967 to wholesale prices based on average branch production cost plus a standard rate of return on capital, based on costs and capital assets in that year. These prices were essentially frozen until 1982, while retail prices did not change at all, officially. Meanwhile prices paid to farms by the state were moved upwards periodically, continuing Khrushchev's attempts to elicit more farm output.

The important priority shifts that took place under Brezhnev included the following: a further increase in the role permitted for trade with the west in the late 1960s to early 1970s, initially emphasizing imports of western machinery and technology but shifting later towards food imports; attempts to cut the investment share of national income from 1975; a slowdown, probably partly intended and partly enforced, in the rate of military hardware procurement between about 1975 and Brezhnev's death in 1982; increasingly heavy resource allocation to the energy sector and the farm sector, the latter culminating in the 'Food Programme' launched in May 1982.

After 1965-7, institutional changes were frequent but minor: examples include the promotion of industrial associations or combines (multi-plant enterprises) in 1973, numerous changes in enterprise 'success indicators', a lengthy and detailed decree on planning and management in 1979 that introduced little that was substantively new, extensive tinkering with science policy and the institutions concerned with it, and so on.

Worsening performance

Meanwhile, economic growth was dwindling and consumer shortages were getting worse. Windfall terms-of-trade gains arising from the OPEC oil price rises were useful but only slightly softened the effects of deteriorating domestic performance. The effectiveness of policies was as much in doubt as it had long been in the British economy – but with the embarrassing difference that the Soviet leaders' formal responsibility for economic performance is well-nigh total and their claim to be guided by a scientific theory of society is part of official doctrine. In a remarkable speech at the November 1978 Central Committee plenum, Mr Brezhnev lamented the failure of branch ministries to control enterprises and of the leadership's decrees to influence ministries (*Pravda*, 28 November 1978). There is a school of thought, with adherents among both Soviet and American economists, which maintains that the strategic policy decision to cut the growth of investment in 1975 was itself a contributory factor in the slowdown.

Perestroika

Policies since Brezhnev have gradually become bolder. The main element in the new policies at first was tougher discipline for both workers and managers, including a purge of senior personnel. This approach, initiated by Andropov (with some tentative beginnings towards the end of Brezhnev's rule) in the form of an anti-corruption drive, was later extended by Gorbachev to include an anti-alcohol campaign. In an authority-intensive system, run as a single hierarchy, such policies are a legitimate weapon of economic management. They have probably produced some gains in X-efficiency, though cuts in alcohol supply, without complementary adjustments in the supply of other consumer items or in money incomes, have also exacerbated consumer shortages and the problems of the state budget.

Gorbachev has also made some important decisions on priorities. So far as planned shares of available inputs are concerned, agriculture and consumption have been down-graded and investment, the engineering sector, and research and development are planned to have a larger share of resources. (Some increases in priority for health services and housing are an important qualification to what has been said about consumption.)

Conclusion

The success of Gorbachev's policies in dealing with the growth slowdown and the inter-connected set of problems in the farm sector and the consumer goods sector has yet to be demonstrated. The standard view, both in the west and in the USSR, is that it is the success or failure of institutional reforms that will in the long run be crucial. These reforms are at a very early stage. They include the introduction of a heavily guided market system in the state sector, the substantial expansion of a legitimate non-state sector (private and co-operative, the latter being a polite form of the former), and a further, more institutionalized opening up to the world economy. The extent to which these measures are implemented should become visible by the early 1990s and their effects on performance should begin to be visible in the late 1990s. So far, under Gorbachev, growth has first improved and then (in 1987–9) slumped again.

The main conclusions to be drawn from the postwar record so far are the following. Priority changes after the death of Stalin yielded the sort of effects that policy-makers were seeking, but later on such changes lost their effectiveness. Institutional changes have been frequent but so far ineffective. Up to the late eighties Soviet policy-makers have tried to work within a system in which their power to change economic performance for the better has dwindled to apparently very low levels. Neither the long-term productivity slowdown nor the structural weaknesses in agriculture and the consumer sector generally have yielded in any detectable way to the attentions of the Soviet leaders and their advisers.

It is tempting to believe that Gorbachev will eventually make a difference. It is none the less far from certain that he will. The radicalism of his economic policies – and indeed much of their general character – is reminiscent of Mrs Thatcher; like her, he is putting the power of government to change national economic performance to as severe a test as can readily be imagined. The obstacles in his way, however, are massive.

Selected dates

1953   Death of Stalin. Khrushchev later emerges as leader.

1954–8	Major expansion of sown area (the 'Virgin Lands Scheme') and higher priority for agriculture.
1957	Switch from branch to regional administration of the economy.
1958	Start of Khrushchev's 'chemicalization' campaign. First postwar turnkey plant deals for western firms.
1962	State retail meat and milk prices raised. Riots.
October 1964	Khrushchev ousted. Brezhnev emerges as new leader.
March 1965	Further agricultural reforms announced.
September 1965	Return to branch-ministry administration. Reforms announced for industry (the 'Kosygin' reforms).
1966	Fiat contract to build car plant at Tolyatti.
1968–9	Loss of momentum of the Kosygin reforms.
May 1972	Soviet–US trade agreements signed in Moscow by Nixon and Brezhnev.
1973	Measures to group Soviet enterprises into associations.
January 1975	USSR abrogates trade agreements with US following conditions for ratification set by US Congress.
November 1982	Death of Brezhnev. Andopov becomes party leader.
February 1984	Death of Andropov. Chernenko becomes party leader.
March 1985	Death of Chernenko. Gorbachev becomes party leader.
January 1987	Western firms allowed to set up joint ventures in USSR.
June 1987	New Law on the State Enterprise approved. Related reform measures follow.
March 1988	Radical draft law on co-operatives announced.

References

Bergson, A. (1983) 'Technological progress', in A. Bergson and H.S. Levine (eds), *The Soviet Economy: Toward the Year 2000*, London: Allen & Unwin.

Bornstein, M. and Fusfeld, D.R. (eds) (1962) *The Soviet Economy: A Book of Readings*, Homewood, Ill.: Irwin.

CIA (1986) *Handbook of Economic Statistics 1986*, Washington, DC: CIA.

Desai, P. (1987) *The Soviet Economy, Problems and Prospects*, Oxford: Blackwell.

Eckstein, A. (1962) 'The background of Soviet economic performance', in M. Bornstein and D.R. Fusfeld (eds), *The Soviet Economy. A Book of Readings*, Homewood, Ill.: Irwin.

Gomulka, S. (1986) 'Soviet growth slowdown: duality, maturity and innovation', *American Economic Review*, May.

Gregory, P. and Stuart, R. (1974) *Soviet Economy: Structure and Performance*, New York: Harper & Row.

Hanson, P. (1984) 'The CIA, the TsSU and the real growth of Soviet investment', *Soviet Studies*, October.

Hanson, P. and Pavitt, K. (1987) *The Comparative Economics of Research, Development and Innovation in East and West: A Survey*, London: Harwood Academic Publishers.

Hardt, J. and Treml, V. (eds) (1972) *Soviet Economic Statistics*, Durham, NC: Duke University Press.

Khanin, G.I. (1981) 'Al'ternativnye otsenki rezul'tatov khozyaistvennoi deyatel'nosti proizvodstvennykh yacheek proizvodstva', *Izvestiya Akademii Nauk SSSR, seriya ekonomicheskaya*, no. 6.

Khanin, G.I. and Selyunin, V. (1987) 'Lukavaya tsifra', *Novyi mir*, no. 2.

Marer, P. (1985) *Dollar GNPs of the USSR and Eastern Europe*, Baltimore, MD: Johns Hopkins University Press for the World Bank.

Pavlov, B. (1988) 'Rost i struktura ekonomiki', *Ekonomicheskaya gazeta*, no. 14.

Pitzer, J. (1982) 'Gross National Product of the USSR, 1950–80', in US Congress Joint Economic Committee, *USSR: Measures of Economic Growth and Development, 1950–80*, Washington DC: US Government Printing Office, 1982.

Treml, V. (1988) '*Perestroyka* and Soviet Statistics', *Soviet Economy*, January–March.

Further reading

Bergson, A. and Levine, H.S. (eds) (1983) *The Soviet Economy: Toward the Year 2000*, London: Allen & Unwin.

Buck, T. and Cole, J. (1987) *Modern Soviet Economic Performance*, Oxford: Blackwell.

Desai, P. (1988) 'Perestroika in perspective: the design and dilemmas of Soviet reform', Columbia University, Department of Economics, Discussion Paper Series, no. 396.

Nove, A. (1969) *An Economic History of the USSR*, Harmondsworth: Penguin.

Nove, A. (1982) *The Soviet Economic System*, Nove, A. 2nd edn, London: Allen & Unwin.

US Congress Joint Economic Committee (1987) *Gorbachev's Economic Plans* (2 vols), Washington, DC: US Government Printing Office.

Weichhardt, R. (ed.) (1987) *The Soviet Economy: A New Course*? Brussels: NATO.

Chapter eleven

The United States

Joseph Hogan and Andrew Graham

Introduction

The United States ended the Second World War as the undoubted leader of the western world. It had, in fact, become the richest country in the world much earlier, surpassing the UK in terms of income per head about 1890, and by 1939 it was the largest economic power and much the wealthiest nation on earth. But it was the Second World War which dramatically reinforced this situation and which brought full realization of US dominance. Unlike the UK, the US had not run down its external assets to pay for the war and unlike the Japanese and continental European economies which suffered massive physical and social disruption, US territory had not been touched, its fixed capital assets had not been damaged and, under the pressure of war-time demand, its output had grown faster than at any other time this century.

Looked at just in terms of GDP per head, by 1947 the US was more than one and a half times richer than the UK, three times richer than West Germany and no less than six times richer than Japan. Moreover, with a population approaching 150 million (at least two to three times that of any other industrial nation), the US had a command over resources several multiples of that of any other country. Yet even these numbers understate the overall disparities in power and influence at the end of the Second World War. One noted US economic commentator describes the situation as follows:

> The United States emerged into the postwar period in a near vacuum of international competition, equipped with the world's only industrial base. Its currency – the only reserve currency – commanded such immense respect that for twenty-five years it was preferred to gold . . . [the result was that] . . . the United States ran a trade surplus in every postwar year until 1971; its first significant deficit on current account was in 1977; its net investment income reached a peak in 1981. (Sommers and Blau, 1988: 6)

The strength of the US was not limited to how it was seen (and saw itself) internationally. Domestically there was a new consensus on what the objectives and instruments of economic policy should be. The contrast between the demoralization and mass unemployment of the depression (at over 25 per cent when Roosevelt became president in 1933) and the return to prosperity, following the New Deal and the expansion of government involvement in the economy, was not lost on the American public. By 1945 continuation of full employment was the priority and government intervention to achieve it more acceptable. The Employment Act of 1946 endorsed this opinion and committed the federal government to the aim of achieving 'maximum employment, production and purchasing power'. This Act and the institutions that accompanied it (especially the Joint Economic Committee in Congress and the Council of Economic Advisers in the Executive Branch) were established to oversee the economy and were the formal recognition of the new public, activist economics.

Yet neither the new consensus nor the position of world dominance was to remain unchallenged. Over the subsequent forty years new ideas, new industrial nations, and new capital markets emerged. As a result the economic performance of the US economy has to be seen as starting from great strength, but with the initial advantage being gradually eroded. Internally political and economic events undermined agreement on how the economy should be run and, externally, there was a gradual realization by the US that it was no longer able to call the tune on international finance and trade.

The objectives and instruments of policy

These changes in the US are readily seen in how US economists and political scientists describe the period. In a symposium held in 1986 to commemorate forty years of existence of the Joint Economic Committee of Congress, the Employment Act of 1946 is described as the ratification of the primary objectives of the New Deal – 'Keynesian demand management, continued development of a social insurance system (e.g., social security, unemployment insurance, later medicare, etc.), and the expansion of equal access to education and job opportunities.' (Obey and Sarbanes 1986:1) At the same time the comment is made that the consensus persisted and even grew in the breadth of its appeal from the 1950s to its high point under the Kennedy administration of the 1960s. However, thereafter it declined in the face of the events and ideas of the 1970s and 1980s and gave way first to monetarism, second to the inactivism of the rational expectations school and third, to supply-side economics. Finally, the growth in the importance of international factors is noted as is the renewed interest in activist economics that occurred at the very end of the period. Thus, at least from one perspective the position has come full circle.

To describe the US economy in this way is to place the emphasis on the climate of ideas and, in particular, on the instruments of policy. Alternatively, the focus could be placed on the changes in objectives. What altered was not the *set* of objectives, but the one given priority. Thus the primary concern under Truman in the immediate postwar years was to avoid a return to unemployment, but when the economy proved all too easy to keep going in the late 1940s and was then further boosted by the Korean War the emphasis shifted under Eisenhower to concern about inflation. This in its turn gave way to Kennedy's concern to boost growth followed by Johnson's goal of reducing inequality. Then, as inflation built up in the late 1960s, the cycle begins again. Nixon's main worry is inflation, Carter's is unemployment and Reagan's is inflation followed later by unemployment. Finally, at the end the US becomes concerned for the first time with its balance of payments position (arguably Nixon's actions in 1971 mark the beginning of this concern, but the worry in 1971 was more to do with the role of the dollar in international finance than with the payments position *per se*).

Looked at like this, the US is remarkably similar to the UK. Governments in both countries often seemed incapable of keeping more than one objective in mind at any one moment. They also seem to have had similar ideas on the instruments to be used. In both cases the Keynesian consensus on demand-side management (primarily through fiscal policy) reached its high point in the 1960s and in both cases this is followed by a greater emphasis on monetary policy and then by a more radical shift, at least as judged by the rhetoric of policy, to supply-side management during the 1980s and a renewed emphasis on markets. There is, it would seem, a greater similarity in the climate of ideas on either side of the Atlantic than on either side of the English Channel.

However, this description of US policy needs much qualification. First, the aim of balancing the budget continued to be a preoccupation of almost all presidents (which is not to say it was often achieved) as it was for much of the business community and many opinion formers in Congress – far more so than was the case in the UK. Second, whilst one objective of policy frequently dominated political discussion, most policy-makers were well aware of the trade-offs involved (and much work was done in the US trying to estimate the empirical significance of these trade-offs). Third, and most important, the constitutional and institutional structure of policy-making is quite different in the US – a fact which has important implications for the ability of the US to run a coherent fiscal policy.

The institutional structure of US policy-making

The shape of US economic policy-making is heavily influenced by three factors. The US is a federal, rather than a unitary, political system; there is a constitutional 'separation of powers' between the executive and legislative branches of government (i.e., between the powers of the president and the powers of Congress); and the US has a Central Bank (the Federal Reserve) which possesses real and independent powers. As a result, economic power is, at least in principle, dispersed and there is much scope for conflict. This is especially true for fiscal policy where there are a series of presidential and congressional procedures that interact sequentially to agree – or disagree – a federal budget, a federal tax regime, and other means for regulating the economy.

President Roosevelt responded to this problem by expanding the capacity of the presidency to manage the economy, mainly by increasing the staff of the presidency and, in 1939, by establishing the Executive Office of the President (the EOP), within which there were a number of specialist economic units. The most important development was the transferral of the Bureau of Budget from the Treasury to the EOP. The Bureau, now called the Office of Management and Budget (the OMB), prepares the president's budget and is his main instrument for imposing his fiscal policies upon the executive branch. The Treasury Department undertakes responsibility for managing the tax system, for leading on foreign economic policy, for conducting relations with the International Monetary Fund, and – through the issuing of Treasury bills – is also responsible for managing the government's debt. A third advisory body to the president on economic affairs – also within the EOP – is the Council of Economic Advisers (CEA), which was created by the Employment Act of 1946. It consists of three members who are economics experts; they are assisted by approximately fifteen professionals. The CEA analyses the consequences of economic policy proposals and helps initiate policies desired by the president. In particular it takes the lead in determining the economic assumptions upon which the president's budgetary and economic goals are built (Berman 1979; Clifford 1965; Norton 1977).

The OMB, the CEA and the Treasury are the president's economic 'Troika', meeting regularly to formulate and adjust the president's economic policies. Once the president's fiscal proposals are folded into his budget and submitted to Congress, the first stage of federal fiscal policy-making is completed. The second stage involves congressional examination of the president's budget proposals. This process is both complicated and time-consuming. It involves parcelling out various components of the budget for consideration by just about every committee in Congress and it has to occur, in near duplicate form, in both the House of Representatives and the Senate.

This complex structure creates multiple opportunities for Congress both to resist and to revise, often radically, presidential economic policy proposals. The House of Representatives may also disagree with the Senate. Moreover, partly because of the federal structure and partly for a complex set of historical reasons, there is no equivalent of the discipline of the UK political party within Congress and it is commonly thought that such cohesion as did exist at the end of the war declined in the 1960s and 1970s as more 'cross-cutting' issues appeared (McKay 1985). As a result fiscal policy-making in the US has great potential for conflict and confusion, is at best time consuming and at worst non-existent (Schick 1983).

Determining and managing the monetary component of federal economic policy is also a complicated process because it requires the president, his advisers, and Congress to co-ordinate monetary policy objectives with a central bank which has a significant degree of independence. The Federal Reserve Act of 1913 established the central banking system, which was developed by the Banking Acts of 1933 and 1935. The Federal Reserve Bank is organized into twelve districts and there are two main decision-making forums. The first, the Federal Reserve Board, is composed of seven members appointed by the president for fourteen-year terms (the person designated chairman, holds office for four years at a time on appointment by the president and with the consent of the Senate). The Board exercises exclusive jurisdiction over many factors concerning bank regulation and also sets the discount rate. The second, the Federal Open Market Committee (FOMC), consists of the seven board members and five of the presidents of the district banks. The FOMC is the most important forum for monetary policy decisions. It makes decisions about how to try to influence interest rates, the money supply and, ultimately, inflation and economic growth. At the same time, like all central banks, the Federal Reserve can act as a lender of last resort to forestall national liquidity crises and financial panics (Bach 1971; Woolley 1984).

The degree of independence of central banks is always a relative matter, but there is not much doubt that the 'Fed.' lies at the freer end of the spectrum. Admittedly it reports regularly to Congress on its policies, and meets frequently with the 'Troika', but its decisions do not have to be ratified by the president. Moreover, appointments, once made, cannot be undone. Most importantly, it has proved willing and able in practice to back its own judgements against the wishes of the president on the relatively few occasions when it has felt this to be really necessary.

The fragmentation of economic power and the legitimation of conflict in economic affairs in the US creates the potential for an exceptionally confused and anarchic form of policy. In practice the degree of cohesion or confusion has changed over time and is somewhat different with respect to micro policy, fiscal policy, and monetary policy.

Micro policy, being by it nature more decentralized and (especially in the US) often having a legislative component, has been most subject to the bargaining processes of Congress. It is also variable state by state and even locality by locality. As a result it can be argued that 'there is no federal industrial or regional strategy worth the name, and training and manpower policies are more ameliorative *ad hoc* measures than true labour market strategies'. (McKay 1985: 283). This does not mean the US has no micro policy. There is a powerful framework of law and a large number of regulatory agencies: the US is not at all the free market of economic textbooks. Equally it does not mean that there have been no changes in the thrust of micro policy: in the 1970s and 1980s, for example, there has been the growth of consumer and environmental concerns which US lobbyists have used with skill, but neither this network nor the policies adopted have been strongly influenced by a central leadership.

There is therefore nothing in the US directly comparable with the growth of interest in indicative planning from the centre such as occurred in France and Britain in the 1960s nor any attempt to increase co-ordination either nationally or locally that is comparable to the role played by the Ministry of International Trade and Industry (MITI) in Japan. In fact the one consistent theme of US micro policy has been the extent to which, compared to other countries, planning and co-ordination *between firms* has not been on the agenda – although some authors (Galbraith 1967; and Shonfield 1965), writing when ideas of indicative planning were at their height, suggest that the US compensated for this by having large firms and extensive planning *within* them. The US approach to price and wage policies exhibits the same point. Such policies were used rather infrequently and, even when they were, they took the form primarily of either direct legislative controls or of confrontations with one or two large firms; there is nothing comparable to European corporatism, because corporatism was neither an option desired in the US, nor, it could be argued, one really available.

In contrast, in the case of fiscal policy, while the potential for confusion and conflict existed from the outset, it was, in practice, significantly muted in the first two decades of the postwar era by the fact that the executive and the legislative branches shared something close to a consensus on the goals and instruments of economic policy. At the same time the Roosevelt administration had left in place a series of reforms which buttressed both fiscal and monetary policy.

In the course of the New Deal before the war, Roosevelt had established the Securities and Exchange Commission to regulate the securities market, the Federal Deposit Insurance Corporation was set up to guarantee bank deposits, unemployment compensation was enacted, minimum wage laws were passed, public works programmes were established, and social security was enacted for the elderly. Yet even these developments were not part of any plan to promote recovery, but rather expressed Roosevelt's willingness to experiment in order to rescue American capitalism. Moreover, while these pre-war measures might have been of only a temporary nature, the demands created by global armed conflict had required further and more extensive management of the economy by the federal government. The result of these series of unplanned developments covering the period from the 'great depression' through the Second World War was not just the creation of an extensive and permanent network of federal government institutions for managing the economy but also that a large number of automatic stabilizers had been put in place.

As a result, as we shall see, it was only when the US economy was heavily disturbed, partly by its own fiscal actions and partly by external shocks, at a time when the consensus on fiscal policy was already weakening that the real difficulties in running a 'rational' fiscal policy in the US came to the fore. This, of course, thrust the burden of stabilization onto monetary policy. Here the problem proved to be less one of fragmentation – the independence of the 'Fed.' was probably a positive advantage – and more the difficulty of achieving multiple objectives via a single instrument.

The main phases of economic policy

The postwar recovery: Truman and Eisenhower

As the Second World War drew to a close many economists and law-makers feared a return to economic depression. These fears proved groundless. All three of the main elements of domestic demand (private consumption, public consumption, and investment) were buoyant. The financing of the war, during which the federal deficits in 1943 and 1944 reached more than a quarter of GNP, had produced a massive Keynesian expansion of liquidity which consumers were keen to spend. At the same time public facilities were expanding and business was keen to exploit the technical advances that the war had produced. Added to this was the growth of foreign demand: Europe needed US goods to rebuild. Thus, with the exception of a mild recession in 1948–9, avoiding inflation proved to be more of a problem than avoiding unemployment for most of Truman's two periods of office.

The unexpected outbreak of the Korean War in 1950 exacerbated the problem of inflation. The subsequent explosion of defence spending triggered a new boom. Economic growth was further buoyed up by purchases of cars and houses, and anticipation of consumer goods shortages such as had occurred in the Second World War resulted in wide-spread hoarding. As a result of this rapid and unexpected growth the wholesale price index advanced by 12 per cent from June to December of 1950. To prevent further overheating, taxes were raised and credit tightened. Congress also gave President Truman broad authority to regulate the economy, including the reimposition of price and wage controls (which had been removed in November 1946), during the emergency conditions of the Korean War.

Of greater long-term significance for economic policy was the March 1951 Treasury/Federal Reserve Accord on monetary policy. Until this date

231

the Federal Reserve, under pressure from the president and the Treasury, had agreed to peg bond rates by buying government securities. In effect there was a ceiling on short-term interest rates of about 1.5 per cent and on long rates of about 2.5 per cent. However, as inflation accelerated the Federal Reserve became increasingly reluctant arguing that maintaining interest rates in these circumstances undermined confidence rather than added to it (Stein 1969: 275). Rates were eventually unpegged in April 1951 and monetary policy was restored as an instrument of general economic stabilization.

When the first Republican administration in twenty years came to power in 1953 there was a change in economic policy objectives (with greater priority being given to control of inflation) and also in instruments, but the shift fell well short of either a sea change or the alterations intended by the new president. President Eisenhower pledged himself to maintain 'security with solvency', but, despite the rhetoric as the economy slowed down in 1953 about balancing the budget, the Eisenhower administration was quite content to let the automatic fiscal stabilizers work. They also allowed monetary growth to encourage a recovery.

In fact a gradual shift towards a greater use of monetary policy instruments was evident throughout the Eisenhower administration. This was especially obvious in 1957 when the economy entered its third postwar recession. On this occasion monetary policy took the lead in fighting recession, with the Federal Reserve lowering its discount rate to 3 per cent in November of 1957 and to 1.75 per cent in May of 1958. In spite of this the recession proved to be the sharpest so far of the postwar period. Between August and April of 1958, industrial production dropped by 13 per cent and there was much discussion in Congress of tax cuts, but Eisenhower persisted in his aim of balancing the budget. The economy did eventually recover, but during the Eisenhower period as a whole the economy slowed down and unemployment rose (see Table 11.1). In particular the impression remained that more could have been done sooner to stop the 1958 recession and that fiscal policy could have been more active.

Tax cuts, welfare spending, and Vietnam: Kennedy and Johnson

The arrival of President Kennedy in office in 1960 signalled the new mood of fiscal activism. The new administration quickly pursued expansionary fiscal and monetary policies, which led to an improvement in output and consumer spending in 1961. Unemployment, however, still remained at over 6 per cent. This encouraged the administration to begin pursuing the much heralded strategy – the so-called 'new economics' – of cutting unemployment by a series of tax reductions.

The legislation providing for a 7 per cent tax credit on investment in new machinery and equipment was proposed and enacted in 1962. President

Table 11.1 Economic performance by presidential periods, 1948–88

	Output	Employment	Output per worker	Inflation	Change in unemployment
		Average annual change, %			*%*
1948–52 (Truman)	5.3	1.1	4.2	2.1	−1.1
1952–6 (Eisenhower I)	2.8	1.1	1.6	1.9	+1.1
1956–60 (Eisenhower II)	2.3	0.7	1.6	2.4	+1.4
1960–4 (Kennedy/Johnson)	4.6	1.3	3.2	1.3	−0.4
1964–8 (Johnson)	4.4	2.3	2.0	3.8	−1.5
1968–72 (Nixon I)	2.8	1.8	0.9	4.9	+2.1
1972–6 (Nixon II/Ford)	2.0	1.9	0.1	8.0	+2.0
1976–80 (Carter)	2.9	2.8	0.1	8.0	−0.6
1980–4 (Reagan I)	3.0	1.4	1.6	5.3	+0.4
1984–8 (Reagan II)	2.9	2.2	0.7	3.3	−1.9

Notes: (1) US Presidents are elected every four years in November, but hold office from the following January. The data shown here are therefore measured from the year before they held office until the last year of their period in power

(2) The data for 1988 are partly forecasts

Sources: Maddison 1982, OECD *Economic Outlook, June 1988*, and the OECD database.

Kennedy at the same time also sought legislation to cut personal income taxes. But Congress resisted this request, arguing that any decrease in tax revenues should be accompanied by corresponding cuts in federal spending. In response, the Kennedy administration resolved to secure an across-the-board major cut in personal income taxes to promote economic growth and reduce unemployment and Kennedy, using what would later have been called supply-side language, spoke of 'the restraining effects of the tax system on the economy' and of the choice between 'chronic deficits arising out of a slow rate of economic growth and temporary deficits stemming from a tax program designed to promote fuller use of our resources and more rapid economic growth'. The measure was quickly agreed by the House, but was considered to be too controversial by the Senate and was resisted. It was eventually only passed on the crest of the wave of sympathy that followed President Kennedy's assassination.

This Bill comprised the then biggest tax reduction in American history for individuals and corporations, pumping $14 billion into the economy. The delay limited the measure's effectiveness, but these fiscal measures, together with an expansion of monetary policy, undoubtedly helped to sustain and accelerate the expansion that had begun in 1961.

The accession of Lyndon Johnson to the presidency marked the zenith of the activist view of fiscal policy, with increased public expenditures and frequent changes in income tax rates leading as the central policy tools for managing the economy. Monetary policy, at least at first, was relegated to maintaining a low and stable level of long-term interest rates. The advisers to Kennedy and Johnson argued that using tax and monetary instruments to reduce unemployment would lead to only a moderate acceleration of inflation, and with strong economic growth and an inflation rate of only 3 per cent at the end of 1964 their gamble appeared to have been realized.

This policy framework ran, however, into extremely rough waters from the mid-1960s onwards. There were three main problems.

First, Lyndon Johnson wanted to do everything almost at once. The tax cuts of 1964 were therefore followed virtually immediately by the 'Great Society' initiative with federal programmes expanded to cover the poor, the elderly, the cities, the rural areas and, in order to build support for another round of fiscal activism, the middle class as well. At the same time he extended and accelerated US involvement in Vietnam. More butter *and* more guns were Johnson's requirements.

Second, while the tax cuts of 1964 were seen as a triumph for compensatory finance, the compensation in the opposite direction, as the economy began to overheat in 1966, proved to be a fresh and more difficult battle. Tax cuts were one thing, tax increases another. Thus, although inflation accelerated fairly continuously after 1965 and although, as early as 1966, the Joint Economic Committee recommended a tax surcharge, Johnson did not send a legislative proposal to Congress until August 1967 and the battle between president and Congress was not resolved until well into 1968 – and then only by combining a 10 per cent tax surcharge with a mandatory reduction in federal expenditures and only after an international gold crisis in March 1968 had pushed interest rates to record levels.

Third, the consensus about the role of policy itself began to fall apart. Amongst economists the issue at first was whether fiscal policy was as important as some of the Kennedy Keynesians supposed – was not monetary policy equally powerful, or more powerful? Later it became the much larger question of whether demand management policy had any influence at all in the long run on real output. However, more important in practice than either of these two theoretical disputes (though they undoubtedly played a role) was that the US found itself facing both unemployment and inflation and as this occurred so the consensus in Congress on the management of the economy declined. It was this problem which bedevilled the presidencies of Nixon, Ford, and Carter and which led eventually to the supply-side economics of Reagan.

Struggling with inflation and unemployment: Nixon, Ford, and Carter

As a result of Johnson's legacy, President Nixon inherited in 1969 a stubbornly inflationary economy – at least by the standards of the time (see Table 11.1). During the first two years of his presidency he pursued the traditional, essentially conservative approach adopted by past Republican presidents to tackling inflation. This involved tightening tax and spending policies to accumulate a small budget surplus. In addition, the Nixon administration restrained the supply of money. The administration recognized that tackling inflation meant accepting some increase in unemployment, but believed that by pursuing fiscal policies that sought moderate disinflation they could restrain the rise of unemployment. President Nixon was strongly criticized by congressional Democrats for pursuing disinflation at the expense of a rise in unemployment. This criticism mounted during the summer of 1970, when the administration's economic policy was charged with responsibility for creating a recession in a form that combined inflation and unemployment; and, with the unemployment rate moving in mid-1971 to over 6 per cent, Democratic presidential hopefuls began to savour the prospect of running against Nixon. Faced with the onset of recession and the prospect of losing the presidency Richard Nixon altered course.

On 15 August 1971 President Nixon announced his 'New Economic Policy'. The centrepiece consisted of a ninety-day wage and price freeze, along with the creation of a Pay Board and Price Commission to lead the drive against inflation. At the same time, the administration adopted a stimulative fiscal policy, which involved increasing public expenditure in the second half of the year and reducing taxes. The Federal Reserve Board supported this switch to a stimulative fiscal policy by expanding the money supply. The final component of Richard Nixon's new economic initiative involved abandoning the policy of converting dollars into gold on demand at a price of one ounce of gold for $35, mainly because the amount of foreign-held dollars outstanding had become far larger than the value of the US gold stock at that price. The federal government thus adopted a free, floating exchange rate instead of a fixed one for the dollar. The package stole the political initiative from the Democrats. The programme also achieved good initial results. In the early part of 1972, real output rose strongly, unemployment began to fall, and inflation did move down. In political terms, the package was regarded as a major contributor to President Nixon's landslide re-election in late 1972.

In policy terms, the package was much less successful. The wage and price controls did not usher in a period of disinflation. Instead the controls appeared to set a floor rather than a ceiling on wages and prices, which therefore encouraged inflation. The advent of the two 'supply shocks' in 1973 in the form of an explosion in world food prices due to crop failures and the rise in petroleum prices because of the OPEC cartel were especial and unforeseen factors that further complicated the situation. The administration soon found that it was boxed into controls; their mere existence seemed to encourage the public to anticipate that there would be a rise in inflation once controls were abandoned. To deal with this expectation the administration had to extend the controls several times beyond the initial ninety-day period, with controls actually expiring on 30 April 1974. Sustained and chronic inflation and a sharp reduction in consumer spending pushed the economy into recession again in late 1973.

The problems faced by the Ford and Carter administrations and the policies they used were essentially a continuation of those of Nixon only more so. Unemployment and inflation were both higher at the same time and policy oscillated between giving priority to the cure of one and then the other. Ford, faced with high inflation in 1974, resolved to pursue fiscal and monetary restraint, but, with the knock-on effects of the oil price and the world recession still coming through, he found himself, at first, with both more inflation and more unemployment. However, by 1977, the persistently high level of unemployment was associated with a decline in inflation and President Carter announced in early 1977 that his prime economic objective was fighting unemployment rather than inflation. He stated his intention was to reduce unemployment from 7.4 per cent in January of 1977 to a 'full-employment' target of 4.9 per cent. To do so he proposed a major increase in fiscal expenditures to stimulate the economy. Carter also proposed a package of tax cuts and sought to increase the money supply. This switch to a stimulative fiscal and monetary regime did produce a significant recovery, but it was also followed by further inflationary pressures. In particular, the second OPEC oil supply shock between 1978 and 1979 escalated inflation to record levels. As measured by the consumer price index, inflation reached 13.3 per cent from December of 1978 to December of 1979; the unemployment rate also moved upwards at the same time.

This escalation in the 'misery index' in 1979 signalled the demise of liberal activism in Democratic economic policy and led to a major change of course as the Carter administration made fighting inflation – and fighting inflation at first by monetary means – its prime economic objective.

Paul Volcker, the chairman of the Federal Reserve Board, with the support of the Carter administration, took the lead. On 6 October 1979 he announced, on behalf of the Federal Reserve, a change in procedures in which more attention would be paid to controlling bank reserves and less to controlling interest rates. The effect was immediate. US Treasury Bill rates rose sharply and, following this 'credit crunch', the economy slowed down in early 1980.

Volcker's move was widely interpreted as a move towards monetarism and a sterner determination to check inflation. It also marked, at least temporarily and in one direction, a change in the policy of 'benign neglect' of the dollar which had characterized most of the period since the dollar was floated in 1971. Under this policy, especially from 1973 to 1978, the US refrained from intervening in the foreign exchange market. More fundamentally, the US had always tended to regard domestic economic policy as the priority: the international aspects were no more than a small tail on a large dog.

The one exception to this had been at the end of 1977 when President Carter had shown concern about the US trade deficit and the instability in exchange markets and, following this, there were a series of substantial interventions during 1978, but in spite of these the dollar was again under pressure in 1979. The significance of the Volcker measures of October 1979 was that it marked a turning point for the dollar. For the next five years, especially after the transition from Carter to Reagan, the neglect became that of allowing the dollar to rise rather than failing to hold it up.

Carter did not, however, rely solely on monetary policy. In his January 1980 Economic Report he reaffirmed his support for the Fed.'s new policy and announced a four-point programme for tackling inflation. The fiscal component sought to reduce the federal budget deficit by restraining the growth in federal expenditures. The budget deficit, estimated at $40 billion in fiscal 1980, was set to reduce to a small surplus by the fiscal year 1981–2 (Stein 1985).

The attempts by both Gerald Ford and Jimmy Carter to use restrictive fiscal policies in order to tackle inflation were, however, at odds with both the predominant policy orientation and the economic policy-making structures in Congress which the Kennedy–Johnson era had bequeathed them. Congressional liberals had reformed congressional economic policy-making structures to make the legislature both more open and more accommodating to pressures for increased federal spending. There was greater participation in the legislative process by public pressure groups, who used their access to expand existing spending programmes and to advocate new ones. At the same time Congressmen realized that satisfied claimants were likely to re-elect their representatives and consequently made many spending programmes, particularly those with the most recipients, more secure through the passage of legislation that mandated spending on federal welfare and other benefit programmes irrespective of how the economy was performing.

Congress further reformed its economic policy-making procedures in 1974 when it passed – over a veto from a Watergate-weakened President Nixon – the 1974 Congressional Budget and Impoundment Controls Act. This legislation made significant changes in the involvement and powers of the president in federal budgeting, with Congress seeking to exercise almost total control over budgeting. Congressmen took the new procedures a stage further by adopting an accommodative approach to spending, simply aggregating the spending bids of each congressional committee. Accommodative budgeting produced federal budgets which represented a 'fiscal result' rather than anyone's – certainly not the president's – fiscal blueprint for managing the economy. The pro-spending orientation on Capitol Hill was also reinforced by a post-Watergate and post-Vietnam period of congressional assertiveness and public disenchantment with presidential leadership. The so-called 'imperial presidency' gave way, according to many political commentators, to the 'imperilled presidency' under which the president was increasingly limited in his capacity to set the governing agenda, including the course of economic policy.

Distributive budgeting boomed at the very time when the economy no longer yielded a 'growth dividend' to finance enlarged federal expenditures. In the first half of the 1970s the cost of social insurance and retirement programmes doubled in real terms. Increased spending on electorally popular domestic policies had been financed at the expense of progressive reductions in defence spending and by growth in the federal deficit. Budget deficits averaged about 3 per cent of GNP during the second half of the 1970s (twice the percentage of the previous decade) and the federal deficit doubled during the first seven years of operating the reformed budget procedures.

As the 1970s came to a close it was evident that both ends of Pennsylvania Avenue were seriously divided over the objectives and instruments of economic policy. Successive presidents had made fighting inflation their prime economic objective, and had pursued this policy by seeking monetary and fiscal restraint. Achieving monetary restraint was the more practical objective since it involved only obtaining the support of the Federal Reserve, which in fact often pursued monetary restraint in advance and independent of the presidency. By comparison, Congress had pursued accommodative spending strategies, rejecting – as was largely the response to President Carter – presidential requests for spending restraint. The contradictory mix of periodic monetary restraint and loose fiscal policies was undesirable. In order to restrict spending as part of any attack on the unusually high rates of inflation – induced in part by the second OPEC oil supply shock – in the late 1970s it was clear that a president had also to solve the dilemma of how to wrest political control of the institutions of federal budgeting from Congress (Fisher 1975; Mann and Ornstein 1981).

Supply-side policies: the Reagan years

When President Reagan took office at the beginning of 1981 unemployment stood at more than 7 per cent, consumer prices had risen by 24 per cent over the previous two years, interest rates were high and volatile, and productivity rates were lagging well below America's competitors. The Reagan administration came to office committed to adopting 'supply-side' policies for tackling simultaneously all these economic problems – or so they claimed.

Supply-side economics asserts that the weight of government expenditures and the resulting tax burden has acted as a drag on economic growth. Its supporters claim that by lowering government expenditures and taxes and by reducing regulation of the economy, energies in the marketplace will be unleashed so as to bring about a surge in private economic activity which, they argue, will create economic growth and new prosperity. Revenues will increase along with growth to pay for the essential government services that remain. Hence less becomes more.

It is essentially a capital formation strategy: new capital, it was claimed, would create productive capacity, jobs, and wealth in an accelerating and self-sustaining cycle. The role of government is not to create and respond to demand by generating public spending programmes. Indeed, supply-siders saw Keynesian demand management as responsible in large part for America's economic problems. Rather they believed that the task of government is to help unleash the supply of goods and services in the economy by redirecting them towards the private sector; thereafter it should stand aside and let the interplay of individual initiative promote economic growth.

The advocacy of supply-side tenets by the Reagan administration represented a significant departure from previous presidential economic policies, which could thus expect to encounter resistance from Congress. The president's advisers decided that their best chance for changing America's governing policies lay in 'hitting the ground running' with a comprehensive set of legislative proposals during the first few months of the new administration designed to take maximum advantage of Reagan's initial political honeymoon with Congress. During the transition period the president's advisers therefore put together a four-point programme to be implemented on taking office.

The first three parts of this programme, tax cuts, reduced growth in federal spending, and regulatory relief were intended to provide greater incentives for individuals, corporations, and businesses to work, save, and invest to promote economic growth. The fourth, slower growth in the money supply, was designed to lower inflation. The president's advisers soon encountered difficulties with the fiscal component of this economic plan. David Stockman, the president's designated director of the OMB, found that the plan to cut taxes deeply and to increase sharply the Pentagon's budget would widen the gap between revenue and income and thus lead to enlarged federal deficits rather than Reagan's promise of a balanced budget by 1984. At Stockman's request, the president agreed at the last minute to incorporate a series of further reductions in federal spending to attempt to square the policy circle and Stockman managed to cut such spending by $49 billion over the fiscal year 1981–2, but these cuts were insufficient to balance the budget projected for 1984. The 'solution' was found in the form of the 'magic asterisk' ploy under which Reagan's first budget incorporated 'unidentified spending reductions' amounting to $74 billion over the 1983–4 fiscal years (Greenstein 1983; Stockman 1986).

In the event, what happened to the economy was that there was a further slowdown and then a fall in output beginning in the second half of 1981 and running through 1982 (by the end of 1982 real GNP was lower than it had been three years earlier). Thereafter there was an even more dramatic recovery with the economy growing by 3.6 per cent and 6.8 per cent in 1983 and 1984 respectively, followed by a further expansion at near 3 per cent per year in the subsequent three years. At the same time inflation slowed down sharply from 1981 to 1983 and then stayed at the lower level thereafter.

These developments, together with the growth of employment and the expansion in the number of new small firms, were hailed by the Reagan administration as evidence of the success of its supply-side policies. Whether this is the whole truth (or anything like it) is highly doubtful. There are three main counter arguments.

First, Reagan did not balance the budget by 1984. On the contrary, as many critics had predicted, a combination of deep tax cuts, sharply increased defence spending, and 'hoped for', but unobtained, expenditure reductions produced a rapidly rising deficit. Admittedly the Reagan administration did achieve reductions in domestic expenditures planned for 1982–4, but these amounted to only $130 billion against the $200 billion proposed. Moreover, at the same time, Congress passed much larger tax cuts (for the period 1981–7 the president had requested cuts of about $300 billion, whereas the actual cuts were approximately $1,000 billion).

Second, conventional theory explains what happened perfectly well. The Fed. was able and willing to implement the monetary part of the package and so interest rates were pushed to record levels in 1981 (in the second half of the year nominal rates hovered near 20 per cent and real rates, which had

Table 11.2 The federal budget, the level of debt, and the balance of payments, 1943–84 (selected years)

	Actual budget deficit (−) or surplus (+) ($ billion)	Budget as % of GNP	'Adjusted budget' as % of GNP	Gross federal debt held by the public as % of GNP (end of period)	Current balance as % of GNP
1943	−55	−33			
1945	−48	−22		108.4	
1959	−13	−2.7	+2.9		−0.2
1960			+0.9	47.6	+0.6
1968	−25	−3.0	+0.2		
1969	+3	+0.4	+2.7		
1974	−6	−0.4	+2.0		+0.1
1975	−53	−3.6	−0.5	26.8	+1.1
1980	−74	−2.9	+2.0	27.8	+0.1
1981	−79	−2.7	+1.5		+0.2
1982	−127	−4.2	−2.0		−0.3
1983	−208	−6.5	+0.5		−1.4
1984	−185	−5.2	−2.4	36.7	−2.8

Note: The 'adjusted budget' allows for variations in the level of employment, inflation, and interest rates

Sources: Eisner 1986, *International Financial Statistics* 1977 Supplement, and OECD *Economic Outlook*, June 1988.

not exceeded 4 per cent in the whole of the rest of the postwar period, jumped to over 10 per cent). Then, following the crisis over Mexican debt in mid-1982, monetary policy was substantially relaxed. A similar argument can be made for fiscal policy. To see this we must adjust the deficit for three factors: (a) declines in output and employment which raise the deficit even though net tax rates are unchanged; (b) the effects of inflation which imposes an 'inflation tax', but for which no receipts appear in the official figures; and (c) interest rate changes which alter the real value of the stock of government debt outstanding. Eisner (1986) shows that adjusted for these effects fiscal policy was tight in 1981 and then had the biggest expansion on record (see the swing in the 'Adjusted Budget' from plus 1.5 per cent to minus 2.0 per cent of GDP from 1981 to 1982 in Table 11.2). In short, with both monetary and fiscal policy indicating recession and then recovery it is hardly surprising that this occurred.

Third, falling commodity prices from 1981 to 1985 allowed all countries to improve their inflation performance over this period. Added to this the high interest rates in the US began a long speculative upsurge in the dollar with the result that its rate against the average of all other countries rose by one-third from 1980 to 1985 (against sterling it rose by over 80 per cent). This not only lowered import prices into the US measured in dollars, but also contributed to a huge surge in imports and thus put US industry under much greater competitive pressure.

In other words, there is no need to resort to supply-side explanations to account for either the output or the inflationary experience of the US in this period. Moreover, if a supply-side change had occurred in this period it ought to have shown itself in improved productivity, higher savings, and improved capital formation. Admittedly as Table 11.4 shows there was some improvement in productivity in the years 1979–85 as compared with the period 1973–9 and this may reflect the benefits of supply-side policies. However, productivity still remained below the years before 1973, while investment as a percentage of GDP was slightly lower and personal savings fell sharply as a share of disposable income. Moreover, during the years when supply-side benefits are supposed to be showing, the US continued to perform poorly in international comparisons of investment and savings ratios and in the growth of productivity.

Less controversially there is little doubt that the rapid rise in the deficit and the associated rise in the dollar produced a seriously unbalanced economy. By 1985 the US had a budget deficit and a balance of payments deficit each of which was more than 3 per cent of GDP. Moreover, at the time, both were rising rapidly and beginning to look uncontrollable.

These twin deficits produced conflicting effects on both the US and on the world economy. On the credit side the stimulus to US demand from the expansionary fiscal policy almost certainly contributed to the US recovery. Then, as more and more of the demand leaked abroad, the stimulus shifted to other countries. On the debit side the effect of the large budget deficits, plus, still more, the expectation of larger deficits to come, worried financial markets. As a result even though real money growth had been accelerated in 1982, long-term interest rates fell less than short rates and, with actual inflation remaining low, the net effect was a perception of high real interest rates. Demand in the world economy was therefore being pushed up by the direct effects of the deficits, but pushed down by high real interest rates and, more generally, by the unease which these deficits engendered.

As far as US policy was concerned the effects of the deficits, together with more gradual perceptual changes about the role of the US in the world economy, was to set in train a significant reappraisal. The most obvious outward sign of change was the agreement amongst central banks to bring down the dollar (the Plaza accord of 1985), but this was followed, later in 1985, by the Baker plan for Third World debt and then in 1986 by Reagan's call for international policy co-ordination (see chapter 2). In other words, exchange rates were no longer to be left to the market and demand management, now at the international level, was back on the agenda.

One interpretation of these events would be that the US, having found that it could not run its own demand management, wanted Germany and Japan to do so on their behalf. However, these shifts in the US did also seem to be part of a longer term realization that the US could no longer display such a tendency to ignore the effects of its actions on the rest of the world nor, for that matter, the effect of the rest of the world on the US. With Japanese and German exports having become nearly equal to those of the US and with the market capitalization of Tokyo becoming larger than Wall Street, co-ordination, if it meant anything, was going to be a co-ordination amongst equals much more than in the past.

Assessing economic performance

Assessing economic performance is highly problematic: there are always the vexed questions of what objectives to use, of what importance to attach to each of these, and of what comparisons to draw. Nevertheless Tables 11.1, 11.3, and 11.4 allow a range of comparisons to be made both historically and against other countries for the conventional objectives.

Output, inflation, and unemployment

Table 11.3, drawn from Hibbs (1987), shows that, compared to its own past, the US performed well in the period 1950–80 taken as a whole. The growth of output and the level of unemployment were both significantly better than in the two earlier periods. They also showed much less fluctuation: the standard deviations are well down and so are the coefficients of variation (the better measure since they show the swings relative to the average for each period). Not surprisingly the inflation rate is higher, but this also shows less fluctuation.

Whether all or any of this improvement is the result of policy is impossible to say with certainty. Nevertheless the association of better performance with the period in which stabilization measures were first used consciously is suggestive. This is not to claim that individual acts of stabilization were especially successful (1966–9 and 1981–4 look particularly doubtful). The more plausible argument is that the presence of automatic stabilizers, plus the underpinnings of the monetary system, plus the general expectation that stabilization *was possible*, created an environment that was conducive to growth.

However, if the postwar years are broken up into sub-periods a different impression emerges: Table 11.1 shows a slowdown after the Kennedy/Johnson period of the 1960s – and still more so on productivity (see p. 244). The position is also less favourable relative to other countries: Table 11.4 brings out that the US grew less fast from 1956 to 1973 than the OECD group as a whole (though slightly more rapidly than other countries from 1979 to

Table 11.3 Historical comparison of the level and stability of growth, inflation, and unemployment, 1861–1980

	A. The annual growth rate of real output		
	1891–1929	*1930–49*	*1950–80*
Mean	1.8	1.3	2.2
Standard deviation	6.3	9.2	2.7
Coefficient of variation	3.5	7.0	1.2
	B. The annual rate of inflation of consumer prices		
	1861–1929	*1930–49*	*1950–80*
Mean	0.9	1.7	4.0
Standard deviation	6.3	6.0	3.4
Coefficient of variation	6.7	3.7	0.9
	C. The % level of unemployment		
	1890–1929	*1930–49*	*1950–80*
Mean	6.1	11.8	5.2
Standard deviation	4.1	8.1	1.4
Coefficient of variation	0.7	0.7	0.3

Note: The coefficient of variation is the standard deviation divided by the mean (not always exactly on the data shown above due to rounding)

Source: Hibbs 1987.

1985). The position of inflation is better. Throughout the whole period 1956–85, US inflation has been slightly below that of the OECD group. Taken in conjunction with the low productivity growth (see below) this is more impressive than it would be on its own. Particularly noticeable is the relatively non-inflationary recovery of 1981–5, but, as remarked earlier, some of the success in this period was achieved through the upsurge of the dollar which created well-known difficulties for the balance of payments.

Productivity and employment

The output figures show the US doing better than the OECD group as a whole in the period 1979–85. However, as Table 11.4 shows, this turn round is only true of overall growth and results from the continuing rise in US employment. Measured in terms of the growth rate of productivity (output per worker) the extent to which the US is below the rest of the OECD is not only greater, but also persists throughout the whole period. Moreover, when growth slowed after 1973, the increase in employment in the US actually rose (see Table 11.4: from 1.6 per cent per annum up to 1973 to 2.4 per cent per annum over the years 1973–9).

Table 11.4 US economic performance, 1946–85

		GDP	Employment	Output per worker	Inflation[a]	Unemployment rate[b]
			Average annual changes, %			%
US	1946–56	3.4			3.8	
US	1956–73	3.6	1.6	1.9	3.3	4.8[c]
OECD	1956–73	4.5	1.0	3.5	4.0	3.2[c]
US	1973–9	2.4	2.4	0.0	8.0	6.7[d]
OECD	1973–9	2.6	1.1	1.5	9.0	5.2[d]
US	1979–85	2.5	1.4	1.1	5.6	8.0[e]
OECD	1979–85	2.3	0.6	1.7	7.1	7.8[e]
US	1956–85	3.1	1.8	1.3	4.7	6.0[f]
OECD	1956–85	3.7	0.9	2.7	5.7	4.7[f]

a The consumer price index from 1946–9. The GDP deflator from 1950–85
b The average level in the period as a % of the total labour force
c 1960–73
d 1974–9
e 1980–5
f 1960–85

Note: The OECD totals for GDP and inflation are based on the exchange rates of 1980

Sources: OECD Historical Statistics, 1960–85 and the OECD database.

The implications of these employment figures are striking. The US has done well in terms of providing jobs, in fact better than either the Europeans or the Japanese (though still not well enough to prevent unemployment nearly doubling after 1973). However, this has been at the expense of declines in real wages. Thus, most American families, especially those with children, were significantly worse off in 1984 than in 1973: studies for the Joint Economic Committee found that the real median pre-tax income of families with children which had been growing by 4 per cent per annum between 1947 and 1973 then declined by over 6 per cent per annum between 1973 and 1984 (Marshall 1986: 181).

The productivity slowdown in the US which produced this result started in the 1960s (pre-dating the energy shocks, it should be noted). Why this happened has been a continuing puzzle to US economists. Almost certainly a complex set of factors were involved. Some of the standard economic explanations are probably part of the story. On the supply side the US had a lower ratio of investment to GDP than most other industrialized countries as well as significantly lower growth rates of capital per employee. At the same time, on the demand side, it is well known that recessions reduce productivity and this probably explains part of the sharp fall after 1973. But, while there is some truth in both of these points, they are not satisfactory as a complete explanation. Other countries suffered from the recession but did not exhibit such a large fall in productivity. Moreover the timing of investment is puzzling: capital per person hour accelerated after 1973 when output per person hour was decelerating.

The OECD has suggested that the fall in real wages and the continuing rise in employment which accompanied this decline in productivity has occurred because US labour markets are more 'flexible', in particular by having lower replacement ratios than many European countries. But this perspective also leaves many questions unanswered. For example, a lower replacement ratio may induce workers to seek work more energetically, but it does not make more jobs *available* – especially during a recession. Furthermore an argument about the *level* of the replacement ratio does not translate easily into one about the *rate of growth* of employment, still less does it do anything directly to explain the slowdown in productivity since this is more likely to be affected by decisions about the use of resources within firms than by the number of people applying to firms for work.

It is extraordinarily difficult to measure the effectiveness of firms' internal organization, but a number of studies of the US and Japan (Marshall 1986; Weisskopf *et al*. 1983) have suggested that labour-management relations in the US have been harmful to productivity growth and became more so in the 1960s and the 1970s. For example, Marshall (1986: 194) records that whereas 'only 9 per cent of American workers thought they could benefit personally from improved productivity; 93 per cent of similar Japanese workers thought they would benefit personally from improved productivity' and he links this evidence to greater employee identification, greater worker involvement, and greater job security in Japan. Viewed in this way, the OECD arguments in favour of 'flexible' labour markets might lead to job creation, but at the cost of productivity growth. If so, 'flexibility' would have been a poor long-run strategy for the US to have pursued.

Poverty and inequality

Less impressive than employment, at least in the later years, is the US record on poverty. According to the official definitions there were some 33 per cent of the population in poverty in 1947. This dropped to 22 per cent by 1960, to 19 per cent by 1965, to 12 per cent by 1969 and to 11 per cent by 1973. Thereafter it rose to 12 per cent in 1975, dropped slightly to 1978 and then rose sharply to 15 per cent by 1983 (Heller 1986). These data probably illustrate the effects of overall growth up to 1960, together with the results of the Great Society programmes (see p. 234) during the late 1960s. Also clearly in evidence is the effect of the slowdown after 1973 and the cut-backs in social security spending after 1979.

It is not correct, however, to attribute all of the increase in poverty to the reductions in the welfare spending in the 1980s. Some of it seems to be the result of a greater inequality in pre-tax incomes beginning in the late 1970s. Harrison, Tilly, and Bluestone (1986) find that wage inequality fell dramatically in the expansion of the mid-1960s, continued down more slowly until about 1978 and then turned noticeably upwards and carried on rising until 1983 (the last year of their data). Why this increase in the inequality of pay occurred, and whether it was mainly the rich getting richer or the poor getting poorer, or both of these at the same time is the subject of continuing research. Moreover, while the rise in poverty can be linked to the rise in unemployment (and thus to the recession), the greater inequality of wages cannot – at least not so directly. Nevertheless, whatever the reason, this increase in the inequality of incomes in the 1980s would usually be regarded as a negative factor when evaluating US economic performance.

Two other factors possibly on the negative side are first, the fall in the incomes of families with children that occurred after 1973 that was noted above and, second, and more arguably, the fact that many of the families who were able to maintain income did so through housewives entering the labour market (Council of Economic Advisers 1988). In this latter case families have lost to the extent that two earners are now required to achieve what one provided before, but against this, women may have gained if the choice to work was a free one (though research in progress suggests that this was unlikely to have been generally the case).

The external environment: the balance of payments

A further worrying feature of recent US performance is the balance of payments. Until the 1980s this was not an objective of US economic policy. Even though there was a long-term trend loss in the US share in world export markets (at first to Europe and the Japanese and later to the newly industrialized countries) there were surpluses on the balance of goods and services in most years before the 1980s and, in any case, for much of that period everyone accepted dollars, so deficits, even when they occurred, caused little concern. However, the deficits of the 1980s are rapidly changing this position.

As a share of GDP (approximately 3 per cent in 1985) the deficit is no larger than has been experienced by several other countries, but it is so large absolutely that the US has swung from being the world's largest creditor nation in 1982 to the largest debtor by the end of 1986. This carries the long-term implication for the US of a slower growth of national income as its net income from abroad swings from positive to negative (from its peak of $52 billion in 1981 it had already fallen to $34 billion in 1986 [OECD 1988a]). Even more important is the short to medium-term implication for US consumption: during the period that the balance of payments is corrected the US will have to give up the equivalent of more than one year's growth.

Much of this will have to fall on private consumption and the adjustment will undoubtedly be painful.

Conclusion

The overall impression of the US economy is that at the start of the period it was wealthy, dominant, and energetic. In contrast, at the end, while it is still the richest country in the world, it is less dominant and less energetic. This is not to deny that the US still has a sense of social vitality (mixed, it must be said, with a lot of violence), but, at least economically, other countries have been overhauling it and its own rate of productivity growth has been sluggish for a long time. At the same time, while being a rich country, it is also a country which has become more unequal in the 1980s – and the loss of equality seems to have been without any obvious gain in dynamism (productivity growth, savings, and investment all remain low both historically and compared to other industrial countries).

Of course US performance has to be seen in the context of a longer run adjustment to its changing role in the world economy. It is still a superpower, and some would argue that under Reagan it has regained its sense of self-confidence, but some catch up by other countries was probably inevitable and it no longer dominates world industrial production, world trade, or world finance to anything like the extent it did in 1945. Then it dictated terms to Germany and Japan. Now it is Japan and Germany that determine the level of the dollar.

Within this general picture there are two related sub-themes on the role of policy – both of which suggest the US has lost policy options.

First, over the period as a whole the US has found itself with less room for manoeuvre domestically. The constitutional structure of the US meant that from the outset there was great potential for conflict in policy-making and, in particular, for fiscal policy to be near impossible to run coherently. But at the beginning these difficulties did not fully materialize because there was a bipartisan consensus on the goals and machinery of economic policy. This consensus has been gradually eroded and, part cause and part consequence, there has been a growth of Congressional power which has made the operation of fiscal policy increasingly difficult. As a result, contrary to what was expected in 1946, much of the strain of stabilization has fallen, and will continue to fall, onto monetary policy.

It does not follow that the US cannot or should not operate fiscal policy at all. At the beginning of their terms of office determined presidents can still get some of what they wish through Congress. The same is true in periods of emergency. Thus, where a structural adjustment is required, as seemed to be the situation in the US in the latter half of the 1980s, fiscal action can still be part of a medium-term goal. But, by the same token, the option of using fiscal policy for short-run stabilization does not exist – crisis management is hardly a recipe for good fine-tuning (particularly in today's financial markets). Conversely, these difficulties with short-run action strengthen the case for automatic stabilizers (unlike the Gramm-Rudman-Holdings Act which could just as well de-stabilize).

Second, the US has faced more constraints externally. The concern about the balance of payments deficit in the 1980s is the most obvious example. But other longer-term changes have been occurring: the decline in the role of the dollar, the loss of share in world markets, and the growth of other financial centres. Yet the US remains an extremely important actor on world markets. The most dramatic example of its continuing importance was the effect of the rising dollar and high US interest rates after 1979 on third world debt (with policy on interest rates being reversed in 1982 largely because of the debt crisis).

The interrelation between these two themes is that the US has found itself with a single policy instrument, the interest rate, yet increasingly trying to do three things: to control domestic demand, to achieve equilibrium on the balance of payments, and to avoid a debt crisis. The problem for the US is that policy would be easier if the US were still so large that it could dictate (without worrying about the consequences) or so small as to be able to do its own thing unnoticed by anyone else. In fact the US is now in that difficult intermediate position where everything is strategic.

One interpretation of current US policy is that it is attempting to resolve this dilemma by urging the case for international co-ordination – if other countries will act at your behest this adds another policy instrument. The obvious problem is that they may not. And, as is well known, strategic games do not always produce the collectively desired outcome (though in this case the situation is eased by the obvious self-interest of the lenders to the US, especially Japan, in protecting their investments).

Moreover, even if co-ordination does help with stabilization and the balance of payments, it will not remove the need for painful internal adjustment in the US. Still less will it tackle the problem of low productivity growth. In the long run this is the biggest single factor causing US economic performance to be disappointing.

Selected dates

April 1945	Death of President Roosevelt. Truman succeeds as president.
1946	Employment Act passed.
January 1946	Creation of the Joint Economic Committee of Congress and the Council of Economic Advisers.
November 1948	Truman re-elected.

1948–9	Mild recession.
June 1950	Outbreak of Korean War.
March 1951	Treasury/Federal Reserve Accord on monetary policy.
November 1952	Eisenhower elected.
1953	Second postwar recession.
November 1956	Eisenhower re-elected.
1957–8	Third postwar recession.
November 1960	Kennedy elected.
February 1962	Kennedy proposes cuts in personal income tax.
November 1963	Assassination of Kennedy. Johnson succeeds.
1964	Kennedy tax cuts passed by the Senate.
1965	Escalation of Vietnam War.
March 1968	Gold crisis.
November 1968	Election of Nixon.
August 1971	Nixon announces 'New Economic Policy'.
June 1972	Watergate break-in discovered.
November 1972	Nixon re-elected.
August 1973	Nixon resigns. Ford succeeds.
October 1973	First oil shock.
November 1976	Carter elected.
1979	Second oil shock.
October 1979	Volcker announces switch in US monetary policy to controlling bank reserves.
November 1980	Reagan elected.
August 1981	Economic Recovery Tax Act cuts individual and business taxes. Omnibus Budget Reconciliation Act cuts domestic spending, especially for poor people.
November 1984	Reagan re-elected.
September 1985	Plaza accord amongst central banks.
October 1985	'Baker plan' announced at IMF/World Bank meeting in Seoul.
February 1986	Reagan speaks of 'policy co-ordination' in his State of the Union message.
November 1986	Tax Reform Act reduces individual tax rates.

References

Bach, G. (1971) *Making Monetary and Fiscal Policy*, Washington, DC: The Brookings Institution.

Berman, L. (1979) *The Office of Management and Budget and the Presidency, 1921–1979*, Princeton, NJ: Princeton University Press.

Cagan, P. (1986) *Essays in Contemporary Economic Problems: The Impact of the Reagan Program*, Washington, DC: American Enterprise Institute.

Cagan, P. (1987) *Deficits, Taxes, and Economic Adjustments*, Washington, DC: American Enterprise Institute.

Clifford, J. (1965) *The Independence of the Federal Reserve System*, Philadelphia, PA: University of Philadelphia Press.

Council of Economic Advisers (1988) *Report to the President*, Washington, DC.

Eisner, R. (1986) 'The federal budget crisis', in D. Obey and P. Sarbanes (eds), *The Changing American Economy*, Oxford: Basil Blackwell.

Feldstein, M. (ed.) (1980) *The American Economy in Transition*, Chicago, IL: Chicago University Press.

Fisher, L. (1975) *Presidential Spending Power*, Princeton, NJ: Princeton University Press.

Galbraith, J.K. (1967) *The New Industrial State*, New York, Houghton Mifflin.

Greenstein, F. (ed.) (1983) *The Reagan Presidency: An Early Assessment*, Baltimore, MD: Johns Hopkins University Press.

Hansen, A. (1964) *The Postwar American Economy: Performance and Problems*, New York: W.W. Norton.

Harrison, B., Tilly, C. and Bluestone, B. (1986) 'Rising inequality', in D. Obey and P. Sarbanes (eds), *The Changing American Economy*, Oxford: Basil Blackwell.

Heller, W. (1986) 'The public policy experience', in D. Obey and P. Sarbanes (eds), *The Changing American Economy*, Oxford: Basil Blackwell.

Hibbs, D.A. (1987) *The American Political Economy: Macroeconomics and Electoral Politics in the United States*, Cambridge, Mass.: Harvard University Press.

McKay, D. (1985) *American Politics and Society,* Oxford: Basil Blackwell.

Maddison, A. (1982) *Phases of Capitalist Development*, Oxford: Oxford University Press.

Mann, T. and Ornstein, H. (eds) (1981) *The New Congress*, Washington, DC: American Enterprise Institute.

Marshall, R. (1986) 'Working smarter', in D. Obey and P. Sarbanes (eds), *The Changing American Economy*, Oxford: Basil Blackwell.

Norton, H. (1977) *The Employment Act and the Council of Economic Advisers*, Columbia, SC: University of South Carolina Press.

Obey, D. and Sarbanes, P. (eds) (1986) *The Changing American Economy*, Oxford: Basil Blackwell.

OECD (1988a) *National Accounts: 1960–1986*, Paris.

OECD (1988b) *Economic Outlook, June 1988*, Paris.

Schick, A. (ed.) (1983) *Making Economic Policy in Congress*, Washington, DC: American Enterprise Institute.

Shonfield, A. (1965) *Modern Capitalism: The Changing Balance of Public and Private Power*, Oxford: Oxford University Press.

Sommers, A.T., with Blau, L.R. (1988) *The US Economy Demystified*, Lexington Mass: Lexington Books.

Stein, H. (1969) *The Fiscal Revolution in America*, Chicago, IL: University of Chicago Press.

Stein, H. (1985) *Presidential Economics: The Making of Economic Policy from Roosevelt to Reagan and Beyond*, New York: Simon & Schuster.

Stockman D. (1986) *The Triumph of Politics*, New York: Harper & Row.

Weisskopf, T., Bowles, S. and Gordon, D. (1983) 'Hearts and minds: a social model of US productivity growth', *Brookings Papers on Economic Activity*, no. 2.

Woolley, J. (1984) *Monetary Politics: The Federal Reserve and the Politics of Monetary Policy*, New York: Cambridge University Press.

Guide to further reading

The best introduction to US economic data is Sommers with Blau (1988). An up-to-date view of the US economy and of the contemporary issues is provided by Obey and Sarbanes (1986). Hibbs (1987) gives an excellent empirical study of the relationship between economic policy and US politics. Feldstein (1980) contains many interesting pieces on the US economy. Schick (1983) and McKay (1985) give excellent introductions to the structure of American policy-making and its interaction with other political issues. Stein (1969) is a highly readable and thoughtful account of the influence of Keynesian ideas on US policy and he also gives an up-to-date view of policy in Stein (1985). Hansen (1964) provides useful comment on the US as seen mid-way through the period. Stockman (1986) is a must for an inside view of policy-making under Reagan and Cagan (1986 and 1987) discusses in detail the economics of the Reagan period.

Chapter twelve

Japan

Ian Nish

Introduction

In 1945 Japan had been bombed out of existence. Even by 1947, the first postwar year for which national income data are available, output was not much more than half the level reached during the war and output per worker was only about one-sixth of that of the US. Since then productivity has grown nearly ten-fold and now, in 1989, equals or even on some measures exceeds that of the US. The performance of Japanese exports is even more startling. Since 1950 they have multiplied in volume almost seventy times. As a result, Japan, which was a country facing balance of payments difficulties in the 1950s and early 1960s, moved into structural balance of payments surplus in the early 1970s.

The question is, how did this extraordinary achievement occur? There is no simple answer, but part lies in Japan's early history, part in the institutional structure, and part in the events and policies, both internal and external, of the postwar years.

Early history

When Commodore Perry sailed into Tokyo bay in 1853, he found a country which had already taken the first steps towards the creation of a modern economy. Although Japan was poor in natural resources and had been cut off from contact with most of the outside world since the 1630s, she had developed some modern commercial institutions. To be sure, the standard of living of the ordinary Japanese rose only slowly during this period, but it did provide a solid base on which the new rulers, who took over after the Meiji Restoration of 1868, could build. Determined that they were not going to be dominated by the expanding countries of the west either economically or militarily, they sought to make Japan *fukoku kyohei*, a wealthy country with a strong army and navy. They arranged for the importation of foreign know-how in the industrial, military, and academic spheres. Over the next few decades, they set up factory industries, based largely on imported raw materials. Before long Japan became a formidable exporter of selected manufactured commodities. Between 1885 and 1930 there was a steady growth in Gross National Product though income levels were still well below those of the United States, Germany, and Britain. While Japan lived under a war economy for most of the 1930s, it was generally recognized by the outbreak of the war with the west in 1941 that it was one of the world's leading trading nations, with strong and wealthy trading companies possessing an international network of offices. In the economic development of the home islands and the colonies in Taiwan, Korea, and 'Manchukuo', the state was accustomed to playing a substantial role, and a breed of highly intelligent economic bureaucrats emerged.

The institutional structure of policy-making

Under the constitution which Japan adopted in 1947 it was laid down that the Diet was the supreme organ of state; that the cabinet was the supreme executant of policy; and that the prime minister was the key figure in propounding policies. In general, the Diet has not been an initiator of economic policy; that role has been performed by the cabinet under the guidance of the bureaucracy. Because of the purge of pre-war politicians, the postwar politicians took time to find their feet and it is only since the 1970s that they have been asserting themselves. But they represent constituencies whose interests are affected by economic policy and have tended to intervene from time to time in government planning.

Since 1947 Japanese politics have been dominated by conservative parties and, specifically, by the Liberal-Democratic party (LDP) since 1954. Although the general atmosphere has been one of stability, there have been regular changes in government; and factions within the LDP, united by self-interest rather than ideology, have played a large part in the formation of cabinets. In the economic sphere, much credit for Japan's success is due to the Prime Minister's Office which has taken a primary place in the making of economic policy in conjunction with the Ministry of Finance, the Ministry of International Trade and Industry (MITI), the Economic Planning Agency, and the Bank of Japan.

Businessmen have a role independent of government and the bureaucracy. So much so (MITI argues) that they often lose sight of the national interest. Companies are competitive with one another, and representative industrial institutions like the Federation of Economic Organizations (Keidanren) have varying degrees of influence on policy. As we should expect, businessmen are not all of one mind and do not always accept the 'administrative guidance' of the bureaucrats. The Japanese business tycoon may collaborate with government because he is a disciplined and patriotic Japanese, and also because he can see benefits for his company from that collaboration. While many economic decisions have in postwar years been forged at seemingly endless committees, in which businessmen have played a part alongside the bureaucrats, many are also taken in the board room. Examples of changes that came about without undue involvement of government are the amalgamation of the pre-war industrial and commercial giants (*zaibatsu*) with the help of bankers in the 1950s and the amalgamations within the steel industry in the 1970s.

Bureaucracy was one of the pillars of pre-war Japan, as in the case of many developing societies. This continued after the war when Japan felt that her economy needed protection. As industry has gained confidence it has become increasingly independent of the bureaucracy and, when there is a need for national policy co-ordination, the leadership initiative is increasingly being taken over by politicians and industrialists. But it is still probably true that Japan muddles through politically with the bureaucrats steering the ship of state skilfully in the background. Basically, relations are good between business and officials. MITI is the most prestigious ministry in the industrial field and is most wide-ranging in its contacts and consultations. But different industries have come under different ministries: pharmaceuticals under Health; telecommunications under Post and Telecommunications; aerospace under Transport. This inevitably leads to jealousies and demarcation disputes between ministries. Legislative drafting in Japan is generally broad and vague; considerable powers of interpretation rest with the bureaucrats who can, through regulations, exercise some degree of administrative influence after the legislation has been passed. But the main role as guide appears to have been taken by MITI, especially in doing the groundwork for the economic miracle of the 1960s. The high calibre of the ministry's officials and their skill in persuasion were essential to Japan's postwar development.[1]

It was unlikely that the administrative guidance of earlier decades could continue indefinitely as the major Japanese companies achieved successes. The Japanese bureaucracy is large and there have been inconsistencies between the policies forged by various parts of it. The public hostility towards bureaucrats in general has also applied to their role in the fields of commerce and industry. In particular, politicians grew jealous of the bureaucrats' role in the 1970s. There were malpractices connected with the retirement prospects of senior bureaucrats, especially the entry of senior officials taking retirement employment in top industrial positions (*amakudari*) in which their previous influence could be turned to company advantage. Despite criticism the practice is still widespread. The senior academic and former foreign minister, Okita Saburo, has written:

It is a healthy trend for politicians to take leadership initiative from the bureaucrats even if the US and others are seeking to slow the erosion of bureaucratic power by demanding government administered voluntary export restraints, semi-conductor cartels and other paraphernalia of controlled trade.

It is not easy to make generalizations about the concept of policy-making in Japan any more than it is in any other country. There is however more consensus-building through detailed committee work there than elsewhere, both in government and in companies. Partly it comes from the tolerance for time-consuming discussion. Partly it comes from convenience: it has proved to be beneficial in the past to have exhaustive advance consultation, leading to fewer zigzags of policy and a greater degree of continuity. Since there has not been an alternation of political parties in government, there have not been the sudden reversals of policy found in other countries. On the other hand, consensus-building is not universal. Not every Japanese company management is susceptible to consensual decision-making. Recently more modern management styles have been emerging when there are strong personalities at the top of companies and there are some examples of autocracy in upper managerial hierarchies.[2]

The role of labour in national policy-making has not been conspicuous. On the political plane, the socialist parties have not formed a government since 1947. Trade unions have been fragmented and have not been prominent in the postwar period. Strikes have been infrequent and have often been token affairs as at the time of the annual round of wage bargaining, the so-called 'spring offensive' (*Shunto*). In attempting to explain this lack of industrial conflict, one may point to the union structure whereby workers tend to be organized into company unions and national federations tend to be weak. One may also emphasize the unusual capacity of Japanese for loyalty to their company, and more generally, for co-operation and compromise. One cannot say that unions have played a prominent part over the various recent schemes for rationalizing industries such as steel and shipbuilding or for privatization of telecommunications and Japan National Railways which have come to fruition since 1985. But then government and management have tried to ensure that arrangements are made to find other jobs for redundant workers.[3]

Policy and performance

Japanese society has gone through many phases since 1945. In examining the performance of the Japanese economy, it is helpful to break the story into chronological sections, pausing at 1957 – arguably the point of the so-called postwar economic take-off – and 1973, the start of the oil crisis.

Rehabilitation: 1945–57

Between Japan's defeat in 1945 and the end of the allied occupation in 1952, Japanese industry was obviously affected by its relationship with the United States. After 1945 there emerged, over the years, in effect a trans-Pacific industrial alliance in which Japan borrowed American technology and was encouraged to develop it in order to rehabilitate the Japanese economy which had been seriously destroyed by the war.

At the same time the Japanese often allege that many of the measures encouraged by the allied occupation authorities were not geared towards Japan's economic recovery. The dissolution of the pre-war industrial combines (*zaibatsu*), the anti-trust legislation, the land reform (to name but three) were all aimed at eradicating some of the evils of pre-war capitalism rather than restoring the Japanese economy. To add to the economic difficulties, the number of unemployed in December 1945 was 13 million out of a population of 75,500,000. Every year this was increased by former soldiers repatriated from overseas, last of all from the Soviet Union. Many of these repatriates were militant. This may have been one of the causes for the violent labour movement which became evident in 1947–8. The Japanese government under the prompting of the occupation authorities clamped down on what it saw as an undesirable tendency. It increasingly discouraged militancy in the trade union movement and began to work for the recovery of Japanese capitalist enterprises. The raw materials which Japan needed were supplied, mainly from the United States. Thus Japan was set on the road to economic recovery in which it was greatly assisted by the procurement policies of the Americans during the Korean War. Although, following this war, there was a sharp recession, it is possible to argue that the period of economic recovery had been completed by 1957.

Perhaps the most difficult factor behind the recovery was inflation. The index of wholesale prices (taking 1934 as 1) increased from 15 in April 1946 (just after the currency reform) to 197 in March 1949. Despite the intervention of the high-powered Stabilization Board, violent inflation was holding back any prospect of industrial revival. There was a widespread American belief that Japan's bureaucrats had favoured increasing the national output rather than concentrating on price stabilization. On the recommendation of Dr Joseph Dodge, a Chicago banker called in by the occupation authorities, a drastic deflationary programme was introduced by the Japanese government, involving some measure of unemployment. By the spring of 1950 before the Korean War broke out, manufacturing industry had generally managed to adjust to the changed financial situation.

It was not that Japan was building from scratch. True, industry and the industrial cities had been devastated. But there existed large resources of well-educated manpower with a strong determination to survive. There was fall-out from the wartime technology which had been well-planned from 1931 to 1945. The objects which came on sale remarkably soon after the war – the cameras, the watches, and optical instruments – were products of wartime naval technology. To some extent, it was one of the greatest achievements of the Japanese administration which continued in existence uninterrupted to redirect war-time technology to civilian use. Another long-term achievement was to steer the pre-war economy in new directions and move slowly away from cotton to heavy industry such as iron, steel, ship-building, and chemical production.[4] The steering involved a degree of state intervention: sweeping measures such as tax incentives, financial aid to potential investors, and encouragement of research and imported tech-nology from overseas, especially the United States. At the same time it is generally recognized that part of the reason for the success of these policies lay with the Japanese people who had, as a whole, tasted deprivation and who, as a result, had a strong sense of national will and a strong motivation to return to – and better still exceed – the industrial levels of the 1930s.

An interesting example is the treatment of the cotton textile industry. By 1956 the production of cotton goods had been re-established so successfully that members of a Japanese parliamentary delegation met a barrage of hostility when they visited Manchester in that year. When, however, Japan experienced a boom in 1959–60, cotton remained sluggish. As a result the government took immediate steps. They banned the installation of new and additional production facilities and they curtailed the operation of certain mills to prevent over-production. One consequence of this was that the Toyota Cotton Company diverted successfully into motor car production. The government also made it clear later in its Long-Range Economic Plan for 1961–70 that: 'Japan's object is to further the reorganization of the industrial structure with emphasis on the heavy and chemical industries which has been in progress since the end of World War.[5]

Another relevant incident relates to the pre-war *zaibatsu* (the large indus-trial groups). The allied occupation policy which was endorsed by Japanese governments was to destroy the power of the major *zaibatsu* groups. In 1947 at the prompting of the Allies the Japanese government passed anti-merger legislation, introducing the Deconcentration Act empowering it to dissolve these various *zaibatsu* combines which were duly split up into separate autonomous units. After the occupation ended in 1952, the govern-ment modified the anti-monopoly legislation and enabled these combines to reunite. In the depression which struck Japan after the Korean War boom, the affiliates of the Mitsubishi company were induced to discuss merger into a single firm as a result of the endeavours of the banking groups affiliated with Mitsubishi. Between 1954 and 1956 the last steps were taken in the process by which these interests were amalgamated. In the case of Mitsui the separate units came together at the prompting of the banking interests in the group in 1952, 1955, and finally in 1958 for negotiations which did not prove to be so easy. The negotiator-in-chief in five years of difficult diplomacy between the former affiliated companies was Sato Kiichiro, president of the Mitsui Bank. It was February 1959 before Mitsui Bussan made its comeback and emerged as the largest trading company in Japan. Together Mitsubishi and Mitsui have formed the backbone of the commercial combines (*sogo shosha*) which became one of the keys to Japan's export-led recovery of later years.

The story is related here because these major examples of restructuring of Japan's industry and trade took place, in some cases with decisive interference by government, in other cases without such interference. The party responsible for the commercial mergers was the banking arm, which had not lost its Mitsubishi or Mitsui identity. Thus, banks which had avoided the interventionist zeal of the reforming occupation for breaking up pre-war cartels were able to play a vital part in welding together the fractured parts of these companies and in due course in financing their economic expansion. It would appear that the government did not need to intervene in this aspect of restructuring because someone else co-ordinated it.

High growth: 1958-73

Japan has always been fond of planning, even if also proud of free market economy. In the 1930s there were economic plans for the country; and in Manchukuo where it had a supervisory brief for fifteen years there was an atmosphere of bureaucratic control for the territory. Although growth in the Japanese economy has owed more to private enterprise than bureaucratic or government control, there have been industrial policies and plans which have been skilfully devised, coherent, and effective. As Sir Norman Kipping, the director-general of the Federation of British Industries, said after a visit to Japan in 1962: 'The initiative for Japan's growth has rested in the board-rooms of large-scale industry, but in the closest liaison at every point with government.'[6] The first of these long-range economic plans was drawn up in 1957 by the Economic Planning Agency for the period 1958-62 under the Kishi cabinet. The rates of growth which it contemplated were such that most of the targets had already been attained by 1960 and it was soon necessary to remodel the plan. The next plan was to double the nation's income within ten years. It became the major slogan in the general election campaign fought by prime minister Ikeda in November 1960 and aimed at an economic growth of 9 per cent for the period 1961-3. A revised five-year plan had to be introduced for 1965-70 since the initial growth targets were again speedily outstripped. The Ikeda cabinet was widely criticized for the uneven expansion which resulted.[7] That is, industrial leaders went all out for re-equipment, thus contributing to the over-heating of the Japanese economy, while the government had to try to rein in these developments from time to time. Japan was experiencing the unavoidable strains of high growth in this period.

The government's intervention led to the boom associated with the Olympic Games of 1964. This was followed by recession in 1965-6 and what the world hailed as the Japanese economic miracle at the end of that decade. The miracle was that a country, which had lost a war and lacked raw materials, had attained such a high level of economic growth in such a short period. Although Japan's industrial progress in the high growth period from (say) 1958 to 1970 owed much to government intervention, it was not exclusively brought about by planning. If we accept that Japan was a 'follower economy' in the fifties and sixties, her industrialists were able to follow the model of the United States and adopt the new technologies coming into existence there with skill and determination. Moreover, MITI's industrial policy could afford to concentrate on a limited number of export industries and play a co-ordinating role in some aspects of information exchange and research orientation; and – a crucial additional factor – private enterprise co-operated successfully with these expansionist policies.[8]

For their part, firms set about safeguarding their positions by accelerating their plans for investing in new capital equipment and in particular by importing foreign technology. This heavy investment in plant and machinery was the root cause of the adverse balances of trade which occurred from time to time. The industrial progress of this period reflected the confidence of industrial management in relying on banks which in turn relied on the strong tradition of the people for private saving. Government, in its turn, was ready to cool expansionist policies when they led to national balance of payments crises.

The government was, however, far from all powerful. The story is told that Ikeda, prime minister from 1960 to 1964, opposed the reconstitution of the large *zaibatsu* groups in several speeches on the ground that the *zaibatsu*-controlled banks had not honoured the undertakings they had made to the government to reduce their plant extension programmes by 10 per cent during the fiscal year 1961. The government was in a dilemma: it did not want to discourage the powerful industrial combines who wanted to safeguard their future position by heavy investment in modern technology and had the money to do so; but it had the prime responsibility for maintaining Japan's balance of payments equilibrium and had issued regulations to that end which seemed to have been violated. The ikeda cabinet found it hard to secure the acceptance of the leaders of industry for a policy of monetary stringency. It was at this time that Japanese journalists speculated that 'industry' had taken over from the pre-war military the role of an independent third force in Japanese politics. This was probably an exaggeration. But there were instances where a weak government could not bring a strong 'industry' to heel.

Nevertheless, despite the occasional constraints imposed by the balance of payments, the overall characteristic of the period was a strong and consistent rise in GNP. Between 1957 and 1973 real GDP grew at an average annual rate of almost 10 per cent. Moreover, rapid export growth (at an average rate of nearly 15 per cent per annum over this period) swung the balance of payments from a small deficit in the years 1961 to 1964 to substantial surplus thereafter.

Another characteristic was that by the end of the sixties Japan had achieved significant success in transforming her industrial base into one composed mostly of heavy industry such as machinery and chemicals. Special attention was given to steel, shipbuilding, automobiles, machinery, electrical goods, petrochemicals, and synthetic fibres. This policy was stimulated by fairly generous development loans, fiscal incentives, government contracts, and subsidies. While import restrictions were being slowly liberalized under foreign pressure, government assisted industry to pursue an effective and sustained export promotion campaign, supplying relatively easy credit, depreciation allowances, and tax benefits. These measures often led to what some Japanese call *shuchu gou teki no yushutsu* (concentrated downpour exports) and exports grew so fast that they even generated complaints from foreign importers who claimed to be suffering from 'the deluge' in a limited number of commodities.

Despite these complaints, the government assumed well into the sixties that it was necessary to assist the fertilizer, electric power, steel, coal, and transport industries. Indeed, as high-growth Japan entered the period of new industries, chemicals, petrochemicals, and other intermediate goods qualified for preferential treatment from the state.

However, towards the end of the sixties commercial relations with the United States deteriorated further and, with large surpluses on current account in 1970 and 1971, it was agreed that the yen should undergo revaluation from Y360 to Y308 to the dollar under the Smithsonian Agreement of 1971. While this had a deflationary effect, Japan's current account surplus with the United States (as well as with the world in general) continued to expand.

Adjustment to the new technology: 1974 to the present

The next turning-point in Japan's economic growth was the first oil crisis of 1973. The sudden, steep rise in the price of oil had an especially severe impact on the manufacturing industry which had been rebuilt after the war on the basis of oil dependence. Japan's growth was inevitably restricted when the oil-producing countries (OPEC) initially cut off supplies entirely for a period and later resumed them at quadrupled prices. It was difficult to sustain export-led growth when the increased price of energy in the world market transformed the prices of export commodities. After the oil crisis the Japanese government undertook drastic measures to restrict the demand for oil. Industry showed a remarkable readiness for living with the changed environment although the adjustment took about five years to complete successfully.

The energy crisis led to severe disruption in the Japanese economy. Output fell 1.3 per cent in 1974 (and a great deal of idle capacity followed in 1975); for a short period, 1973–5, there was a two-digit level of inflation; and there were deficits in the balance of payments on current account in 1973, 1974, and 1975. However, exports recovered again in 1976 and the balance of payments went back into even bigger surpluses in the years 1977 and 1978. By rationalization of export industries a painful, but successful adjustment was achieved in which government and industry both had a hand.

It is none the less notable that the degree of state involvement in the seventies stands in marked contrast to that which was practised in the 1950s and 1960s. Though industrial policy was still a factor it was less vigorous, less all-embracing, and less acceptable. The Japanese economy had grown to vast proportions and no longer needed to be protected from outside competition. To that extent the legendary days of MITI power and influence were coming to an end.[9] Japan's businessmen had become increasingly strong, self-confident, and less desirous of government help. Instead they were pressing the politicians for some degree of de-regulation in line with economic currents in the United States and elsewhere.

While Japan was running into problems with United States and the European Community on account of trade surpluses, she was in turn encountering competition from her near neighbours, Korea, Taiwan, and Hong Kong. Where she had previously been a chaser, she was now being chased. Domestically she was suffering from the increased cost of labour which was detracting from her competitive position.[10] Public awareness of pollution grew. Politically the environmental lobbies were active after the casualties suffered as a result of the effluents at the Minamata plant; and there was a call for the phasing out of smoke-stack industries. Companies involved in these adjustments found it opportune to move towards offshore investment in the eighties and ultimately to manufacture increasingly abroad.

Japan's economic performance had to take account of the advice and complaints of those euphemistically called trading partners. Japan was under sustained pressure from abroad to encourage domestic consumption rather than concentrate on export industries. The government accepted that it had to move in the direction of making Japan more open to foreign goods, opening government tenders to foreign companies and breaking up the comfortable harmonious relationships which had previously governed Japanese trading practices. Thus, in one of many packages of economic policy measures announced in the 1980s, the government undertook in 1981 to open the Japanese market further to foreign competition and, in the following year, they set up the office of Trade Ombudsman. On the other hand, the government accepted that there had to be industrial adjustment (*chosei*) and financial restructuring (*zaisei saiken*). But it was difficult to accomplish the second goal in a systematic way while pursuing the first. It was also problematic since the second was politically acceptable to the Liberal-Democratic Party while the first was not universally welcomed and was contested by the protectionist lobbies. Thus, in the case of shipbuilding which had earlier been a boom industry and seemed to have installed capacity well beyond the world's requirements during the slump of the 1970s, drastic but effective programmes were carried out. In 1978-9 capacity was cut by 35 per cent and in the eighties by another 20 per cent, in accordance with the formula worked out between the industry and government.

One policy adopted in the second half of the 1970s was to accumulate large budget deficits in the hope of becoming a 'locomotive of world growth'. In 1977 prime minister Fukuda took the bold step of increasing public works expenditure by more than 35 per cent in one year in the hope that it would increase the growth rate to 7 per cent. This channelling of public works expenditure (*kodo seicho*) is regarded by most Japanese as counter-productive. Certainly the outcome was unsatisfactory: the growth rate receded; the wealth and power of the construction industry increased; and the move did not encourage imports to any appreciable extent. On the other hand it is difficult to know what would have happened without these measures and the slowdown in growth is probably more the result of the second oil price shock of 1979 than of the budget deficit. Nevertheless these policies left the governments of the eighties with an inheritance of large government debts and prime minister Nakasone (1982-7) opted for a strategy of austerity in order to restore government finance.

Industry for its part has had to adjust not only to the second oil price shock, but also to major changes in exchange rates during the 1980s. From 1979 to 1985 Japan's competitive position improved, but from then to 1988 it deteriorated by between 40 and 50 per cent. The cause of this dramatic change was the Plaza Accord of September 1985 (see chapter 2). One of the main aims of this was to bring down the value of the dollar against the yen. Mr Takeshita, who was then finance minister and became prime minister in October 1987, agreed to the formula on behalf of Japan and thereby earned some criticism from the Japanese business community. With the other ministers he agreed to co-operate over exchange rates and also to work for the lowering of interest rates. Since then the yen has risen steadily creating problems for Japanese firms engaged in the export trade.

In February 1987 the Louvre accord pledged the Japanese central bank (among others) to keep exchange rates at the levels they had then reached. Japan again came under pressure to stimulate domestic demand through her fiscal policies and the Bank of Japan's discount rate was reduced immediately afterwards from 3 to 2.5 per cent. Some reliance was also placed on the comprehensive tax reform proposals which were presented by the cabinet to the Diet but were not adopted before prime minister Nakasone retired in October. They were subsequently passed in summer 1988.

The existence of a strong yen for such a long period has led manufacturers yet again to restructure their operations. This restructuring represents a further move away from heavy industry, especially steel and shipbuilding, fields where Japan had hitherto been dominant and the newly industrialized countries were upgrading their technology. The trend has been towards high value-added electronic products like factory automation equipment (machine tools, industrial robots) and office automation equipment (copiers, computers, and word processors). It would appear that this transition to high technology industry has been partly government inspired and partly industry inspired. Government is clearly determined to cosset its high technology industries in the same way as at an earlier stage it had ensured the international competitiveness of Japanese televisions and videos by encouraging high levels of research and development.[12]

A different problem exists for government in dealing with the phasing out of industries where Japan has ceased to enjoy comparative advantage. The political influence of the Liberal-Democratic Party in areas where there are declining and depressed industries forces the government to act with vigilance as it does in areas where the LDP has substantial vested interests in the agrarian sector.

There is also an obligation on government to be responsive in a way which industry does not have to be to foreign complaints. For the past ten years the United States, the European Community and developing countries have been protesting vehemently about export imbalances, huge yen surpluses, and the methods used to promote exports. It has long been accepted by government that the Japanese will have to stimulate domestic demand for their own and foreign products and reduce the energy which has been devoted to exporting. It is hard to convince the established Japanese exporting companies of this. Ministers have not been able to achieve a consensus by their speeches nor have bureaucrats been able to sell the idea. In May 1987 the Japanese government announced (in advance of the Venice summit) a series of measures entailing government procurement overseas and large-scale spending on public works. Possibly the scale of the remedies proposed does not match the scale of the problem. Moreover in 1986 prime minister Nakasone set up a commission under Haruo Maekawa, a former highly respected governor of the Bank of Japan. Mr Nakasone's idea was to keep this commission out of bureaucratic control by selecting figures who were independent but whose reputations would carry weight in the community. It was described as a Blue Riband group. Government adopted its main recommendation to move towards a more diversified economy, focusing on the domestic market and away from export-led growth. In the achievement of this appreciation of the yen has played a great part. But it will certainly take time.

Conclusion

We have made a rough distinction between three periods of growth – rehabilitation (1945–57); high growth (1958–73); and adjustment to the new technology (1974 to the present). Japanese economic performance in these periods had different characteristics but, overall, it has to be judged a success by almost any standard. As Table 12.1 shows Japan performed better on output, productivity, inflation, and unemployment than the OECD as a whole. Indeed its growth was the fastest growth of any country in the postwar period and was faster than any prior period in Japan's own history. This was combined with a rising share of world markets and, as a result, an almost consistently strong balance of payments. Moreover, Japan managed to adjust well after the oil crisis of 1973: unlike most countries her growth in the period 1979–85 was higher than for the period 1973–9.

Some qualifications would have to be made to this overwhelmingly bright picture. Japan's economic performance has had its ups and downs: in each of the periods there were peaks and troughs. There have also been regions which suffered relative to the prosperity elsewhere: hence the need for prime minister Tanaka's Economic Plan for the Japan sea coast which seemed to be losing out economically in the 1960s. In Japan's dual economy the ancillary supplier industries to big business have often suffered disproportionately. Perhaps the priority accorded by the state to economic development has neglected the overall environmental effects on society, notably the issue of pollution. While there was substance to this criticism before the 1970s, impressive steps have since been taken to tackle the

Table 12.1 Japanese economic performance, 1946–85

		GDP	Employment	Output per worker	Inflation[a]	Unemployment rate[b]
		Average annual changes, %				%
Japan	1946–56	8.7[c]			21.4	
Japan	1956–73	9.4	1.4	8.0	5.3	1.3[d]
OECD	1956–73	4.5	1.0	3.5	4.0	3.2[d]
Japan	1973–9	3.6	0.7	2.9	8.1	1.9[e]
OECD	1973–9	2.6	1.1	1.5	9.0	5.2[e]
Japan	1979–85	4.0	1.0	3.0	2.1	2.4[f]
OECD	1979–85	2.3	0.6	1.7	7.1	7.8[f]
Japan	1956–85	7.1	1.1	5.8	5.2	1.7[g]
OECD	1956–85	3.7	0.9	2.7	5.7	4.7[g]

a The consumer price index 1946–52. The GDP deflator from 1953–85
b The average level in the period as a % of the total labour force
c 1947–56
d 1960–73
e 1974–9
f 1980–5
g 1960–85

Note: The OECD totals for GDP and inflation are based on the exchange rates of 1980

Sources: OECD Historical Statistics, 1960–85 and the OECD database.

pollution issue and its anti-pollution regulations are now among the toughest in the world. Overall, however, while Japan has had sustained and spectacular economic growth since the war, the growth has had certain unbalanced features.

This leaves two fundamental questions: why did this happen? and what role (if any) did policy play? These are incredibly difficult and complex questions and the literature on Japanese growth suggests a considerable range of disagreement over the factors at work. The evidence of the three chronological periods described in this essay leads us to take an intermediate position towards the various theories of economic success. Indeed we find ourselves in general agreement with the statement made by Professor Hugh Patrick:

> No one advocates the position that Japanese economic growth has been state-led and that industrial policy has been the integral component, with private business a willing follower of government bureaucratic leadership. On the other hand, no one argues that, although Japan has had an industrial policy, it has been an incoherent and ineffective one.[13]

On this basis, there seems to be substantial agreement between experts, both Japanese and foreign. There cannot, however, be a single, correct explanation of Japan's 'success'.[14]

Nevertheless we can identify a range of factors that have played a part. Most writers draw attention to several permissive factors, e.g., the possibility of catching up on technology, the availability of labour, the weakness of unions, and the availability of savings. Some writers have suggested that much has depended on questions of culture and habits. Thus Michio Morishima has argued in respect of the Japanese ethos that Confucianism, one of the factors in Japanese thinking, is a religion of a 'pro-government type'.[15] Because of this it may be argued that the state in Japan carries much authority which it would not have in other societies and individualism is less prominent. This may be illustrated by the people's acceptance of belt-tightening measures in the interest of the nation. It is but a short way from this to the views associated with the phrase 'Japan Incorporated'[16] – the collaboration of the state, business, and the political parties in pursuit of industrial policy. But this consensus/cultural explanation cannot be the whole story because it does not explain why Japan has done so much better economically than she did in the past when presumably many of the same factors were at work.

An alternative explanation might be that a number of factors acting together allowed this to occur. Leaving a number of qualifications and complexities on one side for the moment, we may select certain fundamental characteristics as follows:

a   Japan was able to combine small-scale and large-scale industry so that each was complementary to the other. The normal way of describing it is to say that the former was clearly keenly competitive and the latter oligopolistic. This is true, but the more important point is that in the Japanese context each acted where it had the comparative advantage: the small-scale units acted as suppliers while the large-scale producers and the *sogo shosha* (trading companies) acted as marketing agents especially in the export sector where scale was required and where the requisite skills (e.g., in foreign languages) were at first in short supply.

b   The oligopolies acted aggressively competing for market share and so maintained a high rate of investment. As Boltho shows, this behaviour can be traced to the cultural emphasis on hierarchy.[17] In economic terms it may well have had the crucial effect of allowing Japanese industry to exploit dynamic economies of scale (economies which are not well captured by profit maximizing firms because the economies are frequently external to the firm yet internal to the industry or economy).

c   At the same time, after hesitant financial beginnings, the trading companies played an important role as financial intermediaries. They borrowed from the banks (who once the trading companies were established viewed them as low risk) and then lent to the smaller firms.[18] The point here is not the cost of finance (the evidence suggests that interest rates to small firms were quite high), but rather the relationship in which the trading companies were both the marketing outlet and the financier of the smaller firm. This relationship may possibly have solved several problems at once. First, the large companies were in an extremely strong position, both in terms of market and in terms of information to *make* the suppliers compete so that they had to keep on searching for gains in efficiency. (The nearest UK analogy, which some people say is modelled on Japan, is the relationship between Marks and Spencer and its suppliers.) Second, the trading companies also had the requisite information both about the suppliers and about potential markets to be able to lend unusually intelligently and to solve one of the problems of market economies. (The point here is that it is not normally worth while for a bank to acquire the kind and quantity of information which the *sogo shosha* necessarily acquired as part of the rest of their business so bank lending to small firms is usually at too high a rate of interest and/or requires collateral as a partial substitute for information.)

As far as government policy is concerned it seems to be agreed that it played a role that was, for the most part, strongly supportive of these developments. After the end of the occupation in 1952 it allowed and even encouraged the re-emergence of trading companies in the first phase of economic rehabilitation. Through the agency of MITI as co-ordinator of information, it made intelligent interventions in the fields of industry and trade by means such as generous depreciation allowances to encourage investment; the various departments of state influenced the direction that economic developments took.

Here interpretations differ widely about the degree of involvement by government. Chalmers Johnson, having said that 'collaboration between the state and big business has long been acknowledged as the defining characteristic of the Japanese economic system', asks whether the role of the state was overweening or merely supportive.[19] Clearly there has to be a distinction drawn between administrative guidance, regular consultation, and merely 'influence'. We can, for example, detect a spectrum of involvement, stretching from positive intervention such as government's role in the mergers of the 1950s (some of which continued for a long time – the old-established Yawata Steel company finally merged with Fuji Steel to form Shin Nippon Steel in 1969) to government's comparatively minor role as a clearing-house for commercial intelligence.

Finally, and less contentiously, there is fairly clear evidence of a change over time in the degree of intervention by government. In the period of rehabilitation MITI still had wide statutory powers of interference. But, when they lost these in the period of super-growth, they resorted instead to administrative guidance. That in turn became less prominent towards the end of the 1970s. In the third period, the decade of high technology, it would appear that government's role has been less pervasive but equally important in new directions, e.g., assisting in the switchover to new technologies and promoting research and development.[20] But one has the feeling that it is not so much the bureaucrats' reticence that accounts for this lesser role for government as the increased confidence of industrial and commercial leaders.

Selected dates

September 1945	Occupation by Allied countries under General MacArthur.
November 1945	*Zaibatsu* holdings frozen.
August 1946	Creation of Economic Stabilization Headquarters.
April 1947	Anti-monopoly law passed.
April 1949	Dodge Plan for Reconstruction.
September 1951	San Francisco Peace Treaty.
April 1952	Allied occupation ends.
1956–7	Jimmu Boom.
1959–60	Iwato Boom.
December 1960	Ikeda's income-doubling plan announced.
November 1962	Anglo-Japanese Commercial Treaty.
April 1964	Japan joins IMF and OECD.
September 1964	Olympic Games in Tokyo.
1970	Nixon textile 'shock'; free-floating yen–dollar rate.
October 1973	Energy crisis results from increase in OPEC oil prices.

1973–8	Sharp inflation leads to period of slump.
February 1976	Lockheed bribery scandal.
April 1979	Sharp appreciation of yen against dollar; tight money policy applied.
1979	Fifth Economic Summit in Tokyo.
December 1981	Measures for further opening the Japanese market announced.
May 1982	Office of Trade Ombudsman established.
September 1985	Plaza Accord covering the exchange rate of the yen.
February 1987	Louvre Accord.
1986–7	Maekawa commission on the long-term restructuring of the Japanese economy.
May 1987	Twelfth Economic Summit in Tokyo.
July 1988	Cabinet approval for new tax legislation, introducing General Consumption Tax.

Notes

1 The fundamental studies are Chalmers Johnson, *MITI and the Japanese Economic Miracle: The Growth of Industrial Policy*, Stanford, 1982 and *The Industrial Policy Debate*, San Francisco, 1984.

2 See, e.g., Akio Morita, *Made in Japan: Akio Morita and Sony*, London, 1987.

3 Sepp Linhart, 'Aspects of social conflict in Japan – the annual spring wage offensive of the trade unions', in I.H. Nish and C. Dunn (eds), *European Studies on Japan*, Tenterden, Kent, 1979, pp. 30–8.

4 Johnson, *MITI*, p. 308, emphasizes that there is continuity between the pre-war and postwar roles of the commercial ministries.

5 Economic Planning Agency, *New Long-Range Economic Plan of Japan, 1961–70*, Tokyo, 1961.

6 R. Cudlipp in *The Anglo-Japanese Economic Journal*, 1977. See also 'Consider Japan', *The Economist*, London, 1963.

7 For a contemporary account, I.H. Nish, 'Japan's economic development, 1951–61', in *Australian Outlook*, 1961, pp. 280–94. It should be emphasized that at the time the income doubling plan was published, many Japanese were highly sceptical about its targets being fulfilled; and Ikeda and his advisers had difficulty in persuading the public of Japan's growth potential.

8 This is a controversial issue. Johnson, *MITI*, p. vii takes a favourable view of MITI's contribution in the high growth period, while H. Patrick, *Japan's High Technology Industries*, Seattle, 1986, views it as 'Having made positive but on the whole quite modest contributions to that rapid of growth'. Each author has supporters for his opinions.

9 Patrick, op. cit., p. xiv, 'Japanese industrial policy . . . is now less pervasive, less strong and less effective, though not non-existent or emasculated'.

10 More than 50 per cent of the labour force in 1945 was engaged in the primary, predominantly rural, sector; by 1955 it had declined to 30 per cent and by 1980 to 11 per cent. In 1980 the tertiary sector absorbed 55 per cent and demand for labour was still high in many industrial cities.

11 Shigeto Tsuru (ed.), *Growth and Resources Problems related to Japan*, Tokyo, 1978, p. 194.

12 Patrick, op. cit., p. xiv: 'By the mid 70s Japan had caught up to the United States in civilian (though not military) technology. For Japan as a "follower economy" in the 50s and 60s, what were new (high) technologies and new industries already existed in the United States. Industrial policy had a clear model to follow; it was relatively easy to catch up by picking "winner" industries.'
13 Patrick, op. cit., pp. xi–xii.
14 M. Morishima, *Why has Japan 'Succeeded'?*, Cambridge, 1982, p. viii.
15 Ibid., p. 195.
16 J. Watanuki, *Politics in Postwar Japanese Society*, Tokyo, 1977, p. 20, who attributes the phrase to *Time*, 10 May 1971.
17 A. Boltho, *Japan: An Economic Survey, 1953–1973*, Oxford, 1975.
18 Yoshihara Kunio, *Sogo Shosha: The Vanguard of the Japanese Economy*, Oxford, 1982, gives an account of the role of the *sogo shosha* as financial intermediaries.
19 Johnson, *MITI*, p. vii.
20 Patrick, op. cit., p. xiv.

Guide to further reading

Useful guides to the state of Japan's postwar economy are: G.C. Allen, *Japan's Economic Expansion*, Oxford, 1965; A. Boltho, *Japan: An Economic Survey, 1953–73*, Oxford, 1975; Takafusa Nakamura, *The Postwar Japanese Economy*, Tokyo, 1981 and *The Economic Development of Modern Japan*, Tokyo, 1985; and Kozo Yamamura and Yasukichi Yasuba (eds), *The Political Economy of Japan*, vol. 1, *Domestic Transformation*, Stanford, 1987.

Central to the themes covered in this essay are the various writings of Chalmers Johnson, especially *MITI and the Japanese Economic Miracle: The Growth of Industrial Policy*, Stanford, 1982, and the various writings of Hugh Patrick, especially *Japan's High Technology Industries: Lessons and Limit Actions of Industrial Policy*, Seattle, 1986.

Further information on matters alluded to in this essay may be sought in Michio Morishima, *Why has Japan 'Succeeded'?: Western Technology and the Japanese Ethos*, Cambridge, 1982; Akio Morita, *Made in Japan: Akio Morita and Sony*, London, 1987; Saburo Okita, *Developing Economies and Japan: Lessons in Growth*, Tokyo, 1980; and Yoshi Tsurumi, *Sogo Shosha*, Montreal, 1980.

The best annual of the Japanese economy is to be found in *The Economic Survey of Japan*, sometimes known as the 'Economic White Paper', which is prepared by the Economic Planning Agency of the Japanese government and published in English by *The Japan Times*. Also useful are the various monographs compiled by the Economic Planning Agency on Japanese Business Behaviour, especially those published between 1977 and 1983.

PART II

Comparative economic performance of the OECD countries, 1950–87: a summary of the evidence

David Henderson

Framework and historical background

This chapter presents some comparative indicators of the economic performance over the past four decades of what are now the OECD countries.[2] Initially, performance is defined and measured with reference to three economy-wide indicators. All of these are rates of growth, expressed for each period in annual average percentage terms. The three growth rates relate to (i) output, as measured by gross domestic product (GDP); (ii) employment; and (iii) output in relation to employment, or 'productivity' for short. Besides these three basic indicators, I refer to inflation rates and unemployment rates, which also bear on economic performance. This is the framework used.

Since performance is examined in terms of actual figures, it is worth asking at the start what specific values for these indicators appear from past long-run experience to be typical: what performance is it reasonable to expect from a representative OECD country? An answer to this question is provided in Angus Maddison's excellent book, *Phases of Capitalist Development* (1982). It is there suggested, on the basis of evidence extending over the period from 1820 to 1980, that the following triad of growth rates has been characteristic of the long-run economic performance of these countries in the capitalist era:

output (GDP) growth   2.4 per cent per annum
population growth   0.9 per cent per annum
growth of GDP per head   1.5 per cent per annum.

Since we are concerned here with employment rather than population, and since round figures are appropriate for the present purpose, I take as a starting-point a slightly different triad: 2½ per cent annual growth for output, 1 per cent for employment, and 1½ per cent for productivity. I shall refer to this pattern of growth rates as the OECD historical norm.

Maddison's analysis covers sixteen countries. All of them are members of the OECD, and between them they account for over 90 per cent of the output of the OECD area as a whole. By way of background, Table 13.1 shows the three key growth rates – in output, employment, and productivity – for the period 1870–1950, both for the sixteen countries taken together and for three country groupings within them, namely the United States, Japan, and OECD Europe. It can be seen that the OECD area growth rates for these decades were close to the historical norm. As between the three regions, output growth was substantially faster in the United States than in the other two. While this was associated with higher growth rates both of employment and of productivity, the first of these was a more important influence than the second. Again, the somewhat faster rate of growth of output in Japan than in OECD Europe was linked with stronger growth in employment rather than in productivity.

Over the period 1870 to 1950, differences in long-run growth rates of productivity were not very marked either between the three regions shown here or within them over time. This relative stability is brought out in Table 13.2, in which separate figures are shown for the two sub-periods 1870–1913 and 1913–50. The growth rates in the table are close to the OECD historic norm except for Europe and Japan in 1913–50, where they are lower; and these latter rates were clearly affected by (in particular) the fact that both in Japan and in several countries of continental Europe output levels in 1950 had not fully recovered from the effects of the Second World War. Thus economic developments in the decades preceding 1950 suggested that productivity growth rates in particular could be expected to be fairly stable over the long run, with the OECD average rate running at around 1.5 per cent

Table 13.1 Comparative growth rates, 1870–1950 (average annual rates of increase, %)

	OECD[a]	US	Japan	OECD Europe[b]
Output (GDP)	2.4	3.6	2.2	1.7
Employment	0.9	1.8	0.9	0.5
Output/employment	1.5	1.8	1.3	1.2

a Sixteen countries only (cf. the note on country groupings pp. 282–3)
b Twelve countries only. Australia and Canada are included in the first column of the table but are excluded in the regional breakdown

Source: Maddison 1982.

Table 13.2 Growth rates of output/employment, 1870–1913 and 1913–50

	1870–1913	1913–50
United States	1.8	1.7
Japan	1.6	0.9
OECD Europe[a]	1.3	1.1

a Twelve countries only

Source: Maddison 1982.

per annum, the United States rate somewhat higher, and rates for Europe and Japan somewhat lower.

In reviewing the period since the end of the Second World War, I follow Maddison's treatment (i) by taking 1950 as the initial date, though a slightly earlier year could be chosen, and (ii) by dividing the period as a whole into two sub-periods, with 1973 as the year when the first of these ends and the second begins. Although turning points are generally less dramatic and more debatable in economic events than in other branches of history, there is good reason to regard 1973 as a watershed year.

The golden age: 1950–73

Table 13.3 shows for the period 1950–73 the three key growth rates for the OECD area as a whole and for the United States, Japan, and OECD Europe. In addition, the first column of the table shows for comparison the OECD historical norm, and in the last two columns separate figures are given, within OECD Europe, for eleven countries of continental Europe and for the United Kingdom.

Taking first the OECD area as a whole, it can be seen that economic performance, as judged by these indicators, was strikingly better than in the past. The rate of growth of output was substantially higher; and since employment grew at an average rate which was close to the past long-run norm, this increase was associated with a sustained rate of productivity growth which was more than double the past norm. This broad pattern of higher output growth, associated largely or entirely with higher growth of productivity, was common to the United States, Japan, and OECD Europe. But in contrast to the period 1870–1950, major differences emerged, as between these three regions, with respect to productivity growth in particular. For the United States, productivity performance in 1950–73 was better than in the past, but not by a wide margin. By comparison, the improvement in productivity growth was much more striking in OECD Europe: the average annual rate of increase, at just over 4 per cent, was more than triple the long-run average for 1870–1950. This improvement within Europe was still more striking in the countries of continental Europe, where output and productivity growth were appreciably stronger than in the United Kingdom – even though British productivity performance during this period was in fact significantly better than in the past. Moreover, if Greece, Portugal, and Spain were included in the group of continental European countries in Table 13.3, the effect would probably be to raise rather than lower the very high growth rates of output and productivity in the penultimate column, since economic performance improved dramatically in all three countries.

Even the continental European achievement, however, pales by comparison with the growth rates of output and productivity which

Table 13.3 Comparative growth rates, 1950–73 (average annual rates of increase, %)

	OECD historical norm	OECD[a]	United States	Japan	OECD Europe[b]	Continental OECD Europe	UK
GDP	2.5	4.7	3.7	9.6	4.7	5.2	3.0
Employment	1	1.2	1.5	1.7	0.6	0.7	0.5
Output/employment	1.5	3.5	2.2	7.8	4.1	4.5	2.5

a Sixteen countries only
b Twelve countries only

Source: Maddison 1982.

characterized the economy of Japan during this period. These rates had no precedent in economic history, though from the late 1950s onwards they were broadly matched by four other smaller East Asian economies, none of them OECD members – namely Hong Kong, the Republic of Korea, Singapore, and Taiwan.

As a result of these marked differences in growth performance, the geographical distribution of output, as also of real income per head, changed quite markedly within the OECD area over the period 1950–73. While output growth in both the United States and the United Kingdom was rapid by past historical standards, both countries fell behind in relation to the rest of the OECD countries taken together. In 1950, they accounted for almost two-thirds of the aggregate GDP of the sixteen countries included in Table 13.1–13.3. By 1973 this share had fallen to little more than a half.

Faster growth of productivity in the OECD countries was not associated with problems of unemployment. On the contrary, if we go beyond the triad of growth rates to look at average rates of unemployment over the period 1950–73, performance again was generally impressive compared with what past experience would have suggested as likely or even possible. A partial exception to this generalization is North America. For both the United States and Canada, average unemployment rates were rather more than 4.5 per cent, a figure which was not out of line with earlier periods of relative prosperity. Hence their performance under this heading, though reasonably good, was not exceptional. By contrast, in Japan and OECD Europe, as also in Australia, unemployment rates were consistently and strikingly low: for the period as a whole, 2 per cent can be taken as a representative figure. By all past standards, this was a remarkable achievement.

The verdict with respect to inflation is more mixed – in fact, inflation emerged in this period as an endemic problem throughout the OECD area. Over the period from 1870 to the Second World War, high inflation rates had been an exceptional and temporary phenomenon, mainly arising in particular countries from the effects of wars. Apart from such infrequent episodes, the general price level showed no clear long-run upward trend, so that inflation was not a continuing preoccupation. After the Second World War this situation changed: price levels rose generally from year to year, right through the period, in all the OECD countries – and indeed in most other countries of the world except for the Soviet Union and Eastern Europe.

Rates of inflation for the seven largest OECD economies for the period 1950–73, and for two sub-periods and the final year within it, are shown in Table 13.4. For the period as a whole, these rates vary from under 3 per cent per annum to just over 5 per cent. Even for the United States, the country with the lowest inflation rate of those included in Table 13.4, the price level in 1973 was over 80 per cent higher than in 1950. In France and Japan, it rose more than threefold over the period. Such general and sustained rates

Table 13.4 Inflation rates in the seven largest OECD economies, 1950–73[a] (average annual rates of increase, %)

	1950–73	1950–65	1965–73	1972–3
United States	2.7	1.8	4.4	6.2
Japan	5.2	4.7	6.2	11.7
Germany	2.7	2.2	3.8	6.9
France	5.0	5.0	5.1	7.3
United Kingdom	4.6	3.9	6.1	9.2
Italy	3.9	3.7	4.4	10.8
Canada	2.8	2.0	4.3	7.6

a Consumer price indices

Sources: Maddison 1982; OECD.

of peacetime price increases had no parallel in the economic history of the previous century. Moreover, as appears from the second and third columns of Table 13.4, and from the final column which gives figures for price increases between 1972 and 1973, there was a clear tendency for rates of inflation to accelerate in the later years of the period. Thus inflation emerged not only as a chronic problem, but as an increasingly acute one. This was reflected in official concerns and actual government policies.

Inflation apart, the economic performance of the OECD countries in the years 1950–73 was outstandingly good. Everywhere it was better than in the past; and in continental Europe and (still more) Japan, output and material standards of living grew over a sustained period at rates which were without precedent. The period thus brought a change of tempo, an unforeseen break with what past experience would have suggested as likely or even possible. In the light both of earlier history and of later developments, the period has become labelled as a golden age; and just as this golden age had been unanticipated, so the extent to which economic performance fell away in the succeeding period was greater than could reasonably have been foreseen.

Stagflation and after: 1973–87

Table 13.5 presents the comparative growth rates of output, employment, and productivity for the OECD area as a whole and its three main constituent regions for the period 1973–87. Looking at the figures in the first column for the OECD countries taken together, two points emerge: first, output growth, and still more productivity growth, fell off considerably as compared with 1950–73; and second, the pattern of growth was very close to the OECD historical norm. At first sight, therefore, a simple interpretation of events suggests itself: that the golden age was an exceptional, once-for-all interlude in economic history, following which the established long-run pattern of growth for capitalist economic systems reasserted itself.

Table 13.5 Comparative growth rates, 1973–87 (average annual rates of increase, %)

	OECD[a]	United States	Japan	OECD Europe[a]
GDP	2.4	2.5	3.8	1.9
Employment	0.8	1.9	0.8	0.1
Output/employment	1.6	0.6	3.0	1.8

a All twenty-four OECD countries are covered in the figures in the first column, and all nineteen countries of OECD Europe in the last

Source: OECD.

However, from the rest of the evidence presented in Table 13.5, it is clear that such an interpretation does not accord with the facts.

The main reason for this is that, much more than in the decades before 1950, but as in the period 1950–73, there have continued to be striking differences in performance as between different regions within the OECD. In Japan, growth rates of output and (still more) productivity fell off markedly from those of the golden age. It is true that these rates remained high in relation to other OECD countries, while the rate of productivity growth, at 3 per cent per annum, was between two and three times that which broadly characterized the Japanese economy in the pre-1950 era. But the growth of Japanese productivity in the post-1973 years has been not only less than half of that achieved in the golden age, but also well below the rate which characterized continental Europe in the years 1950–73.

In the United States, output growth has also fallen off as compared with the golden age, but this has been despite a somewhat higher rate of growth in employment. What is striking about the United States figures in Table 13.5 is the extremely low rate of growth of productivity in recent years: not only has the rate fallen sharply as compared with that of 1950–73, but it is also conspicuously low in relation to the pre-1950 long-run average for the United States, which was between 1.5 and 2 per cent per annum.

For OECD Europe, growth rates of productivity have likewise fallen off, to a figure somewhat exceeding the long-term pre-1950 average; but what is more remarkable, in relation to past performance, is the very low rate of growth in employment since 1973. This has been associated with (i) lower rates of output growth than would otherwise have been possible, and (ii) the emergence in many European countries, and particularly within the European Community, of unemployment rates which have been chronically and disturbingly high.

Some broad interregional differences in labour market developments during the period 1973–87 are illustrated in Tables 13.6 and 13.7. Table 13.6 shows the increase in the total labour force in each region, together with the corresponding division of this increase between the rise in the numbers of those employed and of those unemployed. In the United States, there was a

David Henderson

Table 13.6 Comparative labour market developments, 1973–87 (increases in millions; % in brackets)

	Total labour force	Employed	Unemployed
United States	30.4 (100.0)	27.3 (89.8)	3.1 (10.2)
Japan	7.6 (100.0)	6.5 (85.5)	1.1 (14.5)
OECD Europe	18.2 (100.0)	4.8 (26.4)	13.4 (73.6)

Source: OECD.

rapid growth in the labour force, but also substantial creation of new jobs. As a result, about 90 per cent of the rise in the labour force was matched by an increase in employment. In Japan as compared with the United States, the growth of the labour force was much slower; but the two economies were alike in that the growth of employment was almost as rapid as that of the labour force. The result was that in Japan as in the United States, unemployment rates in 1987 were not much above the level of 1973. OECD Europe, like Japan, had a rather slow proportionate increase in its labour force; but by contrast with both Japan and the United States, the rate of employment growth was much slower in relation to it. As a result, almost three-quarters of the increase in the labour force between 1973 and 1987 was reflected in higher unemployment, rather than in greater numbers of people employed. Between 1973 and 1985 the growth in numbers employed was in fact negligible: only in the last two years of the period has positive employment growth in OECD Europe been resumed.

In Table 13.7 these broad labour-market trends are viewed in relation to changes in average unemployment rates in selected years during the period. In all three regions, unemployment was more of a problem than in the golden age; but in the United States by 1987 it was back to a rate which was not far from the 4.5 to 5 per cent norm of past decades, while in Japan in 1987 it was not much higher than in the golden age. In OECD Europe, on the other hand, average unemployment rates increased over the period 1973–85; nor did they fall – as they did in the United States – during the period of recovery from the slowdown of 1981–2. Although the position in Europe improved slightly over the period 1985–7, the average 1987 unemployment rate was not much below 11 per cent, which historically is a very high figure. Thus in the period 1973–87, as compared with the golden

Table 13.7 Unemployment rates for selected years, 1973–87 (%)

	1973	1979	1982	1985	1987
United States	4.9	5.8	9.7	7.1	6.1
Japan	1.3	2.1	2.3	2.6	2.8
OECD Europe	3.5	6.1	9.6	11.0	10.7

Source: OECD Economic Outlook 44, December 1988.

age, unemployment performance was a good deal worse in the OECD area as a whole, but especially so in OECD Europe.

OECD inflation performance also worsened considerably after 1973, as can be seen from Table 13.8. For the period 1973–87 the average annual rate of increase in prices, of almost 8 per cent, was approximately double that of the golden age. Only in Japan, where inflation rates had tended to be above average before 1973, was inflation performance no worse. Hence the control of inflation became a major and continuing concern in all the OECD countries. However, from about the beginning of the present decade – the precise turning point naturally varies from case to case – inflation rates were brought under more effective control. This can be seen by comparing the second and third columns of Table 13.8, and also from the final column which shows price increases as between 1986 and 1987. The OECD area inflation rate for calendar years, as measured by the consumer price index, reached a peak of 13 per cent for 1980. It then fell in each succeeding year to 1986. For the OECD as a whole, the increase in consumer prices for 1987, at 3.2 per cent, was comparable with the inflation rates of the 1950s and early 1960s.

Because of the widespread and persistent combination of lower growth rates, higher unemployment rates, and higher rates of inflation, the period since 1973 has been characterized as the age of stagflation. To what extent this label is still appropriate, or may continue to be so, is a matter for debate. As to inflation rates, there has been (as noted above) a clear improvement in performance in the 1980s. While it is too early to tell whether this improvement will be maintained, OECD governments, both individually and collectively, have repeatedly emphasized their determination to ensure that rates of inflation are kept under control.

Performance with respect to output growth, productivity growth, and unemployment rates has been slower to improve. As to productivity,

Table 13.8 Inflation rates, 1973–87[a] (average annual rates of increase, %)

7 largest economies	1973–87	1973–81	1981–7	1986–7
United States	6.9	9.4	3.8	3.7
Japan	5.8	9.1	1.5	−0.2
Germany	3.8	5.0	2.2	0.2
France	9.4	11.4	6.7	3.1
United Kingdom	11.0	15.4	5.3	4.2
Italy	14.0	16.9	10.2	4.7
Canada	7.9	9.7	5.5	4.4
OECD Europe	9.6	11.8	6.7	3.6
Total OECD	7.9	10.4	4.7	3.2

a Consumer price indices

Source: OECD.

developments up to 1985 have been analysed in depth in a recent OECD study. This goes well beyond the rather simple definition of productivity used here: labour productivity is measured with reference to changes not only in employment but also in hours worked and the composition of the labour force; and the analysis extends to changes in the productivity of capital, and hence to total factor productivity with labour and capital combined. One conclusion of the study is that: 'Although year-to-year productivity growth has recovered somewhat since the recession of the 1980s, there is little evidence that the slowdown in *trend* productivity growth . . . has been reversed.' (Englander and Mittelstadt 1988: 8)

More recently, and since this assessment was made, developments in the OECD area have taken a somewhat more favourable turn. From about the middle of 1987, output growth accelerated rather unexpectedly; and in part, this has been associated with higher rates of productivity growth, as measured by output in relation to employment. These improvements in productivity appear greater than can be explained by higher output growth in itself, so that there are indications that trend rates of productivity growth may have risen somewhat. At the same time, the recent brisk growth of output has made possible further – albeit modest – reductions in unemployment rates within OECD Europe. Thus performance with respect to output, productivity, and unemployment was showing signs of improvement at the close of the period 1973–87 – though at the time of writing, at the end of 1988, the evidence for this related only to a short period.

As with the fall in inflation rates, it remains to be seen whether these improvements will be consolidated and taken further. Despite the considerable progress that has been made during the present decade, it is too soon to say with confidence that the age of stagflation has come to an end.

A note on country groupings and sources

The OECD has twenty-four member countries. Of these, nineteen are European: the twelve member states which now make up the European Community, together with Austria, Finland, Iceland, Norway, Sweden, Switzerland, and Turkey; the five non-European members are the United States, Canada, Japan, Australia, and New Zealand.

For the period 1973–87 the figures quoted in the text are from OECD sources. These cover all twenty-four member countries, and 'Europe' refers to all nineteen countries listed above. OECD data, however, at present go back only to 1960; and for the period 1950–73, as well as for earlier years, the figures have been taken from Angus Maddison's study (Maddison 1982). For the OECD in general, sixteen countries only are included, covering however some 95 per cent of total GDP. The absentees are Greece, Iceland, Ireland, Luxembourg, New Zealand, Portugal, Spain, and Turkey. Thus up to 1973 the term 'Europe' covers only twelve countries, but this group includes all the four largest economies – Germany, France, Italy and the United Kingdom.

References

Englander, S., and Mittelstadt, A. (1988) 'Total factor productivity: macroeconomic and structural aspects of the slowdown', *OECD Economic Studies*, no. 10, Spring.

Maddison, A. (1982) *Phases of Capitalist Development*, Oxford: Oxford University Press.

OECD *Economic Outlook* 44, December 1988.

Notes

1. The author is Head of the Economics and Statistics Department of the Organization for Economic Co-operation and Development (OECD), and this commentary draws on OECD data and publications. However, the treatment of the subject and the views expressed here reflect the author's personal judgement, and should not be taken to represent the views of the organization. The chapter has benefited from comments and suggestions by Derek Blades and Andrew Dean.
2. A note on country groupings is given on pp. 282-3.

Chapter fourteen

Benefits of backwardness and costs of continuity

Charles Feinstein

Explanations for differences in productivity growth

A commonplace of studies of postwar performance has been the notion of virtuous and vicious circles. At one extreme, Japan exemplified the former. High rates of growth of productivity made possible low rates of change in unit labour costs and prices, and this created a highly competitive position in international trade. Rapid growth of exports meant strong demand and profitable expansion, and at the same time ensured a healthy surplus on current account, so that it was never necessary for the authorities to constrain the level of activity because of balance of payments problems. Swift and profitable expansion generated both the demand for increased capacity and the supply of finance to fund high levels of investment. This, in turn, promoted rapid modernization of the stock of capital, and so completed the circle by stimulating further improvements in productivity. Britain, at the other extreme, suffered repeatedly from comparatively low rates of growth of productivity, inability to compete in international markets, frequent balance of payments crises, and low levels of investment. Export-led growth characterized Japan and also Germany, France, and Italy, but always eluded Britain.

While there was a broad consensus regarding the nature of the disparity, there was very little agreement on the crucial issue of how the process had started. Why had one country entered the virtuous circle while another hurtled round in a vicious orbit? By the early 1950s the more rapid growth rates achieved by so many of Britain's competitors could no longer be attributed simply to their recovery to pre-war peak levels of output. From then onwards a stream of explanations poured forth to account for Britain's persistently low position in a proliferation of international league tables. Among the factors to which her relatively slow growth was attributed were an adversarial two-party electoral system, an inefficient civil service, a divisive class structure, cultural hostility to industrialization, the hegemonic power of the City over industry, failure to join the Common Market, insufficient education and training, excessive taxation, too much government spending, too little planning, the stop-go effects of Keynesian economic management, levels of demand which were either too high or too low, restrictive practices and over-manning, too few MBAs, and too many strikes. Suitably transposed, these factors were held to explain the superior growth rates achieved elsewhere. Some of these explanations were more relevant than others, but one strand of thought was common to all: something in the organization and operation of Britain's economy and society was fatally flawed. If only these faults could be eradicated, Britain would forge ahead as others did. For GDP per worker to increase at only 2 to 3 per cent per annum was a sign of sub-standard performance; there was no necessary reason, it was implied, why Britain should not match the rates of 4 or 5 per cent achieved by her rivals.

An alternative view, advocated here, is that all of these criticisms lacked historical perspective, and persistently overlooked the fundamental importance to subsequent economic performance of the great disparities in *level* of development which were present in 1948, and have persisted – to a diminishing extent – down to the present time. Most of the studies of particular economies in this volume recognize to some degree that the various nations started their postwar development in very different circumstances. But, in general, this consideration quickly fades into the background as a primary explanation for the different rates of economic growth, leaving issues of economic policy, and social and political organization, to hold the spotlight in the centre of the stage. By contrast, the focus of the present comment is on the enduring importance of certain fundamental conditions arising directly from the initial – and continuing – differences in levels of output and productivity. On this view, countries which started at a much higher level could not be expected to grow as rapidly as those which were starting well behind and thus had enormous scope for catching up.

The evolution of these differences in levels of development at selected dates from 1913 to 1987 is documented in the next section. Then the basis for the hypothesis that it is the consequences of this uneven development that have been the principal determinants of fast or slow growth throughout the postwar period is outlined (p. 288). Some further implications of this hypothesis are considered in the final section.

Changing levels of economic development

Disparate postwar starting points were in part the outcome of discrepancies in the levels of development which countries had reached by 1938, and therefore of differences in the pace and pattern of growth in preceding decades. Thus they reflected the very varied way in which countries were affected by the First World War, and by the uneven incidence of postwar recession and recovery in the 1920s and of the great depression in the 1930s.

Superimposed on this was the differential impact of the Second World War, with massive destruction and devastation inflicted on some, and exceptional opportunities for rapid expansion of productive capacity granted to others. A broad indication of the magnitude of these differences, and of their historical context, is given in Table 14.1 for eight of the major market economies covered in this volume. The overall level of economic development is defined in terms of labour productivity, meausred by Gross Domestic Product (GDP) per worker. In the upper panel the absolute level of GDP per worker in each country is shown for selected years in the form of indices, with 1948 = 100. In the lower panel the same information is used to calculate the level for each country relative to that in the United States at those dates. Countries are ranked in the order of their relative position in 1948 as shown in the lower panel.

A number of significant features of the historical record emerge prominently from this table. First, the disparity in the impact of the Second World War is immediately evident from the upper panel. For all countries except the United States and Sweden it represented an immense setback. The deterioration was particularly marked for Japan and Germany, where there was a large absolute fall; and Italy, Denmark, France, and the United Kingdom all made little or no progress between 1938 and 1948. The consequence of this difference in wartime experience, superimposed on the pre-

Table 14.1 Levels of GDP per worker[a] selected years, 1913–87

	1913	1938	1948	1956	1973	1987
1. Indices, 1948 = 100						
United States	59	74	100	127	175	189
United Kingdom	80	94	100	117	186	233
Sweden	52	82	100	136	229	262
Denmark	70	96	100	130	216	254
France	69	97	100	144	323	437
Italy[b]	77	104	100	140	341	444
Germany	99	136	100	186	384	513
Japan	77	169	100	155	572	843
2. US level at each date = 100						
United States	100	100	100	100	100	100
United Kingdom	78	74	58	54	62	72
Sweden	43	55	50	53	65	69
Denmark	58	64	49	50	61	66
France	42	47	36	41	66	83
Italy[b]	43	47	33	37	65	78
Germany	50	55	30	44	66	81
Japan	20	36	16	19	51	70

a The data used here are workers in employment, rather than potential workers (which would include the unemployed)

b The OECD labour force data for Italy from 1956 onwards have been adjusted upwards to maintain comparability with the figures for earlier years; see Maddison 1982: 197

Sources: For 1950–87, OECD 1987a, 1987b, EEC 1988; for 1913–50, Maddison 1982.

war position, is that by 1948 there were vast disparities between the nations (see the lower panel). Output per worker in the United States was 70 per cent higher than in the United Kingdom; double that in Sweden and Denmark; three times the level in France, Italy, and Germany; and as much as six times the Japanese level. We thus have the extremely important finding that the productivity gap separating all countries (except Sweden) from the United States was appreciably greater after the Second World War than it had been before the First World War.

The pattern of growth which flowed from this initial position is very striking. As can be seen from panel 1 of Table 14.1, there is a strong inverse relationship between the level in 1948 (indicated by the order in which countries are listed), and the rate of increase achieved during the subsequent period. The United States, starting with the highest level of output per worker, managed to increase it by only 90 per cent over thirty-nine years (a compound annual growth rate of 1.6 per cent). Japan, starting in the most backward position, raised her standard by 740 per cent (5.6 per cent per annum). All the other countries fall neatly into place between these extremes, with increases of 130 to 160 per cent for the United Kingdom, Sweden, and Denmark in the upper half of the ranking, and of 340 to 410 per cent for France, Italy, and Germany in the lower half. The corresponding annual rates of growth were 2.2 to 2.5 per cent for the former group and 3.8 to 4.3 per cent for the latter.

As a direct consequence of this inverse relationship between levels and rates of growth there was a remarkable convergence towards the United States level of output per worker (see panel 2 of Table 14.1). By 1987, Denmark, Sweden, Japan, and the United Kingdom had all come broadly into line with each other at about 70 per cent of the United States level; Italy, Germany, and France had come to within 80 per cent. By contrast with 1948 (or 1913) the differences both within the group of follower countries, and between them and the United States, were now comparatively modest.

Some further points of interest emerge if we subdivide the postwar period into three shorter phases: the long boom 1948–73, the first period of slower growth, 1973–9, and the most recent phase, 1979–87. In Table 14.2 productivity growth rates over these three periods are shown for the same eight countries. In the first period the rates of growth were high, the discrepancies between countries were large, and the strength of the inverse relationship with the initial postwar level was strongest. In the subsequent phases growth slowed dramatically, with the change especially marked in those countries which had raced ahead most swiftly before 1973. Since then, no country has achieved as much as 3 per cent per annum, and differences between countries have been quite moderate. In three countries (the United States, Sweden, and the United Kingdom) growth rates accelerated in the final phase; in the remaining five they slowed further, most notably in France

Table 14.2 Growth of GDP per worker, 1948–87 (compound growth rates, % per annum)

	1948–73	1973–9	1979–87
United States	2.3	−0.1	1.0
United Kingdom	2.5	1.2	1.9
Sweden	3.4	0.5	1.3
Denmark	3.1	1.5	0.9
France	4.8	2.7	1.8
Italy	5.0	2.0	1.8
Germany	5.5	2.9	1.5
Japan	7.2	2.9	2.8

Sources: See Table 14.1.

and Germany. This is associated with some movement away from the predicted ordering of rates of growth indicated by the 1948 levels. In particular, the United Kingdom has broken rank and in the period 1979–87 the former laggard has shown the second fastest rate of growth.

Late-starters and leaders

With this historical data as background we turn now to consider the explanation for the observed process of convergence towards a common level of output per worker. Our basic hypothesis is that the fundamental factor which served simultaneously to constrain productivity growth in the United States and Britain, and to boost that of their competitors in Europe and Japan, was the different levels from which they started in 1948.

The crucial consequences of these differences in levels have been extensively studied by economic historians and economists (for example, Veblen 1915; Gerschenkron 1962; Gomulka 1971; Marris 1982; Abramovitz 1979, 1986; Baumol 1986; Maddison 1987). The hypothesis drawn from this work recognizes that development cannot proceed until a backward country attains a certain minimum level of economic activity, of education and culture, of social cohesion, and of political and administrative stability. Manifestly, all the countries on our list, including those most disadvantaged in 1948, had long since passed this level. Once over this threshold the latecomer has three powerful advantages as it proceeds to exploit the gap between its actual level of productivity, and the potential level set for it by the prior achievement of the leading countries.

The effects on attitudes and institutions

The first asset is that the economy embarks on its path to modern economic growth with an acute awareness of the need for reform and for sustained exertion. It knows that it starts far behind – indeed, military defeat (or its imminent prospect) has frequently been both an historical consequence of backwardness and a stimulus to subsequent progress. Unless it can cast off old habits of thought and activity, and accomplish the necessary dynamic transformation, the late-starter risks economic and/or political subjugation. Even after an initial phase of vigorous growth, the imperative need to catch up will continue to exercise an influence, and the resulting social attitudes and values will contrast with those prevailing in the leading countries. This divergence in approach will be reflected in hours and conditions of physical effort, expectations of social welfare and housing, appreciation of the necessity for additional equipment and modernization and thus for high levels of investment rather than consumption. Most important of all, it will influence the attitudes of workers and managers to technological progress, with consequent implications for manning levels, and also for changes in perceived custom and practice in the workplace. Institutions are affected as much as individuals. Those which may retard development by protecting past practices or future aspirations will be weak in the countries which start from behind, strong in those which are most advanced.

Given the inherited gap between the group of nations we are considering, these fundamental differences in attitude would have existed in 1948 even without the impact of the Second World War. But they were powerfully reinforced by the economic and psychological conditions which prevailed at the end of the war. For many countries this meant destitute cities, ruined railways, factories, and mines, the humiliation of military defeat or foreign occupation. For a few – and pre-eminently for Great Britain – there was a euphoric mood of victory. The former inevitably approached the task of reconstruction with a great sense of urgency and determination and little prospect of early benefits. The latter saw the course and outcome of the war as a triumph for which they could now expect to be rewarded.

It was not only individual attitudes which were transformed by the war. In countries where the war had ended in ruin and defeat, most of the pre-war institutions – government agencies, professional societies, associations of employers, trade unions – had been discredited or destroyed, and it was usually necessary to start afresh with new or substantially remodelled institutions. By contrast, in countries like Britain and the United States which were neither occupied nor defeated, old institutions survived unchanged, preserving the powers and practices which had accrued to them over centuries. In one context long-established vested interests were shattered, in the other they flourished (Olson 1982). The implications for future growth and change of this divergent structure of attitudes and institutions were immense: the late starters would derive the benefits of backwardness, the already advanced countries would suffer the costs of continuity.

A further important influence on growth was the way in which the competing claims of welfare (including housing), defence, and productive investment were perceived. Here too, underlying differences between leaders and late starters were securely buttressed by the outcome of the war. Those countries which started at a higher level of development, and emerged victorious from the war, thought they were entitled to a high standard of welfare and good housing; and their governments believed they had an obligation and a right to maintain a strong military posture. Those who had been defeated and ruined did not expect generous outlays on welfare and were not permitted large defence budgets. The funds which the latter could allocate to modernization of non-residential infrastructure and productive equipment were accordingly greater, and the effects on economic performance correspondingly large.

Borrowing from the leaders

The second, and perhaps the most crucial, benefit of relative backwardness is that once development is under way, late starters can borrow from more advanced nations. This ability to gain from the experience of the leaders is often discussed solely in relation to technological innovations in physical plant and machinery. The diffusion of such inventions will, indeed, be a significant element in the process of catching-up. But the notion of borrowing from the leaders is much more extensive than this. It also embraces a wide array of economic and social practices and modes of operation; for example, property rights and legal procedures, corporate structures and management hierarchies, banking systems and intermediate sources of finance, forms of taxation and of insurance, industrial relations and personnel management. A substantial process of adaptation will almost invariably be needed to tailor the imported practices to the factor endowments and socio-economic circumstances of the borrowing country, and some may achieve this more successfully than others. Nevertheless, the benefits of this international diffusion of best-practice procedures and techniques are always likely to be a highly significant contribution to growth.

Transfers from agriculture

Finally, relatively backward countries typically have a large proportion of their working population still engaged in agriculture, usually employing little capital, primitive farming methods, and with correspondingly low output per worker. Countries in this condition, therefore, have the possibility of raising average productivity by transferring labour to industry and other sectors of the modern economy. In addition, as long as surplus labour is freely available in agriculture (and related low-income sectors such as domestic service), this transfer will permit rapid growth of labour inputs in the modern sector without immediately putting great pressure on wages and prices (Kindleberger 1967). The surplus-labour countries will thus enjoy a considerable advantage over those which have already completed this process of transition to an urbanized, industrialized economy.

Implications of the backwardness hypothesis

The basic proposition of the backwardness hypothesis is that a very large part of the discrepancy in economic performance of the postwar years can be explained in terms of the lower level from which the fast-growing followers started their advance. The leaders were suffering the costs of continuity, while the late-comers enjoyed the benefits of backwardness. On this view comparable rates of growth were not attainable by Britain and the United States, precisely because they were already at a higher level of development, following a long period of supremacy consolidated by victory in the Second World War. Accordingly, it was not realistic to expect them to attain growth rates of 5 or 6 per cent per annum, and their failure to do so was neither reprehensible nor remediable. No doubt some improvement on the rates actually achieved was feasible, but the margin was very much smaller than most commentators suggested.

Equally, the rapid rates achieved in Germany, Japan, France, and Italy owed far more to their low starting point than to any special merits of their economic and social arrangements. The postwar international agreements – including Bretton Woods, GATT, and the EEC – created exceptionally favourable conditions for world trade. In this very open environment competition flourished, and imitation and diffusion of more productive techniques was strongly promoted.

The backwardness hypothesis does not require that differences between nations should terminate at precisely the point at which the formerly backward countries catch up. Rapid growth develops its own momentum, both psychologically, and in terms of the virtuous circle of economic relationships outlined above, and this will carry the country forward for some time. By the same token, slow progress creates its own obstacles to reform, and a one-time leader is likely to continue – and may even strengthen – patterns of behaviour which inhibit rapid growth, long after its leadership position has been eroded. It is however, an implication of the hypothesis that the leader who falls behind will ultimately respond to the changed circumstances and, in particular, to the increased threat to markets and jobs created by the formerly backward economies. The inbuilt attitudes and ossified institutions will finally be seen to be barriers to progress, and will slowly give way to new and more effective arrangements. The suggestion is not that this is an inevitable process, nor one which will come about smoothly and automatically. It may well require a significant measure of government intervention and pressure, but such intervention will only be effective when the population at large has acquired the fundamental perception that their situation has changed: that *they* are now the relatively backward nation and must make every effort to reform their institutions and attitudes if they are not to sink progressively further behind. The British case is notable for the fact that the initial loss of leadership to the United States occurred well before 1913, but for a variety of reasons did not stimulate such a response. That had to wait until the 1970s and 1980s, when the country as a whole began to realize that it was being overtaken by Germany, France, Japan, and even Italy.

The process of convergence will be strengthened by converse forces at work in the countries which have forged ahead to arrive at last in the front rank. They will now feel entitled to relax their efforts and to claim more of the benefits of their economic advance in leisure and consumption. Their institutions will become more rigid and less well-adapted to the new circumstances. The two groups will thus approach a common level of labour productivity and a common growth path. This will be higher than that managed by the leaders while they believed themselves to be comfortably ahead and had only their own technical and social innovations to rely on; lower than that achieved by the late-comers while they could still derive the benefits of catching up from behind. The speed of advance in these new conditions thus depends on the rate at which innovation (broadly defined) proceeds in the bloc of leading countries as a whole. It is likely that different countries will exercise leadership in different fields, and this may mean that the technological frontier moves forward at a faster rate than in the earlier era with a single leader. But the average rate of growth among this group of countries will slow down as the residual scope for borrowing is progressively eliminated. However, new countries (such as Spain, South Korea, or Brazil) will be moving across the capability threshold, and advancing at the more rapid pace feasible for late-starters.

The backwardness hypothesis thus provides an explanation for both the initial discrepancy in growth rates during the long boom, with its associated process of convergence towards a broadly uniform level of output per head; and for the reversal of performance standards which have been evident since the end of the 1970s. The process is too recent and incomplete to permit confident conclusions, but the evidence of the last decade is consistent with the hypothesis. Sluggish Britain is at last beginning to change its ways: to some extent new attitudes prevail and institutions are being reformed; the United States is currently experiencing some of the problems of a leader slowly becoming aware of the loss of its long-held superiority, but the difficult process of adjustment is only just beginning; and Germany, France, Italy, and Japan are slipping down to a lower rate of growth as they respond to the successful outcome of their long struggle for parity.

References

Abramovitz, M. (1979) 'Rapid growth potential and its realisation: the experience of the capitalist economies in the postwar period', in E. Malinvaud (ed.), *Economic Growth and Resources*, Proceedings of the Fifth World Congress of the International Economic Association, vol. 1, London: Macmillan.

Abramovitz, M. (1986) 'Catching up, forging ahead and falling behind', *Journal of Economic History*, 46: 385–406.

Baumol, W.J. (1986) 'Productivity growth, convergence and welfare: what the long-run data show', *American Economic Review*, 76: 1072–85.

EEC (1988) *Eurostat*, 6, Brussels: EEC.

Gerschenkron, A. (1962) *Economic Backwardness in Historical Perspective*, Cambridge, Mass.: Harvard University Press.

Gomulka, S. (1971) *Inventive Activity, Diffusion and the Stages of Economic Growth*, Aarhus: Institute of Economics.

Kindleberger, C.P. (1967) *Europe's Postwar Growth: The Role of Labour Supply*, London: Oxford University Press.

Maddison, A. (1982) *Phases of Capitalist Development*, Oxford: Oxford University Press.

Maddison, A. (1987) 'Growth and slowdown in advanced capitalist economies: techniques of quantitative assessment', *Journal of Economic Literature*, 25: 649–98.

Marris, R. (1982) 'How much of the slow-down was catch-up?' in R.C.O. Matthews (ed.), *Slower Growth in the Western World*, London: Heinemann.

OECD (1987a) *Labour Force Statistics, 1965–1985*, Paris.

OECD (1987b) *National Accounts, 1960–1985*, Paris.

Olson, M. (1982) *The Rise and Decline of Nations*, New Haven, Conn.: Yale University Press.

Veblen, T. (1915) *Imperial Germany and the Industrial Revolution*, New York: Macmillan.

Chapter fifteen

Economic policies and traditions

Sidney Pollard

Any comparative survey of the major industrial economies since the Second World War is bound to draw attention to the similarities of their experience. There was first, in the 'golden years' of the 1950s and 1960s, a rate of economic growth everywhere, even in the sluggard British economy, at a level never before sustained over so long a period. The countries most ravaged by the war seem to have reacted not very differently from those without damage, reaching something like their long-term growth path in a few years, the loss being borne by current consumption rather than by long-term growth. There was then the break in 1973/4, triggered, even if not fundamentally caused, by the OPEC oil price rise, leading to high inflation and slower growth. And then there was the second oil price rise in 1979, followed by high unemployment and even slower growth amounting almost to stagnation, when 'the economic climate had suddenly become unrecognizable . . . Europe was knocked off balance' (Gaston Thorn, in Dahrendorf 1982: ix–x).

This unity was strengthened by common technical problems, and common possibilities of their solution. The shift out of agriculture into industry, the shift from textiles to metals, machinery, vehicles, and electronics, the consequent need for a different infrastructure and for extended training in the new techniques, all imposed, within limits, similar reactions. Nevertheless, the mechanism that transmits world economic development from one country to another is not clear. International trade alone cannot have done it, for countries exported and imported quite different types of goods; moreover the trading link of the planned economies with the west was quite tenuous, yet they also felt the same phasing of growth. Nor can the oil alone have been responsible either, for not only did the price rise follow a longish period of creeping, yet accelerating inflation on a world scale, but the countries concerned occupied quite different positions as producers, importers, and exporters of oil.

Much may, no doubt, be attributed to the international links between the finance and capital markets, which were increasingly liberalized in the postwar period. Although absolute interest levels varied enormously between one centre and another, and the revaluations of currencies against each other revealed a bewildering kaleidoscope of varying fortunes, the financial markets reacted most sensitively to the international shock waves, as well as to the variable position of each country in regard to the rest, especially as revealed by the balance of payments. Financial policy was in every country under more or less direct control of government, as part of its mechanism of overall economic policy-making, but this latter, in spite of different ideologies and the differences in the political compositions of governments, showed remarkable parallels also. Everywhere there was, in the first place, the 'preoccupation with the creation of full employment and the furthering of the equality of income and wealth' (van der Wee 1986: 54). On the supply side, there were in consequence everywhere massive extensions of the provisions for education and research, and there was some planning and aid to investment in what were considered to be key sectors. Gradually, as the fact of rapid economic growth sank into the consciousness of policy-makers, and as it became clear that that was the precondition of almost every other desirable development, growth itself became a major preoccupation. Later on, the rising tide of inflation added yet a further common feature.

In all this broad stream of world history, was there in fact much room left for independent economic policy-making? Were not the great battles fought in each country with such vigour, a form of shadow boxing, for did not the flood of internationally determined problems, together with the limited technical means of dealing with them, impose their own logic on each government?

The force of opportunity and circumstance has, indeed, often been underrated. Yet in each country there was a band of possibilities, which within its admitted limits still allowed alternative policies with widely varying consequences. The house might have been smaller than has often been assumed, but each government was still master in its own and, as is clear from the country by country accounts, actions and reactions differed. These differences were not purely random or *ad hoc*. On the contrary, inter-national comparison suggests strongly and almost universally that they arose because governments were in effect acting within the clearly discernible, and largely agreed, framework of their own national traditions.

The Soviet Union and the other planned economies of Eastern Europe are clearly somewhat apart. In the case of the former, economic government was conducted less by consent than imposed, by a small, strong-willed, and dogmatic minority on an inert population. The dogma, in turn, had been developed for the quite different circumstances of the most advanced western economies instead of the most backward part of Europe, as Russia was when the Bolsheviks seized power. In the rest of Eastern Europe, including Czechoslovakia, power was exercised by party leaders who, for a variety of reasons, felt constrained to follow the Russian pattern, no matter how well or ill it accorded with the circumstances of their own country.

That the shape which the first experiment of a 'socialist' economy took was much influenced by Russian traditions has often been noted, and need not be further elaborated here. Excessive centralization, a powerful bureaucracy, tight constraints on the liberty and mobility of the individual were features of the Tsar's as well as of Stalin's empire. The immense concentration on capital goods (and armaments) while consumption and standards of living remained abysmally low reminds one of the former Tsarist military strategy of throwing massed, ill-equipped troops into battle, achieving victory by weight rather than by quality.

The emphasis on capital goods survived even into the easier postwar atmosphere – overinvestment for its own sake, almost to the pattern, which J.A. Hobson and Rosa Luxemburg had alleged, was driving the capitalist nations into imperialism. Occasional attempts, by Khrushchev in particular, to plan a decisive shift to consumer goods, foundered on the massive inertia of a centrally planned economy. Similarly the emphasis on quantity rather than quality of goods, and on maximizing output rather than minimizing costs, while clearly derived from the way planning is carried through and activities are rewarded, is not entirely dissociated from the Russian experience: a people used to discrimination would surely, subtly and persistently, have led its planners into other priorities.

The Soviet solution of autarky and heavy capital goods was transferred, for political reasons, to the other eastern nations ill suited to it. Least of all did it suit the Czechs, with their traditions of lively entrepreneurship and small-scale flexibility. Being technically among the most advanced of the planned economies, they did gear their engineering industry to some extent to foreign (eastern) demand, yet they were as vulnerable to the world recession from the 1970s onward as the rest.

Among the other countries, Britain was in many ways the odd man out. By failing to match the fast growth rates of the rest in the quarter century after the war, she was overtaken by one country after another in terms of income per head, while at the same time, by failing to match her imports with sufficient exports, stumbling into crisis after crisis on the balance of payments front, until the North Sea oil provided a temporary respite. This is all the more surprising since at the outset, as a country which had escaped foreign invasion and had emerged among the victors in the war, she was economically and technically well in advance of most of the rest, while her people had in the past been known, and feared, for their technical brilliance and commercial aggressiveness.

In explanation, two fatal flaws in the framework within which Britain's economic policy-makers (and even most of their critics) operated, may be noted. One was the very fact of victory, of former imperial grandeur and commercial success, which had left a legacy in the form of the Sterling

Area, of a large commercial and financial network with London at its centre, of illusions as to world standing and, not least, a certain contempt among British entrepreneurs for, and unwillingness to learn from, foreign experiences with the exception of those of the United States. To maintain great-power status, great economic sacrifices, e.g., in the Korean War, were imposed on the economy, holding back its re-equipment just at the time when the other Europeans and the Japanese were massively installing new machines. Meanwhile, the repeated deflationary, 'stop' measures imposed for the sake of holding the Sterling Area together worked in the same direction. Thus, the limited war destruction had as consequence that reconstruction seemed less urgent than elsewhere, and that higher incomes were demanded and gained, too early for the economy to deliver. Once set on a slower growth path, it proved harder to accelerate it than in countries where recovery from a very low point had forced a high rate of investment and a basic flexibility straight away. Less, perhaps, ought to be made of the other penalty of an early start mentioned in the literature, the absence of a large agricultural labour reservoir out of which labour might be recruited for new industrial sectors, for Britain had several other low-income sectors whence labour could be, and was, transferred, beside the Commonwealth immigrants and the immigrants from Mediterranean countries.

Possibly more destructive still was the other British tradition of making policy by and for the financial and trading sector of the economy, without regard to its productive sector. The reasons for this, in the past, when British industry could look after itself, and the City was a power in the land, are not hard to discern; its survival into the postwar years meant the repeated, and unthinking, sacrifice of output and investment for short-term adjustments, and for the sake of such financial targets as the overseas value of the pound sterling, which alone determined the endless manoeuvring with interest rates, credit squeezes, and tax changes. Only in the immediate postwar years was there some governmental effort to aid the productive sector, and growth rates in those years were satisfactory enough. Since then, British industry has become increasingly antiquated and uncompetitive, an excess of manufactured imports over exports has emerged, and such industries as have survived, have done so because Britain has become a low-wage country.

There were some faint similarities in the American experience. The American growth rate was also low, though not quite as low as the British, but this could be explained, at least in part, by the fact that American industry tended to be at the technical frontier, so that the catching-up element included in the high speed of growth elsewhere, was largely absent. At the same time, the high level of unemployment in the United States, even in the 'golden' years, tends to point to the fact that there, also, not all opportunities to maximize production were used.

The similarity with Britain lies in the high price paid for great-power status, though at least, in contrast to Britain, America did gain immense political power and influence which may well be considered a reasonable way of spending some of a country's wealth. Many of the policy assumptions, including a strong dash of Keynesianism in macro-economic steering, were also common to the two countries. One disadvantage of the Americans was the division of powers between president and Congress (not to mention the Federal Reserve Board) so that fiscal policy in particular had to be worked out in painful compromise as a second or even third best solution instead of being a direct response to a problem, even if seen through party spectacles, as in Britain.

Against this, the lobby system of political influence, as well as the strong local pressures on congressmen, ensured that all interests, not merely those of Wall Street, were fed into the Keynesian decision-making process. Thus the United States came off gold and allowed the dollar to float much sooner, suffering much less damage in the process, than Britain did in the case of similar dilemmas.

As by far the most powerful economy, with its currency as the reserve currency for much of the rest of the world, the United States had different options and opportunities from those open to others. In particular, the country could run up an enormous foreign debt without much fear of loss of control: precisely this formed one basis of the policy for much of the 1980s, in which an expansionary posture, including huge budget deficits, was maintained at the cost of large balance of payment deficits covered by foreign investments in the United States. At the same time, American actions were bound to have excessive effects on other nations, which could not but weigh with the decision-making process. This latter consideration, together with the newly found role of political world leadership, rather worked against the American tradition of isolationism and lack of consideration for the rest of the world, but the former showed that, in need, the tradition still held. With all its power and wealth, the United States has not been prepared to adjust its policies, conceived for purely internal ends, to the needs of the world economy.

At the other end of the scale in terms of size are the four Scandinavian countries. Much unites them, but much also divides them. Common is their long democratic tradition, which tends towards policies of social equality, and the high quality of their labour power and their entrepreneurship. But the degree of *étatisme* differs, as also the role of agriculture, and the timing of their industrialization 'spurts' and of fast growth since the war. Starting, except for Finland, with a high absolute level of national income, their growth rates were good rather than spectacular. Their decline in the 1970s led to the widespread assumption that the highly developed social services of the Nordic countries, based as they were on high levels of taxation, had so undermined entrepreneurship and effort that the *élan* had gone out of the economy, equality acting as a drag on prosperity. The resumption of fast growth rates in the 1980s, combined with low rates of unemployment, except for Denmark, make it clear that, at least in the civilized conditions of Scandinavia, social justice is by no means inimical to rapid expansion.

Possibly the most interesting lessons may be learnt from the three large members of the original EEC – France, West Germany and Italy – and from Japan. Each has in its day, and with some justification, been alleged to have experienced, or performed, an economic 'miracle', and the question naturally arises whether, and to what extent, their governments caused these or contributed to them.

As has often been noted, the main strands of economic policy and their chronological sequence were entirely different in each of these four countries. Germany, defeated, suffering from an immense bomb damage as well as from foreign occupation, left as the truncated part of a formerly closely integrated economic unit, started with what possibly looked like the least favourable conditions. True, the value of the surviving infrastructure, the capital equipment, and the skills of the population, have often been widely underrated. True also, the international political climate, in which Germany moved from a hated enemy to a sought-after ally, changed rapidly and in a most favourable direction. Yet her recovery of the 1950s and 1960s, the best-known economic 'miracle' of all, which made her the most powerful and most dynamic economy of Europe, was astonishing enough. How was it done, and what part did government policy play in it?

The official German doctrine of 'social market economy' has been much quoted, and much misunderstood. On the face of it, it seemed to seek the best of both worlds by leaving to the private sector, the market, the largest possible freedom, so as to produce the largest possible cake, but then super-imposing the 'social' provision to improve the share-out and deal with the victims. There is a large element of truth in this description, yet it misses some of the main elements derived from German traditions.

For one thing, there was never any question of the state abdicating to private enterprise in the Anglo-Saxon manner. The German state has since the days of absolutism always been powerful and always pervasive. In the early days of the federal republic, it intervened, in a restrictive direction not dissimilarly from the British, to hold down inflation and right the payments balance. But beyond it, and more permanently, it proved to be a much more active agent in planning and fostering the infrastructure, especially the transport and communications network, as well as industry and mining itself.

More impressive still, and possibly more influential, were the numerous semi-official, traditional institutions, which almost invariably tended to affect the economic sphere in a positive way. Prominent among them are the schools, colleges, and near-universal apprenticeship schemes, providing not only the skill, but also the confidence and self-discipline which distinguish the German worker. Others are the numerous associations of industries and employers, but above all the trade unions, which have been given various rights firmly anchored in the law, and which, in return, tend far more than most other Europeans, to advance rather than thwart technical and structural change. Lately Germany's growth rate has declined, while her enormous export surplus and her high unemployment rate point to a lack of ability of the home market to absorb all her output. In those circumstances, some of the forms of German social discipline show signs of cracking.

France, also, started with a good and varied industrial base and highly skilled manpower. France is often taken to be the epitome of planning, thus proving that it cannot have been the free market which was responsible for German successes, since France did almost equally well under a large measure of control. A powerful state is, of course, as much a French tradition as a German, as is the tradition of serving her own nation, no matter how much damage it does to others, by using not only tariffs, but prohibitions, quotas, and other forms of discrimination much more actively than her neighbours.

Much of French industry and banking was nationalized early, there were economic plans for other main sectors, as well as government control over credit, prices, foreign exchange, and in part even over trade. This battery of powers was most successful in the early postwar years, when it helped to build up modern basic industries, under the umbrella of which other industries could also be modernized. Given the necessity for structural changes in later years, the planning and statist structure proved, not surprisingly, to be a handicap. In the 1980s the French economic performance was poor by any standards. Government policy was floundering: it has been accused of tending to devalue too late and to place the burdens too unfairly. The traditional picture of a rich, unevenly developed country governed by brilliant civil servants but incompetent politicians, is once again beginning to re-emerge.

Her fascist past tended to drive the politicians of Italy, including her communist ones, in the direction of economic liberalism after the war, but the state by no means abdicated its powers. In the early postwar years Italy used her advantage of cheap labour, whose bargaining power was low because of migrants from the south and because of weak trade unions, to keep her share of foreign markets. The state helped by its regional development policies in the south (with only moderate success), by providing the infrastructure of roads and communications, and by setting up some highly successful companies in certain key sectors, such as steel and oil. Relatively little effort was expended to prevent inflationary pressure at home. In due course, rapid rises in productivity, the building up of modern industries and the beginnings of social services created here, also, a miracle of rapid modernization, while strengthened trade unions, not to mention the indexing of wages, kept up inflationary pressures. In spite of unstable governments and a notoriously inefficient and corrupt public sector, output and exports continue to grow satisfactorily, but at the price of high inflation coupled with repeated devaluations and high unemployment. State planning is negligible: the private sector works largely by ignoring the state.

Japanese economic recovery after the war was remarkable enough; but the country's sustained growth rates since then are unique in world history. Japan is now the third if not the second or even the first economic power in the world, threatening in many fields to overtake even the United States. There is no clear agreement as to how it was done, largely because the traditions and assumptions of Japanese society differ from those of the west in several not easily measurable ways.

The government certainly played an active part, and was guided by industrial efficiency, and the ability to pay with exports for the many necessary imports, as a primary aim. Government went in for some long-term planning, particularly in deciding on the industries that were to be supported because they offered the best chances for the future. But it operates only indirectly, mainly by obstructing foreign imports and by channelling funds to the large combines. It is the combines which have generated Japanese industrial expansion, exports, and foreign investment based on the surplus achieved in foreign trade. In turn, they have benefited by a tradition of attitude to work, of loyalty to one's employer, and of modesty of individual demands which differ in subtle and largely undefinable ways from those current in Europe. The trade unions, which seemed after the war to have introduced European methods into the labour market, have been weakened in part by the very economic success itself. Growth rates have much slowed down lately, but are still the highest in the world, and the population is at last beginning to reap some of the advantages of higher output in higher real incomes. In Japan also, as in Germany, it may well be that it is less the government, than the network of traditional habits and institutions linked only indirectly with the government, which provided the real impetus for a remarkable economic achievement.

In this brief survey, the sequences of phases and their impact on the different countries have, of necessity been omitted, and the emphasis placed on the long-term observation of the period as a whole. The cyclical crisis management of the different governments, which shows interesting differences within a limited spectrum of choices available, could not be pursued here. As far as long-term trends are concerned, government responses mattered, even if operating within the framework of world developments; but these responses, no matter what the party and ideology under which they took place, could be derived to a very large extent from the political culture and the traditions of their society.

References

Dahrendorf, R. (ed.) (1982) *Europe's Economy in Crisis*, London: Weidenfeld & Nicolson.

van der Wee, H. (1986) *Prosperity and Upheaval: The World Economy 1945–1980*, Harmondsworth: Viking.

Chapter sixteen

The meaning of hard work

Michael Rose

How far does willingness to work account for patterns of national economic performance? How does economic development affect this propensity?

Work commitment is regarded as one of the most important aspects of culture – shared social values, standards ('norms') of behaviour, and worldviews. But it is hard to define and measure and reliable comparative data about economic culture have been available only in the last decade or so. Japanese success above all is often attributed to cultural factors – not least by the Japanese themselves, and the chapter on Japan could be usefully read alongside Morishima's (1982) study of the Japanese difference. Britain has become a laboratory for cultural policy, as a 'culture of dependency' (on state welfare or guaranteed employment) is attacked and replaced – perhaps – by more businesslike values.

International studies of work commitment still show work taking a more important place in the lives of Americans or Japanese than of British employees. But commitment varies too between occupations, regardless of country; surveys of multinational companies (for example, the 120,000 employees of International Business Machines in over 100 countries) suggest that those economic values that matter most are trans-cultural (Hofstede 1984). But country comparisons still provide the interesting surprises: in the International Meaning of Work inquiry, Yugoslavs and Israelis appear no less work-centred than Americans, while the 'hard-working' Germans and 'serious' Dutch score fewer points than might be expected (MOW 1987: chapter 5).

But maybe work values – at least, amongst *employees* – in all industrially advanced countries sooner or later follow one common trend. Such an analysis of economic attitudes differs from the 'backwardness hypothesis' cogently stated in Charles Feinstein's commentary (p. 284), where national awareness of 'league position' in development becomes a powerful motivating factor in its own right. This approach, however, applies best to the mentality of policy elites, and the broader politics of production. What might be called 'promotion fever' or 'relegation panic' may affect work behaviour at relatively dramatic historical moments. The more mundane forms of the disposition to work seem relatively resistant to crisis. But the question of how these two kinds of influence are related is worth coming back to after examining other theories about work values under modern industrialism.

The work ethic: abandonment and revival

The most manageable question is, how far did the postwar boom affect readiness to seek employment, regular work habits, and work effort? Did it erode a formerly strong work ethic – a sense of moral obligation to work hard – indispensable to industrial dynamism? And, conversely, have the harsher conditions of more recent years, with high unemployment and collapsing smokestack industries, restored work discipline by producing significant changes in attitudes and values?

In the US, worries that a Protestant work ethic was being stifled (by bureaucratic corporations, not 'top team' complacency) surfaced in the early 1950s (Whyte 1955). From the mid-1960s, American industrial managers and business commentators reported growing labour indiscipline and lower motivation. By 1970, they had been joined by their colleagues in the higher-growth European countries.

Workers' co-operativeness had certainly fallen. Industrial conflict, particularly strikes, rose fast in the late 1960s in many countries and remained high until the first oil crisis in 1973. Turnover had risen so high in some mass-production industries (especially automobile assembly) that recruitment and training could barely keep pace with resignations. Increasingly, large immigrant workforces were being introduced to take the assembly-line work disdained by native workers. Voluntary absenteeism (that not caused by health or personal problems) rose too, pointing to a greater readiness to trade earnings for leisure as incomes rose.

'Discretionary effort' in manual work, or 'optional ingenuity' in the provision of a service, deteriorated noticeably wherever supervision or control were difficult to maintain. Even German workers began to joke that they would never buy the cars they had assembled on a Monday morning or a Friday afternoon. By 1973, the existence of a revolt against work had been officially recognized in the US by the appointment of a Presidential Committee of Inquiry (O'Toole 1981). European countries, from the league leaders to table-bottom strugglers, rapidly followed suit, establishing agencies to recapture workers' involvement by improving the quality of working life (QWL).

There was little hesitation in ascribing this revolt to changing social values and norms, rather than to a changing structure of economic incentives and opportunities (Kanter 1978: 47–78). Might it even presage, as many American observers feared, a rejection of capitalism as well as of a

Protestant work ethic? Here, the alarmists followed Max Weber's classic study of a the link between capitalist dynamism and a Protestant moral discipline (Weber 1930). Yet Weber had examined the interplay of religion and entrepreneurship. Terms such as 'work ethic' or even 'Protestant work ethic' do not appear in his monumental study, and Weber was relatively uninterested in the economic values of wage workers.

These commentators could well have paused to ask whether changed work behaviour needed a cultural explanation in any case. Why not simply regard it as a reflection of a changed balance of power? Wherever they had a following, labour unions had exploited the 1960s prosperity to limit employers' power and ease workplace discipline. Social legislation had further checked management authority and the use of flexible work practices. In this perspective, a change in economic climate ought to have restored discipline and productivity, by increasing workers' sense of insecurity and restoring managerial prerogatives.

But as unemployment climbed steadily in the slowdown years of the late 1970s it became clear that some work attitudes had become relatively immune to market forces. Concern over work commitment in America was now paired with a 'productivity panic'. Surveys of Germany (Noelle Neumann 1981: 46–50), or Sweden (Zeterburg and Frankel 1981: 41–5), pointed to a striking change amongst their workers, who until the mid-1960s had showed consistently high levels of commitment to work and effort. Ten years later, an increasingly large minority of Germans were putting far greater stress on enjoyment of leisure. This was not just an 'age-effect': the younger West Germans of 1985 had become markedly less work-centred than the younger Germans of 1965; an international study of work commitment in the early 1980s by the Aspen Institute concluded that it was surprising to find that the Germans took so little pride in their work given the national stereotype which sees them as particularly hard-working and industrious. However, this finding was qualified by the thought that a low level of German work ethic might not be equated with a low level of actual performance (Yankelovitch *et al.* 1985: 64–5). This conclusion is consistent with the remarks about recent trends in the morale of workers, in the chapter on West Germany (chapter 5). The author's comment that Germans are unhappy unless they have something to worry about may be an oversimplification. But the implied point – that other industrial institutions, notably those affecting training and management, may be strong enough to offset a decline in economic morale – is valid.

Post-industrial theory

Interpretations based simply on market indiscipline did not stand up well to the evidence. Alternative (or supplementary) cultural explanations, based on 'needs theory' or 'post-materialism', claim that a sort of psychological ratchet operates on expectations as higher living standards are achieved. These allegedly became permanently set at such a high level that many economic actors were now developing a 'post-materialist' mentality. Extensive survey data (Inglehart 1977, 1979) did begin to show growing numbers of such post-materialists.

But they were minorities; and the term post-materialist was always a questionable one to apply to their members, who apparently have remained powerfully motivated by rewards (an extra holiday entitlement perhaps, or luxury products such as designer clothes, or opera performances) of which they approve. Some of their members might avoid 'unworthy' occupations (notably manufacturing) or fail to respond to certain sorts of money incentives. But concern for post-materialist needs and rewards – greater leisure, a cleaner environment, personal health, and enjoyment of sport or the arts, as ends in themselves – may not diminish capacity for hard work. Some economic psychologists (Yankelovitch 1985) now claim that the motivation of such people presents managers with no insuperable problems, but rather with opportunities. The advertising industry in the 1980s regards such groups as the key to many growing consumer markets, targeting many of its messages at tastes (whether in food or financial services) which could prove prototypical. In a word, many post-materialists seem closer to yuppies than to hippies.

Again, theories of post-industrialism (Bell 1976) allege that work competence is now built as much upon social and psychological skills – above all, an ability to manipulate people – as on technical ones, outmoding values like independent-mindedness, and old-fashioned ideas of personal responsibility ('conscience'). Simultaneously, the post-industrial economy is seen as inverting the relationship of production and consumption. Production is no longer an urgent, almost 'sacred' focus of life.

Work effort thus ceases to be treated as an expression of personal worth and character. If anything is applauded, it is a general manipulatory competence. Post-industrialism thereby does away with an already ailing Protestant work ethic, of which it has no need. Cultural values and social norms give priority instead to consumer sovereignty and its rewards, putting paid to a traditional insistence upon the 'deferment of gratification'. In western society, deferment of gratification has indeed been a middle-class ('bourgeois') trait with wide economic consequences. Its most common form was thrift. Victorian children were taught that wanting necessarily involved long periods of waiting, until money was earned, or saved up, to purchase utilities outright. Consumption on credit was treated as morally indefensible, no less than as a sign of financial incompetence.

That advanced industrialism does kill off a Protestant work ethic is unproven. But there is an important subsidiary problem. Did most Victorian workers ever share the economic mentalities of the 'bourgeois' middle class? Social historians have only recently taken the question up in

Britain (Joyce 1987), but the American search for a popular Victorian work ethic suggests it was thinly spread, even in Puritan New England, amongst manual workers (Gutman 1977). Cultural historians are now beginning to argue that the British industrial take-off itself depended on a greater readiness to consume in the late eighteenth century, not upon any secularized Protestant ethic held by workers – or by entrepreneurs (Campbell 1987). Underlying changes in values may be much less dramatic than the grand theories of industrial culture make them seem.

At the same time, the post-industrial thesis has been taken very seriously by business managers (Dluglos and Weiermaier 1981), and by commentators in Japan, where official reports and surveys have begun to fret about 'advanced country disease', and the Japanese press about teenager 'spoiled brats' who allegedly are losing respect for Work. As western commentators note (Berger 1987: chapter 3), the real issue is transition to a new type of industrialism, not its disappearance. Structural changes do interact with longer run cultural ones. Neither is yet understood in any but a very sketchy way, except that a new relationship between work competence and work commitment may indeed be necessary. Meanwhile, attention has shifted from the changing economic culture of advanced industrialism as a whole to the question of how far it is moulded – and can be remoulded – within nation-states.

New realism and moral uplift

Since 1979, British economic policy has linked the aim of restoring dynamic economic growth with a crusade to revive traditional social values: the two are seen as interdependent. If the Thatcher Experiment is succeeding on the former count, how far is it doing so because of headway on the latter? Or, paradoxically, is an economic break-through to be bought only at the price of a further erosion of traditional values?

The intellectual axis of the programme has been the doctrine of 'new realism', meaning hard-headed calculation. Yet new realism is also portrayed as as step towards moral reconstruction. The logic of this programme calls for comment. To act more 'realistically' requires a change in behaviour. It may also signal a change in perspectives. It need not signify any change in social values, which are moral objects. Realism (about wage settlements, manning levels, government assistance, accounting procedures, or public finance) is a criterion, and the essential one, of rational economic behaviour. Change in this direction, long overdue, has certainly occurred.

Of the country chapters, that on Britain recognizes best the complex role of inherited patterns of behaviour, organization, and ways of thought in industry. In Britain's case, a demoralizing deadweight of traditionalism stifled the will to innovate on the side of capital, and any general quest for upward mobility on the part of labour. This was most apparent in manufacturing industry, where technical obsolescence was paired with social and cultural archaism. The author shows that the syndrome was reinforced by what groups saw to be their interests, yet cannot be analysed in terms of interest alone.

In the 1980s, new realism was presented as a cultural as much as an economic cure for the British disease. Some notable successes could be claimed in its name – a readiness, certainly, to recognize that change could no longer be evaded, and some striking productivity gains. Yet was new realism the long-awaited cure, or a new form of the disease itself? There was a risk of converting it into a totem. New realism might thus implant a shallow market mentality and foreclose on those attitudinal changes – greater respect for training, for managerial competence, for technical innovation, for product development, for quality, and for investment – essential for future economic development. High unemployment, for example, might have forced higher effort levels. But had it produced genuine commitment to them? The stimulation – or the reinforcement – of narrowly calculative behaviour, producing an opportunist yet still restrictive mentality, would be a poor basis for long-term recovery. New-found co-operation – its existence is beyond question – between workers and employers might be deceptively brittle. The risk has been that of checking the development of the very social values most relevant for building strategically planned industries trading in high quality products – rather than (to speak metaphorically) the cheap tin trays in which British manufacturing came to specialize.

Some findings in the annual *British Social Attitudes* surveys (Jowell *et al.* 1985, 1986, 1987) point soberingly in this direction. But recent research into social change and economic life undertaken for the Economic and Social Research Council, suggests a more complex situation (ESRC 1987, 1988, 1989). It shows that many British employees have been working harder than ten years ago, with large majorities in all occupational groups reporting a growth in the effort they put into their work in the 1980s. (Sizeable minorities report that they are often warned that they work too hard.) Commitment to paid employment also remains high and – an important change, to which we shall return – is growing amongst women. Thatcherite policies have certainly helped force a rise in levels of effort, then. There is also a wide recognition that greater effort was, if only on pragmatic grounds, a legitimate objective. Many employees seem to have been ready at least to modify their values, if not to adopt new ones.

But the values most relevant to the long term will not develop spontaneously. To nurture them calls for highly skilled, even inspired management. Detailed case studies show that many British-run firms, especially in manufacturing, either lack appropriate management skills or do not see the need for them. Fortunately, there are exceptions to this rule, but there are too few of them. Such considerations are relevant when the economic culture of Britain is placed beside that of Japan (Dore 1973, 1986). Large

Japanese companies can count upon high commitment to work effort and high-quality production. This can hardly reflect the influence of Protestantism. That it reflects comparable traditional Japanese religious values (Morishima 1982) is sometimes contended. But Japanese workers (in this sense, they resemble the western 'post-materialists') undoubtedly have high expectations of 'self-realization' – a sense of lifetime achievement – through the act of working.

Larger Japanese companies shape the experience of employment and work to cater for these moral ambitions. They do so in a context of high management skill, excellent worker training, and strategically planned investment policies, seeking to build an atmosphere of trust and an environment of long-term security. In Britain, such aims still seem exotic. The 'economic terror' of the first years of new realism undoubtedly provoked many firms to think more strategically and to build closer bonds with their much reduced workforces. The majority used it in a more traditional, less far-sighted – more British – way, to shed excess labour and eradicate some restrictive practices, without establishing positive personnel and manpower strategies.

Japanese cultural values cannot be transferred directly. But the means adopted by Japanese firms – high levels of training, skilful supervision, 'career' development even for manual workers within firms – can be exported. It is remarkable that Japanese firms often set up and do best in areas of Britain (South Wales, the north east) not just of high unemployment but of high historic labour militancy. One reason is their skill in building worker trust and commitment. Workers in such plants report especially favourably on the high competence of their Japanese managers (White and Trevor 1982) who never seek to offload responsibility for management lapses on to workers. (A substantial number of strikes in British engineering were once provoked in this way.)

Has the opportunity to rebuild British work culture now been lost? Sizeable minorities of people in the Economic Life studies report that they could still substantially increase their own work effort if they wanted to do so. Training, with notable exceptions, remains inadequate. Production engineering is still badly paid – a dustbin career, from a bright graduate's point of view. There are signs, as the current (1988–9) revival begins to generate inflationary heat, that the realist boot, so to speak, is about to change foot, with labour unions in more prosperous firms once again able to exploit skill scarcities and managers' taste for a quiet life.

As aspect of this 'competence-commitment' problem where policy might help is women's employment. Theories of post-material or post-industrial society have been developed during a period when the typical wage-earner of industrialism – a blue-collar worker with a full-time housekeeping wife and dependent children – has been receding. Once almost 40 per cent of employed people in the advanced societies fell in this group. In the United States only 12–13 per cent, and in Britain maybe a few percentage points more, now do so. This change has been caused partly by a modest fall in the participation-rate of adult males, but more by a steady rise in women's labour-market participation. Table 16.1 shows trends for major industrial countries.

Women are usually pictured as possessing much less commitment to employment and lower economic ambition than men. The Economic Life studies show, however, that this partly reflects the structure of employment opportunities for women, as well as the enduring strength of gender roles in social convention. The employment values of better qualified younger women in higher occupational grades approximate more closely to those of men in similar grades. Moreover, there is a growing expectation, already strong in the United States, and even stronger in the Scandinavian countries, that more women will seek a work career broken only – and then, increasingly briefly – by periods of maternity leave.

Feminist agitation may partly account for these changes, through pressure to alter social values, but research suggests that many women utilize the feminist message to justify behaviour resulting from more direct pressures. If more women work it is because their opportunities and their need to do so have steadily been rising. With an increase in divorce and single parenthood, more women need to support themselves. Moreover, there has occurred a continual rise in the expectations and commitments of dual-earner households as consumer units. At the same time, such households can develop more complex strategies towards earning and employment than those of the traditional male-headed single-earner unit.

For example, dual-earner households run on more egalitarian lines result in new pressures on men to share domestic tasks, reducing the effectiveness of some men as employees. At the same time, egalitarianism may add to the effectiveness of many women as employees, by increasing their availability and freeing them from domestic concerns. Theoretically, this should contribute to overall economic effectiveness, by making better use of the human capital (education, training, social skill) of more highly qualified

Table 16.1 Female labour force participation rates[a] 1950–90

	France	W. Germany	Japan	Sweden	UK	US
1950	49.5	44.3	57.6	35.1	40.7	37.2
1960	46.4	49.2	60.0	55.0	46.1	42.2
1970	48.2	48.1	55.3	59.4	50.5	48.9
1980	52.6	49.2	51.6	73.8	58.2	59.1
1990[b]	57.9	52.0	52.8	85.8	61.3	67.8

a Female labour force as % of female population aged 15–64
b Estimates

Source: OECD, Demographic Trends, 1950–90, 1979.

women, and helping to develop it amongst others. If this is so, policy should be aimed at increasing women's availability for work, and discouraging social conventions and values that inhibit it. One way of doing so effectively would be to promote the provision of child care, either privately through tax reliefs (as in the United States) or through public nurseries (as in France).

Dismantling traditional gender roles could now offer one of the better prospects for modifying British economic culture. Yet what is striking is how rapidly the revision of the economic role of women, and the social values bearing on it, have been occurring in Britain regardless of policy. Indeed, in all countries (except, perhaps, Japan) it seems to constitute the single most important labour market development of the second half of the century, interacting with the less well-agreed changes in economic values posited by the various versions of post-industrial theory (which would be better termed 'post-factory' theory). Modification of culture to allow for it to proceed more smoothly could be more productive than trying to administer a kiss of life to the ghost of the work ethic or Victorian family values.

A post-bourgeois capitalism?

How will changes in values in the advanced countries affect performance in the system as a whole? Firstly, those so far defined are thoroughly consistent with dynamic economic growth. Indeed, they may provide a key to a new phase of general expansion. Secondly, handling them may need to vary from one country to another. In Britain, this would seem to call for an attack on those institutions that support archaism in thought and action. So far, only labour unions have experienced such uncompromising social engineering.

It bears repeating that work commitment seems closely connected with technical competence. Recent social research on the link between industrial institutions and performance has been stressing the variety of institutions for creating competence, and indirectly, commitment, from one country to another (Maurice *et al.* 1986; Rose 1985: 65–83). Here, the expectations and perspectives of employers become as important as those of labour unions and the authorities. It is far from clear that new realism in Britain has altered employer policies in the most promising ways for longer term success, rather than reinforcing a less strategically minded type of animal spirits.

This other aspect of British economic culture, the logic and style – not so much the vigour – of British entrepreneurship and business management, need more attention than that given to it here. A standard work on the decline of the industrial spirit amongst English employers in the nineteenth century (Wiener 1981) assumes that industrialists once possessed a strategic and rational approach to production, which they then lost under the counter-attack of languid landed aristocrats and obscurantist pastoral socialists. But, possibly, most British – or at least, most English – entrepreneurs had never become truly scientific industrialists. If so, long-term hope for the British economy might lie in continuing international economic integration, with non-British employers taking a larger role in running the economy. This implies a policy committed to suppressing the narrow nationalism and xenophobia of British popular culture. After all, the extent of international integration already achieved, at least in Europe, makes it worth asking in what sense 'national economies' still exist.

Nation may thus join the traditional family, and such other venerable middle-class virtues as thrift, as a cultural casualty of a thriving post-bourgeois world of contemporary capitalism. And this internationalization calls for a final comment on the question of how far economic mentality can be usefully viewed as a reflection of relative advance or backwardness.

The relevance of 'league table consciousness' is greatest for under-standing some aspects of the politics of economic life. Politicians, and opinion leaders, no doubt think in the 'league table' terms Charles Feinstein attributes to them. The public at large, too, experience a sense of economic rivalry with other nations.

Yet how far this affects their behaviour, as economic actors, even in the dramatic circumstances of the early 1980s economic terror in Britain, is not agreed. That it affects short-term political behaviour may well be correct: an effective election poster of the 1980s showed an oversize bulldog (the British Miracle created by new realism) with a simpering French poodle on one side and a fatuous German dachshund on the other, both lost in admiration. Yet Britain had not overtaken the continentals. On relative rates of growth at the time of writing (1989), its per capita income will take a further eighteen years to equal that of France, around sixty to equal West Germany's. To pretend otherwise, might postpone the day for ever, through reviving complacency. Little reliable research on the effects of such awareness is available. Case-studies of behaviour and attitudes within companies at the time of the 1980–2 economic blizzard suggest that managers and employers merely reacted to their immediate circumstances, as they saw them, and have gone on doing so. To put it bluntly, people resorted to league position arguments or justifications only when it suited their book to do so. For example, where labour productivity doubled, as sometimes it did, this reflected attitudinal change in only very small measure. Often it merely resulted from the dismissal of the 50 per cent of a labour force who had been doing very little truly productive work. There was little need for the active remainder to work very much harder than they had done before – though, statistically speaking, they were now working 'twice as hard'. Those workers who were retained, hardly surprisingly, were more likely to cite relegation peril as a justification for large-scale dismissals than were the dismissed themselves.

When economic explanations are available for economic events, no need arises to resort to one in terms of moral propensities – whether attitudes, values, or norms of behaviour. Yet such factors are of the highest importance in their indirect effects, and in what they tell us of a society's institutions. Work remains less 'central' amongst British workers, and post-bourgeois minorities are smaller in Britain. Policy-makers, suspending their preconceptions, ought to ask why this may be so, and whether their social and economic objectives can be so neatly reconciled in practice as they can be in stirring political rhetoric.

References

Bell, D. (1976) *The Cultural Contradictions of Capitalism*, London: Heinemann.

Berger, P. (1987) *The Capitalist Revolution: Fifty Propositions about Prosperity, Equality, and Liberty*, Aldershot, Hants: Wildwood House.

Campbell, D. (1987) *The Romantic Ethic and the Spirit of Modern Consumerism*, Oxford: Blackwell.

Dluglos, G. and Weiermaier, K. (eds) (1981) *Managing under Different Value Systems*, West Berlin: de Gruyter.

Dore, R. (1973) *British Factory: Japanese Factory*, London: Allen & Unwin.

Dore, R. (1987) *Taking Japan Seriously*, Stanford: Stanford University Press.

ESRC (1987 onwards) *Social Change and Economic Life: Working Papers and Reports*, Swindon.

Gutman, H.G. (1977) *Work, Culture and Society in Industrialising America*, Oxford: Blackwell.

Hofstede, Gert (1984) *Culture's Consequences*, London and Beverley Hills: Sage.

Inglehart, R. (1977) *The Silent Revolution: Changing Values and Political Styles amongst Western Publics*, Princeton, NJ: Princeton University Press.

Inglehart, R. (1979) 'Value priorities and socio-economic change', in S.H. Barnes *et al.*, (eds), *Political Action: Mass Participation in Five Western Democracies*, London and Beverley Hills: Sage.

Jowell, R., *et al.* (1985, 1986, & 1987) *British Social Attitudes*, Annual Reports. Aldershot, Hants: Gower.

Joyce, P. (ed.) (1987) *The Historical Meanings of Work*, Cambridge: Cambridge University Press.

Kanter, R.M. (1978) 'Work in a New America', *Daedalus*, 107.

Marshall, G. (1982) *In Search of the Spirit of Capitalism*, London: Hutchinson, 1982.

Maurice, M. *et al.* (1986) *The Social Foundations of Industrial Power*, MIT Press.

Morishima, M. (1982) *Why Has Japan Succeeded?*, Cambridge: Cambridge University Press.

MOW (International Meaning of Work Team) (1987) *The Meaning of Working*, London: Academic Press.

Noelle Neumann, E. (1981) 'Working less and enjoying it less in Germany', *Public Opinion Quarterly*, 4 (4).

313

O'Toole, J. (1981) *Making America Work: Productivity and Responsibility*, New York: Continuum.

Rose, M. (1985) 'Problems and promise of a societal approach to economic institutions', *European Sociological Review*, 1 (1).

Rose, M. (1985) *Reworking the Work Ethic*, London: Batsford.

Rose, M. (1988) 'Involvement in work', in D. Gallie (ed.), *The Sociology of Employment*, Oxford: Blackwell.

Weber, M. (1930) *The Protestant Ethic and the Spirit of Capitalism*, London: Allen & Unwin.

White, M. and Trevor, M. (1982) *Under Japanese Management*, London: Heinemann.

Whyte, W.H. Jnr (1955) *The Organization Man*, Harmondsworth: Penguin Books.

Wiener, M. (1981) *English Culture and the Decline of the Industrial Spirit, 1850–1980*, Cambridge: Cambridge University Press.

Yankelovitch, D. *et al.* (1983) *Work and Human Values: An International Report on Jobs in the 1980s and 1990s*, New York: The Aspen Institute.

Yankelovitch, D. *et al.* (1985) *A World At Work*, New York: Octagon Books.

Zeterburg, H. and Frankel, O. (1981) 'Working less and enjoying it more in Sweden', *Public Opinion Quarterly*, 4 (4).

Chapter seventeen

Political institutions and economic performance

David Marquand

Since Adam Smith, if not before, writers on economic matters have known that economic performance depends partly on political and institutional factors. Even those who believe that the competitive free market is bound, by definition, to allocate resources more efficiently than any other mechanism, and that public intervention in the market is therefore bound to do the economy more harm than good, accept that governments can affect economic performance for good or ill – for good, by removing barriers to free competition, and for ill by erecting or maintaining them. Other schools of thought believe that state intervention can, at least in principle, improve it. On either view, it is reasonable to suppose that the structure, values, and policies of the state must have something to do with its economic impact.

Unfortunately, attempts to discover how and under what conditions these political or institutional factors impinge on economic performance have not been conspicuously successful. Discussion of this topic rarely gets beyond anecdote, and often falls into the trap of circularity. Seeing a successful economy, and noticing that the political institutions in the society concerned have tried to promote economic success, we are apt to conclude that the success is the product of the institutions. By the same token, if a country's political institutions intervene in the economy, and the economy performs badly, we tend to blame the institutions or their policies. But these are not valid inferences. The successful economy might have been even more successful – and the unsuccessful one even more unsuccessful – if the institutions or policies had been different.

So it is not enough simple-mindedly to compare the political institutions and economic performances of the societies described in this book, in the hope that worthwhile institutional or political generalizations will emerge of their own accord. It might be better to proceed in the opposite way: to begin by looking at possible 'models' of the relationship between institutions and policies on the one hand, and economic performance on the other, and then to see what light they throw on the story told here. Three such 'models' suggest themselves: first, Paul Kennedy's (1988) model of imperial over-stretch; second, Mancur Olson's (1983) model of group-induced economic

315

sclerosis; and third, John Zysman's (1983) model of the role of distributional coalitions in economic development.

Kennedy's is the simplest. Political and military power, Kennedy argues, go hand in hand with economic strength. Wealth translates into power: power both demands and generates wealth. But there is a paradox in the relationship. Great powers cannot rise to greatness unless they possess the resources to achieve it; indeed, the economic processes which give them the resources also make them great. In becoming great, however, they acquire commitments; and if they are to remain great in the face of inevitable competition from potential rivals for greatness, they have to maintain these commitments. All too often, the costs of doing so cut into the economic base which made it possible for them to rise in the first place. As Kennedy puts it:

> An economically expanding Power – Britain in the 1860s, the United States in the 1890s, Japan today – may well prefer to become rich rather than to spend heavily on armaments. A half a century later, priorities may well have altered. The earlier economic expansion has brought with it overseas obligations (dependence on foreign markets and raw materials, military alliances, perhaps bases and colonies). Other, rival Powers are now economically expanding at a faster rate, and wish in turn to extend their influence abroad. The world has become a more competitive place, and market shares are being eroded. Pessimistic observers talk of decline; patriotic statesmen call for 'renewal'.
>
> In these more troubled circumstances, the Great Power is likely to find itself spending much *more* on defence than it did two generations earlier, and yet still discover that the world is a less secure environment – simply because other Powers have grown faster. . . . Great Powers in relative decline instinctively respond by spending more on 'security', and thereby divert potential resources from 'investment' and compound their long-term dilemma. (Kennedy 1988: xxiii)

It is not difficult to pick holes in the argument. It is not clear whether Kennedy is saying that declining great powers always divert resources from investment to military expenditure, or only that they sometimes do so. Either way, he does not explore the mechanisms of the process as fully as one would have liked. Why do priorities switch from wealth to armaments as relative power declines? Is it for emotional (or, to use Kennedy's word, 'instinctive') reasons, or is the explanation institutional? For that matter, do priorities always switch in this way? Britain and the United States may both have followed the trajectory – wealth first, armaments later – sketched out in the quotation above, but what about Imperial Germany? It is well known that Germany was beginning to overtake Britain in at least some crucial indices of economic performance by the late-nineteenth century, but her growing economic success went hand in hand with heavy military expenditures. On a different level, is it necessarily the case that resources allocated to armaments must be 'diverted' from investment in the economic base? On Keynesian assumptions, after all, arms expenditure may sometimes help to take up the slack of an under-employed economy, and so help to stimulate investment which would not otherwise have taken place. Some people think that that is what happened under the Reagan presidency. Even on non-Keynesian assumptions, some forms of arms expenditure – notably on advanced technology – may have a peaceful spin-off and therefore make the civilian economy more productive than it would otherwise have been.

When all the qualifications have been made, however, the Kennedy thesis does throw some light on the story told in the earlier chapters of this book. Of the economies whose experiences they describe, it is most obviously relevant to the Soviet and the American. Indeed, it is its relevance to the United States which has brought its author fame and fortune in that country. For the reasons just given, however, I am not sure that the model tells us as much about the American experience as it appears at first sight. What does seem to me worth exploring is its possible relevance to Britain – and, above all, to the contrast between Britain's postwar, performance and the performances of her competitors on the mainland of western Europe.

Though Britain was not really a great power in the period under discussion here, she was, for much of the time, a would-be great power. Successive British governments made manful efforts to retain as much of her old world role as they could and devoted substantial resources – scarce foreign exchange, an unusually high proportion of her total R and D effort, scarce scientific manpower – to the exercise. As late as the mid-1960s, Harold Wilson insisted that Britain's frontiers were 'on the Himalayas'; and it was not until the post-devaluation expenditure cuts of 1968 that a firm decision was taken to abandon the so-called East of Suez policy. The contrast with the rest of western Europe is patent. Italy and West Germany were cured of pretensions to greatness by defeat in the Second World War. Thereafter, they were content to pursue wealth rather than power. The smaller countries, with no recent experience of greatness to distract them, did the same. And, as everyone knows, Britain experienced a long period of relative economic decline *vis-à-vis* all of these. It would be wrong to suggest that the Kennedy thesis provides a complete explanation, but it is hard to escape the conclusion that it provides part of it.

There is, of course, a counter-example. France was just as reluctant as Britain to give up the trappings of great-power status. If Harold Wilson thought his frontiers were on the Himalayas, there were times when de Gaulle seemed to think his were in Quebec. The French withdrawal from empire was more reluctant, more painful and a good deal more bloody than the British. Yet for most of the postwar period, France's economic performance has been more impressive than Britain's. To complicate matters still further, the fierce determination of French elites to regain great-power status may actually have stimulated the postwar modernization programme which helped to lay the foundations for French economic success later on. But this does not mean that the Kennedy model tells us nothing about the postwar experience of western Europe in general, or about Britain's postwar experience in particular. What it suggests is that we need to know more about the contrasting ways in which postwar British and postwar French governments tried to retain great-power status, and in which their attempts impacted on their respective economies. Since the seventeenth century, French regimes have seen the development of the national economy and the defence of national greatness as different sides of the same coin. The postwar modernization programme belonged to a policy tradition going back to Colbert. The British conception of national greatness, and the British view of the way to achieve it, were associated with a radically different tradition of indirect rule and economic liberalism, to which the notion of state-led development was alien. To put the point another way around, mercantilism was a boo word in Britain, but second nature to the French. And a mercantilist view of national greatness – or, at any rate, of the way to achieve national greatness – is plainly at odds with a liberal one. How far these differences of tradition account for differences in policy, and still more for differences in performance, is an open question. Not the least of Kennedy's merits is that he encourages us to ask it.

The second of my three models is Mancur Olson's. It is more complicated than is sometimes realized. As everyone knows, Olson thinks that organized producer groups – what he calls 'common-interest organizations' – are bound to seek special benefits for their members which are not available to the public at large. In practice, this means that they are bound to make the rate of growth lower than it would otherwise have been. A society with a large number of such groups is therefore likely to have a lower rate of growth than a society with a small number. Since these groups need long periods of stability to establish themselves, moreover, societies which have been stable for a long time will have more of them – and consequently a lower growth rate – than societies which have suffered revolution, dictatorship, or foreign occupation. All this, however, is only part of Olson's story. Gloom is not unalloyed. If the common-interest organization contains a large proportion of the total population – if, in Olson's language, it is 'encompassing' – the built-in conflict between its special interests and the wider public interest disappears. It can pursue the general interest while at the same time pursuing its own particular interest. Thus, 'encompassing' groups are not, by definition, anti-social and do not slow down the rate of growth.

The first leg of the argument has received more attention than the second.

Organized groups slow down growth, Olson has seemed to be saying, so the key to slow growth lies in the presence of organized groups in the society concerned. Britain has grown more slowly than her competitors on the mainland of western Europe because their organized groups were destroyed in the upheavals that preceded and accompanied the Second World War, while hers had centuries of stability in which to establish themselves. That, of course, is Olson's own conclusion. It is not, however, the only possible conclusion; and I doubt if it is the right one. Apart from any other considerations, it is not at all clear that the Second World War did wipe the slate clean of continental organized groups in the way that Olson assumes. Still less is it clear that Britain's more successful continental competitors have all had fewer or weaker groups than she has had. Some have, but some (including some of the belligerents in World War Two) have not. Fortunately, however, the model also suggests a more promising perspective. The key variable, it seems to me, is 'encompassingness'. What matters for economic growth is not the presence or absence of organized groups, but the presence or absence of *encompassing* groups. It follows that the crucial institutional question is whether a given society's organized groups are 'encompassing', and what has made them so if they are.

For Olson himself 'encompassingness' is a function of size. That too seems to me over-simplified. A vast, amorphous, ill-disciplined and uncoordinated organization, like the British TUC, is not rendered encompassing by the mere possession of a large membership. Structure matters too; and structure reflects purposes and values. All this suggests a different set of conclusions from the ones Olson and most of his commentators have drawn. If what matters is 'encompassingness', and if 'encompassingness' is, in part at any rate, a function of purposes and values, then countries with the kind of values that promote 'encompassingness' will do better economically than countries without. Of course, we do not know what these values are. We can, however, make a good guess. It seems fairly clear that 'encompassingness' flourishes most of all in central Europe and Scandinavia, where the industrial culture has been strongly influenced by solidaristic social-democratic and (in the central European case) social-Christian ideologies, which put a high value on group loyalty and social peace. In varying degrees, and for some of the time, it has, of course, gone hand in hand with neo-corporatist institutional arrangements, in which the state has shared control over public policy with 'peak' associations of producer groups. But if the argument advanced here is right, neo-corporatist institutions are the products of solidaristic values rather than vice versa. In Britain and the United States, by contrast, the industrial culture has been shaped by the individualistic values reflected in and legitimized by Benthamite utilitarianism in the one case and Lockean liberalism in the other. As such, it has impeded 'encompassingness' and fostered the fragmented, narrowly self-seeking, ultimately anti-social common-interest organizations which Olson holds responsible for sluggish growth.

A modified Olsonian model of this sort clearly helps to explain the differences between the Anglo-American record on the one hand, and the Central European and Scandinavian records on the other. Are there any other arguments, beside abstract theory, in its favour? I think there may be. The main argument has to do with the relationship between human capital and economic development. The higher the level of technology, the more important is human capital: and the more important human capital, the less appropriate a straightforward market model of economic behaviour. The reason is that as human capital becomes more important, as economic activities become more skill-intensive, it becomes less and less sensible to think of the labour market as a market at all. The mill owners of early-nineteenth-century Lancashire could and did treat their under-educated, unskilled 'hands' as though they were factors of production and nothing more, as subject to the laws of political economy as a bale of cotton. The skilled technicians of an advanced industrial society cannot be treated in this way. If they are seen solely as factors of production, if relations between capital and labour are regulated exclusively by the calculus of the market, they will soon discover that it pays them to use their market power, while they have it, to extract a monopoly rent from the rest of us. In such circumstances, industrial harmony and a social climate conducive to industrial harmony become public goods, for which it is worth paying a price in strict allocative efficiency. And although this is hard to prove, it is intuitively plausible that 'encompassingness' – and the solidaristic values which promote 'encompassingness' – are closely related to industrial harmony: that it is easier to establish co-operative industrial relations and transcend the calculus of the market in a society with solidaristic values and encompassing groups than in one without them.

This leads on to John Zysman's view of the relationship between economic development and distributional coalitions. This springs from the obvious, but easily forgotten, insight that economic growth has costs as well as benefits. These costs and benefits have to be distributed somehow; and the processes of distribution are political as well as economic. It follows that the traditional dichotomy between markets and politics is artificial. 'Market positions are a source of political power and government choices shape the operations of the market' (Zysman 1983: 17). A further conclusion follows as well:

[A] stable settlement for distributing the gains and pain of growth is a political prerequisite for a smoothly functioning economy. If the distributional settlements are not stable, political conflict will continue until a new agreement is reached. Inevitably, the distributional battles will interrupt the routine functioning of the market-place and make the institutions of the economy – such as the structures of finance and labour relations – the scene of overt political conflict . . . [G]overnments can achieve a stable settlement of distribution in several ways: by consciously shaping the market to impose a particular distribution of the costs and pains of growth; by permitting the market to allocate them with only limited government intervention or compensation; or by negotiating an explicit settlement between the producer groups. In essence, the losers in the market must either be compensated by policy or excluded from policy making. (Zysman 1983: 309)

The last point is in some ways the most important. If losers and potential losers are neither compensated nor excluded, they will use their political power to impede the growth processes from which they stand to lose. In that case, growth will not take place. Thus, everything depends on the way in which losers and potential losers are handled. If they cannot be excluded, they must be bought off. If they cannot be bought off, they must be excluded. In practice, of course, the mechanisms are likely to be quite complicated. In Japan and Gaullist France, Zysman argues, a stable winning political coalition bought off some losers – notably, in agriculture – for practical purposes excluded others and imposed its distributional settlement upon them. In Federal Germany, a consensus was established, based on a 'negotiated division of the national product', (Zysman 1983: 256) and embracing the operation of the market as well as the policy of the state. But these are details. Zysman's crucial point, at any rate for our purposes, is that if the distributional issue is not resolved, the result will be paralysis. And that, he argues, is what happened in the United Kingdom. No settlement could be imposed, because no one was strong enough to impose it. No settlement could be negotiated because the putative partners to the negotiation were unwilling or unable to allow their common interests to take precedence over their differences. Though Zysman does not use it, the term, 'encompassingness' once again emerges as the key to the story. The key to Britain's relative economic decline *vis-à-vis* her continental neighbours does not lie in state intervention, producer-group power, or market rigidities. It lies in her inability to find and sustain a substitute for the market-led development of the days of her glory.

Yet it is just conceivable there is light, albeit of a rather paradoxical kind, at the end of the tunnel. The period covered by this book is not all of a piece. There is a lot of evidence to suggest that advanced industrial societies are all moving out of the era of 'organized capitalism', characterized by mass-production manufacturing, macro-economic regulation, and large-scale producer groups, and into an era of flexibility and disorganization. The thrust of this comment is that Britain's economic culture has, for a variety of reasons, been ill-adapted to the era of organization which is now coming to an end. May it be that some, at any rate, of the factors which have made it so will facilitate adaptation to the era which seems likely to follow – that the individualistic and ill-disciplined British will do better in a disorganized world than in an organized one?

References

Kennedy, P. (1988) *The Rise and Fall of the Great Powers: Economic Change and Military Conflict From 1500 to 2000*, London and Sidney: Unwin Hyman.

Olson, M. (1983) *The Rise and Decline of Nations*, London and New Haven, Conn.: Yale University Press.

Zysman, J. (1983) *Governments, Markets and Growth: Financial Systems and the Politics of Industrial Change*, Ithaca, NY and London: Cornell University Press.

Index